When Broadway Was the Runway

When Broadway Was the Runway

Theater, Fashion, and American Culture

Marlis Schweitzer

PENN

University of Pennsylvania Press
Philadelphia

Published by
University of Pennsylvania Press
Philadelphia, Pennsylvania 19104-4112

Printed in the United States of America on acid-free paper

10   9   8   7   6   5   4   3   2   1

Library of Congress Cataloging-in-Publication Data

Schweitzer, Marlis.
  When Broadway was the runway : theater, fashion, and American culture / Marlis Schweitzer.
    p. cm.
  Includes bibliographical references and index.
  ISBN 978-0-8122-4157-0 (alk. paper)
    1. Theater—New York (State)—New York—History—19th century. 2. Theater—New York (State)—New York—History—20th century. 3. Costume—New York (State)—New York—History—19th century. 4. Costume—New York (State)—New York—History—20th century. 5. Fashion—New York (State)—New York—History—19th century. 6. Fashion—New York (State)—New York—History—20th century. 7. Department stores—New York (State)—New York. I. Title.
PN2277.N5S39 2009
792.09747'109041—dc22

                                                                    2008045168

For Dan, who knows me better than I know myself

Does anyone think I am talking too much about clothes? The reason is not because I am a woman, or vain, but because I am in show business. In show business clothes matter.

—Sophie Tucker, *Some of These Days*

Contents

Introduction

On June 13, 1908, thirteen hundred women entered the New Amsterdam Theatre at Broadway and 42nd Street for the 275th performance of *The Merry Widow*, enticed by the promise of a free Merry Widow hat. Three weeks earlier, the *New York Times* had announced the arrival "from Paris" of a consignment of one thousand hats, "all of the most ample variety," which would be distributed to all coupon-bearing theatergoers at the conclusion of the special show.[1] Like other promotional stunts in this period, the giveaway was designed by theatre manager Henry Savage to renew interest in *The Merry Widow* and prolong what was already an impressive run. By June 1908, Savage's American production of the internationally successful operetta by Franz Lehar had made well over one million dollars, launched two road companies, given rise to numerous burlesque versions, and inspired a vast array of tie-in products, ranging from sheet music and cigars to lunches, cocktails, and corsets.[2]

But of all the commodities associated with *The Merry Widow*, it was the Merry Widow hat that attracted the most attention. Originally designed by the couturier Lucile (Lady Duff Gordon) for the 1907 production in London, it was "an immense black crinoline hat, banded round the crown with silver and two huge pink roses nestling under the brim."[3] Within days of the London opening, the fashionable commodity crossed from the footlights to the showroom to the stage, sparking a transnational craze that, according to Lucile, "lasted longer than most fashion crazes" and carried the designer's name "all over Europe and the States."[4] By the spring of 1908, as milliners throughout Europe and North America struggled to meet consumer demand and outperform one another, the hat had ballooned to enormous proportions, reaching spans of three feet or more.[5]

Given the hype surrounding the production and the tie-ins it had inspired, Savage's promise of a Merry Widow hat to all women who attended the 275th performance of *The Merry Widow* was a brilliant marketing tactic, guaranteed to achieve maximum publicity.[6] Yet while Savage had thought carefully about how to distribute the hats to ensure that his patrons remained for the duration of the performance, correctly assuming that there would be little incentive for them to remain once the hats were gone, he failed to anticipate the lengths to which they would go to secure their gifts. As expected, the New Amsterdam Theatre was filled to capacity on the afternoon of June 13 with hundreds of women eager to collect their Merry Widows. Rather than quietly sitting through the performance until the appointed time, however, these fidgety spectators refused to remain seated. After the first act, an excited crowd gathered in the ladies' cloakroom, looking expectantly at the stack of hatboxes arranged on two tables. One woman asked to try her hat on, explaining, "If it doesn't look good on me I don't want to carry it home," but was politely told by the cloakroom attendants that she would have to wait until after the performance. As the end of the second act neared, more and more women trickled out of the auditorium to request their souvenirs in advance, claiming that other obligations prevented them from staying until the end of the performance. By the time the house manager intervened, insisting that no more hats would be given out until the curtain had fallen, hundreds of women had already left their seats. While most returned to the theater at his urging, a stalwart group insisted on waiting outside the cloakroom, determined to be the first to get the hats.[7]

The giveaway finally commenced just before the final curtain and ran smoothly for several minutes while spectators filed out of the house, at which point chaos ensued (figure I.1). Desperate to get their Merry Widows, the normally respectable middle-class audience ignored calls to get into line, overwhelmed the female attendants, pushed aside one of the tables, and began helping themselves to the boxes, blocking those who had already picked up their hats from getting out of the room. "In an instant the confusion was at its height," the *Times* reported somewhat gleefully. "One woman, jammed tight against the one table that still stood in place, tackled the woman next to her with a vim that would have done credit to the world's champion female wrestler." The most adventurous and nimble women managed to climb over the furniture to escape, but others had their gowns and hats trampled as they struggled to get out. After half an hour of pushing, shoving, name-calling, and other, very unladylike behavior, the house manager announced to those who remained that the hats were all gone. Although he promised to give out rain checks, one hundred angry women left the theater empty-handed, with "only the débris and the memory of the struggle" to show for their efforts.[8]

The chaos surrounding the Merry Widow giveaway—or "The Battle of the Hats" as the *Times* dubbed it—was typical of the kind of bargain counter crushes one might expect in a department store, where working- and middle-class women frequently battled over marked-down goods.[9] Such a scene was

Figure I.1. The *New York World*'s depiction of the "Battle of the Hats." "Women in Hard Battle for Free 'Merry Widows,'" *New York World*, June 14, 1908, 1.

highly unusual in a commercial Broadway theater, however, especially in a first-class playhouse like the New Amsterdam Theatre, which catered to an elite audience and expected its patrons to behave in a courteous and respectful manner. In thus bringing the department store into the theater, Henry Savage had aligned female theatrical spectatorship with fashion consumption, advocating a very different way of looking at and relating to theatrical spectacle.

In this, Savage was hardly alone. Beginning in the 1890s and continuing through the first two decades of the twentieth century, theater managers aggressively pursued the imagination and presence of female theatergoers by transforming the stage into a glorious site of consumer spectacle. Acutely aware that their financial solvency hinged on their ability to attract and retain the interest of socially advantaged women, these predominantly male impresarios presented actresses, the dresses they wore, and the objects they used onstage as fantastic commodities, readily available in photographs and magazines, in nearby department stores or, in the case of the Merry Widow giveaway, in the theater lobby just beyond the auditorium. By the 1910s, Broadway theaters had become fully commercialized urban spaces, comparable to any amusement park, department store, or, indeed, the Great White Way itself. Advertisements were everywhere: in the programs, on the curtains, on the scenery, and in the embodied performances of trade-character showgirls. This fusion of theatrical spectatorship and consumption represented a crucial step in the formation of a mass market for consumer goods and the rise of the cult of celebrity, two intertwined cultural projects designed to fuel the American economy and overwrite anxieties about the exploitation of labor and the loss of individuality. Utilizing the rhetoric of democracy and the shining faces of manufactured stars, Savage and his colleagues advocated a consumerist mode of looking, moving, and being in the city, training female consumers to see themselves as patrons of leisure rather than players in a capitalist game.

A number of interrelated economic, social, and cultural developments made collaborations between Broadway theaters, department stores, mass-circulation newspapers and magazines, fashion designers, and consumer goods manufacturers both desirable and necessary. These included New York's prominence as the nation's social, economic, and cultural hub; the emergence of large corporations with enough capital to launch national and international advertising campaigns; increased recognition of the power and influence of female consumers; growing consumer interest in fashion thanks to the large-scale promotional efforts of couturiers in London and Paris; and consumer desire for interesting, attractive, and inspiring role models who could demonstrate how to succeed in the swiftly changing modern world.

Throughout the late nineteenth century and the early twentieth, New York forged its identity as the imaginary if not geographic heart of the United States, the epitome of all things American, and the point of origin for a remarkable range of new products, ideas, and people. Every year, millions of dollars in goods from around the world arrived in New York Harbor, the nation's largest seaport, at which point they were loaded onto trains and distributed throughout the country. Immigrants also moved swiftly in and out of New York, transforming the demographic makeup as well as the sites and sounds of the city; of the twenty-three million Europeans who entered the United States between 1880 and 1919, 75 percent landed in New York.[10] Many of these newcomers remained in the city, where they found employment in clothing factories, stockyards, and other booming industries and became avid consumers of popular entertainment and other forms of mass culture.[11]

By the early twentieth century, New York had become the de facto center of capitalist enterprise in the United States, home to sixty-nine of the nation's one hundred largest corporations. Although the percentage of trade goods moving in and out of the city decreased to just below 50 percent in 1900 from a previous rate of 57 percent, due in part to the migration of heavy industry to less densely populated areas, the city maintained what the historian William R. Taylor describes as a "stranglehold" on credit and banking as well as such "market-sensitive" and mutually dependent industries as fashion and publishing, surpassing Boston and Philadelphia to become the center for trade in "intangible" commodities. By 1904, New York's garment factories produced 65 percent of all ready-made clothes in the United States, accounting for a similar percentage of the total value of women's clothing. The centralized publishing industry helped to promote these and a wide array of other commodities, informing readers throughout the United States of the latest styles and innovations.[12]

Theatrical touring companies, "direct from New York," also played a pivotal role in the distribution of information, ideas, and fashion throughout the United States. Beginning in the 1890s, theater managers and booking agents in vaudeville and the "legitimate" theater moved to consolidate their business interests, extending many of the same processes of rationalization and standardization that characterized modern manufacturing to streamline touring practices and establish greater control over the production, distribution, and consumption of theatrical commodities. These changes would not have been possible without the phenomenal growth of the railway industry and the establishment of New York as a major transportation hub. Between 1870 and 1910, the amount of ground covered by railway tracks increased by almost 500 percent from 52,922 to 249,902 miles. Newly constructed stations in small towns previously cut off from the main lines brought large touring companies to existing theaters and encouraged enterprising businessmen to build new ones.[13]

The incorporation of the theater industry mimicked developments elsewhere. Throughout the 1890s, business leaders in industries ranging from sugar and oil to meatpacking and dry goods participated in a flurry of mergers in an effort to rationalize production processes, ensure financial stability, and outperform the competition. The outcome was a radical transformation of the business and economic landscape; by 1904 approximately three hundred corporations controlled over 40 percent of all manufacturing in the United States and influenced business operations in 80 percent of the nation's industries. Gone was the self-made man of local business; in his place stood corporate giants such as the National Biscuit Company (Nabisco) and Standard Oil. Throughout this period, anxious observers and surviving independents called upon the government to introduce legislation to prevent the new corporations from becoming monopolizing behemoths. Laws such as the Sherman Antitrust Act of 1890 offered some resistance to the merger mania, but a certain laxity in defining such key terms as "combination" and "trust," the absence of an effective structure for enforcing the act, and an administration that turned a blind eye to shadier business dealings did little to stem the tide.[14]

Vilified for their "robber baron" tactics, corporations set about creating a positive public image, promising real benefits to American consumers. With the assistance of leading advertising agencies, most notably N. W. Ayer and Sons and the J. Walter Thompson Company, consumer goods manufacturers used funny names, catchy jingles, and cute or interesting trade characters to create a memorable impression on consumers and convince them that their branded products were far superior to unbranded goods or those of their competitors. "[Overcoming] the growing distance between manufacturer and buyer," the historian Susan Strasser explains, corporations such as Nabisco, Procter and Gamble, Campbell's, and Swift and Co. "surround[ed] their products with a magical aura" and "personal[ized] impersonal commodities."[15] Training consumers to associate brands and corporate logos with quality, they laid the foundation for a mass market that extended from coast to coast.

Although advertising campaigns targeted men as well as women, agencies such as the J. Walter Thompson Company soon recognized the influence of the female consumer and created advertisements that spoke directly to female needs, interests, and desires. In 1915, Thompson opened up its Women's Editorial Department, believing that the best way to reach female consumers was with female copywriters.[16] J. Walter Thompson's advertisements appeared in leading women's magazines, including the *Ladies' Home Journal*, the first magazine to reach a circulation of one million readers, *Women's Home Companion*, and *Good Housekeeping*, as well as prominent fashion journals such as *Vogue* and *Harper's Bazar*. Although magazine editors had previously hesitated to publish large advertisements, wary of the false claims made by many nineteenth-century manufacturers, they now welcomed the attractive ads produced by professional agencies and the revenue that came along with them, going so far as to court advertisers directly.[17] For example, when Condé Nast gained control of *Vogue* in 1909, he introduced a number of measures to emphasize the magazine's "high-class" status in a bid to increase circulation and attract major advertisers.[18]

Vogue and its rival *Harper's Bazar*, which was owned by the publishing magnate William Randolph Hearst, also profited from and played into growing interest in fashion from London and Paris, vying for the American rights to publish sketches and photographs of the latest couture fashions.[19] Although the words "from Paris" had long held considerable cachet for American consumers, the emergence of a group of designers, led by Paul Poiret, revolutionized international fashion. Influenced by modern art and dance, these couturiers tested the limits of fashion, creating bizarre, even awkward, styles that reshaped the look and movement of the female body. Such changes alone would likely have captured international attention, but Poiret and his competitors, perhaps most notably the British designer Lucile—the inventor of the Merry Widow hat—were also experimenting with new and often radical promotional techniques. Styling themselves as artists while utilizing a range of advertising strategies that included commissioning artists to sketch their designs, sending mannequins to highly publicized events, staging highly theatrical fashion shows, and collaborating with theater directors, these designers achieved international recognition.[20]

The problem for many Americans, however, was a time lag between the styles' debuts in London or Paris and their subsequent arrivals in the United States. By the early 1890s, innovations in communication and transportation, including the telephone and the wireless, the transatlantic cable, and impressive new ocean liners, had facilitated the rapid exchange of fashion ideas between Paris and New York.[21] Yet while newspapers published written descriptions of new gowns within a day or two of their appearance, consumers had to wait weeks or even months to see published photographs and sketches. Salon openings in the spring and fall also put Americans at a disadvantage. Those who traveled to Europe in the summer returned to the United States with trunks of expensive gowns only to find that they were now a season behind their Paris counterparts. This lag helps to explain why female audiences across the United States were so eager to see the clothes worn by star actresses, who, thanks to the support of theater managers, possessed the resources to get the gowns first.[22]

Mass-circulation newspapers and class-oriented publications such as *Vogue, Vanity Fair,* and *Harper's Bazar* recognized the theater's importance as a site of fashion spectacle and created special sections devoted to New York stage fashion. In July 1913, *Harper's Bazar* increased its previously sporadic coverage of stage gowns, introducing a special monthly feature entitled "Gowns Seen on the Stage" (later "The Stage as the Mirror of Fashion"). *Vogue* responded in kind, publishing photographs of leading actresses in character and even enlisting their services as fashion models.[23] Former *Vogue* editor Edna Woolman Chase recalled that throughout the 1910s the stage actresses Irene Castle, Mary Nash, Hazel Dawn, and Jeanne Eagels were regular "stand-bys."[24] Unlike many of the anonymous "living models" who posed for fashion photographs, these women possessed a physical confidence and self-awareness that appealed to photographers such as Baron Adolf de Meyer and Ira L. Hill.[25] Perhaps more important, as celebrities, actresses were guaranteed to draw attention not only to the clothes they wore but also to the magazines in which they appeared. In 1913 the newly launched *Vanity Fair* signed a contract guaranteeing to publish a photograph or illustration of the ballroom dancer Irene Castle every month as a strategy to entice new readers to the magazine.[26]

American manufacturers took similar steps to profit from the actress's emerging status as a trendsetter and role model, soliciting testimonials from famous stars or naming new products after their stage characters. As beautiful yet accessible women, actresses represented the perfect solution for breaking into new markets and encouraging new patterns of consumer behavior. Indeed, the increased emphasis on the actress as personality rather than as character—one of the effects of the emerging "star system"—was a crucial factor in testimonial advertising because it positioned the actress as a cultural performer *outside* the limits of her stage roles. By bringing theatrical stars to consumers via the pages of fashion and women's magazines, advertisers succeeded in reaching a much broader segment of the theatergoing and nontheatergoing public. One of the most famous and enduring examples of this promotional strategy was the Peter Pan collar created for Maude Adams, who originated the title role in the J. M. Barrie play in 1905. In 1909, when Adams starred in *What Every Woman Knows*, the *Theatre Magazine*'s fashion columnist assumed that she would continue to set the styles in collars. "[S]he will undoubtedly be [the originator] of the Maggie Wylie collar," the writer noted, "and we may therefore look to a vogue of dainty lace and lingerie collars of this type to begin the warm weather." Manufacturers and designers also named sleeves, hats, slippers, coats, and various other fashion articles after popular actresses, hoping that the star endorsement would equal big profits.[27]

More than selling a single product, actresses' endorsements of clothing items seem to have been part of a much larger attempt to convince female consumers, particularly middle-class women, of the benefits of manufactured clothing. According to the fashion historian Rob Schorman, predominant turn-of-the-century gender ideologies that emphasized the importance of clothing as an expression of female individuality discouraged women from adopting ready-to-wear fashions long after men had accepted this form of clothing. Rather than purchase a blouse or skirt that hundreds of other women were already wearing, women continued to go to their dressmakers for custom-made clothing, even after 1910 when most items of clothing were available ready-made. Consumers frequently dismissed ready-to-wear clothing for its poor quality and strong association with the immigrant working class, preferring to make their own clothes along the lines of the latest styles rather than wear shoddy, factory-produced garments.[28] Actresses' endorsements thus constituted an important part of a larger business strategy to reshape consumer behavior and promote new consumption habits.

But as the mob-like behavior of the thirteen hundred women gathered at the New Amsterdam Theatre suggests, controlling and containing female consumers was no easy task. The surging crowds of supposedly respectable women who showed little respect for managerial requests and even less respect for one another bore an eerie resemblance to the radical suffragists who paraded in the streets and the increasingly militant groups of female laborers who demanded better treatment and working conditions. Rather than standing apart from the urban masses, middle-class female consumers seemed to be joining them in alarming numbers. Indeed, as Elizabeth Wilson observes, "The [early twentieth-century] crowd was increasingly invested with female characteristics," depicted as hysterical, unstable, flood-like. "Like women, crowds were liable to rush to extremes of emotion" and like women, crowds needed to be brought under control to prevent the established order of American society from being swallowed up by the feminine swamp.[29]

Theater managers attempted to do just that, collaborating with department stores and other commercial institutions to promote an idealized vision of the modern consuming woman that would stabilize boundaries of gender, race, and class. But the "liveness" of the actress—that is, the interpretive possibilities of live performance as well as the formation of imaginary bonds between stars and their female fans—made it difficult if not impossible to project a single, coherent vision of female modernity or to prevent existing social boundaries from dissolving.

When Broadway Was the Runway: Theater, Fashion, and American Culture explores the central and largely unacknowledged role of commercial Broadway theater in the explosion of modern American consumer culture, particularly through its influence over tastes in women's fashion and its function as a staging ground for larger issues related to consumption—debates about the loss of individuality, the corporatization and feminization of cultural institutions, the blurring of class and racial boundaries, and the reordering of gender relations. Previous histories of American mass consumption have stressed the importance of commercial institutions, ranging from newspapers and magazines to world's fairs and the cinema, in the formation of a national market for mass-produced goods and the development of a model of modern subjectivity inextricably linked to consumption. Few studies, however, have fully considered the American commercial theater's involvement in this process, beyond noting the transposition of theatrical techniques and staging practices into venues such as the department store.[30]

This book extends previous analyses of theater and commerce in its dual focus on the business decisions that encouraged collaboration between theaters and other consumer institutions, and on the more intimate interactions among theater critics, managers, advertisers, designers, performers, and audiences that influenced the circulation and shaped the meaning of theatrical commodities. This approach illuminates the complicated and often paradoxical processes that produced modern American consumer culture, especially with respect to shifting relationships between producers, distributors, and consumers both within and beyond the theatrical auditorium. Commercial Broadway theater—vaudeville, "legitimate" drama, and musical comedy— did considerably more than display fashion, borrow marketing strategies, and appropriate advertising rhetoric. Through its extensive partnerships with department stores, manufacturers, and mass publications, the theater became a central locus for producing modern consumers, a place where audiences learned how to become discriminating buyers of a wide range of domestic as well as foreign goods and where they imagined themselves as part of a national and increasingly global consumer economy.[31]

What made the theater such an ideal site for exploring these issues was the way it offered a safe, collective environment for audiences and perform- > ers to awaken new hopes and desires and to analyze, debate, and enact new ideas and ways of being. This process of imagination and enactment is rarely smooth, coherent, or homogenous; individual spectators interpret stage performances according to their individual desires and interests, often coming away from a performance having seen or experienced something quite different from that seen or experienced by their fellow spectators. Indeed, as much as each performance can be seen as a reenactment of the previous night's performance—as the celebration of the 275th night of *The Merry Widow* clearly suggests—the actors' moods, their interactions with other performers, the idiosyncrasies of the gathered audience, the specific events of the day, the surrounding environment, and countless other factors color and shape each performance, marking it as a single, irretrievable event. It is this fleeting, ephemeral quality, the experience of living, breathing, sweating, laughing, and crying together in a single room, and the sensation that anything *could* happen even if it doesn't, that separates theater from other mediated performances. Although it can at times produce consensus and often works to maintain dominant cultural ideologies, the theater nevertheless remains an important site of contestation, a place where audiences can debate and work through cultural change and participate in the formation of a very different world.[32]

Chapter 1

The Octopus and the Matinee Girl

[The theater] has passed from the hands that ought to control it—the hands either of actors who love and honor their art, or of men endowed with the temperament of the actor and acquainted with his art and its needs—and, almost entirely, it has fallen into the clutches of sordid, money-grubbing tradesmen, who have degraded it. Throughout the length and breadth of the United States speculators have captured the industry that they call "the Amusement Business" and have made "a Corner in Theatricals."

—William Winter, Theatre Magazine

In 1907 the venerable theater critic William Winter lashed out against the "sordid, money-grubbing tradesmen" who had seized control of the American theater. Playing on the rhetoric of white slavery, Winter depicted American drama as a beleaguered woman held captive by a group of materialistic speculators. Unless strong, virile men, the representatives of elite white society, joined forces to resist this foreign incursion, he insisted, the theater industry would remain "a Corner in Theatricals," a department store trading in dramatic goods.[1] Winter was not alone in lamenting the degradation of the American theater, nor was he alone in developing a narrative of cultural struggle that drew heavily from gender and racial stereotypes. For two decades, literary and theater critics from some of the nation's most influential publications, including *Leslie's Magazine*, *Harper's Weekly*, *Cosmopolitan*, and over eighty major newspapers from the United States, Canada, and England, attacked the businessmen they claimed were responsible for turning American theater from an inspired art form into the "Amusement Business."[2] Their central target was the Theatrical Syndicate, an organization of six booking agents and managers, all but one of whom was Jewish, that controlled hundreds of theaters across the United States and effectively determined the theatrical destiny of most "legitimate" productions. With its stranglehold on the industry, the Syndicate did more than eliminate the competition, the critics argued; it inhibited the development of actors, playwrights, and audiences, thereby threatening the advancement of American society itself. "It is for you to make a stand in the best interests of yourself, and of the theater which can be made the most wholesome, reasonable, clean and uplifting form of amusement, or can be brought even lower than it is at present," the editors of *Leslie's Magazine* warned readers in 1905. "The future of the theater in this country rests with you and you only."[3]

The scope of the anti-Syndicate crusade stands as a testament to the growing prominence of the dramatic critic as a cultural commentator. By the 1890s, most major urban newspapers and many leading literary journals had their own resident critic, an individual whose primary responsibility was observing industry trends and critiquing the latest theatrical fare.[4] Although differing in style according to age and experience, these critics were predominantly well-educated, middle-class, male WASPs united by a desire to preserve cultural hierarchies and a growing aversion to the products and effects of modernity.[5] Styling themselves as protectors of culture, they assumed an active role in what Laurence Levine described as the "sacralization" of culture, distinguishing high-brow "legitimate" theater—canonical plays and other works of literary merit—from low-brow popular amusements such as the circus, burlesque, and, to a lesser extent, vaudeville.[6] Central to this project, as the invocation from *Leslie's Magazine* suggests, was the involvement of respectable, white, middle-class men and women who would support the development of a national endowed theater divorced from the taint of commerce.

But theater critics' hopes for an audience-led theatrical renaissance were dashed when it became apparent that the most powerful audience demographic on Broadway was no longer middle-aged men but juvenile girls. Shifting their attack from the members of the Syndicate who produced and distributed theatrical entertainment to the matinee girl who consumed it, theater critics joined contemporary manufacturers and advertising agents in recognizing the powerful influence of the female consumer.[7] Yet whereas advertisers used this discovery to encourage the gendering of consumption, confident in their belief that they could control and manipulate female desire, theater critics seemed disheartened by this turn of events, uncertain whether they could do anything to stem the tide of affluent, independent, consumer-oriented young women flooding the theater. They tried nonetheless. With such evocatively titled articles as "The Brutality of the Matinee Girl," "The American Girl's Damaging Influence on the Drama," and "The Young Person Is the Tyrant of the Theatre," critics reversed their previous position on the cause of theatrical decline, arguing that female theatergoers' incessant demands for spectacle and entertainment prevented theater managers from producing serious, artistically sound work. "Unless people of high standing in America get together to support good, respectable productions," warned the actor and lecturer Wilton Lackaye in 1910, "something terrible may happen to the theatre."[8]

In juxtaposing the critics' initial vilification of "sordid, money-grubbing tradesmen" with their later focus on "illiterate, candy-eating" women, this chapter weaves together recent historiographic explorations of the cultural and racial biases that informed critical reception of early twentieth-century commercial entertainment with continuing work on the feminization of mass culture and the devaluation of female tastes and interests.[9] Theater historians have exposed the aggressive anti-Semitism and class-based prejudices that colored many of the critics' rejection of commercial theater practices, but this important revisionist work has tended to frame the pro- and anti-commercial confrontation as a struggle between men. By bringing matinee girls into the conversation, I hope to emphasize the complicated triangular relationships that developed between critics, managers, and audiences as each group struggled to assert its voice and get what it wanted. This bizarre triad became caught up in a complex web of competing discourses on the relationship between art and commerce; the standardization and rationalization of labor processes; the effect of foreign commodities on American industry; the growing influence of the female consumer; the perceived feminization of mass culture; and the role of the critic as a cultural arbiter. In tugging at the various threads in this web, what ultimately emerges is the story of a group of well-meaning men (and, to a lesser extent, women) who feared that within the rationalized world of commercial Broadway theater, they were swiftly becoming obsolete.

Incorporating the American Theater

In February 1896, six of the most influential booking agents and theatrical managers in the United States met at New York's Holland House to discuss terms for consolidating their business interests. Although later represented as a happy coincidence, the gathering of Charles Frohman, Al Hayman, Marc Klaw, A. L. Erlanger, J. Frederick Zimmerman, and Samuel Nixon was no accident. In an effort to forestall the effects of economic recession, these men agreed to create a national booking agency that would streamline the cumbersome process of theatrical touring. At the time of the meeting, Charles

Frohman and his partner Al Hayman owned several theaters in New York and ran a booking agency in the West that controlled approximately three hundred theaters. Marc Klaw, a former lawyer and his partner A.L. Erlanger owned a comparable number of first-class theaters across the country and oversaw the booking arrangements for another 200 theaters in the Southeast. J. Frederick Zimmerman and Samuel Nixon operated out of Philadelphia and owned or controlled most of the important theaters in the mid-Atlantic region. According to the terms laid out over lunch, the members of the newly formed Theatrical Syndicate would pool sixteen theaters that they either owned or leased along with an additional seventeen independently managed theaters held under exclusive arrangements with Klaw and Erlanger. Located in major cities throughout the country, these thirty-three theaters would form the backbone of a national theater chain. In the years that followed, the Syndicate pursued an aggressive and at times ethically questionable strategy to monopolize theatrical touring in the United States (a subject I will return to later). By 1903, it controlled or otherwise influenced five hundred theaters, seventy of which it owned and managed outright, one for every major stop on the theatrical touring circuit, and all but two or three of the first-class theaters in New York, the center of theatrical production. Such an extensive network gave the Syndicate a staggering monopoly over theatrical touring in the United States.[10]

Although loudly lamented by critics, the establishment of a centrally controlled, national chain of theaters was, in many respects, the inevitable outcome of a series of changes that dated back to the 1870s. In the mid-nineteenth century, most towns in the United States had their own resident stock company led by a manager who either owned or leased the local theater and oversaw all aspects of production, from casting actors and conducting rehearsals to planning the season plays and coordinating all aspects of production. Stock performers acted in different plays throughout the season and filled supporting roles whenever a touring star from New York, London, or Paris came to town. But as more stars recognized the financial rewards of touring and took to the road, they fed local appetites for celebrities, a situation that compelled local managers to devote more resources to attracting talent, much to the detriment of the local company and facilities. By the mid-1860s, many stars were opting to travel with their own company of actors and perform the same play throughout the season instead of traveling alone and performing plays in repertory with a local company. These "combination companies," as they became known, usually originated in New York, Boston, or Philadelphia and drew from the talent located there, an arrangement that effectively shifted power from the local manager to the star, who now acted in the capacity of actor-manager to ensure that all aspects of the production were to his or her liking. When the Panic of 1873 hit, many stock companies could not withstand the financial pressure to attract stars and maintain a regular company, and within three years more than thirty of the existing fifty-plus stock companies had folded. By contrast, the economically efficient combination company flourished, more than doubling the number of stock companies in this period. By the 1880s, 282 combination companies were touring the country while only 8 stock companies remained.[11]

More than providing a more efficient and cost effective approach to theatrical production, the combination system and the corresponding introduction of "duplicate companies"—a franchised version of the original production sent out on the road long before the first had closed—initiated an important shift in the collective experiences of American theatergoers. In the early 1880s, as many as fourteen companies toured the country with Steele Mackaye's *Hazel Kirke*, making it possible for thousands of theatergoers across the United States to consume a single commercial spectacle simultaneously. Anticipating the nationalizing power of radio, film, and television, the combination company participated in the transformation of heterogeneous local audiences into a more cohesive if not homogenized national audience. By 1905, over three hundred "first-class" shows were touring the nation with an additional one hundred to two hundred "second-rate" shows originating out of cities like Chicago. From Portland, Maine to Portland, Oregon, combination companies traversed the nation, bringing with them new plays, new performers, and new ideas.[12]

Throughout this period of restructuring, New York achieved new prominence as both a site of theatrical production and the official headquarters of the converging theater industries.[13] Although by the mid-1870s theatrical newspapers, photography studios, costume shops, play publishers, and booking agencies had all congregated around Union Square, transforming the area into a theatrical "Rialto" for commercial transactions, the rise of booking agencies in the 1880s and 1890s transformed the daily operations of theatrical business, centralizing control in the hands of a few.[14] Prior to the rationalization of the booking process, actors, managers, and theater owners had acted independently, discussing business arrangements over a pint or in a stroll down Broadway, sealing deals with handshakes instead of contracts. In the area of Union Square commonly referred to as the "Slave Market," would-be actors and established stars announced their professional status and their availability through dress and demeanor. "They wanted all who saw to know that they trod the boards," one contemporary observer recalled. "[T]hey attracted attention wherever they went and they dressed conspicuously, often loudly."[15] Commodity and seller in one, the actor, like the prostitute, showed off his (and less frequently her) wares, hoping to catch the eye of an interested manager (figure 1.1). These displays became most elaborate between the months of June and September, when theater managers from around the country descended on Union Square, hoping to book enough combination companies for a complete season.[16]

Although appealing in its sociability, from a business perspective the system was cumbersome at best and financially disastrous at worst. Managers who could not afford to make the trip to New York had to secure business arrangements by correspondence, a risky venture that often resulted in confusion and empty theaters. Even those who could afford to travel often found the relaxed congeniality of the Union Square Rialto less than conducive for business. Without a legally binding contract, combination companies could cancel their bookings with little or no notice; managers in turn often booked more than one company for the same performance dates, a practice that inevitably led to double bookings. With approximately 250 combination companies touring the country by 1880, the prospect of booking these companies into 5,000 theaters in 3,500 cities became an administrative nightmare.[17]

One solution involved organizing several theaters in the same geographic region into a circuit, a move that improved the bargaining power of the individual theaters while saving time and money. Working collectively, a group of seven or eight theaters in the Northwest stood a far better chance of attracting a successful hit than they did on their own; even better, they avoided heavy costs by selecting a single representative to act on their behalf. Throughout the 1880s, enterprising businessmen organized more and more theaters into circuits, bringing together small-town music halls with big-city palaces. Their ventures were so successful that in 1888, the ever watchful *New York Dramatic Mirror* expressed concerns about circuit monopolies. Still, while theatrical circuits represented a more systematic approach to theatrical booking, traveling theater companies continued to face the arduous task of organizing an entire season on the road. Centralized booking agencies promised to solve this problem by coordinating all of the booking arrangements for each show, requiring all participants to agree to a signed contract, thereby eliminating the problem of double bookings and cancelled appearances. A process that had once been informal, unreliable, and expensive was now legally binding, standardized, and cost-effective.[18]

Booking agencies increasingly dominated the daily business of theat-

ON THE RIALTO.

Figure 1.1. "On the Rialto," 1899. Fashionably dressed actors and actresses parade their wares in Union Square. Picture Collection, The Branch Libraries, The New York Public Library, Astor, Lenox and Tilden Foundations.

rical production, opening up new opportunities for business-minded men and women with little or no previous theater experience or knowledge. For a former copyright lawyer like Marc Klaw or a real estate agent like Henry Savage, the transition to theatrical booking was relatively easy and surprisingly logical. Although other members of the Syndicate, most notably Charles Frohman, had worked as agents and road managers earlier in their careers and therefore understood the practical realities of road life, their greatest strength lay in their ability to anticipate and enforce new business practices. By the early 1890s, several dominant agencies, led by Klaw and Erlanger in the Southeast and Frohman and Hayman in the West, controlled most theatrical booking arrangements. From a business perspective, combining these agencies into a single, national booking agency was the logical next step; it simplified the booking process, reduced connecting times between "desirable attractions in all the largest cities," and prevented competing companies from "[killing] each other's profits."[19]

Initial reactions to news of the Syndicate's formation were mixed. Some managers approved of it, believing that "[t]he scheme will expedite business transactions, and for that reason will be beneficial," but others preferred to stand "aloof from any syndicate or trust." Responding to a request from the *Dramatic Mirror* for managers to share their views, Fred G. Berger, the manager of Sol Smith Russell, wrote that in his experience the Syndicate was "inclined to be more fair and just in arranging terms for Mr. Russell" than "many of the local managers." George Bowles, the manager of the Chimmie Fadden Company, likewise noted that "the effect of the systematic and business-like concentration of theatrical affairs seems to me to be favorable to the managers of first-class traveling attractions." Fred W. Bert wasn't convinced. Although willing to concede some benefits to the new system, he worried that it was open to monopolistic abuses and feared that touring managers and theater owners had made themselves vulnerable to the whims and fancies of the Syndicate.[20]

By the fall of 1897, Harrison Grey Fiske, the editor of the *Dramatic Mirror* and the husband of the star actress Minnie Maddern Fiske, decided that he had seen enough of the Syndicate. On November 13 he published the first of fifteen "Theatrical 'Trust' Supplements" dedicated to exposing the abuses of the Syndicate and its members. These supplements included Fiske's own lengthy editorials and reprints of editorials, articles, and letters from newspapers from around the country—"proof" that anti-Syndicate sentiment was growing. With such headlines as "Another City Disgusted," "Tied Hand and Foot," "It Means Slavery," "It Will Not Be Tolerated," and "It Is Feared and

Detested," Fiske left readers with little doubt of his own position.[21] The Syndicate hit back hard and fast, launching a libel lawsuit against Fiske, withdrawing advertisements from the *Mirror* and other newspapers supporting his campaign, and pressuring distributors who sold the *Mirror*. Although Fiske and others continued to rage against the Syndicate for close to two decades, it would ultimately take the much nimbler corporation headed up by the Shubert brothers, who enlisted the support of venture capitalists and adopted an "open-door" policy for independent touring companies, to challenge the great "octopus."[22]

Until that time, however, the Syndicate continued to extend its business tentacles throughout the continent, securing its dominance over the production, distribution, and consumption of theatrical commodities by controlling the booking processes and acquiring theaters in key locations. Many of its tactics were undoubtedly ruthless. In addition to charging a commission of 5 to 10 percent, the Syndicate insisted that all productions traveling along its circuit should play in Syndicate-controlled houses.[23] Where the Syndicate did not own theaters, it refused to book any shows until local managers agreed that they would book shows *only* through its New York-based offices. Confronted with the prospect of an empty house or a tour in second-rate theaters, managers, producers, and players yielded, often begrudgingly, to these demands. Those who challenged the Syndicate or who otherwise refused to play by its rules faced punishment in the form of an "unsatisfactory route that will make railway fare more than eat up all the profits."[24] When a small group of stars led by Nat Goodwin, Richard Mansfield, Francis Wilson, Fanny Davenport, and Minnie Maddern Fiske organized a revolt against the Syndicate in January 1898, they soon discovered that audiences accustomed to seeing their favorites perform in first-class houses would not follow them into vaudeville or other second-rate venues. Faced with the choice of yielding to the Syndicate's demands or playing second- and third-rate houses for the rest of their careers, they chose the former.[25]

Yet while the Syndicate maintained power through its centralized control of theatrical booking and its ownership of dozens of theaters across the United States, it extended its control through the theatrical productions of its constituent members. From the 1890s well into the 1910s, Charles Frohman and the producing team of Klaw and Erlanger staged everything from society plays and period dramas to musical comedies and French farces, operating independently of other Syndicate members but remaining confident in their support. Frohman alone produced an average of thirty to forty shows each season, hiring between five hundred and six hundred performers, not including chorus members, and overseeing a production staff of approximately ten thousand people. "He seems like nothing so much as an engine of industry and application, far in advance of anybody about him, and with his eye steadily fixed upon a still more distant vantage point," the *New York Times* remarked in 1908.[26] Inevitably, shows produced by Syndicate members got the best routes regardless of quality and critical reception, a situation that had negative consequences for independently produced shows. In 1903 Klaw and Erlanger deliberately booked David Belasco's hit production *Darling of the Gods* on a terrible route so that their own copycat production, *The Japanese Nightingale*, would benefit from the advance publicity Belasco's show had received. They even went so far as to block *Darling* from appearing in St. Louis during the World's Fair.[27]

Of central importance to the Syndicate's aesthetic domination was its influence over the nation's leading newspapers, most effectively realized by Frohman, who used personal connections to secure good press. "All the gossip, all the serious interests, of the world in which most dramatic critics breathe, center in the doings of Mr. Frohman, his associates and dependents," the theater critic Norman Hapgood explained in 1901. As a result, Frohman's weakest plays received high praise while strong shows produced by his less influential rivals did not. The Syndicate's "control of most of the plays [gave] them exceptional opportunities to pay dramatic critics to write and rewrite certain acts or plays, and to give opinions."[28] Although many critics simply refused to play the Syndicate's game and wrote scathing editorials on its tactics, those with playwriting aspirations or dreams of heading up a press department gave into the Syndicate's requests, trusting that their loyalty would be rewarded later.[29] With these "press representatives" placed in an "authoritative position," Montrose Moses reiterated, the Syndicate was poised to "establish a chain of papers willing to print any news emanating from the theatre office."[30]

The Syndicate's strategic deployment of reviews and other forms of media coverage signaled an important change in publicity tactics. Although in preparing to take a show on the road, most producers still hired an advance agent to arrange publicity and chat up newspaper editors a week or two ahead of the show's arrival, the expanding network of news services like the Associated Press and the growing dominance of newspaper chains like the one organized by William Randolph Hearst simplified the agent's work. By 1901, as many as twelve million people saw New York papers on a regular basis, meaning that within a matter of days Syndicate attractions "[became] known through the land."[31] "Connected through print" to big-city audiences, small-town theatergoers constituted what Benedict Anderson describes as "the embryo of the nationally imagined community."[32]

Frohman and his colleagues played to local audience's aspirational desires for big-city culture and the goods associated with it, often keeping slow-selling shows running in New York until they had built up enough advance publicity to guarantee a successful road tour. Mimicking the evolving strategies of consumer goods manufacturers, who in the 1890s and early 1900s used brand names and trade characters to distinguish their products from the almost identical goods sold by their rivals, the Syndicate ensured that, when given the choice between three traveling shows, local audiences would opt for the one they had read about.[33] In fact, one of the major complaints launched against the Syndicate was that the "Number 2" companies that played in smaller towns and developing urban centers were inferior to the original productions. Audiences went to the theater expecting to see the original cast members "direct from New York" but instead found "no-name" performers and often inferior production values.[34] Educated about the politics of false advertising and the need to look for trademarks as a proof of quality by government agencies and businesses such as the Eastman Company, small-town audiences cried foul when the Syndicate's Number 2 companies failed to deliver and insisted on receiving what they had paid for.[35] For these theatergoers, the issue was not the Syndicate's existence per se or its monopolistic practices but rather its attempt to pass off third-rate goods as first-rate. Indeed, while Fiske cited consumer frustration as further evidence of the Syndicate's corruption, local reactions to its perceived failure to deliver brand-name goods indicate that audiences outside New York were actually quite *willing* to see standardized goods from Broadway as long as they were the *real* thing.[36]

Before turning to theater audiences, however, I want to focus further on the anti-commercial stance represented by Fiske and the critics who similarly believed it was their job to combat the Syndicate and reshape the tastes of American audiences. This is not to suggest that the critics' complaints about the Syndicate were unfounded—clearly the group's monopolistic tendencies and often unethical business practices were cause for alarm. What interests me, though, is how the anti-commercial rhetoric used to frame the anti-Syndicate campaign exposes deep-seated fears that legitimate Broadway theater was becoming a feminized commercial paradise dominated by foreign commodities.

The Campaign against the "Manipulators of Unsavory Merchandise"

In waging their attack on the Syndicate, theater critics and their supporters drew extensively from existing anti-Semitic discourses and the language
of contemporary muckrakers, representing the members of the Syndicate as
purveyors of tainted goods (figure 1.2). In December 1897, a writer identified
only as A.S.A. wrote to the *Dramatic Mirror* to describe how his blood had
"come almost to the boiling point . . . while contemplating the usurpers of
power, the Shylocks and the vampires who are at the throat of the theatrical world in this country." Invoking cultural associations between vampirism
and Judaism, this self-declared "native American" insisted that "[e]veryone
who fails to raise his voice against this system of avarice, cowardice, deception
and brow-beating is equally culpable with the members of this most ignoble
Syndicate *in taking the public's money under false pretenses* [my emphasis]."[37]
Harrison Grey Fiske took this rhetoric further, framing the fight against the
"smut and manipulators of unsavory merchandise" as a religious crusade.
"The salvation of the American theatre lies in two things," he explained: "The
vigorous seed of rebellion that has been sown by the disinterested leaders
of this crusade: the splendid missionary work of the press, and the internal
weakness and rottenness of the unholy combination."[38] Casting himself in the
role of righteous crusader, Fiske enjoined his fellow Christians to follow him
into the fray, imitating the militant language used by muckrakers such as Edward Bok, the editor of the *Ladies' Home Journal*, in the campaign to regulate
patent medicines—a campaign that culminated in the Pure Food and Drug
Act of 1906.[39] Like Bok, Fiske and his supporters worried that Americans were
being duped by amoral producers into consuming dangerous products that
jeopardized the nation's health. Where he differed from Bok, however, was in
his staunchly anti-Semitic perspective and his fundamental refusal to allow
commerce to interfere with artistic production.

    William Winter echoed Fiske in playing up contemporary stereotypes
of the thieving Jewish businessman and the ubiquitous Jewish peddler to
disparage the Syndicate's strategies. Conjuring images of Lower East Side
markets, he complained in 1907 that the Syndicate "dispens[ed] dramatic
performances precisely as vendors dispense vegetables," and on another occasion insisted that "it is one thing to sell boots or pickles, and another to
disseminate thoughts and emotions."[40] But Winter's favorite metaphor to
describe the Syndicate's rampant commercialism seems to have been the department store. In a 1905 lecture entitled "The Theatre and the Public" he
spoke at length about "the Department Store Theatre" and its trade in worth-

THE THEATRICAL TRUST.

(Reproduced by permission of the World.)

A Cartoon Drawn for The World by Francis Wilson.

Figure 1.2. The actor Francis Wilson's depiction of the monstrous Theatrical Syndicate. "Theatrical Trust Supplement" no. 7, *New York Dramatic Mirror*, December 25, 1897, 1.

less commodities. Such a theater, he claimed, "means no more to the public than a factory of soap and candles . . . [it] represents nothing but the fang of commercialism and the pot-banger of vulgar traffic."[41]

The overt hatred that characterizes so many of the anti-Syndicate attacks suggests that at the root of it all lay contemporary fears about Jewish influence on American business and society. By 1910, 1.2 million Jews lived in New York City alone, bringing with them new tastes, attitudes, and political ideologies.[42] Proclaiming socialist ideas about labor protests and unionization, Jewish laborers in the textile and clothing industries threatened to disrupt American business with strikes and protests.[43] Jewish financiers also came under attack following the economic turmoil of 1893, facing charges that an international cabal of Jews was responsible for the rapid inflation that was crippling American business.[44]

Against this backdrop of paranoia, the rise of a group of Jewish theater managers and booking agents, "useless middlemen," "insolent jobbers," and "crooked *entrepreneurs*," who had not followed the traditional path to theatrical success and who went so far as to admit that art was *not* their primary motivation, represented a serious threat to American culture and society.[45] "Not merely one industry, but civilization itself is concerned," insisted the author and critic William Dean Howells, "for the morals and education of the public are directly influenced by the stage."[46] For Howells, the theater's potential to civilize, its ability (in the words of William Winter) "to instill, and to maintain purity, sweetness, and refinement in our feelings, our manner, our language, and our national character," distinguished it from other industries.[47] One might tolerate the incorporation of the iron, coal, sugar, or oil industry because the public was not "personally, directly influenced by the matter" and such consolidations seemed almost inevitable. "But," Howells argued "with art it is different." The theater was an art form not a business and actors were artists not laborers; to define them as such threatened the very foundation of American civilization and the future of the white race. It was therefore incumbent upon every self-respecting American to resist the efforts of the Syndicate to turn art into a mass-produced consumer good.

This adamant denial of theater's commercial aspect formed the central core of many anti-Syndicate arguments.[48] Rather than debate the merits of a coordinated booking system or acknowledge the necessary and inevitable relationship between business and theater, Fiske, Winter, Howells, and others sought to distance the legitimate theater from any taint of commercialism.[49] For these critics, as the following section details, the Syndicate's promotion of star personalities, its interest in foreign playwrights, its willingness to cater to the lowest common denominator, and its involvement in the development of new consumer behaviors signaled the "disintegration" if not the complete destruction of theater as an art form.

Star-Making Factories and the Problem with Foreign Imports

In 1906, Alan Dale, the resident *Cosmopolitan* critic, cynically compared Broadway's "star-making" factory to the "jam industry of London and the sausage profession of Chicago." "Every season," he explained, "we drop at least half a dozen meek young people who can neither talk distinctly, act convincingly, nor give any evidence of dramatic fitness, into that fine, open-mouthed machine, and out they come at the other end as 'star,' full fledged."[50] Unlike the self-made performers of the previous decade, the new stars were manufactured products, carefully packaged commodities who, with the requisite publicity and the right vehicle, appealed to the public on the basis of appearance and style. Theater insiders would have had little trouble identifying the unnamed target of Dale's rant as Charles Frohman, the most prolific theater manager within the Syndicate. Since forming the Empire Theatre Stock Company in 1892, Frohman had elevated numerous performers to theatrical stardom, believing that stars brought "a unique value" to a play by "concentrat[ing] interest."[51] Unlike nineteenth-century stock company managers such as Augustin Daly, who had rejected the star system for fear that it would undermine his managerial authority, Frohman chose to present himself as a "star maker," a magician of sorts who transformed unknown individuals into household names while maintaining an almost invisible presence behind the scenes.[52] "In a country where a public character may as well think of escaping the light of the day as the man with the camera, Charles Frohman is the great unphotographed," the *New York Times* observed in 1908. According to contemporary accounts, Frohman's public profile was so low that very few people recognized him when he appeared in public.[53]

Despite this apparent reluctance to appear before the camera, however, Frohman was an astute observer of new technologies who skillfully employed recent developments in commercial advertising, including electric lighting and large billboards, to promote his performers and manipulate public opinion.[54] Frohman's biographers insist that his greatest strength as a "star maker" was selecting vehicles that amplified his performers' personalities. In the case of the actress Billie Burke, an attractive strawberry blonde with a limited acting range, he took pains to "adapt her personal appearance, humor, and temperament to her plays," commissioning new works to showcase her "peculiar gifts." As Burke herself admitted, "I was amusing onstage because I had delightful costumes, because I had witty lines to say, written by the wittiest authors, and because I worked."[55]

Frohman's biographers claim that in reviving the star system, Frohman was simply meeting public demand. He recognized that the public, "the new generation," wanted "younger people, popular names—somebody to talk about," and he gave them what they wanted: a series of fresh faces and interesting personalities.[56] Critics like Alan Dale, however, were less convinced and voiced fears that the star system severely limited opportunities for emerging performers. Whereas actors had once been rewarded for their years of servitude, now those who failed to catch a manager's eye were doomed "to be hewers of wood and drawers of water for other actors."[57] The situation was equally grim for star performers, who became comfortable and rich playing the same or similar roles year after year and failed to expand their repertoire. *Leslie's Magazine* warned that even the brightest stars had "degenerated into mere acting machines," "slaves" and "automatons" who had traded their identities and individualities for a chance at stardom and were now reduced to flitting about the stage in frivolous comedies and dramas.[58] "[T]he race of actors is slowly dying out," the *Theatre Magazine* concluded in 1907, "and the general drift is downwards towards the commonplace and the vulgar."[59]

In comparing the star system to sausage manufacturing or actors to automatons, theater critics tapped into prevailing debates about the rationalization of labor and its effects on individual subjectivity, particularly as it affected men.[60] Indeed, their frequent use of male pronouns as well as their exclusive use of the term "actor" in a period when female performers were commonly referred to as "actresses" indicates that it was the commodification and corresponding feminization of *male* stars that most troubled the critics.[61] Although leading men such as John Drew and matinee idols such as Kirle Bellow and E. H. Sothern continued to attract adoring audiences, they were hardly the models of strong, virile "self-made manhood" typified by nineteenth-century actors, who had managed their own companies, built their own theaters, and generally assumed control over all aspects of their business. Limited by the whims of the box office, by the casting decisions of managers more concerned with profit than art, and by the privileging of female performers—who despite enduring sexism in the workplace made the most of their elevation within the "star system"—male performers had fewer opportunities to assert authority and seemed disturbingly emasculated as a result.[62]

Critics' comments about the "dying race" of actors and the degradation of audiences also recalled Theodore Roosevelt's dire predictions of "race suicide" in the wake of mass immigration.[63] In a speech to the National Congress of Mothers in 1905, Roosevelt warned that "[i]f either a race or an individual prefers the pleasure of more effortless ease, of self-indulgence, to the infinitely deeper, the infinitely higher pleasures that come to those who know the toil and the weariness, but also the joy, of hard duty well done, why, that race or that individual must inevitably in the end pay the penalty of leading a life both vapid and ignoble."[64] Theater critics transposed Theodore Roosevelt's concerns about "race suicide" into a theatrical context, claiming that the American stage would soon be overrun by alien hordes.[65] "The race of trained, accomplished, competent actors, rapidly dwindling, will soon have passed away, and no new actors of equal qualification are going to fill the void," William Winter warned in 1907.[66] Although census statistics for 1910 show that the racial composition of the acting profession was remarkably unchanged from nineteenth-century statistics, with 78 percent of actors and 81 percent of actresses identifying as native-born whites, the critics' warnings about dying races and racial pollution suggest that they had a very different impression of demographics.[67] Certainly Irish and Jewish performers—both members of racial groups teetering on the cusp of whiteness—were assuming a much more dominant presence in this period.[68] Although access to white, middle-class audiences often hinged on performers' willingness to exploit ethnic stereotypes or appear in blackface, the ascendancy of such stars as Eddie Cantor, Al Jolson, Sophie Tucker, Fanny Brice, and Blanche Yurka fueled the dreams of would-be players.[69] The phenomenal American success of the French star Sarah Bernhardt, who, as Susan Glenn explains, deliberately played up her Jewishness "to provoke and captivate," offered further evidence that the demographic makeup of the profession was changing and audience tastes along with them.[70]

The influx of foreign performers into the United States, a number of whom entered the country from England on a salary from Frohman, was a source of great concern for many critics.[71] Although in 1895, the *Times* claimed that "the supremacy of the foreign stars as an attraction for American audiences is becoming a thing of the past," a 1897 editorial in the *Dramatic Mirror* indicates that "alien performers" continued to "shine resplendent" on American stages.[72] By 1904, Franklin Fyles was suggesting that so many artists from Great Britain, France, and Italy would be "invading" Broadway during the upcoming season that theatergoers might embark on their own theatrical "Grand Tour" without leaving the comforts of home.[73] Although the actual number of foreign performers touring the United States in this period was relatively low compared to the flood of immigrants entering the country—ranging between 15 and 17 percent—the attention they received from the American press stirred resentment among native-born actors and critics, who unfavorably compared foreign players to foreign goods and complained that "it is only necessary for an artist to bear a foreign label to evoke enthusiastic comment."[74]

Critics similarly disparaged Charles Frohman's preference for foreign plays, arguing that they impeded the development of American playwrights.[75] Indeed, with the assistance of the play broker and literary agent Elisabeth Marbury, Frohman all but cornered the playwriting market in Europe and the United States, importing hit plays from London and Paris, including works by Oscar Wilde, Henry Arthur Jones, and Haddon Chambers, and commissioning translations and new works from such leading American playwrights as Augustus Thomas, William Gillette, Bronson Howard, and Clyde Fitch. "I wonder whether there are any English actor-managers, or English managers that produce more English plays than I do," he pondered in a letter of 1901 to the playwright Haddon Chambers.[76]

Frohman did little to endear his critics to him, openly admitting that he was not interested in developing native talent for its own sake (figure 1.3). "My object in life is to give the public incessant novelty—even if it fails," he told Alan Dale in 1905. "I am proud to say that I have produced more failures than any other living man, because I have produced more plays."[77] When asked whether negative reviews bothered him, he explained to the critic Samuel Moffett that "[t]he only comment that is worth anything is that which speaks through the box-office."[78] Despite continuing to insist that the box office should speak for itself, Frohman addressed critics' complaints that he ignored American playwrights, writing in a 1909 *Times* editorial that "[m]anagers do not import plays out of preference, but out of a habit of taking good dramatic material wherever it is to be found. There are no national boundaries for play-writing or to any other art." Arguing from a universalist position, Frohman implied that the nativist cry for a uniquely American theater was antithetical to good art, insisting that American critics and playwrights might do better to learn from foreign authors: "The greatest benefit that can befall an American playwright is to see his play fail in a theatre next door to a success fresh from the Paris stage—and not only to see it, but to see why."[79] Those who refused to acknowledge foreign skill and artistry, he concluded, did so at the expense of their own development.

American critics disagreed. "It is the English playmakers who have

Figure 1.3. The theater manager Charles Frohman aboard the *Lusitania* in 1915. Frohman was one of the passengers on board the ship when it was sunk by a German U-boat. Photography Collection, Miriam and Ira D. Wallach Division of Art, Prints and Photographs, The New York Public Library, Astor, Lenox and Tilden Foundations.

cause to be grateful to Charles Frohman and the Syndicate," the editors of *Leslie's Monthly Magazine* snarled in 1904. "He buys their commonplace stuff, their tawdry adaptations from the French, their witless, soulless, snobbish, botched work, and pays a big price for it." Echoing the rhetoric of economic nationalism, they argued that Frohman's poorly made foreign commodities were flooding the American theatrical market, leaving no room for the native playwright. "[F]ew native born dramatists are admitted within the sacred precincts of the Frohman circle, as that manager prefers to import a success from London rather than risk the work of an unknown fellow countryman," continued the editors. Other critics went so far as to argue that foreign plays were responsible for "all the filth, vulgarity, and immorality of our fast degenerating stage" and demanded some kind of action to prevent their importation.[80]

In rejecting foreign plays and players, theater critics joined a growing chorus of anxious voices worried about the influence of foreign products on American consumers, especially women. Throughout the late nineteenth century and the early twentieth, leading proponents of economic nationalism—government officials, business leaders, and other cultural arbiters—introduced measures to limit imports of luxury goods from Europe, concerned that preferences for foreign goods were inhibiting the development of American industry and negatively affecting consumer taste. Despite growing calls to "buy American," however, most female consumers viewed themselves as members of an "imagined community" of consumers that extended beyond national borders and embraced a modern transnational aesthetic that defied traditional American values.[81] Hoping to forestall the invasion of foreign goods and ideas, and fresh from his victory over the patent medicine industry, Edward Bok, the editor of the *Ladies' Home Journal*, launched an "American Fashions for American Women" campaign in 1909, through which he urged his female readers to throw off the shackles of Paris and embrace their republican roots. "[W]e have a New World cleverness that the [others] have not," he declared in an October 1910 editorial, reiterating the notion that each nation possessed a unique national character that could only be appreciated by its citizens.[82] Bok's passionate editorials suggest that what he feared most was that in wearing the "freakish" creations of Parisian couturiers, American women were becoming freaks themselves. Polluted by consumption, they would no longer be capable of producing the healthy, hearty stock necessary for the advancement of American culture and society.[83]

The situation was equally dire for American theater audiences consuming foreign plays. In 1910, the actress Mrs. Leslie Carter proposed a five-year ban on foreign plays, which she hoped would shame managers like Frohman who "without nerve or patriotism . . . spend most of their time abroad watching the foreign producer take the risks of original production, only to swoop down upon the cream of the result, buy it up for home consumption, and, returning here, demand veneration for wonderful acumen and managerial ability."[84] While Carter's proposed boycott did not come to fruition, critics continued to uphold the long-standing dream of an endowed theater that would allow native playwrights to develop in an environment unhampered by commercial interests. Although they debated whether the endowed theater should be publicly or privately supported, they nevertheless agreed that its primary objective should be "to present only dramas which are good literature and which represent the life and manners of the present time."[85] Such a theater would stand against the commercial influence, provide sanctuary for those disgusted by the excesses of the Syndicate, and uplift those who had succumbed to its lures. "In the matter of correct theatrical taste the American public has no standard at present," a 1901 editorial in the *Theatre Magazine* explained. "An endowed or independent theater could create one, and in my humble opinion this should be its chief mission. Then consider, for a moment, the blessing that such a theatre would be as an educator."[86] Other advocates of the endowed theater expressed similar views about theater's civilizing function, firm in their belief that with the appropriate venue audiences could be trained and educated. "The public is more discriminating each year," Harrison Grey Fiske insisted in January 1898. "There is no longer hope for mediocrities in [a] calling that requires well defined ability, and in this discrimination we find a bow of promise."[87] Victory was assured; it was only a matter of time.

But finding the right venue proved a difficult challenge. The first experiment with a subscription-endowed theater in Chicago during the 1906-7 season was a failure. Poor business management, mediocre production values, and inexperienced actors disappointed audiences and the theater was forced to close after only twenty weeks.[88] Although the 1909 opening of the New Theatre in New York achieved greater success, plans for a full-scale national theater remained a distant dream.[89] Audiences continued to patronize the commercial theaters and did not experience the kind of cultural uplift expected by the supporters of the endowed theater.

Indeed, for many critics, one of the most distressing signs of the Syndicate's degradation of the stage was its effect on theater audiences. "The theatrical audience of this period is largely composed of vulgarians, who know nothing about art or literature and who care for nothing but the solace of their common tastes and animal appetites," William Winter railed. He urged "thoughtful observer[s]" to notice the "faces and manners of the multitude" and warned that if the Syndicate continued to have its way, "[t]he stage, already 'orientalized,' will, more and more, be devoted to ornate spectacle, 'crank' experiment, and all forms of fad and folly that the ingenuity of the 'amusement' monger can invent." *Leslie's Magazine* agreed: "The theater-going public is now recruited from the lowest ranks of our nation—the cultured class prefers grand opera to the spectacles which appeal only to the baser senses." With few alternatives to "worthless plays [and] vulgar, showy productions," civilized patrons were abandoning the theater, leaving it to the tastes of less "cultivated" minds.[90] John Corbin compared the commercial theater to dime magazines such as *McClure's* and *Munsey's*, which had lowered their cover prices in the mid-1890s to appeal to a more predominantly middle-class market. "The drama is in precisely the condition in which literature would be if the reading public were limited to the ten-cent magazines," he argued. Rather than challenge audiences with material of high literary standing, managers catered to base interests with light-hearted comedies and insubstantial fluff. Corbin admitted that the Syndicate did "good work in giving the play-going public what it wants," but he doubted whether it would ever produce lasting works of art.[91] The solution, according to the *Theatre Magazine*'s Charlton Andrews, was an "Admittance Commission" of experts who would conduct interviews with prospective theatergoers to assess their mental, physical, and social status. Such a commission would ensure the proper "elevation" of American audiences and "keep out the intellectually unfit."[92]

The image that emerges from Andrew's social Darwinist proposition and Winter's overblown references to "common tastes," "animal appetites," and "orientalized" dens of iniquity is one of a predominantly ethnic, working-class, male audience. Yet this image is surprisingly inconsistent with the image of giggling matinee girls that appear in so many other accounts. In fact, while greater numbers of working-class immigrants did attend the theater in this period, most immigrant men frequented music halls and vaudeville, *not* the legitimate theater. How, then, are we to account for these clashing images? One possible answer is that the older generation of theater critics, represented by William Winter, was unwilling to blame middle-class white women for the degradation of the stage and preferred to point the finger at less sympathetic culprits. An immigrant audience that resembled the Syndicate in its behavior and outlook was a much more convincing villain than an audience of juvenile school girls. More problematically, to admit that women were responsible for the degradation of the stage was to admit that these same women were shirking their duties as the spiritual guardians of the home and the nation. Such an acknowledgment threatened to undo the critics' allegorical association between the debasement of the stage and the corruption of gentile womanhood.[93] For those who had exploited stereotypes of white slavery for years, this was not an argument they could easily make.

The newer generation of theater critics seems to have held no such reservations, however, and shifted the terms of the anti-commercial argument from an attack on thieving Jewish managers to an attack on matinee girls. Eschewing the genteel tradition of seasoned critics like Winter in favor of pithy and sometimes acerbic commentary, they recognized what Charles Frohman and other defenders of the Syndicate had been arguing for years: that theater managers were bound by the whims and fancies of their audiences.[94] "[A] manager's business is dependent upon the will of the people, however much he may dictate terms," Montrose Moses argued in 1911. "They like what they like, and just as soon as they discriminate in their liking, the manager's stand will have to change."[95] Although some critics adopted a laissez-faire stance, believing that the market would eventually right itself, others refused to sit by and let women ruin the American theater. In a 1908 article in the *Ladies' Home Journal*, an unnamed actor showed little restraint in identifying the root cause of theatrical decline:

If I Were Asked: "What is the most pernicious tendency of the American playhouse?" I should unhesitatingly say the bad influence of the matinee girl. And by matinee girl I do not necessarily mean the young girls who are allowed too much freedom by devoted but misguided parents, but in that category I place the indolent woman who passes for an intelligent person, but who is in truth an illiterate, candy-eating woman whose idea of amusement is found in omnivorous theatregoing.[96]

Rather than perform their traditional responsibilities as the spiritual guardians of elite white culture, these "illiterate, candy-eating" women voraciously consumed the foreign plays, performers, and commodities imported by the Syndicate and indulged their base desires for pleasure and escape. What is striking about the theater critics' virulent response to the matinee girl is their apparent unwillingness to allow the theater to become yet another site of female-centered amusement. In refusing to yield to the whims and fancies of juvenile girls, these men identified the legitimate theater as their last stand.[97]

The Tyranny of the Matinee Girl

In 1897, *Munsey's* contemplated the phenomenon known as the "matinee girl." "That she is *fin de siècle* does not need to be proved," the magazine observed, "for it is well known that only in recent years has the privilege of attending theaters been allowed to young women unescorted by brother or father, or the creature known by the elastic and accommodating term 'cousin.' "[98] The matinee girl's emergence was the result of a number of interrelated factors that included women's increased economic self-sufficiency, higher levels of education, new leisure opportunities, and a growing willingness to allow young women to participate in public life. Throughout the 1880s and 1890s, thousands of middle-class women pursued college degrees, infiltrating male-dominated professions such as medicine, law, and engineering, often at the expense of the traditional marriage. Working women similarly abandoned the traditional route to domesticity, finding employment in department stores, hotels, restaurants, offices, and factories, which allowed them to partake more directly of the many "cheap amusements" on offer in the modern city.[99] In 1909, a matinee girl could purchase a ticket in the gallery of a "high-priced theatre" for between fifty and seventy-five cents, much less than the two dollar charge for orchestra seats. Unlike the galleries in less reputable variety houses, these were "clean and orderly" and therefore appropriate for respectable women.[100] Yet while working women regularly attended the theater, most matinee girls were white, middle-class suburban dwellers in their teens and twenties—high school students, college girls, young brides—who did not work and had few responsibilities outside of the home. On Wednesday and Saturday afternoons, these women descended on the theater district, crowding the highways, thoroughfares, streetcars, subways, and elevated trains as they rushed to meet their friends outside one of Broadway's many theaters (figure 1.4).[101]

The matinee girl phenomenon marked the final stage in what the historian Richard Butsch calls the "re-gendering" of theater audiences, a process that had begun in the mid-nineteenth century. Throughout this period, the rowdy, male-dominated audiences that characterized the late republican and early nineteenth-century theater slowly gave way to increasing numbers of respectable, well-behaved female theatergoers.[102] Theater managers addressed women's concerns for respectability in the 1840s by instituting new rules to tame unruly crowds, holding special weekday matinees for women and children, and otherwise promoting their establishments as a safe and comfortable home away from home. This transformation of the theater from

Figure 1.4. Matinee girls flood out of a theater and onto Broadway, enjoying their newfound freedom to enter public spaces without a male escort, 1901. Picture Collection, The Branch Libraries, The New York Public Library, Astor, Lenox and Tilden Foundations.

a "male club" to a "female parlor" was consistent with a larger shift in the gendered geography of the modern city, whereby public spaces that had once been considered too dangerous or disreputable for women began to accommodate and even encourage female patronage. Along with department stores and ice cream parlors, reformed theaters, with their offering of plays such as the anti-slavery melodrama *Uncle Tom's Cabin*, were the first commercial establishments to cater specifically to women and were instrumental in the development of female-centered retail districts—a subject I will return to in Chapter 2.[103]

Although the rhetoric of respectability continued to be important in the mid-nineteenth century, theater managers began placing greater emphasis on visual pleasures and other sensory delights, selling the theater as an exciting, glamorous site of consumption and spectacle, where women could temporarily escape their domestic obligations and the surveying eyes of fathers and husbands.[104] New attitudes toward theatricality and a more expressive model of femininity also played into this transition. During her 1868 performances at Niblo's Garden's, the British burlesque performer Lydia Thompson lampooned the liberated "Girl of the Period" and posed in character for a publicity photograph wearing a stuffed squirrel hat and smoking a cigarette. When Thompson and her troupe of "British Blondes" later toured the country, they popularized a rounder, fuller figure for women and sparked a craze for dyed blonde hair; the widespread distribution of their photographs likewise contributed to the gradual standardization of beauty ideals throughout the country.[105]

By 1910, the critic Walter Prichard Eaton estimated that women constituted 75 percent of all "legitimate" theater audiences. Independent surveys conducted in the same period by the Shubert brothers and Charles Frohman suggest that the percentage of female theatergoers was slightly lower, ranging between 66 percent and 68 percent, while an article in the *Green Book Album* in 1910 reported that 85 percent of the audiences at Wednesday matinees were women.[106] Regardless of their discrepancies, these surveys indicate that female theatergoers, many of whom were young, single women, had assumed a significant presence in the commercial theater. "Drama totters on the verge of becoming a noun of feminine gender!" the theater critic Clayton Hamilton proclaimed in 1909. "Appeal to the petticoats has been the dominant note in nearly all our productions, from 'Votes for Women,' which argued that women really ought to be men, to 'The Newlyweds and Their Baby,' which reminded us that they can't be."[107]

Not surprisingly, the rapid increase in the number of women at the legitimate theater corresponded with a sharp decline in male attendance. "Very few men go to the theater unattached," Clayton Hamilton observed in 1907, "and these few are not important enough, from the theoretic standpoint, to alter the psychologic aspect of the audience."[108] "[M]ere man has been considered not a bit in thirty-days quota of simple, simpering, tea-and-biscuit, drawing room comedy," he complained two years later. Advertisements declaring "Every girl will want to see it" and "The sweetest story ever told" left little doubt about the identity of the target audience.[109] Although the percentage of men at evening performances was much higher than the percentage at matinees, other observers claimed that most men would rather be somewhere else. "[H]alf the men who do come to see the plays would, if left to themselves, either go to their club or drop in on a vaudeville show or musical comedy," explained one critic. "They come [to the theater] because their wives or sweethearts want to."[110] Despite ceding the legitimate theater to matinee girls, however, men continued to seek theatrical amusement elsewhere. In 1906, *Variety* reported that 65 percent of the vaudeville audience at Hammerstein's or the Fifth Avenue was "made up of the sterner sex" at both evening and matinee performances. "Men whose appearance proclaimed them merchants, bookkeepers and other workers were devoting the busiest part of the day to witnessing a variety performance," the writer noted with surprise.[111] To the critics, the male theatergoer's preference for loud, brash vaudeville acts and sexually provocative musical comedies was a direct response to the feminization of the legitimate stage.

Although most working-class audiences patronized vaudeville and cinema, growing numbers of working-class women were also beginning to attend the legitimate theater. Unable to attend matinees, these women often lined up after work to buy gallery tickets for an evening show, eating the remnants of their lunch as they waited for the box office to open. "It gives me a better chance for a front seat," explained one working girl when asked why she was willing to stand in line for such a long time.[112] For working-class women, however, the freedom to attend the theater alone was often complicated by their financial dependency on men. Those who could not afford to pay for their own theater tickets were often expected to repay their male companions with sexual favors. Although "treating," the name given to this form of exchange, allowed women to escape the drudgery of their everyday lives, it also left them dependent on the whims and fancies of their companions.[113]

In 1902, Marion Earle, a young working woman, wrote a letter to the *Evening World* proposing the formation of a "little club of wage-earning girls who, like myself, [long] occasionally for an evening's diversion [of opera] or theatre, and who [do] not wish to depend upon an invitation from time to time from a man." Earle hoped to attract a group of eight to ten girls, but when her letter was published in the *Evening World*, over one hundred women responded. After a preliminary meeting, attended by one hundred and fifty women from throughout the Greater New York area, the "Bachelor Girls' Club" was officially formed with fifty-seven members enrolled. Most of these women were "members of skilled professions—stenographers, bookkeepers, trained nurses, milliners, dressmakers, all well educated, many of them highly accomplished." When the actress Elsie de Wolfe learned of the Bachelor Girls' Club, she offered the women free tickets to attend her production of *The Way of the World*, much to their delight. "Girls who work every day in the year don't get invitations to the theatre any too often," explained Earle, "and to see Miss De Wolfe, of whom they had all read and heard so much, was a totally undreamed of pleasure."[114] In proposing the Bachelor Girls' Club, Earle offered a positive alternative for those who wished to make their own theater choices and avoid the sexual politics that an invitation from a man could entail. Her club gave working women an opportunity to declare their economic independence, express pride in themselves as single, professional women, and perhaps most important, indulge their own tastes and interests. No longer beholden to the choices, expectations, or permission of male companions, young women were free to see the theater *they* wanted to see.[115]

From the theater critic's perspective, however, women's growing demands for light-hearted entertainment spelled disaster for the development of modern American drama. Writing in newspapers and literary magazines, these educated men and women made a point of representing female theatergoers as irrational, emotionally vulnerable, culturally deficient, and prone to hysteria, positioning themselves as rational and sensible, the protectors of the American art and culture.[116] "[W]oman glories in hysteria and loves the tears she sheds over the sorrows of the stage heroine," one male commentator observed in 1908. "I can see where this emotional safety-valve is of inestimable value to women."[117] Without such a safety valve, he implied, women's pent-up emotions might lead them to behave in inappropriate ways elsewhere. In a 1902 article published in the *Atlantic Monthly*, the writer Elizabeth McCracken used similarly disparaging language to describe the college sophomore seated beside her at a matinee performance of *The Pride of Jennico*. According to McCracken, the girl "wept copiously, she laughed most wildly, she shuddered, and she applauded Mr. [James K.] Hackett, whenever he appeared or disappeared, with an exaggerated but delightful fervor." At the intermission, the sophomore talked to McCracken about her love for Julia Marlowe and E. H.

Sothern and admitted that she had "cried quarts" at *Barbara Frietchie*; when asked whether she found "the theatre very interesting," she responded in the affirmative, "especially since I have begun to read psychology." McCracken's following remarks, intended for the well-educated, culturally sophisticated readers of the *Atlantic Monthly*, represent the effusive matinee girl as flighty, misguided, and curiously out-of-touch with her emotions:

> That sophomore undoubtedly does find the theatre interesting; but could Professor [William] James himself discover any connection between what she finds in it of most evident interest and her study of psychology? With all her confidences, she still was canny when it came to the delicate point. *She possibly does not know just why she goes to the play; she may actually believe that her motive has something to do with the study of psychology* [my emphasis].[118]

In questioning the girl's self-awareness and implying that her interest in psychology is as insubstantial as her devotion to Julia Marlowe, McCracken sets the stage for the real subject of her article: the theatergoing practices of female tenement house residents. As the theater historian Shannon Jackson has shown, reformers like Jane Addams made theatrical training and perfor-mances an active part of their social work, believing that "the embodied, en-vironmental, and enacted nature of the medium itself . . . uniquely facilitated the transformation in sensibility and behavior."[119] In line with this philosophy, McCracken celebrates theater's potential for cultural advancement and social uplift and portrays tenement house residents as ideal spectators: "They are influenced; they are made greater or less; and, simple as the influence may be, its result is surely felt by their associates and their surroundings." To illustrate her point, McCracken recalls one resident, "whose life had been very hard," who proclaimed her love of the British actress Ellen Terry and proudly dis-played a magazine photograph of Terry as Portia on a shelf in her room. "It's been a long time since I saw her," the woman told McCracken, "but I've never forgot the things she said 'bout having mercy, and how she looked when she said 'em. People ain't always had mercy for me; and when I've wanted to pay 'em back for it or be mean to anybody, I jes' remember her and what she said 'bout havin' mercy—and I don't want to be mean 'cause of her."[120] Behind McCracken's representation of tenement house residents as earnest devotees of "the drama," women whose lives have been transformed by their contem-plation of serious theatrical art, lies a none-too-subtle critique of middle-class matinee girls and their predisposition for excessive emotional display and fluffy, inconsequential plays.

Yet while tenement house residents may have represented the ideal salvation for the American theater, their low economic status presented a problem. Indeed, the real issue, theater critics realized, was a financial one: matinee girls could not be ignored because they effectively controlled the box office. In the months following the Crash of 1907, when the producing members of the Syndicate had difficulty filling their theaters, they renewed their effort to cater to female tastes for fantasy and escape.[121] "To-day I take advantage of a general feminine desire to view Miss Tottie Coughdrop," Charles Frohman confessed to the playwright Paul Potter, noting that the men who attended his productions were almost always there at the behest of their female companions.[122] Managers who might otherwise produce experimental or more "artistic" work discovered that their success hinged on their ability to please female patrons. "If women do not like a play, it is doomed," George A. Kingsbury, the manager of the Chicago Opera House, observed in 1910, "[b]ut if it appeals to them and they flock to it, its prosperity is assured."[123] In fact, by 1914, legitimate theater managers had recognized that box office receipts for matinee performances were exceeding those for evening performances and that more than ever their fate was in the hands of female theatergoers.[124]

Although Frohman and Kingsbury approached the issue of female patronage from a pragmatic perspective, theater critics were frustrated by the amount of influence wielded by women. In their view, managerial dependence on female patronage privileged musical comedies and other light material over serious drama, preventing promising work from being staged and requiring playwrights to "dumb down" their plays. "The real cause of the insipidity of the American dramatic art," a male critic announced in 1907, "is she whom Christy and Gibson have fashioned, the American Girl. Our plays . . . are not written for thinking men and women, but appeal chiefly to the limited intelligence of immature girlhood."[125] The theater critic Alan Dale likewise worried that female audiences had been "vulgarized" by the "overdressed drama" to such an extent that managers were now obliged to select plays on the basis of costuming opportunities.[126] According to Walter Prichard Eaton, the producers of Joseph Medill Paterson's *The Fourth Estate* (1909) were so dismayed by poor box office receipts that after overhearing female theatergoers complain about the depressing ending they asked Paterson to rewrite it. "Business in fact, did at once increase," Eaton observed. "Yet the play was measurably weaker as a work of art, measurably less effective as a weapon for good."[127] Indeed, as the playwright Henry Arthur Jones warned, the "Young Person's" tyrannical tastes led to "plays that do not tell the truth, but would form a suitable entertainment for matinee girls."[128]

Clayton Hamilton identified women's inherent irrationality and inability to focus for prolonged periods of time as the source of the problem. "[S]ince women are by nature inattentive," he explained, "the femininity of the modern theatre audience forces the dramatist to employ the elementary technical tricks of repetition and parallelism, in order to keep his play clear though much of it be unattended to."[129] The underlying issue for Hamilton and many of his peers was the matinee girl's failure to watch theater in a manner they deemed appropriate for engaging with serious (read: legitimate) theater.[130] In 1897, *Munsey's* similarly implied that matinee girls were ill-equipped to think critically about what they were seeing, offering the following description of a typical matinee girl's journal: "The first act is almost invariably indicated by a long series of truly feminine ejaculations, such as: 'Too sweet for anything!' 'Just perfect!' 'Simply great!' The second is even more intense: 'Superb!' 'Wonderful!' 'Magnificent!' 'Oh!' But the third act is the climax. Exclamation points alone fill the lines, and the paper has bubbled up here and there, where evidently blinding tears have fallen."[131] What is perhaps most striking about this presumably fictionalized account is the way it represents the matinee girl's experience as an erotic journey, a slowly building swell of emotion culminating in a climax of tears that renders her incapable of speaking or writing. The speechless, overwrought, matinee girl is the antithesis of the calm, intellectually astute theater critic who produces witty, eloquent critiques even with the pressure of a publication deadline.

Yet for reform-minded observers like Edward Bok, matinee girls' voracious consumption of theatrical fare, especially the "problem plays" of playwrights like Shaw, and their deep emotional investment in stage players was cause for concern, *not* because it undermined the development of American drama but rather because it threatened to damage innocent minds: "One will see at these matinees seats and boxes full of sweet young girls ranging from twelve to sixteen years of age. They are not there by the few, nor by the score, but literally by the hundreds . . . it is enough to make a man burn with shame and indignation to see hundreds of young girls sitting in the theater, and, with open mouths, literally drinking in remarks and conversations to which no young girl in her teens should listen."[132] Bok worried that the matinee girl's indiscriminate taste for plays with mature content threatened to undermine parental authority, arguing that "[n]o young girl needs to have her mind soiled by having it dragged through realistic dirt and mire for two or three hours to learn a moral lesson which her mother should have taught her at home."[133] Ever the paternalist, he used his editorial position with the *Ladies' Home Journal* to urge mothers to pay closer attention to their daughters' theatergoing habits, preferably by attending the theater with them.

Bok's position on the phenomenon of the matinee girl is striking for several reasons. First, his concern about "problem plays," a term often used to describe Ibsen's controversial dramas, and his description of the young audience's focused concentration are strangely at odds with other critics' complaints about matinee girls' inattentive presence at "dumbed down" plays. These anxieties seem to suggest, contrary to the complaints of Hamilton and Arthur Jones, that young women may have been attending some of the most innovative theater of the modern era. Second, by directing his comments toward female readers and calling upon them to take action, Bok shifts responsibility from the girls to their mothers on the assumption that these women *will* take action. Unlike other critics, who categorically dismissed all women as problematic consumers, Bok had greater faith in his readers' tastes and their willingness to advocate for appropriate consumer goods. Writing about the theater while simultaneously leading the charge against the patent medicine industry in the pages of the *Journal*, he clearly trusted in his ability to sway consumer opinion.

But while Bok continued to see matinee girls as young if frivolous innocents in need of firm guidance, others saw them as tyrannous, inhuman monsters, "illiterate, candy-eating" women who behaved terribly at the theater.[134] "Women behave here just as they do when shopping," one box office clerk complained. "They demand to know what seats are to be had in the various part of the house and the prices thereof. A selection is often a matter of the slowest imaginable consideration, even though it keeps a line of persons waiting."[135] Such inconsiderate behavior at the box office was hardly comparable to women's behavior inside the theater. In the "conversational scrap" below (presumably overheard by an "Actor" and later published in the *Theatre Magazine*), "feminine auditors" thought nothing of carrying on a conversation throughout a performance: "Oh, I think Mr. A is just splendid! Did you know he's married? Oh, yes—he has a suite of apartments at the Elysian. I know a girl whose brother meets him every day at his club. Doesn't his coat fit just perfect. He goes to London every summer for his clothes. Do you like the leading woman? I think her dress is a sight! I mean to do my hair the way she does, though. You too?"[136] Rejecting the model of focused concentration upheld as the ideal by theater critics, these women exchange information about "Mr. A's" offstage life and offer a critical assessment of the leading woman's clothes and hairstyle. The 1908 cartoon, entitled "What the Cartoonist Saw of Maxine Elliott at the Matinee," offers a similar glimpse of women's problematic theatergoing practices, depicting an audience of stylishly coifed female heads gazing and dissecting the various characteristics of their idol—her hair, clothing, and so forth—with little consideration for the male cartoonist seated behind them (figure 1.5).[137]

Despite their extensive complaints and unflattering representations, critics could do little to stop women from behaving inappropriately in the theater. In a 1907 article entitled "The Brutality of the Matinee Girl," Juliet Wilbor Tompkins accused matinee girls of laughing at inappropriate moments and making fun of poor acting. "An emotional scene where the stage personage is carried out of the conventional tones and postures of daily life by some overwhelming feeling will rouse her to open mirth, no matter how well it is done," she explained. If the play or performance failed to please her, "she is whole-heartedly gay, pelting it with laughter and comments without a qualm." What most seems to have alarmed Tompkins was that these misbehaving women were "not common, in the usual acceptance of the term" but rather "[p]rosperous and educated Anglo-Saxons" who had apparently abandoned the characteristic traits of good breeding in their pursuit of pleasure. These not "quite human" women did not respect the artistry of the stage but rather behaved as they saw fit, rejecting traditional stereotypes of "the sympathetic and emotional sex."[138]

Tompkins was not alone in fearing that white, middle-class women were shirking their traditional roles and responsibilities. By the early twentieth century, a growing chorus of conservative critics warned that the rise of a new group of highly educated and economically independent women, who preferred the intellectual stimulation of work and friendships with other women to the obligations of marriage and motherhood, spelled disaster for the dominant white society. Active participants in Progressive Era politics, these New Women agitated for social reform, called for the legalization of trade unions, opened settlement houses for underprivileged women, and staged suffrage protests. For conservatives already worried about declining birth rates among the social elite and the possibility of "race suicide," women's preference for the company of other women and their apparent willingness to forego motherhood threatened the health and future of the nation.[139] Although juvenile matinee girls did not represent the same threat as militant suffragists or settlement house workers, their frivolous, self-centered behavior, unquenchable appetite for stage spectacle, and avid consumption of fashion and other consumer goods signaled a distressing moral decline. In a 1910 address, the lecturer Mrs. John Logan warned that young women were shirking their duties as mothers and wives, "becoming careless, mentally supine, and morally slipshod." To Logan, the site of "women promenading upon Broadway or Fifth Avenue" dressed in the height of fashion constituted

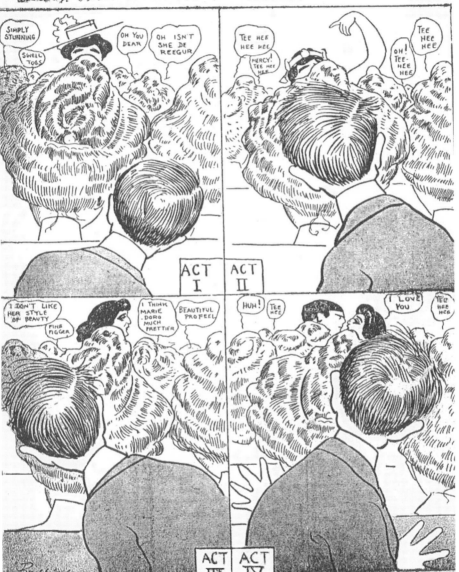

Figure 1.5. "What the Cartoonist Saw of Maxine Elliott at the Matinee." This comic strip depicts the hapless male artist's attempt to see the stage from behind the well-coiffed heads of female audience members. Billy Rose Theatre Division, The New York Public Library for the Performing Arts, Astor, Lenox, and Tilden Foundations.

a "very shocking spectacle" that did not bode well for the advancement of American society.[140]

A "vinegar valentine" of 1902 from Raphael Tuck and Sons (figure 1.6) confirms that for many male observers the matinee girl's obsession with fashion signaled "a tremendous waste of money, waste of brains, and waste of morals."[141] Beside the sketch of a haughty young woman dressed in a large feather hat and tailored suit, her tightly corseted body shaped into an approximation of the letter 'S' in keeping with the prevailing silhouette of the period, the vinegar poet launches his attack:

O, yes, we know your ruling passion,
It is to dress in height of fashion,
And try when walking 'long the street
To flirt with every man you meet.
Dear girl, though stylish you may be,
Your style is not the style for me.

Matinee girls are inverting traditional courting rituals, the poet implies, flirting with men in the streets and making themselves into sexualized spectacles. A second vinegar valentine, also from 1902, offers further evidence that the phenomenon of the matinee girl raised fears that women were usurping the rights and privileges of respectable, white, middle-class men. This card depicts a fashionably dressed and obviously infatuated matinee girl waiting outside a stage door to catch a glimpse of her favorite matinee idol. Rather than teasing the girl for her youthful passion, however, the anonymous poet cruelly suggests that she is wasting her time:

Your joy and your pleasure is day after day
To sit through the acts of a poor trashy play,
Admiring some ham-fatter filling the part
Of a lover without the least atom of art.
But be advised, silly gusher, and drop your fool fad;
Choose a man to admire, not a loafer and cad.

Characterizing actors as unworthy romantic objects, artless cads, and feminized loafers, the valentine urges matinee girls to limit their dating pool to their own kind.

Yet as much as matinee girls dressed to attract male attention in the street and at the stage door, their primary goal seems to have been out-dressing their female friends.[142] "[T]he promenade up and down Broadway" before the matinee was one of its greatest charms for women, *Munsey's* remarked in

TO MY VALENTINE

Matinee
Girl.

O, yes, we know
        your ruling passion,
It is to dress in
            height of fashion,
And try when walking
            'long the street,
To. flirt with every man you meet.
    Dear girl, though
    stylish you may be,
Your style is not
        the style for me.

Figure 1.6. A "vinegar valentine" attacking matinee girls for their obsession with fashion, ca. 1902. Author's collection.

1897, "each woman striving to outshine her fellow promenaders in beauty or daintiness, and sometimes in showiness of attire."[143] Of all the fashion items worn by female theatergoers, the matinee girl's hat was the most important and the most controversial. From the 1890s through the first decade of the twentieth century, the vogue for large-brimmed hats, often two or three times as large as the average woman's head, predominated. These were generally worn for afternoon outings, especially shopping excursions and matinee performances, and were a source of great pleasure and pride.[144] "I'd rather any time see some of these pretty hats than the faces under them," explained one woman when her male companion asked why women did not remove their hats in restaurants.[145]

The magnitude of these hats presented a major challenge for theater managers, who regularly fielded complaints from angry male theatergoers who could not see the stage. These men soon took the matter into their own hands, lobbying for state legislators to pass "high hat" bills that would outlaw millinery spectacles from all places of amusement. Rather than charging the actual women wearing the hats, however, most of these bills held management accountable, presumably out of respect for middle-class women whom the legislators perceived as fashion victims incapable of controlling their consumer desires. Indeed, while a number of state governments, including those of California, Wisconsin, and Ohio, succeeded in passing "high hat" laws, others debated whether it was fair to penalize management while the "real offender . . . may retain her seat and enjoy the performance without let or hindrance."[146] A bill introduced into the Albany legislature in 1897 offered a very different perspective on the rights and responsibilities of female consumers, proposing to fine "any person wearing a hat, bonnet, or a head-dress comprising feathers which shall obstruct the view of any other person in the theatre . . . $5, recoverable in civil proceedings." Although the bill dispensed with the blatant paternalism of its predecessors, seeing women as capable of controlling their urges and paying for their crimes, the *Dramatic Mirror* dismissed it as "amusingly weak and technically to no avail."[147] Too impractical to implement, most of the proposed high hat bills fell by the wayside by 1900 (figure 1.7).

Managers nevertheless continued to struggle with female patrons over their hats, posting announcements reading "Ladies, Please Remove Your Hats" on the backs of seats, in programs, and on tickets.[148] Most women complied with managers' requests by pinning their hats to the upholstered back of the seats in front of them, but others feared that their hats would be damaged and refused. In 1908, the Shuberts tried to resolve this problem by installing a

A SUGGESTION

Figure 1.7. The cartoonist proposes an alternative to the "high hat" laws. Picture Collection, The Branch Libraries, The New York Public Library, Astor, Lenox and Tilden Foundations.

hat rack in the lobby of Daly's Theatre that was attended by a "regular milliner's assistant."[149] Despite managers' efforts to reach a compromise, however, some women stubbornly insisted on wearing their hats, challenging managerial attempts to dictate their appearance and behavior. In 1897, the *Dramatic Mirror* told the shocking story of a Chicago theatergoer, who when asked to remove her hat "not only refused, but drew a razor and slashed the officer who had spoken to her." That the woman had so publicly committed a violent act—and with an item most commonly associated with men—signaled a troubling inversion of gender hierarchies. "What next?" the *Mirror* pondered.[150] Although most examples of female resistance paled in comparison to this one, matinee girls nevertheless continued to flout managerial requests; some even went so far as to insist that male theatergoers should similarly be required to change their behavior.[151] As late as 1915, *Variety* reported that "at the Colonial Monday afternoon over [fifty] women kept on their hats during the performance. This is too bad, for it took a long while for the managers to educate the women in removing their hats."[152]

For theater critics who had fervently believed that well-educated theater audiences would prevent the theater from becoming a commercial paradise, the ascendancy of the matinee girl was an enormous disappointment. Instead of demanding better plays and supporting the development of a dramatic canon that would cement the international reputation of the United States, spoiled middle-class girls attended the theater as they would the department store, intent on satisfying their personal desires. Comfortable in their role as consumers, these girls threatened the theater's traditional gender hierarchy by becoming the stars of their own dramas and declaring their right to see the theater they wanted to see. As much as the critics continued to rail against the dangerous feminization of Broadway, they were ultimately unable to wrest control from the juvenile tyrants who filled its theaters.

In contrast to the majority of theater critics, who generally refused to acknowledge the positive aspects of feminized entertainment, commercial theater managers remained acutely aware that their survival depended on women. Indeed, while many critics assumed that women were inherently drawn to frothy stage confections and displays of bright commodities, theater managers recognized that controlling how and what female audiences consumed was much more difficult than it looked. Through their associations with department stores, advertising agents, and other commercial institutions, as the next chapter will show, they worked aggressively to secure and maintain female interest and to naturalize the relationship between female spectatorship and consumption.

Chapter 2

The "Department Store Theater" and the Gendering of Consumption

Although the theater critic William Winter despaired that a " 'department-store' administration" had overrun the American theater, other observers looked favorably on the commercialization of Broadway, noting with interest the similarities between theaters and department stores. In 1905, for example, the architect Fred Thompson described the newly opened Hippodrome as "a department store in theatricals," an enormous entertainment emporium that played to spectators' desire for fun and escape with a wide-ranging bill that promised something for everyone.[1] "A big department store has much in common with a theatre," the *Theatre Magazine* echoed in 1917. "The backers of each, to succeed, must be good 'showmen' to say nothing of being artists in their lines. They must know what wares to choose and display to the current taste, and particularly how to stage them. They must plan to change the bill frequently in some cases and give long runs in others."[2] Such metaphoric associations between theaters and department stores were not only evocative but also remarkably apt given the increasingly symbiotic nature of their relationship. From the mid-nineteenth century onward, these two urban institutions played a central role in the development of the Ladies' Mile, the female-centered retail district along Broadway from 14th Street to 23rd Street, swapping display strategies and marketing techniques to arouse consumer desire and secure their own financial stability.[3]

As the most dominant, widespread entertainment forms in the United States, with a demographic and geographic reach much greater than that of the individual department store, the legitimate theater and vaudeville, its popular counterpart, were well positioned to shape modern American consumer culture, especially tastes in fashion.[4] Through the centralization of theatrical booking, the systemization of theatrical production, and the exploitation of new promotional techniques, Broadway managers and booking agents borrowed from and helped to shape key elements of the emerging mass culture. Although complaints about the poor quality of touring productions and evidence that performers often adapted their material to account for regional differences suggest that this process was far from homogenous, the organization of once disparate local theaters into national chains represented a huge step in the formation of a mass market.

More than merely selling their own products, Broadway managers played a central role in the promotion and distribution of new products and product categories, ranging from automobiles and soda pop to the latest fashion designs from Paris. "Many a woman throughout the country who cannot get about herself finds in the new stage settings many an idea that might otherwise never have reached her," the *Theatre Magazine* enthused in 1916. "In the clever drapery of a window, in the new arrangement of flowers, she finds the inspiration for a bit of welcome change in her own home."[5] Two years later, the magazine again asserted that "the stage to-day is the best publicity means of putting anything before the public and getting it over; especially a new note that can be visualized—such as fashions and interior decorations."[6] By the early 1900s, theater audiences had come to expect displays of shiny new goods at a Broadway show, so much so that they expressed disappointment when a star actress wore outdated fashions or failed to update her costumes on a regular basis.[7]

The construction of a mode of spectatorship intended to arouse consumer desire was hardly unique to the theater. Driven by anxieties about overproduction and labor unrest, and bolstered by statistical evidence that claimed that women made 85 percent of all consumer purchases, manufacturers joined forces with advertising agents to manipulate consumer behavior. Against a backdrop of progressively violent strikes and protests, this group trained Americans to turn a blind eye to social inequities, to construct individual subjectivities around the purchase of commodities, and to view democracy as the freedom to choose between brands.[8] Still, the formation of a social imaginary oriented around the realization of individual consumer desires was fraught with challenges. Manufacturers found it difficult, if not impossible, to predict how consumers would react to their advertisements. Clinging to nineteenth-century perceptions of the relationship between retailer and customer, some preferred to think that they could simply dictate consumer tastes and desires, but new research into consumer behavior showed otherwise. "Manufacturer, wholesaler, retailer—all must observe the buying habits and listen to the demands of the consumer," insisted the N. W. Ayer and Sons agency.[9] Companies who hoped to win consumer trust and loyalty could no longer afford to ignore what their consumers were saying, these agents urged. Yet despite acknowledging the influence that women wielded both in the home and in American markets, advertising agents tended to look disparagingly on female consumers, depicting them as sensitive, irrational creatures in need of guidance. Adapting psychological theories for their purposes, they moved away from the straightforward, "reason why" copy that had dominated earlier advertisements toward "soft sell" copy that played to emotion, producing "powerful gender prescriptions and images" designed to keep women consuming.[10]

Theater and department store managers in Manhattan similarly recognized the challenges of dictating to consumers and worked hard to feminize consumption and choreograph female movement between their respective establishments.[11] Along with the emerging tourist industry, these institutions created an image of the city that encouraged middle-class consumers to bypass its most troubling districts and to instead see New York as a "navigable, legible, and ultimately playful space."[12] This is not to suggest that New York was an exclusive site for the gendering of consumption, or that collaboration between theaters and department stores did not occur elsewhere, but rather that many of the business partnerships forged in New York in response to shifting economic conditions directly influenced consumer practices throughout the United States.[13] Studying the evolution of these symbiotic relationships as well as the behavioral patterns that developed in response to them therefore offers a fascinating new perspective on the production of the modern female consumer.

The Ladies' Mile

In 1866, the English tourist Samuel Osgood commented on the unique juxtaposition of New York's theaters with other businesses along Broadway: "With few exceptions, the American theaters are not distinguishable from the surrounding houses until a close proximity reveals the name, lights, and other outside paraphernalia of a place of amusement; for on either side of the spacious entrances are usually to be found shops or cafes, and above, the windows of a hotel or retail store."[14] Unlike London's geographically disparate theater district, New York's closely situated playhouses enjoyed "a continual stream of life passing backward and forward before their doors," such that "the overflow of one house finds another theater ready at hand." This convergence of theaters, specialty shops, department stores, hotels, restaurants, and cafes fostered strong cross-industry ties, making Broadway the "center of urban life" for the latter half of the nineteenth century. For visitors like

Osgood, the experience of walking down Broadway was one of excitement and confusion, as stores and theaters became distinguishable only when one approached their doors.[15]

Like the buildings themselves, the history of New York's urban department stores is closely intertwined with the history of commercial Broadway theater.[16] Indeed, many of the innovations made by commercial theater managers in the nineteenth century were inspired or otherwise influenced by the department stores and retail shops that surrounded them. For example, the introduction of the weekday matinee, a strategy to entice respectable middle-class women to the theater, closely coincided with the 1846 opening of New York's first major department store: A. T. Stewart's "Marble Palace" at Chambers and Broadway (figure 2.1). With its white marble façade, wide circular staircase, thirteen-foot mirrors, mahogany counters, and plate-glass show windows—the first of their kind—this large emporium was a destination unto itself. "There is nothing in Paris or London to compare with this dry-goods palace," the former New York mayor Philip Hone noted in his journals.[17] The Marble Palace maintained its status as New York's shopping mecca until 1862, when Stewart decided to build a new establishment, this time an elaborate cast iron structure at Broadway between Ninth and Tenth Streets.[18] Presumably emboldened by success, he next decided to move into the commercial realm of theater construction and hired the architect J. H. Hackett to convert the Unitarian Church of the Messiah at 728 Broadway into a theater for his protégé Lucy Rushton. Although visually impressive, the newly renovated Athenaeum failed to attract sufficient audiences and Stewart was forced to give up his dream of becoming a theatrical impresario.[19]

That a department store entrepreneur should even consider moving into the realm of commercial theater suggests a great deal about the blurring of geographic and aesthetic boundaries between these two worlds. But close proximity to a luxury shop or a new department store had its disadvantages as well. In 1860, an editorial in the *New York Times* remarked that compared to the rest of Broadway, theaters such as Niblo's Garden, located just off the main thoroughfare, seemed drab and dusty, especially in the daytime. The writer describes leaving the brilliance of Broadway with its "golden signs and plate-glass windows flashing in the sunlight," its "banners floating over its principal hotels," and "busy clerks using all their powers of persuasion over glittering counters" to entice "more than ten thousand modern Eves hankering after such forbidden apples of dry goods, jewelry and music," to enter Niblo's Garden, only to find that the "white paint on the pillars and box-fronts [did] not look so dazzling as at night; the gilded sculpture-wreaths [were] fly-marked

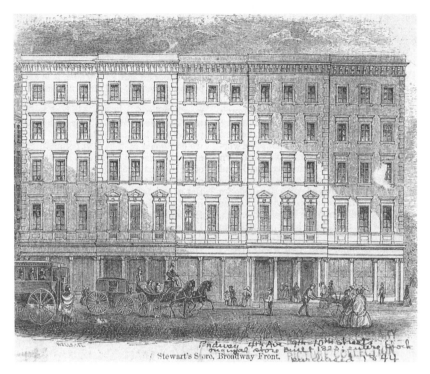

Figure 2.1. A. T. Stewart's "Marble Palace" at Chambers and Broadway. Picture Collection, The Branch Libraries, The New York Public Library, Astor, Lenox and Tilden Foundations.

and faded; we [saw] cracks in the paint on the drop curtain; the floors [had] an unsavory nastiness both to eye and nose; the red merino used for covering the seats betray[ed] evidence that hair-oil [was] popular, and that hands grow moist in hot assemblages." Instead of ten thousand Eves in attendance, the writer observed "ladies in very gay bonnets," a sly reference to prostitutes.[20] Although an anonymous letter to the editor, ostensibly written by a middle-class woman but likely written by Niblo's management, later challenged the claim of the *Times*, insisting that the majority of women in attendance were in fact respectable ladies, there could be little doubt that next to the glitter and glamor of Broadway, the theater left much to be desired.[21]

Buttressed by the visual spectacle of commerce, theater managers moved to create environments that could compete with the brilliance of Broadway's other sites. In 1866, William Wheatley, the new lessee of Niblo's Gardens, had it "cleaned, redecorated, regilded, and put in apple-pie order" in preparation

for the opening of the ballet extravaganza *The Black Crook*. The newly renovated theater succeeded in attracting "upscale, 'first class' assemblies" and was
an ideal complement for the fairy tale spectacle and its corps of scantily clad
dancers.[22] With its unique combination of music, dance, melodramatic plot,
and female spectacle, *The Black Crook* became "the event of this spectacular
age," and "the greatest dramatic sensation of the day."[23] Indeed, despite the
New York Clipper's warning that the show's "nudities" would "drive away the
ladies," women remained a dominant presence at the show, accounting at one
point for almost 50 percent of the audience.[24] "[T]he scenery and the legs are
everything," the writer Mark Twain enthused, observing that while the "beauties arrayed in dazzling half-costumes" captivated male audiences, it was the
lights, sets, and costumes that attracted the women.[25]

As Twain's comments suggest, the visual splendor of *The Black Crook* encouraged a gendered division in audience spectatorship, effectively rendering
the potentially offensive or exploitative aspects of the performance acceptable. Unlike their male companions, who were all too aware of the dancers'
bodies—and often showed up at the performance halfway through for the
express purpose of watching the racy "Demon Dance"—the women who attended *The Black Crook* seem to have ignored or looked beyond the bodies
of the performers onstage, professing instead their interest in the scenery and
costumes. *The Black Crook* thus marks an important moment in the often
complicated relationship between female spectatorship and female spectacle:
female audiences gained access to a form of entertainment previously associated with men on the condition that they did not look beyond the costumes
and scenery, while justifying, through their presence, the sexual objectification of female bodies onstage.[26] Managers would continue to encourage this
tacit agreement with female spectators well into the twentieth century, using
fashion and other commodities to legitimize sexual display.

Periods of economic hardship tightened the bonds between theaters and
department stores.[27] During the Panic of 1873, as stock companies around the
country collapsed under the weight of economic strain, New York companies survived, thanks in large part to their association with local department
stores, costumers, milliners, and dressmakers. Indeed, whereas combination
companies generally avoided costume spectacles for fear that the costumes
would be damaged or lost on the road, stock companies spent large sums on
costuming and sets, seeking to distinguish themselves as sites of consumer
splendor. After losing two theaters in the panic, the theater manager Augustin
Daly contracted Lord and Taylor to make the costumes for his upcoming production of *Charity*, in the hope that the association would attract audiences.

The following year, with the country in the midst of a depression, he printed playbills for *Pique* that announced "every costume new" and named Lord and Taylor, A. T. Stewart and Company, and Arnold Constable and Company as costume providers in the production program. This cross-promotional strategy seems to have worked; Daly survived the panic and, as later playbills for Wallack's and the Lyceum indicate, his rivals followed suit.[28]

"Redressing" a production partway through a run also proved to be both a cost-efficient alternative to mounting a new production and an effective strategy for convincing female audiences to see a play for a second or third time. For the one hundredth performance of *Divorce* in 1871, Daly instructed his entire company to purchase new costumes "to stir up fresh interest." "[W]e must have something to draw the people," he explained, "and they will come to see the new dresses."[29] Popular adaptations of French society comedies and farces such as *Frou Frou*, *Fedora*, and *Fernade* also provided ample opportunity for contemporary costuming in the 1880s and further "whetted the appetite for handsomely dressed women."[30] "None of the modern plays was of great substance," the actor Otis Skinner wrote of Daly's productions: "they were, however, excellent vehicles for the exploitation of the company with a background of attractive stage settings and fine clothes. The dressing of the women had become famous."[31]

Broadway theaters continued to forge strong relationships with other commercial establishments along the Ladies' Mile in the 1880s. When the vaudeville manager Tony Pastor opened a season of vaudeville at the 14th Street Theatre in 1881, he extended the world of nearby department stores by sponsoring "Ladies' Invitation Nights," offering everything from dress patterns and bonnets to hams and flour as door prizes. Other vaudeville managers followed Pastor's lead, building theaters close to department stores to ensure a steady stream of patrons and even staging vaudeville acts in commercial spaces. By 1896, department stores were beginning to break into show business themselves; according to the *New York Dramatic Mirror*, one impresario announced plans to construct his own vaudeville theater "within the walls of the new building."[32]

The marketing tactics of Augustin Daly, Tony Pastor, and their colleagues highlight the close connections between the gendering of theater audiences and the naturalization of consumption as a female pursuit. By the end of the nineteenth century, theater managers considered a focus on consumption and spectacle essential for attracting female audiences. But, as they soon discovered, the continued success of this strategy depended largely on steering female bodies and imaginations along carefully constructed paths, away from a direct confrontation with labor. Ultimately, it was this need that eventually drove theaters and department stores away from their close-knit partnerships along the Ladies' Mile.

Northward Bound

Developers pressed northward along Broadway in the 1870s and 1880s as the city's growing population put greater demands on public space and new modes of transportation opened up previously inaccessible areas of the city. Theaters were often at the forefront of this movement, motivated by cheaper land prices and a desire to remain close to the social elite, who were building elaborate new homes along nearby Fifth Avenue. In 1881, the theater manager Lester Wallack built a lavish theater on the northeast corner of 30th Street, next to Henry Engelbert's Grand Hotel, that rivaled society homes in size and appearance. The *New York Daily Graphic* reported that the interior was "already one of the sights of the metropolis and the exterior, when completed, will be one of the ornaments of upper Broadway."[33] In addition to sixteen murals detailing the history of dramatic art, the auditorium featured a large cast-iron dome covered in gold leaf, from which hung an enormous chandelier with four large dragons and three thousand lights. Steele Mackaye's Lyceum, on Fourth Avenue between 23rd and 24th Streets, boasted a similarly striking interior by Louis Comfort Tiffany, whose own decorating concern was a block away from the theater. Tiffany was apparently so keen to secure the Lyceum job that he waived his fee in exchange for a share of the theater's profits. Under the electric lights installed by none other than Thomas Edison, Tiffany's interior made the Lyceum one of the most impressive theaters on Broadway.[34]

Unlike their theatrical counterparts, department stores were much slower to relocate, grounded by issues of size, inventory, and concerns about customer accessibility. Following the Panic of 1873, retailers were understandably reluctant to invest in infrastructure and it was only in 1881, with the construction of the rug and carpet emporium W. and J. Sloane at Broadway and 19th Street, that major retailers actively joined the uptown exodus. By this point, smaller shops had already begun to move north, motivated by the construction in 1878 of an elevated railroad along Sixth Avenue. This new transportation route dramatically reshaped New York's shopping district, creating one of the world's longest and most diverse continuous shopping circuits. Although several large emporiums including A. T. Stewart's and Mc-

Creery's remained at their locations on 14th Street, most of the city's major retailers moved north to 23rd Street from Fifth Avenue to Seventh Avenue to remain close to the carriage trade.[35] Catering to their clients' perceived desires, many retailers knocked down older buildings, including abandoned theaters, to construct new sites that displayed the latest architectural innovations; others renovated dwellings that had once been home to New York's social elite, inviting customers into an environment previously hidden to the outside world.[36]

Improvements in transportation also meant that "theatres no longer had to depend exclusively on the immediate surrounding regions for their audiences."[37] By the 1890s, theaters stretched for twenty-five blocks along Broadway from Union Square up to Longacre Square at 42nd Street. Although clusters of theaters and support shops remained at Madison and Herald Squares— vestiges of the theatrical "Rialto" at Union Square—the particular geographic arrangement that had struck Samuel Osgood as one of New York's unique characteristics was starting to dissipate. Given these improvements, the fact that New York's theater district actually coalesced around Longacre Square— later renamed Times Square—while fashion salons and other ateliers moved further north along Fifth Avenue, calls attention to the influence of social and economic factors in the reordering of urban geography. Indeed, while New York's developing transportation system made it theoretically possible for theaters and department stores to remain where they were, increased pressure from the rapidly expanding garment industry, with its constant reminders of working-class labor, pushed these establishments further north.

From the middle of the nineteenth century, clothing production had been one of New York's largest industries, employing one-third of all manufacturing laborers. Between 1870 and 1900 capital investment increased threefold from $54 million to $169 million while the size of the labor force nearly doubled from 120,000 to 206,000 workers.[38] Physical expansion accompanied economic growth. By the early 1880s, the garment industry was assuming a more visible presence in lower Manhattan, as developers sought to maximize their gains by building lofts that could easily be converted into factories.[39] From the manufacturers' perspective, staying close to department stores and other major buyers was necessary to lower the costs of transportation and remain well-apprised of the latest stylistic developments. "Those industries which produced products of a standard pattern can locate anywhere," one manufacturer explained in 1910, "but [those that produced women's clothing and other luxury goods must be] in or very near their market, in order to be under the constant supervision of their customers."[40] Despite the looming spectacle of labor, garment manufacturers simply could not afford to set up shop away from the fashion center.[41]

But from the perspective of the retailers and other commercial institutions, all too aware of the need to play to consumer fantasy, the very real presence of overflowing sweatshops and working-class laborers posed a major problem.[42] Fearing that female shoppers would abandon the Ladies' Mile altogether, department stores and specialty shops moved further north, laying the foundation for two distinct yet closely connected commercial districts. Elite stores such as Lord and Taylor, B. Altman, Stern Brothers, and Arnold Constable and Co. relocated along Fifth Avenue, where they hoped to capitalize on "the prestige left by an earlier generation of fashionable homes, churches, and clubs." Broadway theater managers, however, moved into the Tenderloin, a red-light district north of 42nd Street, motivated by cheap land and the potential for promoting a wide range of theatrical experiences.[43]

Although not exactly thrilled with their new neighbors, entrepreneurs such as T. Henry French, Oscar Hammerstein I, Rudolph Aronson, and Charles Frohman used their location to attract elite audiences in pursuit of a more expressive way of life.[44] Whereas the drudgery of factory labor threatened to undermine theatrical fantasies, the nearby presence of brothels and other sites dedicated to male pleasure encouraged audiences to engage more fully in the city's emerging nightlife. Brothels had in fact existed in close proximity to theaters for decades, creating what the theater historian Katie N. Johnson describes as "an interstitial space in which identity, particularly female identity, became destabilized . . . it was often impossible to distinguish society women from prostitutes as both groups engaged in their Broadway promenades."[45] Within this environment of unfixed social identity, New York's smart set experimented with new forms of social interaction, as Lewis Erenberg has shown, breaking away from the "confinement, restrictions, and conventions of urban industrial society and the code of gentility" to enjoy all that the city had to offer.[46] In many respects, these public displays of wealth and privilege were a direct response to the spectacles of mass unemployment and labor unrest that had erupted following the Panic of 1893. With their cultural authority in question, the social elite could no longer afford to sequester themselves within the safety and privacy of their stately homes. Led by the flamboyant Mrs. Stuyvesant Fish, the "four hundred" met the threat of the "great unwashed" with carefully staged appearances in the hotels, restaurants, and theaters springing up along Broadway and Fifth Avenue.[47]

The exhibitionary tendencies of the social elite had a dramatic effect on the social and economic landscape. By the turn of the century, the seedier aspects of the new theater district were beginning to disappear as a group of aggressive vice commissioners, headed by the notoriously vigilant Anthony Comstock, forced prostitution and other illicit activities underground.[48] Electric street lighting and electric billboards along the newly christened Great White Way made it much safer to attend the theater in the evening (figure 2.2). And the completion of the interborough subway in 1904, which brought thousands of people into Times Square, secured the space for the safe passage of middle-class women and girls during the day.[49] These events coincided with a huge theatrical building boom, spurred by the newly arrived Shubert brothers, who decided that they would rather build their own theaters than concede to the terms set by the Syndicate. In 1900, there were twenty-two theaters in Manhattan, only one of which was north of Longacre Square; by 1920, most of the city's fifty theaters were in Times Square and its immediate arteries (figure 2.3).[50]

In little more than a decade then, theaters, department stores, and other retail establishments had abandoned the Ladies' Mile, radically altering the appearance of the city and the experiences of its inhabitants (figure 2.4). Although theaters continued to cluster around Broadway and its immediate arteries, department stores, fashion salons, and other elite ateliers dominated Fifth Avenue from 34th Street to Central Park South.[51] Yet rather than diminishing, the business deals, strategic arrangements, and aesthetic conversations that had long characterized the relationship between theaters and department stores intensified. Why? What kept them together? As the rest of this chapter shows, changing audience tastes, economic uncertainty, industry rivalries, accusations of trust building, and growing awareness of labor exploitation motivated theaters, department stores, and consumer goods retailers to maintain their close ties. Anticipating the joint efforts of film exhibitors and merchants in the 1930s to "coordinate desire and decision so that they occurred at the same moment and in the proximity of department store or motion picture theater, local florist shop, hardware store, or car dealer showroom," Broadway producers, department stores, and their advertising partners joined forces to arouse and direct consumer desire toward brand-name goods at nearby stores, creating a seamless "buyway" between the two districts.[52]

The Revolution in Modern Gowns

The popularity of theatrical realism with American audiences and directors— a development that placed heightened emphasis on accurate and expensive

Figure 2.2. "After Dark on Broadway." Broadway revelers stroll through the newly illuminated theater district. Sam DeVincent Collection of Illustrated Sheet Music, Archives Center, National Museum of American History, Behring Center, Smithsonian Institution.

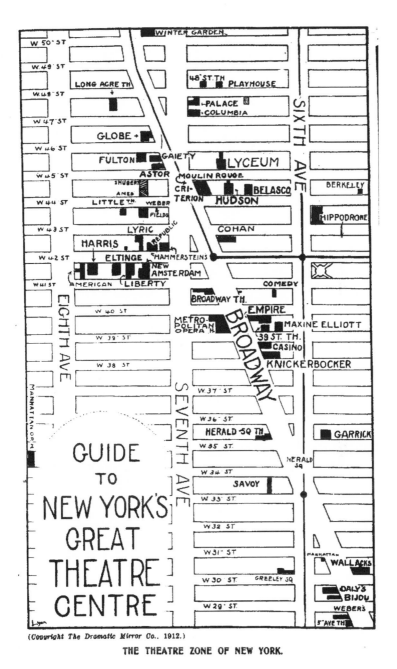

WINTER GARDEN

W 50 ST
W 49 ST
LONG ACRE TH
W 48 ST
W 47 ST
GLOBE
W 46 ST
FULTON
W 45 ST
ASTOR
SHUBERT
ANES
W 44 ST
LITTLE TH. WEBER
FIELDS
W 43 ST
LYRIC
HARRIS
W 42 ST
ELTINGE
W 41 ST
AMERICAN
LIBERTY

48 ST. TH PLAYHOUSE
·PALACE
·COLUMBIA

GAIETY
LYCEUM
MOULIN ROUGE
CRI-
TERION
HUDSON
BELASCO
COHAN

HAMMERSTEINS
NEW
AMSTERDAM

SIXTH AVE

BERKELEY

HIPPODROME

COMEDY

EIGHTH AVE
W 40 ST
W 39 ST
W 38 ST

MANHATTAN OPERA

GUIDE
TO
NEW YORK'S
GREAT
THEATRE
CENTRE

BROADWAY TH.
EMPIRE
METRO-
POLITAN
OPERA H.
39 ST. TH.
CASINO
KNICKERBOCKER

MAXINE ELLIOTT

BROADWAY

SEVENTH AVE

W 37 ST
W 36 ST
HERALD SQ TH
W 35 ST
W 34 ST
SAVOY
W 33 ST
W 32 ST
W 31 ST
W 30 ST GREELEY SQ
W 29 ST

GARRICK

HERALD
SQ

WALLACKS

DALY'S
BIJOU
WEBER'S
5 AVE TH

Lyon

(Copyright The Dramatic Mirror Co., 1912.)

THE THEATRE ZONE OF NEW YORK.

Figure 2.3. New York's booming Times Square theater district, 1912. *New York Dramatic Mirror*, September 11, 1912, 15.

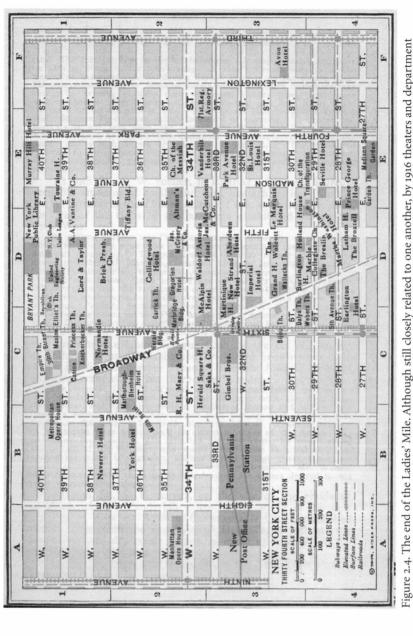

Figure 2.4. The end of the Ladies' Mile. Although still closely related to one another, by 1916 theaters and department stores were no longer part of the same commercial district. Courtesy of the University of Texas Libraries, The University of Texas at Austin.

stage costumes, backdrops, and sets—was one of the most obvious and immediate incentives for theater managers to maintain a close relationship with department stores.[53] " 'Tawdry tinsel!' can no longer be applied to stage costumery," wrote the stage manager and producer Max Freeman in 1897. "This is the age of realism in the dramatic as well as in the other arts," he continued, "and in the march of progress with the playwright, the scene painter, the stage carpenter, the property man, and the costumer have all kept step together."[54] Other writers similarly claimed that a "revolution in modern gowns" was underway. "The actress in make-believe drawing rooms must not only *appear* as richly dressed as the society leader she impersonates, but she must *actually be* as well dressed and wear, not make-believe gowns, but gowns costing the same and turned out by the same dressmakers as those worn by the millionaire dames of Fifth Avenue," the *Theatre Magazine* explained.[55] Actresses who had once appeared in imitations of designer fashion now wore the real thing.

The contemporary writer Vanderheyden Fyles dated the "revolution in modern gowns" to 1894, when Charles Frohman first agreed to subsidize his female performers' gowns in *The Masqueraders*, a contemporary society play by the British author Henry Arthur Jones.[56] According to Fyles, Frohman "argued simply that if [a] manager paid for handsome costumes when they happened to be in the Elizabethan and Arthurian period, why should he allow his actresses to dress in a London drawing room only according to their several resources[?]"[57] Yet while altruism may have influenced Frohman's decision, other factors, including economic fallout from the Panic of 1893 and a need to attract an elite clientele to the newly opened Empire Theatre at Broadway and 40th Street, made fashion spectacle an appealing business strategy. By providing each actress with the financial support "to buy handsomer dresses than she could otherwise afford," Frohman raised the overall standard of costuming in his productions and kept a loyal audience of middle- and upper-class women coming to his theater.[58]

What most distinguished Frohman's approach to costuming was his emphasis on stylish contemporary dress and his willingness to let his actresses select their own stage clothes. While the nineteenth-century stock managers Augustin Daly and Lester Wallack had similarly encouraged costume spectacle, spending upward of thirty thousand dollars on a single production, they had devoted most of their resources to historical plays, requiring performers to pay for their own contemporary clothes when needed. By contrast, Frohman paid for his leading actresses to order gowns from the leading dressmakers and couture houses in New York, London, and Paris and encouraged them to "redress" their stage roles as often as they wished.[59] Throughout the 1890s, his prize "clotheshorse" Elsie de Wolfe spent several months in Paris each summer, where she purchased many of her stage gowns at the house of Callot Soeurs. Upon her return to New York each fall, a group of reporters greeted her at the docks, eager to learn about the gowns she had purchased during her time abroad. "Miss De Wolf [sic] has a number of gorgeous new gowns especially designed for her by a famous Parisian dressmaker," one paper reported, "and will doubtless cause a sensation."[60]

In 1905, Gustav Kobbé observed that the stage had become "a school of fashion," and that an "Annie Russell, Ethel Barrymore, Mary Mannering or Maxine Elliott 'first night' " was now comparable to a dressmaker's or milliner's opening.[61] Society women went so far as to send their maids to the theater to take notes on the costumes, and New York dressmakers and milliners attended the first performances of a new society play with the specific intention of copying the costumes. "On the first Saturday of any play that I appeared in," Elsie de Wolfe later recalled, "they came in a mob, sitting close to the front and jotting down notes on my costumes."[62] Ready-to-wear designers similarly attended the openings of new plays with the hope of "finding new material for models salable in metropolitan shops."[63]

While society dramas continued to provide an ideal venue for fashion display, the vogue for contemporary costuming soon spilled over into other theatrical genres, most notably musical comedy and vaudeville.[64] The musical comedy *Florodora*, a fantasy diversion of 1900 best known for the number "Tell Me, Pretty Ladies" starring the Florodora Girls, six tall, fashionably dressed showgirls, was probably "the first of the musical comedies to go in for the evening gown as a sort of mental shock—that is a climactic episode of the play."[65] Other musical comedies followed *Florodora*'s lead, introducing audiences to a dazzling array of beautifully costumed chorus girls.[66] Although vaudeville was slower to respond to the fashion craze, the press agent Anna Marble noted in 1906 that "women's dress on the variety stage has been revolutionized within the past year or so. . . . There is no excuse for the ill appearance of any woman on the stage nowadays." By 1914, the *Variety* columnist "the Skirt" was pleased to point out that although "the legitimate stage has always led the fashions . . . vaudeville is giving it a close run."[67]

The cross-industry focus on accurate and expensive fashion encouraged the proliferation of costuming companies in New York City—between 1900 and 1920 there were approximately seventy-five costume-making companies in New York alone—and a range of collaborations between theaters and department stores.[68] Although stores such as Lord and Taylor, Arnold

Constable, and R. H. Macy had long provided costumes for managers like Augustin Daly, the growing demand for elegant and stylistically accurate costumes encouraged them to establish special departments or "annexes" exclusively devoted to stage costuming and staffed by individuals whose primary responsibility was liaising with Broadway. Theater managers continued to rely on traditional theater suppliers such as Max and Mahieu, Dazian's, and Eames Costume Company for period costumes, dress clothes for men, accessories, shoes, and on occasion contemporary dress gowns, but they increasingly turned to stores such as B. Altman, J. M. Gidding and Co., Wanamaker's, and Lord and Taylor when they had to outfit a large chorus in contemporary dress. With their economies of scale, teams of traveling buyers, and close ties to the couture houses of Paris and London, department stores were equipped to provide up-to-date fashions in a way that most theatrical costume houses were not. Such an arrangement meant that managers could send performers for fittings during rehearsals and did not have to worry about paying custom duties on imported gowns, an important consideration during a period when tariffs on luxury goods were extremely high.[69]

Given that a star's gown often ranged between $150 and $600 while gowns for a single chorus number could cost upward of $1,500, department stores and specialty shops stood to benefit considerably from their theatrical clients and kept managers well apprised of special reductions in model gowns.[70] Some stores nevertheless seem to have exploited the generosity of managers like Charles Frohman, overcharging or refusing to provide estimates. In 1910 Frohman's business manager, Alf Hayman, was alarmed to receive the bills from Lord and Taylor and the Lichtenstein Millinery Co. for the new wardrobes ordered by Billie Burke and Ethel Barrymore for their respective performances in *Mrs. Dot* and *Mid-Channel*.[71] Although Frohman yielded to his stars' requests, Hayman urged him to curb their reckless spending habits:

Wrote you that Miss Burke's new dresses would cost $800. The bills are now in. They cost $1203,—the dress from Lichtenstein $607, the other dresses from Lord & Taylor, $595. I hope next year you will induce Miss Burke and Miss Barrymore never to go near Lichtenstein,—they are the biggest robbers in the world and when people like ours go in their store they put up the prices fifty to sixty percent knowing that they can get what they please. They are famous for this sort of dirty work. They won't furnish estimates.[72]

The Shuberts were much more rigorous in their dealings with department stores and other retailers. When the Lichtenstein Millinery Co., the "biggest robbers in the world," presented the Shubert management with a bill for several gowns ordered by the actress Fritzi Scheff, they issued a curt response: "When Madame Scheff orders clothes, let Madame Scheff pay for them. We allow no one to order things without a written order from our offices. We are, therefore, returning you your bill."[73]

Despite these struggles, most department stores seem to have worked hard to maintain good relations with theater managers, aware that in addition to the sales up front, they stood to benefit from program acknowledgments and write-ups in trade and fashion publications. In 1909, for example, the *Theatre Magazine* informed readers that the Lord and Taylor gowns used in Frederic Thompson's *A Fool There Was* were "suitable to the occasions on which they are worn, and while they bear the stamp of the new season's fashions they are by no means freakish in style, but such as may be copied outright by a woman of good taste."[74] Lord and Taylor's reputation as one of the city's most elegant stores gave special credence to *A Fool There Was*, transforming the moral melodrama about a man who succumbs to the lures of a female vampire into a fashion event.[75]

Battling for Consumers

If the Panic of 1893 sparked the revolution in modern gowns, the growing rivalry between the Syndicate and the newcomer Shuberts kept it going. For years, the three brothers from Syracuse, New York—Sam, Lee, and J. J.—had been expanding their theatrical interests, producing shows and acquiring a small chain of theaters in Rochester, Syracuse, Utica, and Troy. By 1905, they controlled fifteen theaters in Boston, Philadelphia, Chicago, and St. Louis, and they were ready to make the move to Broadway.[76] The most significant factor in the Shuberts' swift success was their decision to structure their organization as a bona fide corporation. Whereas the Syndicate had organized as a pool, a decentralized and relatively unstable arrangement between agreeable partners who retained their individual interests and therefore lacked the ability to develop collective long-term goals or a cohesive corporate image, the Shuberts collaborated with a group of silent partners—clothiers, factory owners, and venture capitalists—who gave them the financial support they needed to expand quickly while still allowing them to maintain a central management structure through which they oversaw all aspects of their business.[77] The flexibility and efficiency of this corporate structure made it possible for the Shuberts, who had previously booked their theatrical tours through Klaw and Erlanger, to resist the Syndicate's terms and forge an alliance with its fiercest opponents, including Mrs. Fiske and David Belasco. According to Jack Poggi, the Shuberts' "chief weapon" against the Syndicate was its adoption of an "open-door policy" whereby they permitted any production to play in their theaters and made their own productions available to non-Shubert theaters. This reversal of the Syndicate's monopolistic tactics made the Shuberts much more attractive to independent managers and theater owners, although Poggi suggests that it was in fact "an economic necessity, since the Shuberts were not yet strong enough to use monopolistic techniques." With their financial backers' assistance, the Shuberts' empire grew quickly. By the spring of 1906, they had built eighteen new theaters and had a controlling interest in another seventeen; by the fall of 1910, they directly controlled seventy theaters, thirteen of which were in New York City, and oversaw more than fifty dramatic and musical companies.[78]

The ongoing competition between the Syndicate and the Shuberts kept both groups in close contact with department stores and encouraged creative arrangements with advertisers and consumer goods manufacturers. After a short reprieve in 1907, during which time the rivals had briefly joined forces in a bid to break into vaudeville, they were once again battling for theatrical turf.[79] One of the greatest weapons in the Syndicate's arsenal was its close ties to newspapers like the *Morning Telegraph*, through which it published gossipy lies about the Shubert organization. With no comparable newspaper on their side, in August 1909 the Shuberts launched the *New York Review*, a weekly trade paper with industry news and glossy photographs that would be theirs to control. But attracting and retaining advertisers for this new venture proved difficult, especially when initial advertisers complained that the Shuberts did not patronize their businesses as expected or published advertisements for rival firms. The costumers Max and Mahieu wrote to the Shuberts explaining, "We know very well that you rather would like to see our Ad enlargened [*sic*] but for an argument we call our attention to one fact, in the last program of the Wintergarden [*sic*], you find for instance, Paquin, Callot & Worth, Paris; . . . Hugo Baruch & Co., Berlin; Miller, New York. . . . We couldn't find any ad of them in The Review."[80] Like other advertisers, Max and Mahieu expected the Shuberts to reciprocate for their advertising investment and forego patronizing the competition. Perhaps driven by these pressures, the Shuberts began offering potential advertisers a promotional spot in one of their many stage productions in exchange for advertising in the *Review*. Charles Daniel, the *Review*'s advertising and business manager, attended rehearsals for the Winter Garden shows, hoping to identify potential advertising opportunities that he could use to approach a new advertiser. In

1911, for example, the manufacturers of the New England Button Shoe indicated that they would be willing to sign an advertising contract worth $2,000 if the "button shoe number" in the upcoming Winter Garden show proved satisfactory. Scenes set in public spaces such as a dressmaking shop, street, or subway worked especially well, and Daniel frequently instructed performers to insert specific brand names into their dialogue.[81]

The rivalry between the Shuberts and the Syndicate reached a détente in 1913, but by that time the *New York Review* had become such an integral part of the Shubert empire, as both a source of revenue and a "ready-made vanity press," that Lee Shubert decided to keep it running.[82] Although the paper had presumably managed to secure a number of long-term advertisers since its inception, Daniel continued to explore new ways to bring advertisements onstage. In May 1916, J. J. Shubert urged him to find advertisers to sponsor thirteen "City Girls" for a number in the *Passing Show of 1916*. For thirty dollars a week, sponsors would have the dual honor of "naming" one of the showgirls and representing the location of their head office.[83] Over the next month, Daniel contacted a number of prominent corporations including Procter and Gamble, the Fleischmann Co., the Coca-Cola Company, Pillsbury Flour Mills Company, and Colgate and Company, all of which turned down his offer to participate in the show.[84] Positive responses came from the Lackawanna Railroad, a long-standing advertiser with the Shuberts, which requested a Phoebe Snow Girl to represent Buffalo, and the Waterman Fountain Pen Co., which wished to represent New York.[85]

Perhaps the most interesting response came from the J. Walter Thompson Company, as it prepared to launch the famous "A Skin You Love to Touch" campaign for Woodbury's Facial Soap. The Thompson manager James W. Young was enthusiastic about the proposition of a "Woodbury Girl" in the Winter Garden show, but he emphasized that the showgirl chosen to portray the "Woodbury Girl" should be appropriate for the campaign. As he outlined in a letter to Daniel, J. Walter Thompson would agree to the Shubert's proposition, "provided we can be assured that the girl representing Woodbury's Facial Soap will be clearly recognizable as such, and also that she represent the product in a way that will be in keeping with the high class atmosphere with which we try to surround the soap. In other words, we wish to reserve the right to approve the costuming and appearance of this girl."[86] Young included a color print of the first "A Skin You Love to Touch" advertisement, which depicted an attractive, smiling woman with an attentive man at her side, and suggested that the costuming and appearance of the girl cast to play the "Woodbury Girl" should be as close to the illustration as possible.

Although the "Woodbury Girl" never appeared in the *Passing Show of 1916*, presumably because the Shuberts refused to yield casting decisions to a corporate sponsor, extant costume designs for the "City Girls" number demonstrate the extent to which the Shuberts cemented their relationships with advertisers through the literal commodification of female performers.[87] Created by Homer Conant, these designs playfully showcase the sexual aspects of the performers' bodies while disguising them as recognizable objects. Conant's sketch of the St. Paul, Minnesota "girl," for example, includes detailed instructions for transforming the performer into a locomotive, with specific notes for a "headdress with black smoke stack," "white tight[s] with railway tracks painted on one leg," and a "white taffeta cape with train painted on in black" (figure 2.5).[88] Although the costume is undeniably whimsical, the various toy train elements, most notably the bra-like top, short shorts, and "train track" tights, sexualize the performer's body and suggest that like the unnamed railway company she represents, she can be taken for a "ride." Conant's "Detroit girl" sketch similarly sexualized the female performer in a playful yet suggestive manner by turning her into a Cadillac. In his notes beneath the sketch, Conant instructed the Shubert wardrobe department to make the costume from actual car parts—the bodice from skidding chains, the bottom of the skirt from a "Detroit Cadillac 8" tire, and the bracelet from "a normal mirror attached to chains." The most provocative element of Conant's "Detroit girl" design was his deliberate placement of the car door and handle in the middle of the performer's body. "What would happen if someone opened the 'door'?" he seemed to ask, drawing attention to the unseen body beneath the costume.[89]

Conant's designs for the "City Girls" number offer a striking example of the objectification and commodification of the Broadway chorus girl—a subject I will return to in Chapter 5—and call attention to the underlying gender politics that shaped the rivalry between the Syndicate and the Shuberts. Through their partnerships with department stores, specialty shops, and consumer goods manufacturers, theater managers encouraged audiences to associate theatrical spectatorship with consumption and to view female performers as models and commodities. Such ties proved problematic, however, when emerging consumer activist organizations led by well-educated, middle-class female reformers began to accuse department stores and garment manufacturers of labor exploitation.

Figure 2.5. Homer Conant's "St. Paul Girl" for the *Passing Show of 1916*. Costume sketch by Homer Conant. Courtesy Shubert Archives.

Staging the Department Store

Beginning in the 1890s, disgruntled merchants across the United States pro-
tested that "all-devouring" department stores, with their economies of scale,
huge advertising budgets, and enormous physical presence, were putting
them out of business.[90] Along the same lines as the anti-Syndicate critics and
other opponents of "trust building," the merchants argued that they were
"victims," "little [men]" cowering before the "all-devouring monster," of the
department store, that "octopus which has stretched out its tentacles in every
direction, grasping in its slimy folds the specialist or one-line man."[91] The
most vocal opponents, often butchers and liquor salesman, accused department store owners of trust building and lobbied for legislation to slow their
progress. Yet when smaller businesses continued to protest even after state
intervention, department store magnates began to fight back. In 1898, Robert
Ogden, the head of Wanamaker's New York store, responded to accusations
of trust building by the Downtown Business Men's Association, arguing that
department stores represented a modern way of conducting business that
brought convenience into the lives of millions and gave jobs to thousands.
Those who refused to recognize all the advantages of the department store
were simply backward in their thinking. "Hamper its working, forbid its very
existence, and this modern labor-saver yet will find means to obey the inexorable demands of social economy," echoed the *Illustrated American*. The
department store was inevitable.[92]

By 1900, organized efforts to shut down department stores were subsiding but middle-class female reformers, many of whom were active participants in the settlement movement, placed new pressure on store managers.[93]
Since 1890, the New York Consumers' League had closely observed the treatment of saleswomen and cash girls in the city's stores and agitated for reform
through lobbying and petitions (figure 2.6). The league called upon the state
government to legislate a shorter work week and introduced the White List
of stores that met its "standards of a fair house." These standards included
"equal pay for equal work; a minimum wage for sales girls of $6.00 weekly;
paid overtime, and at least one week paid vacation during the summer."[94] Of
the approximately one thousand contracts sent out to merchants, only thirty
were returned; of these, only four passed the league's inspection. In 1898, the
Mercantile Inspection Act "provided for a 60 hour week for women under 21"
and "a provision for sanitary rest rooms," representing a major victory for the
league, but it still wasn't enough.[95]

In 1899, the sociologist Annie M. MacLean published a shocking exposé

Figure 2.6. This 1910 depiction of fashionably dressed department store employees calls attention to the blurring of boundaries between laborers and consumers. Picture Collection, The Branch Libraries, The New York Public Library, Astor, Lenox and Tilden Foundations.

in the *Journal of Sociology* after working undercover for two weeks in several major Chicago department stores. Her detailed account, complete with a breakdown of how she had used her meager salary to pay for lodging and food, alerted many middle-class readers to a hitherto unseen side of the department store. MacLean warned that without social reform, department stores would continue to exploit women and children or drive them to prostitution: "So long as the consumer will patronize bad stores," she wrote, "so long will they exist; so long as people will buy clothing produced under inhuman conditions, so long will they continue to be produced under just those conditions." But power for change rested with the consumer. "Those who have not already considered the matter would do well to . . . ask themselves whether or not they can do something to lessen the hardships of the salespeople's lives. . . . We should not rest until the bad stores improve or go out of business."[96] Playing into class and racial stereotypes, MacLean concluded by calling upon her "intelligent and educated" readers to stand up for change.

Several months after MacLean's exposé, the Consumers' League of Illinois, to which she belonged, amalgamated with existing leagues in New York, New Jersey, Massachusetts, Pennsylvania, Minnesota, and Wisconsin to form the National Consumers' League. Led by Florence Kelley, a driven reformer who had spent several years at Jane Addams's Hull House, the league devoted its resources to improving the deplorable sweatshop conditions that prevailed in most garment districts. Although continuing to keep a close eye on department stores' treatment of sales staff, Kelley felt that a national campaign focused on the production of specific goods would be a more effective strategy for educating consumers and enlisting their support. Adapting the idea of the White List, she introduced the Consumers' White Label to endorse the manufacturers who met the league's standards. Like MacLean, Kelley emphasized the power of consumer choice and pressed her readers to make the ethical decision. "We can have cheap underwear righteously made and clean; or we can have cheap underwear degradingly made and unclean," she wrote in 1901. "Henceforth we are responsible for our choice." Under Kelley's leadership, the league grew rapidly, attracting the support of the General Federation of Women's Clubs, with a membership of over 155,000 women, to become "[t]he single most politically effective organization of middle-class women in the decades before World War I."[97]

Rather than fight the league, John Wanamaker, the owner of the Wanamaker's chain of department stores, decided to join the campaign to improve conditions for laborers producing women's and children's underwear. In addition to selling White Label products, he arranged to display photographs of laborers working under sweatshop conditions juxtaposed with laborers working for Wanamaker's. These photographs became the centerpiece of an exhibit that toured state and international trade fairs, conferring a "moral aura" upon Wanamaker and his enterprise while allowing him to "consolidate his economic power."[98] But for department store managers who lacked Wanamaker's foresight or who believed that they could avoid the White Label altogether, the National Consumers' League and its army of white middle-class reformers remained a source of frustration.

Within such a hostile environment, musical comedies that celebrated department stores as places of glamour, excitement, and adventure, where anything and everything could happen, instead of denigrating them as sites of exploitation, must have provided a welcome public relations boost for beleaguered store managers. The majority of these "shop-girl" musicals originated in England, where department stores found themselves locked in similar battles, and made their way to the United States thanks to transnationally oriented producers like Charles Frohman and the Shuberts.[99] The "shop-girl" fad reached New York in 1895 with the success of *The Shop Girl*, a long-running London hit that had been imported by Charles Frohman and Al Hayman and starred the original cast from British manager George Edwardes's extremely popular Gaiety Burlesque Company. Originally conceived in response to public demand for the "local and the real," the musical was one of the first to dispense with the practice of dressing female performers in over-the-top burlesque costumes in favor of contemporary dress.[100] Opening in New York two years after the Panic of 1893, during an economic recession that forced many small businesses to the verge of collapse, *The Shop Girl*'s light-hearted music, comedic plot, impressive settings, and spectacular costumes challenged the merchants' stereotypical depiction of department stores as "all-devouring monsters."[101] As the retail wars raged, a string of equally frothy musicals followed, helping to secure the hegemony of the urban department store and assist individual store owners as they vied for control of local and national markets.[102]

One of the most successful shop-girl musicals was the American production in 1907 of *The Girl Behind the Counter*, another British import arranged by Edgar Smith and produced by the Shuberts, which, like many of its predecessors, told the story of a wealthy society girl masquerading as a shop girl. This "bright and snappy Americanized version" of the London hit starred the comedian Lew Fields as the floorwalker Henry Schniff—a likely reference to Henry Siegel, who by 1907 owned and operated a syndicate of Siegel-Cooper stores in New York, Boston, and Chicago. Although the highlight of the show was the "soda fountain" scene wherein Fields successfully matched sodas to the color of his customer's clothing, the attractive chorus girls were another major draw. These "excellent specimens of feminine youth and beauty . . . work[ed] hard to support the principals—(on the stage understand)," the *New York Times* critic quipped, slyly alluding to the sexual labor these "specimens" *might* be performing offstage.[103] Indeed, as Katie N. Johnson argues, the department store setting encouraged the sexual objectification of female performers by eliding existing stereotypes of the promiscuous chorus girl with similar shop-girl stereotypes.[104] Playing simultaneously to male scopic desire and female consumer fantasy, theater managers produced a highly appealing spectacle that combated stories about labor exploitation by department stores.[105]

Shop-girl musicals may have provided psychic support for department stores besieged by the National Consumers' League, but they could do little to prevent real-world shop girls and factory laborers from coming dangerously close to the theater and shopping districts. In 1910, the recently established Fifth Avenue Association, a group that included many of the major retailers along the avenue, complained that thousands of "loitering" factory workers on their lunch breaks "almost paralyzed" business between 14th and 23rd Streets, making it "impossible" for shoppers to enter or exit their establishments.[106] The association hoped that Fifth Avenue would soon "eclipse Broadway" with a "Blaze of Illuminations" and "Isles of Safety," but the obvious presence of an estimated forty thousand laborers stood in their way.[107] Early attempts to divert the lunching laborers to side streets or nearby Union Square proved ineffective and it was only the threat of a boycott that kept the sweatshops from pushing beyond 34th Street.[108] In 1914, the passage of a labor law limiting the number of employees in commercial spaces "according to floor space and safety measures against fire" offered some relief, forcing sweatshop owners to relocate. Still, the largest retail block in the city, with 974 employees, was located mere steps away from Broadway, at 45th and 46th Streets between Fifth and Sixth Avenues.[109]

Despite the large number of women working in the garment industry throughout this period, the association's campaign focused almost exclusively on the problem of male laborers in retail environments.[110] This curious gender bias may mean that female garment workers were able to disguise their status as laborers on lunch breaks and blend in with middle-class shoppers; certainly the women in figure 2.7, with their attractive shirtwaists and stylish hats, are curiously alike the crowds of matinee girls exiting the theater depicted in figure 1.4 (p. 36). The differences between matinee girls and gar-

Figure 2.7. Striking shirtwaist factory employees, 1909. Courtesy of the Library of Congress Prints and Photographs Division.

ment workers became all too clear, however, when factory women stepped out on the picket line, adding sandwich boards and union banners to their stylish ensembles.

Mass spectacles of labor unrest complicated matters for department stores and other shops along Fifth Avenue by reminding consumers that many of the clothes and other goods they purchased were products of sweatshop labor. Between 1909 and 1920, thousands of striking garment workers in New York and major cities across the United States staged mass demonstrations, parades, strikes, and rallies to protest their low wages, long working hours, and horrendous working conditions. During the shirtwaist strike of 1909, for example, over twenty thousand factory laborers, many of them Jewish and Italian women, withstood public taunts, police beatings, and arrests to fight for better treatment. Well-versed in popular culture and fashion, these strikers resisted the dehumanizing forces of labor by appearing in stylish outfits, creating a bizarre fusion of labor and capital that many middle-class observers found disconcerting.[111]

Sympathetic society women extended the spectacle of the shirtwaist strike by holding meetings and fundraisers in performance venues. In December 1909, for example, Mrs. O. H. P. Belmont rented the Hippodrome for a Sunday afternoon meeting of the Ladies' Shirtwaist Makers' Union, a gesture that transformed a site described as the "department store in theatricals" into a labor union hall.[112] That same month, society matrons and striking women convened at Carnegie Hall to protest police brutality against picketers. This union of "Fifth Avenue and the lower east side, both represented chiefly by women and girls," signaled a temporary erasure of geographic boundaries drawn along class lines. Within the recital hall auditorium, the female audience behaved as they would at a vaudeville show or melodrama, hissing whenever a representative from the police was named, while onstage a group of over 350 women gathered behind the speakers, wearing paper signs that read "Arrested." Union flags, banners, and other paraphernalia completed the transformation of the hall into a glorious spectacle of labor solidarity.[113]

Perhaps worried that their own labor practices would be called into question, the Syndicate and the Shuberts offered public support to the striking women. Klaw and Erlanger sent a letter to the Carnegie Hall meeting, promising free tickets to the women for one of their upcoming productions. They nevertheless took pains to point out that "[they] didn't know anything about the merits of the strike," but rather wished to offer something to the women "who were badly in need of money for the necessaries of life." The Shubert brothers showed greater generosity, agreeing to donate 50 percent of the receipts from one of their New York houses to the cause, a supportive gesture that was clearly intended to show up their rivals.[114] At the time of the meeting, the *New York Review* had only been operational for three months and the Shuberts were looking to trump the Syndicate in any way possible. Paradoxically, one of the consequences of the intensifying rivalry between the Shuberts and the Syndicate was a decline in working conditions for performers, a shift noted by the actor Wilton Lackaye upon the formation of the Actors' Equity Association in 1913. "We simply wish to return to the spirit that existed prior to about five years ago," he explained at a meeting of his peers, "when the relation between actor and manager was one of cooperation."[115] Locked in a fierce war, the Shuberts and the Syndicate paid little attention to the plight of the men and women in their employ, despite their apparent sympathy for striking garment workers.

The Department Store as Theater

Both before and throughout the war between the Syndicate and the Shuberts, theater managers continued to work with their department store counterparts to keep consumers moving between their respective commercial districts and away from a confrontation with loitering or striking factory employees, utilizing a range of strategies including tie-ins, product placement, promotional appearances, and window displays.[116] Streetcars and the newly completed subway system were of some assistance in the formation of this imaginary Ladies' Mile, as they safely transported shoppers from one site of consumption to another. Like the modern railroad, New York's transit system "annihilat[ed] in-between spaces" by "juxtapos[ing] the most disparate images into one unity," making it possible to ignore or erase areas of the city that might otherwise lead the traveler to stop or ask troubling questions.[117] Along the way, display windows in subway terminals, advertisements in streetcars and trains, and hundreds of colorful posters pasted on building walls and billboards reminded consumers of their ultimate destinations. As the historian Betty Blackmar explains, the "novelty, spontaneity, and crowds promoted by commercial districts were geared to courting impulse, inviting people to spend their time and money freely, to indulge themselves, and to condone the indulgences of others."[118] Intent on diverting attention away from scenes of social strife, theaters and department stores encouraged the formation of a new social imaginary that privileged individual choice and expression over collective social advancement.[119]

As knowledgeable consumers of and partners with Broadway theater, department store managers envisioned the sales floor as "the stage upon which the play is enacted" and sought to keep all "backstage" aspects of production hidden from view.[120] They moved bookkeepers and other clerks not directly associated with selling to office floors, and they relocated warehouses, laundries, garages, shipping and receiving, and other auxiliary departments off-site. With attractive displays, they revitalized corners that had previously been used for these business practices and used mirrors to disguise those parts of the store that still needed refurbishing.[121] The overall objective was to streamline business practices while presenting the department store sales floors as "a sheltered refuge for itinerant lookers, a sanctuary for consumption kept separate from the domain of production."[122] Nothing should prevent consumers from feeling that they had entered a world of delight and privilege; nothing should remind them that their desires were responsible for the exploitation of others. The historian Elaine Abelson describes how department store interiors welcomed customers into "an environment dedicated to sensory stimulation and unfettered abundance," complete with marble floors and columns, wood paneling, and bright chandeliers that kept women moving from one department to another on a pilgrimage of intensifying desire.[123] Wide aisles and revolving doors helped maintain a steady stream of shoppers in and out of the store, while centrally located elevators and escalators directed women past luxury items on their way to the more prosaic staple goods departments.[124] Glass display cases and carefully arranged show windows enticed consumers further by endowing goods with an aura of glamour and excitement that was within reach yet remained untouchable behind the glass. By offering visual access to such delightful commodities, store managers aroused deep longings that could only be eased through consumption. It was immaterial whether the women bought the goods on the spot or deliberated for days as long as they bought sometime.[125]

To extend this illusion, the prominent decorators L. Frank Baum (of *Wizard of Oz* fame) and Arthur Fraser drew from their experiences as performers and theatergoers to revolutionize department store displays.[126] The son of a prosperous businessman with interests in the oil and dry goods industries, Baum had toured the Midwest in the 1880s, alternately performing in his own plays and working as a merchandiser and traveling salesman. In 1897, after several years in Chicago as a newspaper writer, he combined his previous experiences in showmanship and sales to launch the *Show Window*, a "monthly journal of decorative art" that offered tips to merchants who knew very little about display strategies to help them make goods "come alive." As an editor and regular columnist, Baum offered straightforward technical advice, but he also urged window trimmers to consider using electrical devices and other modern inventions and to display goods singly rather than en masse to give commodities the appearance of glamorous individuality.[127]

Arthur Fraser, the head of display at Marshall Field's first in Chicago and later in New York, shared Baum's love of theater. "We would dramatize our merchandise—really stage work," he told an interviewer in 1946. "I went to the New York theater a lot. I derived more from the theater than anything else."[128] Taking a page from the press agent's book, Fraser stirred up hype for his displays by drawing curtains over the windows each Sunday, apparently "out of respect" for the Christian day of rest. In fact, Fraser and his team used these Sundays to install new displays. When the curtains parted on Monday, thousands of people gathered to see his newest creation, prompting *Women's Wear Daily* to compare the "changing of the windows at Field's . . . [to] . . . the opening of a new show."[129] Incorporating elements of stage realism into his window designs, Fraser created evocative backdrops that conferred a unique aura on the goods displayed.[130] Under his direction, the Field's show windows became stages where commodities performed before an audience of delighted consumers.

Press agents for the Shuberts and the Syndicate recognized the show window's ability to reach thousands of people every day and frequently arranged to have star photographs, endorsements, costumes, posters, and other publicity materials displayed in New York's major department stores.[131] In 1910, show windows along Fifth Avenue and 34th Street celebrated the opening of Edmond de Rostand's *Chantecler*, a French import produced by Charles Frohman and starring Maude Adams, with swaths of bright red fabric and chanticleer lace.[132] That fall, the head of the Shubert's press department, presumably inspired by the *Chantecler* windows, suggested that displaying the cloak worn by Julia Marlowe in *Macbeth* in a show window would be "a good scheme."[133] Behind the show window glass, Marlowe's cloak became an exotic commodity, an object that at once conjured the body of the star actress, the character she played, and the world she inhabited on and offstage. Later correspondence between the Shuberts and their traveling advance agents offers further evidence that the rivalry between the Syndicate and the Shuberts encouraged promotional one-upmanship. In 1912, the Shubert agent Nellie Revell complained that press agents for Klaw and Erlanger's touring productions of *Madame Sherry* and *The Red Widow* were stealing the department store fashion show scheme she had developed in Chicago.[134]

Yet while displays of theatrical props, costumes, and commodities created a bridge between theaters and department stores, it was the staging techniques of the director David Belasco and his peers as interpreted by window dressers like Arthur Fraser that perhaps did the most to unite the shop window with the theatrical proscenium. Throughout the late nineteenth century and the early twentieth, Belasco thrilled audiences with his detailed stage recreations of modern living rooms, street scenes, restaurants, and boarding houses, going so far as to purchase the bedroom furnishings from a rundown tenement building in New York's Tenderloin district for the production of *The Easiest Way* in 1909.[135] In purposefully blurring the boundaries between reality and fiction, Belasco aimed to make his audience "forget that it is not looking into a real place." A "correct stage setting . . . [w]ith the right effects in color, scenery, and costume" was just as important as the actors in a production, he argued, in that it transported audiences out of their seats and into the fictional world onstage.[136] In 1912, Belasco received thunderous applause for his detailed recreation of Child's Restaurant, one of New York's preeminent leisure spots, for the epilogue of *The Governor's Lady*. "It is as if he had taken the audience between the intermission, walked them around the corner of Seventh Avenue, and seated them to one side of the Childs' restaurant [*sic*] at that location and let the last act be played there," the *Theatre Magazine* enthused. In fact, Belasco had obtained many of the stage properties, including tables, chairs, hat and coat racks, dishes, coffee boilers, and a "griddle-cake cooker" from the actual Child's Restaurant Company.[137]

Fraser and his colleagues adapted Belasco's hyper-realism to create impressive show windows and display rooms that positioned audiences in the midst of a fantastic world. The 1906 opening of the new Wanamaker's store in New York, for example, revealed show windows as large as "the average dwelling room," capable of displaying entire libraries, drawing rooms, bedrooms, and dining rooms.[138] Department store designers took Belasco's ideas even further by transforming entire floors into elaborate show rooms. In 1908 Wanamaker's opened its two-story, twenty-four-room "House Palatial," complete with "staircases, a butler's pantry, a servant's dining quarters, an Elizabethan library decorated with tiger skins, a Jacobean dining room, a Louis XIV salon, and even a large Italian garden off the dining room." Occupying the store's sixth, seventh, and eighth floors, the "House Palatial" rivaled anything that Belasco had achieved.[139]

By incorporating Belasco's ideas, department store designers encouraged a mode of spectatorship that fluctuated between complete absorption in the display and bemused awareness of its construction.[140] Caught in the fantasy, audiences could "vicariously consume a fictitious representation of intimate society life" but only on the condition that they did nothing to disrupt the illusion.[141] As Maurya Wickstrom explains in her analysis of corporate "brandscapes" such as Niketown and Ralph Lauren, "really made up" spectacles insist that consumers look but don't touch, that they discipline their bodies while freeing their minds to inhabit the imaginary world on offer. In exchange for this physical restraint, consumers are encouraged to feel *"as if"* they can move; they are led to believe, if only fleetingly, in the possibility of social mobility and escape from the mundane reality of everyday life. "The mimetic nature of our immaterial labor is such that we take intense pleasure in the really made up, that bodily experienced spectrum between facticity and invention, which is the space of movement and change," argues Wickstrom.[142] In other words, brandscapes and similar consumer spectacles provoke the sensation of movement, social advancement, and individual transformation while actual bodies remain static, immobilized by consumer fantasy.

Early twentieth-century department store show windows and display rooms built on the promise of social mobility, referring consumers back to the "real" world where they could partake of the spectacle through consumption. Rather than facilitate the democratization of society through the redistribution of wealth, these displays promoted the "democratization of desire," granting temporary visual access to "a dream world of mass consumption," a place where the common woman could envision herself as a society matron through her purchases.[143] Moreover, by encouraging what the historian Ellen Gruber Garvey describes as a "moment-by-moment multiple focus," whereby "concentration on any one thing is segmented, and distraction is a natural and pleasing element," department stores, along with magazines, mail order catalogs, and other sites of public entertainment, facilitated a continually shifting form of spectatorship that was always directed toward consumption.[144]

The Theater as Department Store

Broadway's commercial theaters similarly created environments conducive to aspirational role-playing, urging women to view actresses as idealized mirror images and to refrain from thinking about social inequities and their role in the exploitation of others.[145] Like modern corporations, New York's leading managers hired prominent architects to build "flagship" theaters in a bid to assert their authority within the industry and attract the city's most respectable audiences. The jewel in Charles Frohman's theatrical crown was the appropriately named Empire Theatre at 40th Street and Broadway, an impressive structure seating 1,099, which, as Kim Marra explains, "echo[ed] the beaux arts style popularized by the Chicago World's Fair as the architecture of American imperialism."[146] Since its opening in 1893, the Empire Theatre had been both home to the preeminent Empire Stock Company and the functional center of Frohman's business operations, boasting an impressive double lobby and two balconies (figure 2.8).[147] Klaw and Erlanger's $1.25 million New Amsterdam Theatre on 42nd Street, completed in 1903, was an equally striking playhouse with excellent acoustics, state of the art facilities, and a bold art nouveau façade that represented an exciting departure from earlier architectural styles.[148] Even Harrison Grey Fiske's *New York Dramatic Mirror* could not help admiring the theater: "The New Amsterdam Theatre is beyond question the most gorgeous playhouse in New York. Architecturally it is near perfection."[149] Not to be outdone, Lee and J. J. Shubert also built lavish theaters, most notably the Sam S. Shubert Theatre on 45th Street in honor of their brother, who had died in a train crash in 1905.[150]

igure 2.8. Charles Frohman's Empire Theatre at 40th Street and Broadway. Note the huge electric
ign on the roof. Picture Collection, The Branch Libraries, The New York Public Library, Astor,
enox and Tilden Foundations.

Vaudeville theaters similarly played to audience fantasies with exteriors adapted from the academic or classical style that evoked "an air of respectability" and interiors that including rooms designated for lounging, smoking, writing, promenading, primping, and socializing. Although, as the historian Charlotte Herzog notes, vaudeville managers' propensity for electric lights, flashy posters, and other signage often clashed with the architectural details, undermining the "cool and stately" exteriors, their lavish environments nevertheless encouraged dreams of upward mobility and represented an attempt "to share the prestige of the legitimate theater."[151] Opening in 1913, B. F. Albee's Palace Theatre on Broadway between 46th and 47th Streets became the nation's preeminent vaudeville house. Its expansive marble lobby, cretonne covered seats, finely appointed powder and smoking rooms, and crystal chandeliers "bespoke the grandeur of royalty" and gave theatergoers the impression that they had entered an entirely different world.[152]

Expansive, finely decorated theater lobbies "neither fully public nor fully given over to private viewing" facilitated audience's transitions into the theatrical world, functioning in the words of the film historian Shelley Stamp "as liminal spaces" between the street and the auditorium.[153] For women attending the theater alone or waiting for friends, the lobby was a safe haven where they could make new acquaintances and renew old ones.[154] "You could be blindfolded and know it was a matinée by the chatter!" a box office clerk reported in 1910.[155] Standing in a crowded theater lobby, women shared a collective feeling of anticipation and excitement as they observed one another's clothing in the large mirrors mounted on the walls and moved through rooms decorated with fine art. Within this performative space, theatergoers could also shift their gazes from the people surrounding them to the framed photographs of the actors who were about to appear onstage. An 1893 photograph of the inner lobby of the Empire Theatre shows large portraits of Charles Frohman's greatest stars, most visibly Ethel Barrymore, mounted on the wall alongside a series of smaller photographs, presumably of supporting players (figure 2.9). In addition to introducing audiences to the members of the Empire Stock Company, this constellation of photographs inverted the theatrical relationship, transforming the stationery actors on the wall into spectators of the theatergoers' lively performances. In theaters where a lobby was extremely small or nonexistent this liminal zone often extended out into the street, "surround[ing] both audiences and passersby with a festive glow."[156] Bordering the two worlds, audience members became living advertisements for the theatrical entertainment they were consuming.[157]

Theater managers also appropriated department store advertising slo-

Figure 2.9. The vestibule of the Empire Theatre where portraits of Charles Frohman's stars were prominently displayed. Ethel Barrymore is visible in the portrait on the far left. Photography Collection, Miriam and Ira D. Wallach Division of Art, Prints and Photographs, the New York Public Library, Astor, Lenox and Tilden Foundations.

gans to appeal to female theatergoers' consumer desires, making frequent use of the words "bargain," "special," and "marked down," and holding special "Bargain Matinees" on Wednesdays. "Whenever a woman sees any of those signs," observed a writer in the *Green Book Album*, "she stops and considers an investment."[158] Free giveaways likewise aligned female theatergoers' viewing practices with a consumer gaze. Although Tony Pastor had used door prizes to attract female consumers to his "Ladies Club Theater" as early as the 1880s, early twentieth-century managers developed sophisticated promotional schemes that made a more explicit connection between the gifts being distributed and the production onstage. Although few giveaways could compare with Henry Savage's *Merry Widow* hat stunt, the managers of the 1909 hit *The*

Chocolate Soldier delighted matinee audiences with "boxes of real chocolate soldiers." Two years later, management for *The Deep Purple* gave away purple silk stockings for the forty-fifth matinee performance of the popular play, a gift that effectively turned female theatergoers into walking billboards when the stockings were worn outside the theatrical context.[159]

In 1913, William Morris, the manager of the New York Theatre, went even further to bring the department store into the theater, opening a "New York Store" in what had once been the smoking room, where women could use coupons to select from "an assortment of gaudy looking glassware."[160] Morris's clever scheme negated any need for female theatergoers to look elsewhere for fun little trinkets to take home with them. Indeed, as *Variety* quipped, "Woolworth . . . may yet declare the New York Store opposition." This transformation of a space once intended exclusively for male leisure into a "store" where female theatergoers "making purchases of daytime seats [could] take their choice of most of the articles," illustrates how the gendering of theatrical spectatorship both supported and was sustained by the gendering of consumption.[161]

A photograph of the 1906 "Blanche Bates Bazar" held in the Belasco Theatre as a fundraiser for the victims of the San Francisco earthquake offers similar evidence of a scheme that blurred the boundaries between department store and theater (figure 2.10). The two fashionably dressed women at the far left of the image hold items that they are about to purchase from the two "saleswomen" standing at the counter. An array of goods, including photographs and glassware, are arranged on a shelf behind them, where they may be easily seen by others in the lobby. In fact, the only evidence that this scene occurred outside a retail environment is the caption beneath the photograph, which identifies the sum raised by the event as an impressive $2,272.[162] Not surprisingly, there are no men present in this photograph. In fact, men rarely seemed to have factored into the managers' promotional schemes. In 1897, the *Dramatic Mirror* columnist "The Callboy" complained about "the absurd practice of providing theatre souvenirs for the women and of slighting everlastingly the men who pay the freight" and reminded managers that male theatergoers might appreciate something other than the "alleged all tobacco cigarettes which have long represented the only special favors a man might expect of a theatre."[163] But there is little evidence to suggest that managers ever listened to this complaint.

Theater managers and their commercial partners continued to play to female desires once they had crossed from the lobby into the auditorium, presenting advertisements in programs, on curtains, and even on the scen-

Figure 2.10. The "Blanche Bates Bazar" at the Belasco Theatre, 1906. The theater lobby was transformed into a department store salesroom. *Broadway Magazine* (May 1906): 119, Theodore Dreiser Papers, Rare Book and Manuscript Library, University of Pennsylvania.

ery. By 1912, the average program was over thirty pages long, with plenty of room for quarter-, half-, and full-page advertisements.[164] Not all advertisers were sold on this method, however, as a debate in the pages of the advertising trade journal *Printers' Ink* suggests. Some companies questioned whether theatergoers actually read programs, let alone program advertisements, and thought that they could better invest their money elsewhere. In 1909 *Printers' Ink* attempted to resolve the issue by sending an undercover journalist into a theater to study audience behavior. The journalist's report confirmed advertisers' suspicions; although several men and women skimmed through their programs, most preferred to chat with their companions or watch other theatergoers. On the basis of this report, *Printers' Ink* concluded that program advertising was an ineffective strategy.[165]

Printers' Ink did, however, favor the practice of advertising on stage curtains, explaining that this method offered "such splendid opportunities to the advertiser to check up definitely not only the number, but also the class of readers of his copy."[166] Companies such as Mennen, Adams' Chewing Gum, and Beeman reportedly preferred the stage curtain to other advertising mediums, placing ads in "almost every house in the United States and Canada." The predominance of products targeted at male consumers suggests that this strategy was most effectively used in theaters that catered to mixed audiences, although legitimate theaters also seem to have sold curtain advertising.[167] Legitimate theater owners were nevertheless cautious about the kind of advertisements they accepted lest they "deface" their theaters and displease audiences. In 1908, Clyde W. Riley, the president of a Chicago advertising agency specializing in theater programs and advertising curtains, wrote to Charles A. Bird, the Shuberts' business manager, urging him to get Lee Shubert to approve the new curtain at the Garrick Theatre in Chicago. Riley reassured Bird that the new automobile advertisement would be "just as classical as the bank advertisement we have been running on the steel curtain or the bank advertisement we have been running in the main drop."[168] After viewing a sketch of the proposed curtain, Shubert finally gave his approval, presumably convinced that the "classical" design would not detract from the atmosphere of genteel refinement he wished to preserve.[169]

Moving beyond the stage curtain, theater producers also began to invite advertisers to post advertisements on stage scenery. As the following joke from 1908 suggests, some considered this development yet another example of the advertising industry's colonization of public spaces:

"Advertisements on the scenery!" exclaimed the star. "That's carrying commercialism entirely too far."
"It isn't commercialism," explained the manager. "We want the scene to look like a real meadow, don't we?"[170]

Poking fun at the hyper-realistic tendencies of managers like David Belasco, the author here suggests that painting ads on theatrical scenery was necessary for those who wished to offer an accurate representation of urban life. Indeed, by the turn of the century, no public space was considered too sacred for advertising purposes. Advertisers hung posters in streetcars, subways, town halls, and city streets, and they positioned billboards for brand-name products across gorges, near national monuments, and beside natural wonders—including Niagara Falls.[171]

Forward-thinking advertisers also used the theater to display a range of goods, from hats and petticoats to toothbrushes, alcohol, and cigarettes. Society dramas, musical comedies, and revues, all of which represented urban life, were especially suited to this early form of product placement. In 1901, the actress Elsie de Wolfe delighted audiences when she drove a real Automobile Roundabout by the Baker Company of New York onto the stage in the first scene of the society drama *The Way of the World*. Reports that de Wolfe had experienced difficulties learning to drive the car and had actually driven it into the orchestra pit during a dress rehearsal only heightened the publicity surrounding her novel entrance.[172] As these examples suggest, the model of absorbed spectatorship normally associated with realistic stage settings was strictly at odds with the distracted "moment-by-moment" mode of spectatorship that commercial theater managers encouraged by displaying real commodities onstage. Rather than draw audiences further into the fictional stage world, realistic stage sets, furniture, and designer gowns called attention to their status as real, undermining the theatrical illusion by encouraging fantasies of consumption.[173]

Theater managers strengthened their relationships with advertisers and gained free advertising in trade and popular publications through tie-in arrangements that played directly to what one advertising agent described as women's "emulative eagerness."[174] In 1915, A. G. Hyde and Sons, makers of the Heatherbloom petticoat, launched an intensive campaign to connect their product with *Our Mrs. McChesney*, the new vehicle for Ethel Barrymore. Inspired by Edna Ferber's magazine stories about Edna McChesney, an ambitious petticoat saleswoman, the play centered on Edna McChesney's attempt to "put [the] near-bankrupt manufacturer [of the "Featherloom" petticoat] on his feet through unusual foresight and initiative." Rather than object to the obvious allusion to its Heatherbloom brand, A. G. Hyde and Sons made the most of the connection. The day before the play opened, the company published an advertisement titled "The Plot of a Petticoat," which urged consumers to "remember, it's Heatherbloom that made the play possible." Magazine advertisements included a photograph of Ethel Barrymore, presumably wearing a Heatherbloom petticoat, which implied that both "Edna McChesney" and Ethel Barrymore were satisfied users of the product.[175]

The liveness of the theatrical event and the charismatic presence of star performers like Elsie de Wolfe and Ethel Barrymore made theater an ideal site for promoting new commodities and shaping consumer behavior. Worn or used by a star onstage, the tie-in product became inextricably bound up with the star herself, giving female spectators a practical way to possess the luxurious images displayed onstage and to position themselves alongside their stage favorites.[176] "We want to copy those whom we deem superior in taste or knowledge or experience," Stanley Resor, the president of the

J. Walter Thompson Company advertising agency, observed in the 1920s.[177] Like testimonial advertisements—a subject I will return to in the following chapter—theatrical tie-ins succeed because they not only offer consumers advice from someone they admire, but also imply "that part of the endorser's fame, beauty, wealth [etc.] . . . is linked in some way to the product offered."[178] For manufacturers of fashion and beauty products in particular, the theatrical tie-in's implicit promise to consumers was a powerful selling tool.[179]

The Imaginary Ladies' Mile

Theatrical tie-ins, product placements, and other forms of advertising would not have been possible without the assistance of the nation's leading newspapers and fashion magazines. As the primary means through which news of theatrical fashions and department stores sales reached middle-class audiences, these publications helped naturalize the relationship between going to the theater and shopping. In 1905 the *Theatre Magazine* became the first American magazine to introduce a special department "devoted to the fashions of the stage," explaining its hope that "an intelligent description of some of [the stage's] sartorial masterpieces, accompanied by pictures showing the detail of each gown or wrap, will be much appreciated by our women readers."[180] Unlike the industry newspapers *Variety*, the *New York Clipper*, and the *Dramatic Mirror*, which also reported on stage clothing, the *Theatre Magazine* was a glossy periodical with bright color covers and full-page photographs of stars, aimed primarily at middle- and upper-class female theatergoers. In addition to providing general fashion information, "Footlight Fashions" offered readers detailed descriptions of the clothes actresses wore on- *and* offstage, often with accompanying photographs or sketches, and featured interviews with leading performers on the subject of stage costuming.[181]

As an intermediary between the professional world of the theater and the suburban home of the matinee girl, the *Theatre Magazine* also helped script consumers' movements between Broadway and Fifth Avenue. In June 1915, for example, the fashion writer Anne Archbald took readers on a virtual tour of New York's theater and shopping districts in an article entitled "Clothes Seen on the Stage." Beginning her journey in the dressing room of Julia Dean at the Forty-Eighth Street Theatre, Archbald quickly shifts focus and geographical location to describe her quest for one of the simple dresses Dean had designed for "personal use." To illustrate her visits to Franklin Simon's, Lord and Taylor's, and Russek's, Archbald includes sketches of the different dresses available at each store, informing readers that "all the prices . . . were quite surprising for the loveliness of the models, very much 'value received' if I may be allowed the expression."[182] On the last page of the article, an ad inviting readers to make use of the *Theatre Magazine*'s shopping service appears above the text, drawing an explicit connection between Archbald's interview and readers' shopping experiences. Functioning as a guidebook for readers' excursions into the city, this story and others like it encouraged a way of moving in and seeing the urban environment that effectively bypassed the uglier sides of production. With the latest issue in hand, a housewife from Newark might visit Manhattan for the matinee performance of a new hit play before heading to Lord and Taylor or the Fifth Avenue Toggery Shop, an establishment favored by "famous stars" like Billie Burke for "personal and stage apparel."[183] If she had to run to catch the train home, she could contact the *Theatre Magazine*'s shopping service to make her purchases for her.

By the 1910s, prominent fashion magazines including *Vogue*, *Harper's Bazar*, and even the *Ladies' Home Journal* offered extensive coverage of "gowns seen on the stage," complete with photographs and articles on actress's clothing preferences.[184] More than supporting a particular geographic experience of the city, these magazines facilitated a consumerist way of looking at and interpreting actresses' bodies within the context of the magazine and the Broadway stage.[185] Every month, *Harper's Bazar* offered readers two pages filled with full-length photographs of actresses dressed in their latest stage gowns (figure 2.11). Set against a white or contrasting background, presumably to highlight design details, the actresses seem to float in a fantasy world devoid of character or plot.[186] The cut-out photographs that fill the page draw attention to the performers' clothing, not their talent, effectively reducing them to commodified *object lessons.*[187] The captions similarly guide the reader's eye up and down the actress's body, providing information about the fabric, cut, color, and construction of her costume. In November 1913, for example, readers learned that "May de Sousa, in 'Miss Caprice' at the Casino, wears a costume of white lace with burnt-onion crepe which is very effective. The oddly draped tunic of lace has a border of the burnt-onion crepe with two long tassels in the front. The high girdle is also of the crepe. The very small hat is of brown velvet with a plume the same shade as the girdle."[188] The fashion theorist Leslie W. Rabine argues that such captions "invite a look that scrutinizes and analyzes the photograph in a state of mental concentration so as to permit a future embodiment of the fantasy."[189] The captions beneath the actresses' photographs in *Harper's Bazar* and *Vogue* thus served as blueprints

Figure 2.11. *Harper's Bazar* was one of the first American fashion magazines to feature photographs of actresses in their stage clothes. Actresses shown on this page (clockwise from left) are Jane Cowl, Edna Wallace Hopper, Mlle. Wiche, Margaret Wycherly, and Irene Boudian. "Gowns on the Stage," *Harper's Bazar* (October 1915): 30.

for fashion-conscious women and helped prepare them for the experience of seeing the clothing onstage.[190]

But in training female audiences to read actresses' bodies for design details, fashion magazines also helped to normalize the commodification and objectification of female performers, obscuring the labor that went into their production as stars. Represented as cut-out dolls, the actresses in *Harper's Bazar* became playthings, toys for female consumers to manipulate and then toss aside as they strolled along the imaginary Ladies' Mile. As the following chapter will show, this objectifying gaze had real-life consequences for stage actresses, especially for novice performers trying to make their way onto the Great White Way.

Chapter 3
"The Cult of Clothes" and the Performance of Class

The advancement of the actress as a fashion innovator in Broadway theaters and in the pages of *Vogue* and *Harper's Bazar* had a profound effect on female performers. "I never can wear old clothes," Jane Cowl told the *American Magazine*, "no matter how fondly I may be attached to a dress or a suit. . . . I don't dare to be seen unless I am absolutely spic and span."[1] "Remember," she later warned the novice Blanche Yurka, "you are in the public eye until you shut the door of your bedroom at night. Never feel that you can afford to look anything but your best, on or offstage."[2] By the turn of the century, a star-struck public and an increasingly aggressive group of reporters, gossip columnists, and photographers kept actresses under constant surveillance. As Ruth Shepley explained to the readers of the *Green Book Magazine*:

When the average woman dresses, she primps herself out for the few other women who'll chance to notice her. With us, there is no chance: we know we are going to be picked to pieces, bit by bit, by every woman in the audience. Every detail must have its individual care; we must dress modishly (for many, many women gather their style-hints at the theatre), dress effectively and becomingly, emphasizing our best points; and, it being necessary for us to instruct our dear sisters, we must give them novelty.[3]

Shepley's comments hint at the underlying violence that defined the relationship between early twentieth-century actresses and their female fans. These audiences "pick" their favorites "to pieces, bit by bit," reading their bodies as a series of commodities they can handle, admire, or reject as they would items on a bargain basement table.

Laboring to perfect their image, actresses appeared on multiple stages—theaters, streets, restaurants, newspapers, and magazines—and adopted new and often radical dress styles to please fans and stave off challenges from other performers. Those who took "unfashionable" roles or appeared in public in an unflattering outfit did so at the risk of their reputations and their careers. Indeed, while female audiences regularly applauded actresses for their fashionable appearances—sometimes even stopping the show to reward a particularly bold or beautiful wardrobe decision—they did not hesitate to express disappointment when performers failed to deliver an expected "sartorial treat." In 1908, the *Theatre Magazine*'s Mlle. Sartoris commented disfavorably on Maxine Elliott's "white satin ball gown . . . of the vintage of 1905," rebuking the normally stylish actress for failing to uphold her image.[4] That same year, society women watching Ethel Barrymore in *Alice, Sit by the Fire* wondered why the actress would choose to "play such an ugly character." "Of course, we don't expect Ethel to do any great acting," one observed, "but she might at least wear some good clothes when her friends come to see her."[5] The pressure to put forward a fashionable appearance was so intense that, as one actress told the critic Alan Dale, "I don't mind looking like a fright in the early part of a play. . . . But in the last act I must come into my own. I don't want the audience to go home carrying away that character-picture. I want to be remembered as a good-looker, responding to the 'last cry' of fashion, and that is purely for business reasons too."[6] Audiences disapproved of stars who failed to uphold a particular image, but they reserved their greatest disapproval for those who appeared in imitations of designer fashion.[7] When Blanche Walsh "presented herself in sables [that were] unmistakably imitation" she provoked "howl[s]" from audience members who viewed her false attempt at finery as an affront to the high standards of stage costuming. Audiences that had once been content with a well-crafted imitation were now quick to scorn anything that suggested "imitation and sham."[8]

Technological developments in theatrical staging, coupled with an emphasis on authenticity in the midst of growing class tension, offer some explanation for female theatregoers' insistence on seeing "the real thing." The actress Clara Morris cited the transition from gas to electric lighting, "which brought out the color and details of the costumes and scenery," and the widespread use of opera glasses as two reasons why audiences were more likely to reject stage settings and costumes they perceived as "deceptions."[9] Other contemporaries linked the changes in contemporary costuming to concurrent developments in stage scenery, characterized by the impressive work of directors like David Belasco, whose hyper-realistic experiments reproduced recognizable urban settings onstage.[10] The cultural historian Miles Orvell interprets this desire to stage "real life" as part of a much larger response to changing definitions of authenticity and reality in a period when class boundaries were shifting and the rapid circulation of mass-produced goods made it increasingly difficult to distinguish between an imitation and "the real thing." Those who had once celebrated "the arts of imitation and illusion" now prized displays of authenticity and discernible realism like those offered by Belasco, seeing them as a representation of life as they *desired* it to be.[11]

But female audience members' intensive examination of costume detail and their demands for the "real thing" suggest that an escape into the fictional dream world onstage was the last thing they desired; rather, what seems to have prompted these reactions was a perceived need to assert class status. Turn-of-the-century developments in clothing production, including innovations in the ready-to-wear and fashion industries, the production of cheap fashion products, and the widespread publication of fashion information in newspapers and magazines, made it increasingly difficult for the average city dweller to distinguish class and respectability through dress.[12] Although historians have recently complicated earlier accounts of the "democratization of fashion," qualifying claims of uniformity by noting the number of women who continued to order custom-made clothing, they nevertheless agree that by the turn of the century the once easy equation of clothing with social status was no longer tenable.[13]

"Purposeless imitation!" the home economist Bertha Richardson exclaimed in an article in 1904, noting with disdain the process whereby fashions trickled down from exclusive shops on Fifth Avenue to pushcarts on Hester Street:

The Fourth Avenue shop says to the Fourth Avenue buyer: "Behold my clever imitation. For less than you could pay in a Fifth Avenue shop, I can give you a perfect imitation. You would not be behind the styles, I know. I can make you look like the real peacock." The Third Avenue shop scans the windows of the Fourth Avenue shop and returns the same to its customers. The First Avenue shop has a still cheaper imitation, and in Hester Street, on the pushcarts, ghosts of the real are "Going, going, going" for thirty-nine cents.[14]

For Richardson, working women's clothes were merely "ghosts of the real," imitations of imitations. Yet while she presumably had little trouble distinguishing between "ghosts" and the "real," others found it incredibly challenging. Reporting on her experiences at a Lower East Side dance hall, Rose Pastor confided to the readers of the Jewish newspaper *Yiddishes Tageblatt*: "If I didn't know that all the girls here are working girls, I would think her papa was a railroad magnate or someone who owned a few millions at the least."[15] Pastor's remarks foreground the performativity and fluidity of class as a cultural construct and further suggest that working-class women took pleasure in disrupting social hierarchies through fashion.[16] Given the new challenges of reading class through fashion, then, women's angry responses to stage gowns and jewels they perceived as fake suggest that they saw the theater as a place where they could acquire the necessary skills to continue policing class borders.

Despite their enforced investment in dress and appearance, many actresses shared middle-class women's concerns about the disruption of the nineteenth-century semiotics of fashion and the destabilization of class and racial boundaries. For decades, stage performers had struggled to uplift the profession and were finally gaining the respectability they desired; but the flood of stage-struck girls from diverse class and racial backgrounds rushing to Broadway threatened to lower their status in much the same way that the millions of immigrants from eastern and southern Europe threatened to destabilize white American society.[17] The heightened visibility of African American performers, who enjoyed new opportunities for theatrical stardom thanks in part to the assistance of white managers who recognized their box office potential, further challenged traditional hierarchies. In the 1890s, the black comedy duo of Bert Williams and George Walker found success in B. F. Keith's vaudeville houses, where they entertained black and white theatergoers with jokes, songs, and dances that played on but also critiqued racial stereotypes. They later went on to produce a series of popular full-length musical comedies, extensions of their vaudeville "coon act" that featured all-black casts and played to white middle-class theatergoers. Walker's wife, the dancer and choreographer Aida Overton Walker, successfully negotiated passage into the ballrooms of New York's social elite as a cakewalk instructor in the 1890s and continued to appeal to mixed audiences into the 1910s through her appearances in the Walker and Williams musical comedies. "Negroes were at last on Broadway, and there to stay!" the African American composer Will Marion Cook declared in 1898 after his show *Clorindy* had become a mainstream hit.[18]

In light of these developments, the stakes of theatrical stardom were particularly high for white, middle-class performers, especially women. As this chapter will show, female performers sought to protect the whiteness of the Great White Way by making fashionable dress and a stylish body a prerequisite of stage success. In her book *Stage Confidences* of 1902, a series of "talks" addressed to curious theatergoers and stage-struck girls, the retired actress Clara Morris pleaded with young women to resist "the cult of clothes" overtaking Broadway, calling upon independently wealthy actresses to avoid "the mad extravagance that those who are dependent on their salaries alone will surely try to emulate."[19] But Morris's pleas fell on deaf ears. Working alongside male producers interested in exploiting young talent to boost their theatrical empires, star actresses continued to spend thousands of dollars on their stage wardrobes each year—often advertising the amount they had spent on a single gown to impress their fans and other actresses—to ensure their positions within the profession and prevent undesirable performers from gaining access to the stage.[20]

Still, as many actresses were also aware, their social position hinged on their ability to present an image that was simultaneously flawless and accessible. Audiences warmed to performers who were "just like them" only better. In fact, what made these women so appealing to the public was the knowledge that behind the seamless, public image was a fallible human being laboring to keep up appearances. An actress's ability to maintain a fashionable façade, to mold and shape her body into an appealing form, reassured female audiences that they too might become beautiful or stylish if they worked hard enough and acquired the appropriate goods. Represented by turns as perfect images, calculated constructs, natural beauties, and skilled technicians, actresses overcame centuries of prejudice toward the stage by promising that anyone could achieve similar success with a bit of luck. This belief in the democratization of beauty played a central role in the formation of a culture of mass consumption. By continuing to emphasize the importance of designer clothing and upholding a standard of living that lay beyond that of most Americans, actresses encouraged audiences to associate status with commodities; to overlook the politics of exclusion that defined both the acting profession and American society; to accept an increasingly narrow beauty ideal that privileged thin, white bodies; and to embrace the products and systems that would guarantee their transformation.

Stage-Struck Girls and Personality Performers

Between 1890 and 1920, thousands of stage-struck girls—working-class immigrants, farm girls, middle-class wives, society debutantes—arrived in New York City hoping to find success on the Broadway stage. Census statistics indicate that the number of women identifying themselves as actresses increased by 332 percent between 1890 and 1910, from 4,652 to 15,436—numbers that reflect both the rapid growth of the theater industry and the desirability of a performing career for women.[21] David Belasco estimated that he saw as many as 4,000 stage-struck women every year, with an average of 10 a day.[22] Stage-struck girls came to New York from villages, towns, and cities throughout the

United States, "from Augusta to San Diego, and from Seattle to Savannah."[23] Nearly half of these performers were in fact *girls* in their teens and early twenties, but older women also pursued stage careers.[24] "There are times when I am half inclined to believe that every unmarried female in the country—and many a married one—between the ages of fifteen and fifty, pants for a stage career," the actress Ethel Barrymore commented in 1906.[25]

For some women, a theatrical career represented an escape from the drudgery of other employment and an opportunity for higher wages. The stage "contains visions of independence and diversion, not afforded by the unromantic environs of a counter or hashery," *Variety* explained in 1908.[26] The *Dramatic Mirror* agreed that the "theatre alone of all the public institutions of civilization offers to her sisters a field in which they may and do stand absolutely and equally with man."[27] As boosters for the profession, these papers emphasized that an actress's chance of doubling and tripling her income was significantly higher than that of women in most other professions.[28] Reports that vaudeville's leading performers earned as much as $2,500 and $3,500 each week and that even chorus girls and bit players averaged a weekly wage between $8 and $15, slightly higher than what most women made in a department store or office and certainly more than what most factory workers received, made the stage a highly appealing alternative for the thousands of rural and immigrant women arriving in New York.[29]

But high wages alone do not explain the number of women from diverse social, cultural, and ethnic backgrounds that flooded the theatrical market. More than the prospect of financial gain, it was the growing respectability and glamour of the acting profession that made a stage career attractive. Like Theodore Dreiser's Sister Carrie, stage-struck girls everywhere "wondered at the greatness of the names upon the billboards, the marvel of the long notices in the papers, the beauty of the dresses upon the stage, the atmosphere of carriages, flowers, refinement."[30] Magazine and newspaper articles rich in detail about star actresses' private rail cars, wardrobes, pets, and most recent public appearances created the impression that the theater was a dream world of luxury and romance.[31] Such an impression was markedly different from previous perceptions of the stage in general and actresses in particular. For much of the nineteenth century, many Americans had viewed the actress as a woman who consorted with dangerous men, engaged in raucous public behavior, and played up her physical appearance to advance her career, perhaps even to the point of selling her body.[32] By the turn of the century, however, actresses had graduated from social pariahs into trendsetters, thanks to a series of developments that included the widespread distribution of actresses' photographs both in and out of costume; the proliferation of theatrical newspapers such as the *New York Clipper, Variety*, and the *New York Dramatic Mirror*; the professionalization of the dramatic critic and the press agent who often had close ties to management; and the creation of acting clubs and schools dedicated to providing stage-struck individuals with some degree of formal training.[33] With these changes, theatrical performers finally began to achieve a higher level of social respectability and increasingly came to represent youth, vitality, and success to their growing audiences of middle-class women and men.

In an ironic if not unforeseen turn of events, the influx of stage-struck girls also facilitated the rise of male directors who built their reputations on the transformation of unskilled yet emotionally sensitive women. These Svengali-like figures promoted themselves as the creative geniuses behind weak and yielding female vessels who, through their intervention, became the shining lights of the stage. The artistic, and possibly romantic, partnership between David Belasco and Mrs. Leslie Carter is perhaps the most vivid example of this new relationship. In 1893 the newly divorced and financially destitute Mrs. Leslie Carter auditioned for Belasco, hoping to support herself through a career on the stage. Although awkward, she revealed a promising emotional capacity and Belasco agreed to take her on as his protégé. During a two-year period, she rehearsed forty roles under his tutelage in plays ranging from Shakespeare and old comedy to French melodrama and modern farce. Through intensive study, Belasco later explained, "one deficiency after another was detected and corrected" until she was finally ready to emerge from seclusion as a serious, emotional actress, scoring her first major success in 1895 as Maryland Calvert in Belasco's own play *The Heart of Maryland*. In subsequent productions, such as *Zaza* in 1899, he continued to capitalize on Carter's status as a socialite and divorcée, foregrounding the similarities between her own experiences and those of the musical hall performer Zaza to represent both as honorable and respectable if fallible women.[34] The much publicized story of Carter's transformation from an unskilled amateur into an accomplished artist propelled the actress to stardom and advanced Belasco's career as well. Although their partnership ended a decade later in a bitter and very public split, Belasco continued to tell this "creation myth" in newspaper and magazine articles, advertising himself as the force behind Carter's phenomenal success.[35]

Belasco's deliberate attempt to blur the lines between actress and character marks a major shift in the representation of the actress as a public figure. Whereas nineteenth-century actresses had achieved fame for portraying a wide range of characters, turn-of-the-century actresses attracted notice for displaying an attractive or amusing personality. What made these stars so appealing to modern audiences was the way that they addressed contemporary anxieties about the loss of individuality by offering a reassuring depiction of a self that could be improved upon but which nevertheless maintained an essential core.[36] As thousands of men and women worried that they were becoming mere cogs in the wheel of corporate America, stars who achieved great fame by playing variations of the same character season after season demonstrated that all that was needed for success was an amusing or interesting personality. Just as contemporary self-help literature stressed the importance of expressing an interesting personality through "clothing, personal appearance, and 'good manners,'" in the historian Warren Susman's formulation, actors and actresses seemed to suggest that with enough practice, the otherwise anonymous member of the crowd could transform himself or herself from a nobody into a "Somebody."[37] Moreover, during a period when cultural critics feared that the self had become "discontinuous and fragmented," the always predictable performances of stars like Billie Burke suggested that some inner core remained. Unlike the protean nineteenth-century actress, who raised troubling questions about the relationship between appearance and identity through her various onstage incarnations, the twentieth-century star showcased different aspects of her personality but continued to give audiences the impression that they were seeing the "real" star underneath.[38]

For many traditionally trained performers, however, the emphasis on personality over artistry and the suggestion that anyone could achieve success on the stage if he or she possessed charm or the right look threatened to undermine all efforts to uplift the profession. Underlying these anxieties was a series of questions about the nature of personality itself: Was personality something that you were born with or could it be developed? Was it the product of nature or the outcome of years of nurturing? "Just now we are making a fetish of personality," the character actor E. M. Holland observed in a 1911 article titled "Personality vs. Technique." "[I]t is the explanation of the unthinking for all success in life."[39] Holland was just one of a number of actors and theater critics who made a concerted effort to understand the acting process in relation to the individual psychology of the actor, and to establish new criteria for distinguishing between good acting and bad.[40] Part of the challenge for these writers, though, was the very word personality. "It is extremely difficult to arrive at the exact meaning of 'personality,'" Lady Randolph Churchill explained to the readers of *Harper's Bazar* in 1916, noting that the word itself was rife with contradictions: "If we go to the dictionary, it is not much help to find that the Latin 'persona' means 'mask,' or 'one who wears a mask—an actor,' in fact it rather confuses us, as to most people the idea of personality could not exist without the dropping of the mask and the showing of the real individual. This contradiction has been explained by the suggestion that the showing or manifestation of one's self is akin to the actor's art of expression."[41] In Churchill's reading, individuals perform their personalities as a way of revealing their inner selves; personality is thus both the performance of self *and* the "real" self. Other writers interpreted personality differently. The theater critic Walter Prichard Eaton stressed that personality was something bestowed upon an individual by "God and his grandparents," but nevertheless argued that "[y]ou can train and direct it, you can even develop it, perhaps, as so many men unconsciously do who give their lives to a certain occupation," allowing for a more flexible, shifting notion of the self.[42] Unlike the actor William Collier, who expressed his "opinion that the actor does not create but interprets, and the good actor develops the personality of the character instead of his own personality," Eaton was careful not to dismiss the importance of individual personality, stressing instead the need for actors to develop as many facets of themselves as possible.[43]

Eaton nevertheless took pains to distinguish between "personality" performers and skilled artists. "Nobody disputes that personality plays an enormous part in the popular success of an actor or actress," he explained in 1916. "But to differentiate between the actor with a strong personality who is also an artist, and one who is not an artist, frequently overtaxes the lay critic."[44] Actors who possessed charm and little else, he argued, succeeded only when they played roles that allowed them to show off the most pleasing aspects of their personalities. Limited in range and ability, these stars capitalized upon their unique or admirable qualities and always played variations of themselves. Actresses such as Billie Burke, Marie Tempest, Mabel Taliaferro, and Marie Doro (all products of Charles Frohman's star-making machine) possessed personal qualities, many of them physical, that "capture[d] our fancy and move[d] us" into the story regardless of the quality of the acting.[45] True artists, by contrast, were those who skillfully selected the most interesting or relevant aspects of their personalities to illuminate the characters they were playing. These actors possessed the skill to reveal more than one side of their personalities and excelled at playing a variety of character types. Eaton praised Doris Keane for creating two contrasting characters in *Romance* and *The Hypocrites*, noting her willingness in each role to suppress aspects of her personality that were incompatible with the character she was playing. A "rich" personality combined with the "technical expertness to utilize those sides of it properly adapted to each character she plays" allowed her to play a variety of different roles well.[46] Performers like Keane were few in number, however, compared to the endless series of carefully packaged stars produced by Frohman, Belasco, and others. Rather than supporting more traditional actors' contention that acting was an art form achieved through long hours of specialized training and rehearsal, the star system promised success to those who were beautiful or amusing or who possessed a certain charm or charisma that drew others to them.

Despite the apparent "democratization" of the acting profession, however, the newly emerging star system was hardly democratic. In their capacity as knowable, likeable personalities, stars like Billie Burke and Marie Doro enticed women from diverse class and racial backgrounds to dream about a stage career; but as easily consumable images of genteel, white American girl-hood they also upheld traditional definitions of race and class.[47] The active involvement of Jewish managers like Charles Frohman in such a project may seem peculiar given the frequent anti-Semitic attacks they endured; yet as Kim Marra has convincingly shown, Frohman and Belasco used their association with respectable, white actresses to challenge Judeophobic stereotypes and to represent themselves as upstanding businessmen.[48] Through their insistence on the importance of stage dress, they supported actresses in their efforts to uplift the stage and through their rigorous and often sexist casting practices, they ensured that only the "right" women had a chance for success.

Belonging to Broadway

A stage-struck girl might possess an amusing or interesting personality, but as the Jewish singer Sophie Tucker discovered when she first arrived in New York, if she didn't look or dress the right way, she stood little change of getting a job. "[W]ith my hair-do and the kind of dress I wore," Tucker recalls, "I looked just what I was, a big, gawky country girl, and not more than seventeen." After several managers dismissed her as a "nice-looking country girl," Tucker "began to look closely at the girls sauntering along Broadway." According to Tucker, "They all looked well dressed. Nothing of the country girl about any of *them*. I took to looking into the shop windows, sizing up the clothes, comparing them with my own. There was a hell of a lot of difference. I guessed, if you wanted to go places in New York, you had to look like New York." Determined to "go places," Tucker transformed her image. She purchased a ten-dollar outfit on consignment, set her hair in a more mature style, and headed out to Times Square, confident that she now looked "as if

she belonged to Broadway." She was soon rewarded for her efforts with a singing job in a German rathskeller.[49]

As Tucker's account suggests, finding a job in New York hinged on a
performer's willingness to participate in her own commodification, to reproduce herself as a desirable and saleable object by demonstrating her ability to dress well. "The appeal to the manager: 'I can afford to dress the part
handsomely,' is seldom in vain," the *Theatre Magazine* explained, "and the girl
with only talent is hopelessly handicapped."[50] "Clothes impress the managers," Billie Burke reiterated, "and for this reason most actresses wear their best
bib and tucker when they go to the manager to talk about an engagement.
Some even appear in borrowed plumage."[51] The message was simple: without
fashionable dress even the most talented stage-struck girl had little chance of
being noticed or hired.[52] "The girl who does not dress expensively might just
as well give up the business," a chorus girl writing in *The Independent* advised.
"If she is not finely gowned she may haunt the managers' office day after day
in vain, for she will get no engagement."[53] Stage-struck girls therefore had to
acquire the right clothes and the confidence to wear them if they wanted to
find success on the Broadway stage.

Performers who more comfortably fell into culturally sanctioned definitions of white femininity had an easier time gaining access to the stage and the
roles they desired; but becoming and remaining a fashionable actress necessitated a continual process of reevaluation, reinvestment, and reinvention. Few
beginning actresses could afford to pay for their own clothes without going
into debt, especially as they were often required to purchase these clothes
before receiving their first paycheck. Billie Burke concluded that it was often
more difficult for a young actress to "get the gowns" necessary for a role than
it was to get the role in the first place.[54] Indeed, while managers like Frohman
gave their stars the freedom to spend as they wished, they rarely extended this
courtesy to supporting players. With thousands of eager young women at the
doorsteps and crowds of fashion-hungry women at their plays, managers had
little incentive to discourage the "cult of clothes." As late as 1910, Annie Russell
explained to the readers of the *Ladies' Home Journal*, "Some managements
provide them all, others furnish one out of three; some share the cost; often
the actress provides them entirely."[55] While still a novice earning thirty-five
dollars a week, Ethel Barrymore learned that the two costumes she had to
wear in Charles Frohman's production of *Catherine* cost one hundred dollars
each. "The result," she explains, "was that I was mortgaged, so to speak, for
the entire season to the tailor and the dressmaker." Although Frohman paid
for her costumes up front, a small amount was deducted from her salary each

week until she had paid her debts.[56] "One of the sad things about the theater," she concluded, "is that when you are beginning, trying to make a very little money go a long way, you have to pay for your own clothes; when you're a star, relatively rich, they're provided for you."[57] For those who never achieved stardom, however, a theatrical career often meant living as a mortgaged commodity (figure 3.1).

Poor conditions backstage and unwieldy business onstage meant that expensive gowns were often ruined and needed replacing in the middle of a run, wreaking further havoc on an actress's already strained budget. As Viola Allen explained, "There is much wear in the hurried fastening and unfastening of a gown eight times a week, and perhaps trailing them up and down uncarpeted stairs."[58] A costume made of delicate fabrics, such as the negligee of "the sheerest of chiffons and laces" worn by Ray Cox in *Twin Beds*, had to be replaced several times during the run.[59] Greasepaint stains and unfinished floorboards backstage also damaged costumes. These problems plagued all actresses, but they had the greatest impact on young actresses who paid for their own costumes. Despite these risks, however, stage-struck girls shied away from roles that did not give them an opportunity to appear in fashionable dress, aware that "the first impression they make is the lasting one with the audience."[60] The Jewish actress Blanche Yurka was so eager to get onto the stage that she actually *paid* an agent one hundred dollars to find her a role in a society drama. As a lady of quality in *An Old New Yorker* she had her first opportunity to dress fashionably, but when the play closed after one week, she found that she had little but the bill to show for her efforts.[61] Young actresses nevertheless continued to spend hundreds of dollars on their stage wardrobes for shows opening outside New York, hoping that when, or indeed *if*, they came to Broadway, their clothes would attract the attention of a big-time manager.[62]

Yet while acquiring stylish clothes presented the most obvious challenge for many women, purchasing an expensive gown was no guarantee of stage success. Not only did stage-struck girls have to select tasteful and flattering gowns that evinced an air of distinction, they also had to acquire the bodily awareness and discipline to display them to good effect.[63] The long trains and tight corsets that characterized turn-of-the-century fashion, later replaced by hobble skirts and sleeveless tea gowns, placed specific physical demands on the female body that required time and practice to master.[64] As Sophie Tucker learned when she made her first appearance in fashionable dress, it was one thing to wear a stylish gown, quite another to possess the knowledge, skill, and physical requirements to attract attention and avert disaster.[65] Stepping

"*Gets eighteen dollars per week for wearing a five hundred dollar gown*"

Figure 3.1. Chorus girls, show girls, and other supporting players often went into debt to pay for the stage clothes they needed. Illustration by Warren Rockwell. Channing Pollock, *The Footlights Fore and Aft* (Boston: Gorham Press, 1911).

onstage in a "tightly laced black velvet gown" borrowed from a friend, she did not anticipate the challenges of moving in the restrictive, trained garment. At the conclusion of her act, her heel became caught in the ruffles of the dress when she stepped back to bow. "I hopped back, trying to loosen it," she explains, "and kerplunk, down I went on my fanny like a ton of bricks." Unable to get back on her feet, she was forced to shuffle offstage on her backside, much to the delight of the audience, who thought it was part of the act. "And that," she concludes, "was the climax of my elegant performance."[66]

A further condition of achieving a fashionable reputation was developing an appropriately fashionable body. As early as 1897, the *Dramatic Mirror*'s Matinee Girl noted that "an epidemic of slim and slender girls [had] arisen on the stage." Whereas actresses like Lillian Russell had once impressed audiences with their stately "figures" and Amazonian measurements, those who did not conform to the new physical ideal "languished among the supes."[67] " 'Be thin, ye stars, and let who will shout paniers,' is Broadway's apostrophe," Magda Frances West wrote fifteen years later in an article entitled "Nobody Stars a Fat Woman." "The pressure of the sheath gown," she continued, "is felt in the theatre now just as for several years past it has been leaving its impress on the manufacturers."[68] This close-fitting style flattered tall, thin actresses like Ruth Chatterton and Elsie Ferguson, but it exposed the flaws of older or plumper performers. As a result, West argued, while "all the famous, but fat, deposed [actresses] sit gnashing their teeth in the darkness of 'on tour,' the unknown juvenile hopes are soaring to fortunes on clouds of chiffon."[69]

The implication that all stars could and should work to acquire such a look was consistent with the modern conception of the body as a malleable form. "While the body incorporates fixed capacities such as height and bone structure, the tendency within consumer culture is for ascribed bodily qualities to become regarded as plastic," Mike Featherstone argues, "[W]ith effort and 'body work' individuals are persuaded that they can achieve a certain desired appearance."[70] Upheld as role models, actresses who did not already possess the desired body had to perform "body maintenance," treating their bodies as machines that required "servicing, regular care, and attention to preserve maximum efficiency."[71] But as historians of dieting culture and the body have shown, the early twentieth-century celebration of a thin ideal constituted yet another part of an ongoing cultural project to equate beauty with whiteness. According to Marie Griffith, the modern "doctrine of slimness" did not account for cultures that viewed the thin body as a sign of poverty, disease, and famine, and the fat body as a sign of health and prosperity. This politics of exclusion sets apart the thin, white, middle-class body from other bodies, coded as deviant or sinful, creating a troubling equation between whiteness, physical perfection, and spiritual goodness.[72]

In their pursuit of the perfect image, managers often rejected fat or problematically ethnic women outright or, in the case of performers like Sophie Tucker, required them to hide behind a mask of burnt cork. As the theater historian M. Alison Kibler explains, "Racial masquerade was one route to success and celebrity in vaudeville for women who were not conventionally attractive (particularly for women who were fat)."[73] Tucker writes at length about her early experiences as a blackface performer, claiming that she adopted the guise after being told that she was too "big and ugly" for the crowd at Chris Brown's amateur night.[74] Recalling her first experience, she explains, "The burnt cork stuck in my ears and in the roots of my hair. It had ruined my best white shirtwaist." The new makeup apparently clashed with Tucker's perception of herself as a performer and became an all too constant reminder of her unappealing body.[75]

Tucker's anxieties about blackface may also have arisen out of a fear of being identified as black. "My greatest difficulty," she explains, "was convincing the audience I was a white girl." At the end of every performance, she playfully revealed her whiteness, removing one of her gloves—a parodic gesture reminiscent of burlesque—and exposing a white arm beneath. At this point, "there'd be a sort of surprised gasp [from the audience], then a howl of laughter."[76] Much more than a bid for a laugh, the removal of the glove signaled Tucker's whiteness and foregrounded the distance between the actress and her skillful racial performance.[77] Offstage, Tucker invested in her whiteness by working to improve her physical appearance and overcome Brown's condemning words: "too big and too ugly." Motivated by the thought that once she had developed a more pleasing appearance, she would no longer be required to black up, she worked to create herself as an attractive, white woman. By 1909, she explains, "My hands were smooth and white now. No one would suspect them of long association with the dishpan and scrub pail. My own hair under the wig was a mass of burnished gold curls. Nature and my Crimean ancestors had done that for me. They had given me, too, my smooth, fine skin, that was pleasingly white now, since I had learned to care for it."[78] According to this account, Tucker distanced herself from her working-class home through a carefully constructed physical transformation. Rather than obscuring her Jewish heritage, however, she gained self-confidence by identifying with her ancestors and learning to accentuate the physical traits she had inherited from them. It was through her Jewishness, in fact, that Tucker became more acceptable; by emphasizing her whiteness—the white hands, the "pleasing white" skin—she clearly delineated between her onstage "false black" self and her offstage "true white" self.[79]

In 1909, after years on the burlesque circuit as a blackface performer, Tucker finally had an opportunity to appear *as herself* when the trunk containing all her stage makeup failed to arrive at the theater in Boston where she was to perform. Despite panicking at first, she soon realized, "If I could put my act across without the coon shouter's make-up . . . [m]aybe I would be through with blackface forever." Dressed in her street clothes, a tailored suit and white linen shirtwaist, she stood before the audience and revealed her "true" identity: "You-all can see I'm a white girl. Well, I'll tell you something more: I'm not Southern. I grew up right here in Boston, at 22 Salem Street. I'm a Jewish girl, and I just learned this Southern accent doing a blackface act for two years."[80] Finally free of the blackface mask, Tucker publicly reclaimed her identity as both white and Jewish. The audience's warm acceptance of her whiteface persona confirmed what she had always believed: that she could appeal to an audience without the racial disguise.

In becoming a white performer, Tucker resolved to recreate her personal and professional identity through fashion. Determined to "show 'em" she could "make good in whiteface," she explains that her first thought was to acquire "a swell evening gown." Although this account challenges the limits of believability, her association between fashionable dress and whiteface is nevertheless significant in that it suggests that appearing in a stylish gown was the visual analogue to appearing in blackface; both enabled a kind of racialized performance. Tucker's photographic appearances on sheet music covers from 1909 onward offer a visual record of her attempt to uplift herself and become an attractive, fashion conscious woman (figure 3.2).[81] She nevertheless admits that her early fashion attempts were skewed by a desire for acceptance and recognition. "I was sure a loud baby," she recalls. Dressed in a prized sealskin coat with seal cuffs and a leopard-skin bow, "[I] advertised to the whole world that I was a performer. You could see me coming five blocks off." Over time, however, she refined her sense of style, resolving, "No more loud, showy clothes."[82]

More than simply acquiring the "right" body or the right to wear expensive clothes, then, female performers had to learn to dress in a manner that conveyed class and suited their body types. "I have seen short, stout women in 'Minaret' gowns and stiff taffetas made with frills and huge puffs around the hips and small flat bonnets on the head," the *Variety* columnist "Plain Mary" (Vesta Powell) reported in 1914, "while tall, slender women have worn soft, clinging gowns made on straight lines and high head-dresses a contrast

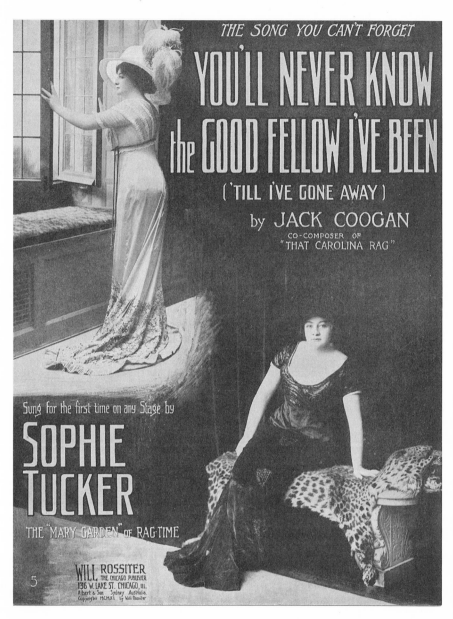

Figure 3.2. Sophie Tucker, ca. 1912. In moving away from blackface performance, Tucker used her sheet music covers to present herself as a fashionable performer. "You'll Never Know the Good Fellow I've Been," Sam DeVincent Collection of Illustrated Sheet Music, Archives Center, National Museum of American History, Behring Center, Smithsonian Institution.

almost grotesque."[83] Without the self-awareness or training to select flattering styles, these women often fell into the hands of aggressive saleswomen hoping for an easy sale. Early in her career, the comedian Marie Dressler reportedly spent hundreds of dollars on inappropriate outfits: pink dresses [that fought] with [her] red hair" and "a tailored suit that surpassed any effect [she had] ever been able to achieve in [her] wildest comedy make-ups" at the urging of a pushy saleswoman.[84] Although she later learned to choose more flattering styles, other performers were less fortunate.

In 1906, *Variety* extended a helping hand to sartorially challenged performers by introducing a weekly gossip and fashion column called "The Woman in Variety." Originally written by the press agent Anna Marble and later taken over by Hattie Silverman, the wife of *Variety* publisher Sime Silverman, this column offered detailed descriptions and critiques of the clothes worn by female vaudeville artists.[85] Both Marble and "the Skirt" (Silverman's pseudonym) promoted higher clothing standards and encouraged performers to consider their stage clothes carefully. Enjoying a kind of panopticonic gaze, they singled out women who appeared in shabby costumes, ill-matching accessories, or distasteful gowns. In 1913, for example, "the Skirt" suggested that Miss Miller of the Marvelous Millers "should glance around and secure some ideas of dressing. The costume worn Monday will never do for the 'Big Time.' The shoes made the feet appear fearfully clumsy."[86] "The Skirt" urged other performers to change the color of their costumes, invest more money in their wardrobes, or discard obsolete or inappropriate fashions.[87] By offering tips on what to wear (or *not* wear), "the Skirt" shaped dress codes on the vaudeville circuit and assisted performers in becoming fashionable. Yet her scornful and at times dismissive comments on unfashionable performers also helped to ensure that costuming standards privileged those who could afford to spend lavishly.

In spite of the class and racial biases that informed costuming practices on Broadway, young novices occasionally benefited from a close friendship with an experienced performer who instructed them in the intricacies of stage fashion. Blanche Yurka admitted that she was prone to "seediness" until her friend and mentor Jane Cowl taught her how to select a more attractive and suitable wardrobe.[88] The Jewish comedian and singer Fanny Brice similarly acknowledged that her previous shopping experiences in the Lower East Side hindered her early attempts to create a fashionable appearance until she received assistance: "I was in the habit of turning my pay envelope over to my mother intact. Her Grand Street ideas of what an evening dress should cost did not agree with mine, so I was forced to nose out a secondhand shop where the maids of fashionable ladies disposed of their mistresses wardrobes. . . . These dresses, however, did not teach me enough about choosing clothes."[89] While on tour with the *Ziegfeld Follies* in 1910, Brice showed up for dinner with Florenz Ziegfeld and his paramour, Lillian Lorraine, dressed "in a terrific sapphire-blue satin with a delirious bright orange velvet coat and a blue velvet hat with an orange plume." "Ziegfeld gave me one shocked look," she recalls, "and handed Lillian two hundred dollars to buy me new dresses." Chastised for her poor taste, Brice accepted Lorraine's assistance, selling her outfit to Lillian's maid. "When our train arrived back in New York and [Ziegfeld] met us, there was Lora behind, arrayed like Sheba's queen in the blue headgear!"[90]

Brice's vivid (and possibly exaggerated) account of her transformation from working-class Jewish girl to *Follies* star highlights the class and racial tensions inherent in the process. In rejecting her mother's "Grand Street ideas" of fashion, she positioned herself above the Jewish and Italian working-class women who frequented Grand Street, the major shopping avenue on the Lower East Side. Yet the sapphire-blue and orange ensemble she selected threatened to expose her class and ethnic roots by confirming stereotypes of the flashily dressed Jewish immigrant.[91] Brice's subsequent decision to sell the outfit to Lorraine's presumably black maid therefore represented her rejection of the ethnic aesthetic and an attempt to move toward a more acceptable, that is, middle-class and WASP, sense of style. With this practical joke, she not only reclaimed her pride at Ziegfeld's (and the maid's) expense, but also paradoxically joined Ziegfeld in acknowledging the maid's bizarre and inappropriate appearance—confirming stereotypes of African Americans' predisposition toward bold colors.[92] In much the same way that immigrants affirmed their status as "Americans" by labeling obvious newcomers "greenhorns," Brice participated in a form of "displaced abjection," calling attention to her new status as a fashionable actress by laughing at the maid's garish apparel.[93]

The behind-the-scenes stories of the Jewish performers Sophie Tucker, Blanche Yurka, and Fanny Brice suggest that learning to "look like Broadway" was akin to learning to look like white, middle-class Americans. While their experiences can hardly be considered typical in light of their phenomenal careers, they nevertheless offer insight into the constraints that ethnic performers experienced in pursuing a spot on the Great White Way. What is perhaps most striking about their personal narratives is the way they represent themselves as neophytes who learn in a Cinderella-like manner to become fashionable white women. By foregrounding the labor involved in the production of the white ideal, they call attention to the performativity of class and ethnic categories and highlight fashion's potential for both upholding and dismantling such categories.

For African American performers, however, the stakes involved in selecting and wearing an appropriate stage wardrobe were much higher. "[T]he power of dress and appearance to convey authentic respectability on an African American woman and to grant her authority as a public figure was always tenuous," writes Pamela Klassen in her study of African American Methodist women's use of dress in the nineteenth century. Although improvements in ready-to-wear fashion and the widespread publication of fashion information from Paris and New York made it possible for socially advantaged African American women to sport the latest styles, the continued circulation of "stereotypes of wanton Jezebels and pious Mammies" meant that dressing fashionably was not necessarily the path to social acceptance and respectability.[94]

Despite these challenges, African American performers used dress to appeal to black and white audiences and present themselves as respectable artists. In the late nineteenth century, the singer Mme. Sisseretta Jones—often billed as "Black Patti" in reference to the internationally renowned diva Adelina Patti—posed for photographic portraits in expensive-looking gowns that confirmed her reputation as "[t]he most popular prima donna in the world with the people of all nations and races."[95] The vaudeville performers Dora Dean and Charles Johnson also dressed strategically, becoming "the first dance team, white or black, to wear evening clothes onstage" (figure 3.3).[96] At a performance at New York's American Theatre in 1909, Johnson appeared wearing "a full dress suit of the latest pattern, while Miss Dean wore a pretty evening coat of costly appearance with a beautiful pair of diamond earrings in her ears."[97] Promoted as the "best dressed team in vaudeville," they cultivated an elegant performance style that captivated audiences even when managers gave them low placement on the bill.[98]

Still, while African American female performers experimented with contemporary fashions and challenged white perceptions of "authentic" blackness—offering a powerful image for black audiences—they had to be careful to signal their blackness to white audiences, especially when they appeared alongside other black performers. Light-skinned performers like Miss Carita Day, of the Rufus Rastus Company, who rejected demands to "darken up" so that white audiences could more easily recognize her race, may have been refusing to accept white stereotypes, but they also put their fellow performers in danger. "[T]his is a problem for the public to solve," the critic for the *Indianapolis Freeman* explained, "when they see Ernest Hogan, made up

Figure 3.3. The elegant cakewalk dance team of Dora Dean and Charles Johnson, 1901. Photographs and Prints Division, Schomburg Center for Research in Black Culture, The New York Public Library, Astor, Lenox and Tilden Foundations.

as black as possible, making love to Miss Day, who just dotes on looking as white as she can." Day's refusal to make her body legible called attention to race as a cultural construct; but at a time when any hint of sexual attraction let alone an active sexual relationship between a white woman and a black man was enough to provoke violence, she also placed Hogan and her fellow cast members in an incredibly dangerous position. Indeed, when a western newspaper incorrectly reported that Day was white, Hogan's private secretary immediately wrote to the paper denying the claim.[99] Unlike Jewish women, for whom cultivating a fashionable appearance was often a crucial step in their assimilation into white America, dressing fashionably was a potentially risky, even life-threatening, act for African American performers.

The Art of Fashionable Dressing

In 1914 the *Theatre Magazine* classified an actress's gowns as "part and parcel of her tools of trade, like the carpenter's kit or the surgeon's case of instruments," defining the actress by extension as a well-practiced craftsman, the compeer of the masculine carpenter and surgeon and the antithesis of the unskilled, untrained, and imminently replaceable factory laborer.[100] Although striking in its acknowledgment of women's work, the *Theatre Magazine*'s analogy breaks down upon further consideration of the actress's actual relationship with her tools. Unlike the carpenter and the surgeon, who use their tools as extensions of their hands to transform *other* objects or bodies, the actress uses her tools to transform herself. With her clothing, she brings her body into being by making it legible as an *actress's* body, illustrating how, in the words of the fashion theorists Alexandra Warwick and Dani Cavallaro, "inanimate" and "powerless item[s] of clothing" can "furnish the body with signifying powers that the unclothed subject would lack."[101] Simultaneously acting and acted upon, the fashionably dressed actress *becomes* an actress both in and through the clothes she wears.

Yet while early twentieth-century actresses spoke openly to reporters about the work required to maintain a fashionable appearance, most denied that such work constituted labor, preferring instead to represent themselves as professional "clothes artists." For these women, as for many of the overwhelmingly white, middle-class members of the acting profession, an association with sweaty, working-class laborers was highly undesirable, especially in light of recent debates over unionization. Even after the formation of Actor's Equity in 1913, which promised to represent the interests of "legitimate" performers, many actors continued to see an association with labor as antithetical to the acting profession.[102] "We are not laborers with calloused hands," Blanche Bates argued in 1919. "[W]e use our hearts and souls in this work, it is our life. We are not laborers, and what we have is something that cannot be capitalized."[103] Effacing the actor's body and any labor associated with it—actors do not "work with their hands," they create with their hearts and souls—Bates reaffirmed class boundaries and echoed anti-commercial critics by refusing to accept the co-mingling of art and commerce, acting and labor.

The competing discourses of art and labor found their way into actresses' discussions of stage fashion, most noticeably in articles where they claimed to have designed their own gowns.[104] "I dressed myself into celebrity," the former *Ziegfeld Follies* showgirl Lillian Lorraine explained in 1914. "From the first day I stepped upon the stage I have myself designed everything I wear."[105] The ballroom dancer Irene Castle similarly emphasized her role in the design process, representing herself as the creator rather than the maker of the clothing. "Ideas for gowns sometimes come to me in the middle of the night," she told the journalist Brian Dureyea in the fall of 1915. "I get up and jot them down. The next day I make drawings of them, in my crude way. Then the modiste's artist draws them over again in the colors I pick. I virtually design all my gowns."[106] Castle envisioned the costume, but she played no role in its actual construction; the "modiste's" unseen hands performed that labor.

Not surprisingly, some of the most detailed accounts of the design process came from actresses playing working-class characters. Ever aware of the need to secure their position as skilled artists and consumers of fashion, these women spoke at length about the steps they had taken to achieve their realistic costumes. "I had a great time getting Mary Turner's costume ready," Jane Cowl enthused when discussing her shop-girl character in *Within the Law*. "I bought everything new before I went to Europe last summer and then I made my maid wear the things out for me so that they'd be ready for me when I got back. The black suede gloves she wore while digging in the seashore sands; the suit she never brushed or cleaned—those were her orders—and the shoes she wore until, oh, they're glorious now, all blowsy in the seams."[107] In referencing the trip to Europe and the maid she orders about, Cowl portrays herself as a privileged lady of leisure and offers a textbook lesson in class detection. She delights in the "glorious" realism achieved by her maid, the "blowsy" shoes, the unbrushed suit, the sand-covered gloves, all legible signs of Mary's economic position, implying that a well-trained eye should be able to determine an individual's social standing through dress. But she simultaneously removes herself both from the labor that had produced the clothes and the labor of the poor little shop girls she had observed while preparing for her role, thereby preserving her status as a fashionable woman and a consummate artist.

Frances Starr shared a similar faith in female theatergoers' abilities to interpret costume details as she described her role in David Belasco's production of *The Easiest Way* (figure 3.4):

> My dress of pale broadcloth accords with the character of *Laura Murdock*, as well as with her present condition in life. Any woman in the audience can see that it has been "cropped" off at the bottom. In other words, it conveys the fact that, now in hard luck, *Laura Murdock* is wearing out the finery which she sported in easier and less virtuous days than those in which she is now living. . . . Every woman in the audience discerns that my short walking-skirt was once part of a trained afternoon dress, and she knows that *Laura Murdock's* own hands altered it for everyday wear.[108]

Starr's approach to costuming was likely influenced by her association with Belasco, who insisted on realistic costumes and settings in his productions.

Figure 3.4. Marion Kerby, Frances Starr, in one of her adjusted gowns, and Laura Nelson Hall in *The Easiest Way*. Museum of the City of New York 37.399.1534.

Educated to think about the effect of environment on character, she used small details such as the cut or color of a gown to indicate her character's social status and assumed that an audience of fashion-savvy women would interpret her costuming decisions correctly. In fact, audience responses to Starr's skillful costuming were sometimes so effusive that they interrupted the dramatic narrative, much to the dismay of male critics seated in the house. For example, at a matinee performance of *The Easiest Way*, the theater critic Walter Prichard Eaton was startled when women suddenly began applauding Starr as Murdock as she packed her trunk in preparation for deceiving her "honest lover." "A more inappropriate time for sartorial interest and enthusiasm could not well be conceived," Eaton complained. "It betokened a complete failure on the part of the audience to enter into the real significance and power of the scene. For the actress it must have been disheartening."[109] What Eaton failed to recognize was that for the women watching Starr—and perhaps even for Starr herself—the "real significance and power of the scene" extended beyond the narrative realm.

Despite offering exercises in class detection, Cowl and Starr paradoxically alerted audiences—if only inadvertently—to fashion's potential for disguise and class passing. As Rachel Moseley suggests in her analysis of the film icon Audrey Hepburn, lurking behind an actress's performance of lower-class characters is the question "whether class can ever really be acquired, or whether it can only ever be performed, more or less successfully?"[110] Indeed, as much as Broadway actresses positioned themselves as "clothes artists," rival performers often undermined their claims to creative ingenuity by copying innovative designs, openly defying the nineteenth-century code of conduct governing stage costumes.[111] According to the traditional code, star performers had the right to choose the style and color of the gowns they would wear onstage while supporting actresses were expected to select complementary gowns; those who attempted to forego tradition were duly censured.[112] But by the turn of the century, supporting performers were disregarding the older costuming code, aware that the fuss raised by outraged stars would attract attention, notoriety, and possibly even fame. "Some new actress of your particular style and manner gets a better part than you, and she begins coming to the fore," Ruth Shepley warned. "She copies your gowns; she uses your tricks of speech and gesture, but—she has a better part, and because she has a better part, you soon get the reputation of copying *her*!"[113]

In what is possibly the most extreme case of backstage fashion rivalry, Valeska Suratt, the star of *The Belle of Mayfair* (1907), attacked the chorus girl Jeanette Horton for wearing the "identical double of [her] yellow princesse [*sic*]" onstage. "I have designed a cord effect over the bosom and arms of my gowns that is all my own and it just took my breath to see she had copied it," Suratt later explained to the press. Confronting the girl after the performance, she ripped the offending copy and reportedly "clawed" her presumptuous rival. Horton responded by taking Suratt to court, much to the delight of the yellow newspapers covering the case. Although a hearing date was set and both parties arrived at the courthouse, a last minute consultation in the judge's chambers resolved matters and the case never reached open court.[114] Later in the year, the *New York Telegraph* cheekily reported that young Broadway actresses continued to copy Suratt's "little originalities in dress" because they hoped that "Valeska will be indignant and give them a frightful slap right on the face and a lot of free advertising."[115] For underpaid and underappreciated chorus girls, a scandal was one way to attract attention and perhaps move up the theatrical hierarchy.

Actresses' insistence on presenting themselves as fashion originators and their subsequent anxieties about copying recall similar struggles in consumer goods manufacturing, whereby corporations such as Uneeda Biscuit, Kellogg's, and Kodak enlisted the support of large advertising agencies to create readily identifiable images that were both stable enough to attract and sustain consumer loyalty and malleable enough to maintain consumer interest.[116] A performer's status as a fashionable woman similarly depended on her ability to continually appear and *reappear* in the latest styles, to make and remake herself as a commodity, all while remaining recognizable. To achieve this effect, however, the actress had to disguise the labor that went into her production, and so she turned to the press agent—an individual who labored on her behalf but remained invisible to the public eye.[117]

With the press agent's assistance, actresses presented themselves and their clothes as originals, reassuring audiences that they were getting the real thing. From the 1890s on, general interest magazines such as *Cosmopolitan* and *Collier's*, and women's magazines such as the *Ladies' Home Journal*, *Harper's Bazar*, and *The Delineator* regularly featured stories, interviews, and photographs that offered readers a glimpse into the world of the theater.[118] "If the actor-folk fail to get into the newspapers, it is largely their own fault," the press agent Nellie Revell explained in 1911. "The general public fairly revels in the absorption of news of the theatre and of the men and women connected with it."[119] Still, while press agents worked on behalf of performers, accentuating their best features by praising their "looks, or charm, or dressiness," actresses were ultimately responsible for creating and maintaining the image. "[H]e announces to the world that you are the best-dressed woman on the stage, and keeps you in poverty the rest of your natural existence buying clothes to live up to that reputation," Ruth Shepley explained.[120] Jane Cowl similarly complained that a press agent's "announcement that I was the most beautiful woman on the stage" had made her a slave to her billing.[121]

For actresses intent on presenting themselves as versatile fashion leaders, photography presented one of the most effective tools for keeping their images in circulation. Whereas most nineteenth-century stage portraits featured performers in character, turn-of-the-century portraits depicted actresses "as themselves," dressed in the latest fashion—a change brought about by the heightened emphasis on modern costuming in society dramas and musical comedies, theatergoers' growing interest in performers' personal lives, and editors' preferences for photographs of attractive, stylish women.[122] In 1906, the press agent Anna Marble advised female vaudeville performers who wore "grotesque or character clothes" in their acts to "have 'straight' pictures taken in an effective gown, other than what you are using. Remember that newspapers like *pretty* pictures of women."[123] Other writers reminded readers that photos in magazines and newspapers were an actress's "most important form of advertisement."[124] Posing for photographs was as much a part of an actress's professional life as learning lines or purchasing costumes. It was therefore necessary "to have ever on hand a large and constantly renewed stock of photographs." "If she fails to do this," *Cosmopolitan* observed in 1903, "she is subject to the criticism that the public is tired of seeing her in one pose."[125]

To meet this demand for a continually fresh image, female performers spent long hours in photography studios in New York and on the road, changing their clothes several times in a single session to demonstrate their versatility and sense of style (figure 3.5).[126] According to the actress Margaret Illington Banes, "[W]hen [an actress] goes to have her photograph taken, [she] takes a whole day for the ordeal, and the operator, instead of snapping at most a dozen negatives, take hundreds of these, all are discarded except those few which show the sitter at her best."[127] Maxine Elliott was notorious for her exacting approach with photographers. Before every portrait session, she demanded to look through the camera to ensure that the background was to her liking; once the session was underway, she rarely smiled or altered her somber facial expression, insisting that she knew what worked best.[128] Still, while her facial expressions remained the same from photo to photo, Elliott responded to the dictates of consumer culture by remaking her image through clothing changes. In thus representing herself as a fixed subject who could nevertheless play with the surface of her body through fashion, Elliott reassured those concerned about fashion's transformative potential and the

JULIA MARLOWE.

1899

Klein & Guttenstein
164 WIS. ST.   MILWAUKEE.

Figure 3.5. The actress Julia Marlowe had this studio portrait taken in
Milwaukee in 1899 by the local photographers Klein and Guttenstein,
who would have distributed the image from their studio and perhaps
made it available at local stationery stores. Courtesy of the Philip H. Ward
Collection of Theatrical Images, 1868–1910, Ms. Coll. 331, Rare Book and
Manuscript Library, University of Pennsylvania.

corresponding loss of individuality that consumption would not lead to a wasting away of the self.

Posing for magazine fashion spreads and other publicity articles was a particularly effective strategy for actresses who did not appear onstage in fashionable dress but nevertheless wished to present themselves as stylish. In 1909, Mary Mannering invited the *Theatre Magazine* along for her fitting with the Paris couturiers Martial and Armand. "I have come to Paris just to buy clothes," Mary Mannering told the interviewer. "For some years now, I have played parts which gave me no opportunity for dressing in modern, up-to-date gowns, that I am determined to find a new play in which I can wear the stunning gowns that Martial and Armand are making for me now."[129] The *Theatre Magazine's* detailed descriptions and photographs of the "stunning gowns" Mannering purchased helped the actress to remodel her image. In 1913, while starring in *Within the Law*, Jane Cowl invited *Harper's Bazar* to her apartment to photograph the gowns she had just purchased for her own use.[130] The following year, Louise Dresser tried the same strategy. "I love clothes—pretty clothes I mean," she told the *Harper's Bazar* reporter, "but the authors of my plays never give me an opportunity to wear them."[131] Her appearance in one of the nation's most reputable fashion magazines was clearly intended to convince both her authors and her public otherwise.

Undoubtedly influenced by the speed with which they could reshape their images through photography, actresses also updated their stage wardrobes on a regular basis. Unlike British actresses, who "redressed" once every few months or possibly only once a year in long-running productions, American actresses changed gowns multiple times during a production run.[132] In March 1916, the *Theatre Magazine* reported that the actress Ruth Shepley was preparing to change her evening gown in *Boomerang* for the third time since opening the previous August.[133] Other actresses opted to change costumes on a *daily* basis, as a strategy to show up their rivals and keep female audiences coming back to the theater even when the play itself was not particularly good. In 1909 Maxine Elliot alternated among several outfits when she appeared in *The Barber of New Orleans*, "sometimes wear[ing] one gown, sometimes another" (figure 3.6).[134] Underlying these redressing practices was the assumption that changing clothes was not antithetical to character interpretation. Although many actresses insisted on selecting costumes that demonstrated their character's psychological complexity (as the following chapter will detail), they clearly believed that they did not need to be tied to a single costume. Their clothing might change but presumably the character (and the actress portraying it) remained the same.

Figure 3.6. Maxine Elliott backstage, 1902. Note the costumes hung on the wall behind her, presumably in preparation for a quick change. Photograph by Byron. Library of Congress Prints and Photographs Division.

Female vaudeville performers similarly promoted the notion that making over the self through fashion did not preclude losing or changing one's individuality but was rather a necessary condition of success. *Variety*'s fashion and gossip columnist "the Skirt" reminded women playing big-time vaudeville that they should consider whether they had "enough clothes to play a circuit of theatres around New York" and singled out "repeat offenders" who did not change their clothes regularly enough.[135] In 1914, she applauded Corinne Sales for wearing different outfits for her two appearances at Hammerstein's and the Colonial, commenting, "This shows versatility."[136] An actress's ability to change gowns quickly and effectively was just as, if not more, important than her actual performance. Indeed, versatility in dress could make up for the absence of versatility in other areas. The typical vaudeville act usually ranged from ten to twenty minutes, and most female vaudeville performers made multiple changes. "The style of a 'small time' single woman is stereotyped," *Variety* quipped in 1911. "There must be at least three songs and three changes."[137] Consistent with vaudeville's fast pace and kaleidoscopic structure, headliners on the big-time circuit made as many as seven or eight changes for each twenty-minute appearance, impressing audiences with their versatile taste and smooth transitions from one outfit to the next. Eva Tanguay, best known for her cyclonic, over-the-top performance style, frequently displayed "a riot of wardrobe" onstage (figure 3.7).[138] To accommodate these multiple changes, performers used under-dressing techniques, often starting the act in a coat or wrap that could be removed to reveal a dress underneath.[139] Changing looks every two or three minutes, stars like Tanguay effectively embodied a speeded up version of the fashion system at work.

This malleable model of fashion performance was again highly consistent with modern consumer culture in that it promoted external change without the threat of internal transformation. Female quick-change artists presented an exception to this general rule, however, with a perspective on dress, fashion, and character that called into question the stability of the self.[140] A vestige of the nineteenth-century preoccupation with "transformational performance," quick-change artists "assumed a series of widely different personae that varied wildly in gender, age, social class, and occupation." According to the historian Matthew Solomon, "Much of the appeal of protean [or quick-change] artistry hinged on the speed with which an individual performer could make costume changes that effected complete and striking transformations of character."[141] Although male artists seem to have dominated the genre in Europe, female performers achieved a much higher profile in the United States. Their performances not only emphasized the versatility

Figure 3.7. The vaudeville performer Eva Tanguay in one of her many elaborate (and costly) ensembles. The juxtaposition of the photograph with the song title "What Money Can't Buy" was obviously intended as a joke. Sam DeVincent Collection of Illustrated Sheet Music, Archives Center, National Museum of American History, Behring Center, Smithsonian Institution.

of the individual artist but also her taste in clothing. In 1911, *Variety* described how the popular vaudeville comedienne Carrie De Mar, the "Only Woman Who Makes Complete Change of Dress, Hat, Gloves, Shoes and Stockings," transformed herself eight times before the audience: "Miss De Mar makes her entrance in a white tailored suit trimmed in black. After a verse, Miss De Mar rips off the skirt, revealing a pair of black and white striped bloomers. . . . A change is made to a black and white chiffon, over which is a jacket of salmon pink. . . . As a widow, Miss De Mar looked stately, and with a turning back of a reveres, a turning down of a hem, ripping off a hat covering, Miss De Mar was a charming soubret [*sic*] in a cerise gown and hat."[142] Slipping in and out of costume and character in quick succession, De Mar is by turns playful, "stateful," and "charming," a girl, a widow, and a soubrette. Indeed, part of the thrill for vaudeville audiences must have been watching De Mar "strip down" from one costume to another in a peculiar parody of burlesque "disrobing acts."[143] But more than this, De Mar's act called attention to fashion's potential for disguise and transformation, showing how boundaries of class, age, race, and gender might be dissolved by adopting a new look. Unlike Eva Tanguay, who remained Eva Tanguay in spite of, or perhaps because of, her "riot of wardrobe," Carrie De Mar impersonated a series of characters who were presumably nothing like the *real* Carrie De Mar.

In their challenge to essentialist perceptions of individual subjectivity, quick-change artists shared a great deal with female mimics such as Gertrude Hoffman, Cissie Loftus, and Elsie Janis, who likewise executed a series of rapid transformations onstage through facial, vocal, and bodily manipulations. As the historian Susan Glenn has shown, these women "posited a radical new environmentalist model in which social experience rather than fixed or innate qualities explained human development."[144] Their "transformational performances" complemented ongoing research in the social sciences, which aimed to replace "traditional notions of a fixed, immutable, and intrinsic human character" with "the more fluid concept of personality as something to be learned or performed."[145] Although, actors and theater critics continued to debate the extent to which personality could be developed, with some clinging to older definitions of an inherent self, performers like De Mar pushed audiences to reconsider traditional views. Yet in their emphasis on speed and the mechanics of performance, quick-change artists also quite paradoxically seem to have addressed concerns about the unfixing of the self.[146] By calling attention to the actual *labor* involved in the performance and positioning themselves as skilled technicians rather than identity chameleons, these women appealed to audiences on the basis of what Neil Harris calls "the operational aesthetic," "a delight in observing process and examining for literal truth."[147] The structure of the quick-change act urged audiences to delight in the skill of the performer as performer, to watch for gaps or slips in the execution, and to contemplate the "methods of transformation" rather than the implications of the transformation for those watching.[148]

Thinking about quick-change acts as magic demonstrations helps to explain the popularity of the drag performer Julian Eltinge, who delighted female audiences with his high-fashion performances (figure 3.8). "Mr. Eltinge's costumes make the rest of the women's dresses look like a bargain sale," the "Skirt" enthused in 1909.[149] In 1910, a columnist noted that Eltinge's "Spanish costume will be the envy of every actress whose part calls for such a dress."[150] Women drew inspiration from Eltinge's performances, so much so that in 1913 he launched the *Julian Eltinge Magazine and Beauty Hints*. For ten cents readers could learn about the "gentle art" of boxing and read advertisements for Julian Eltinge Cold Cream that promised "A Chance for Every Woman to Be as Beautiful as Julian Eltinge."[151] But in cultivating his profile as a beauty expert, Eltinge took pains to distinguish himself from the pretty, feminine creatures he played onstage. The historian John Kasson compares Eltinge to the magician Harry Houdini in the way that he highlighted the skill and technique of his performance rather than aspects of gender transgression.[152] Publicity articles depicted Eltinge as a burly man's man—working on a farm, taking up boxing as an athletic pursuit, and so forth—who underwent incredible tortures to transform into a wasp-waisted female. In backstage interviews, he emphasized the relief he felt once he had escaped the tight corsetry and other confining garments that enabled his transformations. "The first thing I do after appearing in a play is to throw these objectionable garments into a far corner and have a good smoke," he boasted in 1907, conjuring the image of a hearty club man.[153] "[If] my interrogators could see with what pleasure I throw aside my 'creations' at the end of every performance and return to man life," he reiterated in 1913, "they would realize that I was sufficiently punished for wearing such clothes without the additional ordeal of telling how I was able to wear them."[154]

Eltinge nevertheless seems to have enjoyed describing his stage preparations, leaving reporters to puzzle over how he compressed his thirty-eight inch chest into a twenty-six inch corset, squeezed his man's size 7 shoe into a woman's size 4 1/2, or transformed his masculine features into a near-perfect approximation of a Gibson Girl.[155] These writers helped Eltinge construct this image, regularly interpreting his chameleon-like transformations as a sign of artistry, not as proof of sexual deviancy. Even when playing a female

Figure 3.8. Julian Eltinge in fashionable dress, ca. 1912. Picture Collection, The Branch Libraries, The New York Public Library, Astor, Lenox and Tilden Foundations.

role, Eltinge stressed that his "true" gender was never in question: "I feel just as much like smoking a good cigar and quaffing a big one—on a hot night—when I am in my stage clothes as I do when I am wearing the habitual costume of my sex," he explained. "I do not find that a curly wig and high-heeled slippers, dresses and—well all the things that girls wear—make any difference in my feelings and I am just as ready to enter a boxing or wrestling match when I have on the feminine garb as I do when parading in trousers."[156] In laying claim to a fixed gender identity, Eltinge argued that "clothes did not make the man [or woman]" but rather provided an opportunity for play and fun. Any woman could achieve the same look of flawless fashionability he presented if she worked at it; all that was needed was time and practice.

While exposing the labor involved in the artistic process, the transformational performances of De Mar and Eltinge obscured the workings of capitalism by suggesting that practice, hard work, and a serious commitment to investing in the self were all that were needed to acquire fame and fortune, or at the very least, a happier, more successful life. Articles claiming to reveal the "truth" about the work that went into producing an actress's flawless image likewise urged readers to believe in the possibility of the "democratization of beauty." Instead of urging audiences to abandon their dreams, this discursive emphasis on surface change played directly into the hands of fashion and beauty product manufacturers.

The Mad Search for Beauty

"Actresses as a rule know no more about making themselves beautiful than does the average woman; neither are they naturally more beautiful," the actress Margaret Illington Banes wrote in an article in 1912 entitled "The Mad Search for Beauty." "[N]o actress—or any woman—can impart the secrets of beauty to another, any more than the rich man can impart the secrets of business success to some other man." Disturbed by recent trends in whereby "the woman who would achieve newspaper notice as an actress must be a 'beauty specialist' as well," Banes sought to dispel the "tradition that all actresses are lovely" by exposing the constructed nature of the actress's on- and offstage performances. Cast in parts "which compliment her good looks" and dressed in "the finest of fine raiment," the actress succeeds in captivating her fans, she explained, when in fact, "nine-tenths of the women in the audience would look quite as well under the same circumstances."[157]

While intended to halt consumers "mad" emulation of stage beauties, Banes's revelations echoed the promotional strategies of beauty product manufacturers, who in their bid for new consumers, emphasized the *artificial* processes that transformed actresses from attractive women into exceptional beauties, implying that their products could do the same. Between 1911 and 1918, actresses appeared in advertisements for numerous beauty companies, promoting products ranging from soap and perfume to rouge and depilatories, playing an integral part of the industry's attempt to address the competing discourses of natural and artificial beauty.[158]

By the 1910s, hostile attitudes toward cosmetics, predominant throughout most of the nineteenth century, were subsiding. Most women, from working girls to society ladies, used some form of facial cream or powder, and more adventurous women were also beginning to apply color to their cheeks and lips. Despite this growing acceptance, however, many middle-class men and women continued to question the morality of "making up." Unlike working and society women, who seem to have enjoyed opportunities to play and experiment with appearance as a strategy for surviving the challenges of modern life, middle-class women hesitated to change their look, uncomfortable with the notion that beauty could be acquired artificially and the semiotic indeterminacy that such transformations encouraged.[159] It was one thing to apply cold cream to protect the skin; it was quite another to transform the face by applying color to the eyes, lips, and cheeks.[160] Manufacturers desperate to expand into the lucrative middle-class market had to convince women that using beauty products was a morally and socially acceptable practice. Through the persona of the actress, cosmetics companies promoted the idea that every woman could and should make herself beautiful, while underscoring the need to embrace certain beauty regimes to achieve the desired look. Anticipating concerns about lost individuality, they played up the celebration of personality in and of itself, arguing that women could express their individual personalities *through* consumption by developing a personal relationship with the goods they purchased.[161]

The notion that every woman could be beautiful if she learned to use the right beauty products was a radical departure from the nineteenth-century belief that physical beauty was an expression of an individual's soul and could only be achieved through honest and virtuous living.[162] Whereas nineteenth-century writers emphasized the importance of seeing true beauty in the homeliest of women, twentieth-century beauty culturists argued that the homeliest of women need not be homely anymore. Physical appearance was no longer a direct reflection of a woman's interior life, but was rather something she could alter to express her individuality and could be acquired not through good works but through good purchases.[163]

Not surprisingly, given their personal investment in physical appearance, most actresses strongly supported the new doctrine of beauty, stressing that it was a woman's right and responsibility to be beautiful as possible.[164] In 1918, the physical culturist and vaudeville performer Annette Kellerman wrote a book praising "[t]he new and true gospel of a woman's right to remain beautiful," and she encouraged women to do what they could to highlight their best attributes.[165] The musical comedy star Anna Held, the former wife of Florenz Ziegfeld, argued in 1916 that it was a woman's duty to herself "and to the world to appear as attractive as arts and artifices will permit" and further suggested that those who refused to help themselves by "eschew[ing] make-up" were "vulgar."[166] The actresses' emphasis on beautification as a social responsibility and their subsequent condemnation of those who "eschewed" cosmetics as "vulgar" indicates the degree to which issues of class were interwoven with the democratization of beauty.

In October 1911, the Brooklyn-based beauty specialist Forrest D. Pullen launched a major campaign to introduce Créme Nerol [*sic*], a new cold cream. The first full-page ad appeared in the October 15 issue of *Vogue* and displayed testimonials, photographs, and signatures from Broadway's most admired and respectable stars: the actresses Margaret Anglin, Julia Marlowe, Billie Burke, Maxine Elliott, Mrs. Fiske, Frances Starr, and Julie Opp, and the opera divas Luisa Tetrazzini, Geraldine Farrar, and Mabel Taliaferro. The performers' statements characterize Créme Nerol as "an unsurpassed preparation," "a most agreeable cleanser and food for the skin," and "exceptional both as to quality and results." As the ad copy suggests, Pullen knew that consumers were more likely to believe statements from respected, fashionable actresses than the words of an unknown, faceless *male* beauty specialist. "The efficacy of Créme Nerol does not depend on what I *say* Créme Nerol *is*," he explains, "but on what Créme Nerol actually *does* for those who use it." His comments further imply that Créme Nerol is responsible for restoring and maintaining the natural beauty of stage favorites like Billie Burke and Julia Marlowe. Significantly, while Pullen promotes the "efficacious" properties of Créme Nerol, his emphasis is on restoration, not transformation. His cold cream "softens, whitens, refines and beautifies . . . the sallow, rough or impaired complexion," returning it to its former (more natural) state.[167]

Other beauty businesses followed Pullen's lead in soliciting testimonials from actresses. Although many of these ads targeted society women, as suggested by their price—for example, jars of Helena Rubinstein's actress-endorsed Valaze ranged from one dollar to six dollars—and appearance in *Vogue* and *Harper's Bazar*, they are nevertheless notable for the way that they combine testimonials with the rhetoric of democracy.[168] "If women who are not born beauties would give as much care to their appearance as those who are, this would be a world of beautiful women," declared an advertisement in 1912 for Le Secret Gaby Deslys, a line of beauty products named after the fashionable French musical comedy star. Playing up to the idea that every woman could and *should* be beautiful, the Importers Company, manufacturers of Le Secret, advertised its products as "the means of *acquiring* beauty as well as the best method of *preserving* and *accentuating* it [my emphasis]." Although the ad promotes the notion that women who are not naturally beautiful can become beautiful by using Le Secret, it emphasizes preservation and accentuation over actual transformation. Women who use Le Secret are not "making up" as much as they are highlighting their natural physical assets, just like Gaby Deslys. The ad alludes to Deslys's artful performance of beauty by pointing out that "even on close view and under glaring lights," the beauty products "absolutely defy detection." Furthermore, as the name Le Secret implies, women who purchased the beauty products shared a trade secret with the French star. Like Gaby, they could enhance their natural beauty without being caught in the act.[169]

This paradoxical emphasis on the actress's skillful employment of artificial means to achieve natural beauty is perhaps most noticeable in the advertisements created for Pond's Vanishing Cream in the mid- to late 1910s. In 1914, the Pond's Extract Company became one of the first major cosmetics companies to launch a national campaign directed at a predominantly middle-class market. Under the guidance of the J. Walter Thompson Company, its long-time advertising agency, Pond's stopped advertising its signature product, Pond's Extract, and focused instead on promoting Pond's Vanishing Cream and Pond's Cold Cream. Between 1914 and 1916, Pond's advertised these products separately until the Thompson copywriter Helen Landsdowne Resor developed an innovative strategy to encourage women to incorporate both creams into their daily beauty regimens. Ads bearing the slogan "Every normal skin needs these two creams" appeared in major newspapers and magazines throughout the country, including both *Vogue* and the *Ladies' Home Journal*.[170] By 1920, sales for both creams had tripled, firmly establishing Pond's as one of the leading beauty businesses in the United States.

Historians have shown that the success of the "two creams" campaign rested on Pond's ability to convince middle-class women, including those who had never used cosmetics, to try new products and adopt new practices. What these historians tend to overlook, however, is the J. Walter Thompson Company's strategic deployment of actresses' testimonials to demonstrate how Pond's Vanishing Cream enhanced rather than transformed the women who used it.[171] In 1914, the company introduced celebrity testimonials into the ads for Pond's Vanishing Cream, enlisting the aid of popular performers such as Elsie Janis, Frances Starr, and Anna Pavlova. Photographs of these and other prominent stage stars (most ads featured two or three performers) appeared in half- and full-page magazine advertisements, often embedded in the copy beneath a larger illustration.[172] The decision to feature performers from different artistic fields, including vaudeville, musical comedy, drama, and ballet, suggests that the J. Walter Thompson Company wished to appeal to diverse tastes rather than rely on a single performer's ability to attract consumers. Women could identify with one or all of the performers in the ads, depending on their personal and artistic preferences. At the same time, the actresses' collective testimony leant an air of distinction to the advertised product and stood as an authoritative proof of its quality.[173]

Perhaps more importantly, actresses' testimonials implied that women could improve their complexions and achieve a natural glow without compromising themselves or dramatically altering their appearances. These ads emphasized the actress's professional responsibility to maintain a healthy, glowing complexion and characterized her as a knowledgeable and skillful consumer. "Actresses and dancers, whose skin must always be at its loveliest . . . get from Pond's Vanishing Cream just the effect they have always wanted," explained one ad from 1915.[174] Another praised Pond's Vanishing Cream for helping actresses maintain a "fresh, clear and brilliant" complexion despite the "demanding" and "exhaustive" nature of their work.[175] A third ad, published in the *Ladies' Home Journal* with the banner headline "The Charm Every Actress Knows," invited women to discover for themselves "why it is used by more women on the stage than any other cream," with the promise that they too would "obtain just the effect so marvelously attained on the stage" (figure 3.9).[176] The use of the word "effect" here is significant. Without suggesting that women who use Pond's Vanishing Cream will look like the actresses appearing in the ads, it nevertheless implies that their skin (if nothing else) will look similar. The word "effect" also alludes to the invisibility of the product, and its attendant magical qualities. Women who use Pond's Vanishing Cream do not look like they are wearing cosmetics (the product "immediately sinks in—vanishes") yet the "effect" of the cream, its ability to enhance and restore the skin to achieve a natural appearance, is evident. The

FRANCES STARR writes: "I have been using your Vanishing Cream and want to recommend it to everyone. It is delightful."

ELSIE JANIS says "I have never had a better cream than Pond's Vanishing Cream—I always use it."

PAVLOWA says: "I have used Pond's Vanishing Cream and find it very good for softening and whitening my skin."

The charm every actress knows

Every actress realizes that in loveliness nothing can compare with a skin of exquisite texture, of soft delicate bloom. She knows that it is the purity and clearness of the skin which give lovely arms, gleaming satiny neck, and soft white hands, their power to attract.

Every actress will tell you that she could not possibly get this wonderful effect without the cream bath. Mrs. James Brown Potter, in "Beauty and Health," says that this bath of cream is the secret of how actresses preserve the transparent clearness and youthfulness of their skin so much longer than other people.

How easily *you* can have it

Tonight when you dress, bathe your neck, arms and hands, as well as your face, with Pond's Vanishing Cream. Being entirely without grease or oil, it is readily absorbed—vanishes—it leaves no shine, never reappears on the skin, and has a wonderfully refreshing effect on the skin. *Then apply the powder over this base.* You will obtain just the effect so marvelously attained on the stage.

Try Pond's Vanishing Cream. Write for free trial tube. Know why it is used by more women on the stage than any other cream. See how your skin responds to one application. Or send four cents and get a generous *two weeks' supply.* Address Pond's Extract Co., 121 Hudson Street, New York.

Pond's Extract should be in every household for use in emergency, for everyday injuries, cuts, bruises, etc. Get a bottle today.

Free

POND'S EXTRACT COMPANY'S VANISHING CREAM

Sold in 25c and 50c jars and 25c tubes

Figure 3.9. "The Charm Every Actress Knows." Stylish female performers like Anna Pavlova, Elsie Janis, and Frances Starr were an important part of Pond's strategy to encourage middle-class consumers to incorporate "two creams" into their daily beauty regimes. Courtesy Unilever and the John W. Hartman Center for Sales, Advertising and Marketing History, Duke University Rare Book, Manuscript, and Special Collections Library.

underlying message is that women anxious about questionable beauty products like rouge had nothing to fear from vanishing cream.

Returning to New York from Paris in 1916, the actress Anna Held observed that attitudes toward the use of artificial beauty products had changed considerably. "No woman of to-day," she explained, "sees a fresh-blown complexion but what she asks her self, 'I wonder where she buys it,' or says, 'How well she puts it on!' " Cosmetics were now considered a necessary part of daily life, and beauty was something found in a jar rather than within. But the costs of the so-called democratization of beauty were incredibly high. By redefining the natural beauty as the woman who used cosmetics, beauty product manufacturers urged female consumers to commit, like the actresses they admired, to a lifetime of labor and to associate their individual self-worth with chemicals in a bottle.

Yet while manufacturers did all that they could to exploit actresses' testimonials and shape the particular meanings associated with their products, ultimately they could do little to control the actual (and imaginary) relationships that developed between female consumers and star actresses. Unlike illustrations or fictional trade characters—other popular techniques for developing brand identity—actresses who slipped in and out of character onstage were impossible to control.[177] Through their experimentation with the semiotics of fashion, as the following chapter shows, they demonstrated how women of all classes might challenge inscription within consumer society and continue to make meanings for themselves.

Chapter 4
Fashioning the Modern Woman

Fashion is one among many forms of aesthetic creativity which makes pos-sible the exploration of alternatives. For after all, fashion is more than a game; it is an art form and symbolic social system.

—Elizabeth Wilson, The Sphinx in the City

In 1914 *Printers' Ink* surveyed leading advertisers on the relative merits of using a star's name for advertising purposes. Although several re-spondents worried that "the value to sales of the name of an actress or promi-nent person is only of a temporary nature," others used star names to great effect. For the "Parisian perfumer" V. Rigaud, the decision to name its new perfume after the popular American opera singer Mary Garden proved to be a highly effective strategy for breaking into the American market. Playing into the public's perception of Garden as a stylish and respectable yet unde-niably modern woman, Rigaud launched a multimedia promotional cam-paign that included advertisements in *Vogue, Vanity Fair*, and the *Criterion of Fashion*, and window displays with a full-length photograph of Garden as Salome, along with booklets, folders, envelope inserts, counter cards, and window cards "to aid dealers in selling."[1] "As it is," explained *Printers' Ink*, "Mary Garden isn't so classical that she appeals only to the 'high-brows,' and still she isn't of the musical comedy sort whose followers may desert her in a season." The Rigaud example illustrates the extreme care with which advertis-ers selected performers to represent their brands. As an attractive, stylish, and perhaps most importantly, *American* opera star, Garden represented a classy yet accessible image. Garden's dual status as a star and an artist distinguished her from other, lesser players and musical comedy performers, thereby reaf-firming her social position and opera's superiority to commercial Broadway theater.[2]

The American beauty manufacturer Swift and Co. enjoyed similar suc-cess with the launch of Maxine Elliott Toilet Soap in 1912, emphasizing Elliott's distinctive beauty, acting abilities, and business acumen as the owner and manager of the Maxine Elliott Theatre in print ads and displays (figure 4.1). One of the company's most memorable window displays was a miniature reproduction of the front of the Maxine Elliott Theatre, complete with electric lights, depicting several scenes from the actress's most recent play.[3] The company further highlighted its close relationship with Elliott by distributing product samples in the theaters where she appeared on tour. Swift and Co. was nevertheless careful to "[avoid] a too strong featuring of the actress to the detriment of the Swift product." While the company sent dealers photographs of Elliott for display purposes, the newspaper cuts simply showed boxes of the soap *without* a picture of the actress. *Printers' Ink* reported that many dealers preferred these cuts, believing that her picture would distract consumers from the actual product. In thus privileging the product over the image of the actress, Swift and Co. demonstrated how a company could successfully use a celebrity's name and image without becoming dependent on "the pulling power of the name."[4]

Swift and Co. implicitly recognized the dynamic and often unstable nature of turn-of-the-century theatergoers' imaginary relationships with stage stars.[5] As Susan Torrey Barstow has shown, while male performers stirred matinee girls' desires for love and romance, female players also occupied a "prominent position in the imaginative lives of young women" and may even have "made a greater impression" than their male counterparts.[6] In New York and other major cities throughout the United States, actresses such as Ethel Barrymore, Billie Burke, Lillian Russell, Julia Marlowe, and Maxine Elliott attracted loyal followings of women from diverse backgrounds.[7] Detailed accounts of performers' offstage lives published in newspapers and magazines gave many theatergoers the impression that they knew and understood their favorite actresses and encouraged the development of strong emotional bonds.[8] Although theatrical conventions and audience propriety prevented most spectators from bridging the physical distance between stage and auditorium, actual contact with performers remained a distinct and enticingly present possibility. Advertisers like Rigaud and Swift and Co. usefully exploited these bonds for their own purposes, but they also risked alienating their markets if consumers changed their minds about the stars featured in the advertisements.

While actresses attracted female fans for a variety of reasons (often related to age or class), their widespread popularity can be explained, in part, by their successful negotiation of modern life.[9] As women who lived their lives in public and onstage, actresses offered multiple strategies for appearing in

Maxine Elliott Toilet Soap
is for tender, delicate skins.
Swift & Company

Figure 4.1. One of the print ads for Maxine Elliott Toilet Soap. Most dealers preferred advertising cuts without Elliott's image. *Theatre Magazine* (October 1915): 209.

public, demonstrating through their ever-changing wardrobes that experimenting with new looks was both fun and liberating. Maxine Elliott's biographer (and niece), Diana Forbes-Robertson, writes that Elliot's "appeal lay in the creation of glamour particularly attractive to women; she gave them a vision of themselves as they would like to be."[10] To the growing number of women who were asserting their right to occupy male-dominated spaces, entering professions that had once been exclusively male, taking to the streets to demand equal rights, organizing strikes to protest poor working conditions, and otherwise transforming the public sphere, actresses like Elliott showed that stepping into an office or a factory was just as much a performance as stepping onstage. As professional, working women, they proved that it was not only possible for women to make a place for themselves in the male-dominated business world, but that they could do so with grace and style. In their well-publicized disputes with male management over matters like costuming and contracts, female stars asserted the right to receive fair and equal treatment, offering a powerful and inspiring example to thousands of women engaged in their own struggles for autonomy and recognition.

Indeed, despite promoting a beauty ideal that privileged thin, white, upper-class women and necessitated a continual process of self-surveillance and body management, actresses also challenged their inscription within consumer society as laborers and commodities by advancing a vision of modern female subjectivity that negotiated rather than yielded to the lures of mass consumption. In modeling modern gowns, modern bodies, and modern ideas, female performers convincingly demonstrated how women might use commodities as a form of personal and political expression, countering those who insisted that women's obsession with fashion threatened the advancement of American society.

For those who were already active participants in radical protests, marches, and strikes as well as for those who were intrigued but too scared or intimidated to participate, the theater offered a place to witness and rehearse ideas of change, to imagine a world that didn't or wouldn't or *couldn't* exist outside the theater walls. The literal and symbolic confines of the theater also gave actresses, wary of making overtly political statements, an opportunity to express a political point of view. As several historians have shown, most actresses did not become politically active in the woman's suffrage movement until the 1910s, when the movement had already moved away from the fringes and was gaining widespread support.[11] Yet by stirring the imaginations of their female fans with their exploration of the semiotics of dress, turn-of-the-century actresses called attention to themselves as creative and psychologically complex individuals and opened up a space for reflection, critique, and rebellion.[12]

Witnessing the Modern Body

By the late nineteenth century, most Americans were well apprised of the latest trends in fashion, thanks to frequent reports in newspapers and magazines. What made the theater such a unique site of fashion spectacle, however, was the "liveness" of the actress and the ease with which she modeled the clothes. "[On the stage] as nowhere else to such advantage, can one observe the effect and mark the shortcomings of a new style of gown," *Harper's Bazar* observed in 1909. While seeing real fashions worn by a real woman hardly seems revolutionary today, it was an exciting novelty at the turn of the century. Prior to 1910, department stores rarely displayed clothing, and when they did it was usually on a "headless dummy," a common dress form without arms, legs, or head. Stores occasionally used wax models similar to those seen in museum anthropology exhibits, although William Leach argues that it was only "with the rise of ready-to-wear clothes and the production of fully prepared garments" in the 1910s that full-bodied mannequins became popular.[13] Yet despite the introduction of more realistic facial expressions to make these mannequins appear lifelike, wax mannequins could hardly compete with flesh and blood.[14]

The actress's role as fashion model and style arbiter intensified in the early twentieth century in large part as a response to the American public's growing interest in and awareness of Paris fashion. More than simply showing the gowns, fashionable actresses demonstrated the appropriate way to wear and move in the new styles. "If the average woman would study and copy the way women of the stage wear this style of [bowl-shaped] hat the public would sooner become reconciled to it," the *Theatre Magazine* urged in 1909.[15] "Nowhere else are costumes displayed to such wonderful advantage," it reiterated in 1914, "for they are the result of studied perfection, and are considered, by the actress herself, a part of the business of life, which they most certainly are."[16] At the theater women saw the latest styles on bodies specifically trained for the purpose and learned through observation how they too might perfect the modern look.[17] Ironically, as much as actresses' fashionable performances worked to maintain class boundaries by providing middle-class and society women with the necessary tools to distinguish between "authentic" and "imitation" fashions, these same performances threatened to blur class distinctions by giving immigrant and working-class theatergoers lessons in style, comportment, and self-advancement. "A woman, too, may educate herself in the proper things to do, say, and wear, by carefully observing the best actresses on the stage," the author Alfred Mason advised in 1909. "Some women with ambitions for self-cultivation do not have any other means of knowing what is proper for a street-gown, a house-gown, or a reception-gown. They may never have any use for some of them, but they like to know the right thing in the right place, just the same."[18]

But seeing modern fashion live on actual living, breathing, moving women was about much more than satisfying curiosity; it was also about witnessing the emergence of the modern female body—a body that was not only self-aware and sexually desiring but also ready and eager to move into male-dominated spaces: offices, universities, government buildings, city streets. Beginning in 1907, Paris designers introduced a dramatic and controversial reinvention of the female silhouette, abandoning the S-curve corset, which accentuated the breasts and hips by shaping the torso into an approximation of the letter "S," in favor of a straighter, more tubular, high-waisted silhouette that evoked the Directoire style of the Napoleonic era. This new silhouette radically transformed the appearance and movement of the female body. Gone were the puffed sleeves and bell-like skirt made popular by the Gibson Girl drawings of Charles Dana Gibson; in their place was a sleeker, form-fitting style that emphasized the legs and lower torso over the breasts and hips (figure 4.2).

Consistent with its name, the new sheath gown quite literally "sheathed" the body, necessitating a high slit in the skirt, which offered a revealing glimpse of the calf and upper thigh accentuated by brightly colored stockings. In addition to this glimpse of leg, part of what was so shocking about the sheath was the sheerness required in the accompanying undergarments; a woman walking into the wind gave passersby a detailed glimpse of the body beneath the skirt.[19] The tightness of the sheath gown also marked a shift in attitudes toward the body brought about by the growing movement to abandon corsetry; we see here the embrace of a thin ideal and the corresponding emphasis on maintaining the body through dieting and exercise rather than a carefully constructed corset.[20] The sheath's focus on the lower half of the female body also represented an important psychological shift. Rather than highlight the maternal and reproductive aspects of a woman's body—breasts and waist—as earlier fashions had done, the sheath skirt emphasized the legs, transforming the female body into a mobile and potentially dangerous site of sexual power.[21] Far from the maternal ideal, the sheathed woman was an ac-

Figure 4.2. The shocking sheath (Directoire) gown worn by Mlle. De Joire. Picture Collection, The Branch Libraries, The New York Public Library, Astor, Lenox and Tilden Foundations.

tive, sexual being—living proof of the sexologist Havelock Ellis's contention that women were not the timid and passionless individuals that nineteenth-century medical discourse held them to be, but were passionate and desiring individuals.[22] At a time when Victorian ideals of restraint and modesty were only beginning to give way to a more modern sensibility, the sheath's explicit exposure of female limbs and its tight encasement of the torso aroused both fascination and horror.

Not surprisingly, many women were uncertain about how to or even whether they should adopt the new styles from Paris. Conservative critics railed against what they viewed as the "freakish fashions" of Paris and urged American women to reject the obscene transformation of the female body. In 1908 the Reverend W. A. Bartlett of Chicago's First Congregational Church condemned the new styles, drawing comparisons between the fashion-obsessed young woman and the alcoholic. "This passion for dress becomes as inexorable as the drink habit," he argued. "It takes the mind of the young from good books, it induces an artificial life, and the whole trend of it is away from stability of character and success in study or work."[23] For Bartlett, fashion threatened to transform American women into sinful hedonists, more concerned with appearance than spiritual well-being. More disturbing, fashion would divert women's attention from the domestic realm, undermining the stability of American society, initiating cultural decline and "race suicide."[24] These anxieties were certainly nothing new. The fashion historian Valerie Steele writes that Americans were "always somewhat schizophrenic" when it came to Paris fashion, which they characterized as decadent and antithetical to the sobriety and virtue of republicanism.[25] However, as more and more women acquired the means to dress fashionably, contemporary observers became alarmed by what they perceived as the American woman's obsession with fashion and her distressing lack of individuality in dress.[26] The arrival of the sheath gown, with its attendant emphasis on a highly public form of female sexuality, brought these concerns to the forefront.

Despite, or perhaps because of, conservative anxieties about foreign influence, many actresses embraced Paris fashion in all of its extremity, modeling even the most bizarre styles on- and offstage.[27] In doing so, they presented themselves as daring, adventurous, modern women who were unwilling to yield to calls for restraint or the remonstrations of the pulpit. Dressed in Paris fashion, their bodies became public stages for dramatizing a series of collisions: between foreign and domestic markets; between the private world of the home and the public world of the city street; and between nineteenth-century morality and twentieth-century modernity (figure 4.3).

Figure 4.3. This sheath-wearing woman may have been a stage performer trying to advance her way to theatrical stardom. Courtesy Library of Congress, Prints and Photographs Division.

On May 23, 1908, less than a week after news of the sheath reached American shores, the chorus girl Bertha Carlisle of the *Merry Widow* Company, walked down Chicago's State Street dressed in what was reportedly a sheath gown.[28] According to the *New York Times*, word of her "impromptu" fashion show spread quickly and soon a "pushing, scrambling mob of 10,000 persons" surrounded the actress, forcing her to retreat into the safety of a jeweler's shop.[29] Two months later the vaudeville performer Madelaine Capretta drew a crowd of 5,000 people in Toledo, Ohio when she too appeared in public wearing the sheath. As *Variety* reported, the fashion spectacle "stopped car traffic; caused a riot; called out the police and fire departments; caused injuries to many people in the crush; stopped business for an hour, and gave Chefalo and Capretta the biggest advertisement any act ever received in this city."[30] Although Capretta presumably emerged from the stunt unscathed, others did not. In fact, actresses' willingness to exploit their bodies for promotional purposes may have made urban spaces even more dangerous for other women. Only a week after Capretta's stunt in Toledo, 5,000 people swarmed a young woman in Harlem, believing—incorrectly, as it turned out—that she too was wearing a sheath.[31] The woman retreated into a nearby shop for safety, but the curious onlookers refused to disperse until the army reserves arrived and forcibly beat them back with fists and clubs.[32] This rather disturbing account throws into relief the tension surrounding women's incursions into public space and the dangers of sexualized female spectacle. The pushing Harlem crowds seem to have been motivated more by a desire to punish the woman for transgressing gender norms than by any interest in seeing her gown.

Paradoxically then, while new fashions like the sheath envisioned an active public body, most American fashion debuts occurred within the semi-public, safe environment of the theater. Indeed, despite the examples of Carlisle and Capretta, most contemporaries argued that controversial styles like the sheath were not appropriate for street wear and should *only* be worn in the theater.[33] Within the confines of the theater—a public yet domesticated space governed by clear rules for audience behavior—actresses did not have to worry about undesired physical contact with spectators. The literal and conventional distance between stage and auditorium, marked by the decorative proscenium arch and the corresponding fiction of the "fourth wall," as well as the representational logic of the theater, which transformed a stage gown into a sign of a sign, protected actresses from awkward or threatening encounters with audiences. As theater semioticians explain, an object onstage represents not a material object per se but rather the *idea* of an object to which it may or may not bear any direct relationship. A chair on the stage *may* signify the generic category "chair," but it may also signify an infinite variety of objects or beings, depending on the context of the scene and the style of performance.[34] This quality of "transformability" made the theater a uniquely safe place to introduce controversial styles and shocking representations of the female body and, as Jill Dolan suggests, an ideal "site for working through some of the gender troubles that would be too dangerous, in different ways, on the street."[35]

Behind the mask of character and the literal structure of the proscenium arch, the actress dressed in a sheath gown did not represent herself nor was she necessarily wearing a sheath. Still, as Gay McAuley observes, "Although the theatrical 'frame' necessarily transforms any object placed within it into a sign, the object in the theater is always simultaneously a real, material presence."[36] Therefore, while the theatrical context may have muted the effect of the shocking sheath, the potentially transgressive elements of the gown did not disappear nor, I would argue, were they imperceptible to an audience of fashion-conscious women. Educated in the semiotics of dress through long hours spent reading fashion columns in newspapers and magazines, these women saw considerably more than their male companions and used this knowledge to advance their own agendas. Actresses relied on this shared, gendered knowledge—an example of what Peter Bailey refers to elsewhere as "knowingness"—to encourage female spectators to embrace a more expressive form of female sexuality without fear of public censure, humiliation, or physical violation.[37]

In August 1908, the "American Beauty" Lillian Russell, now in her late forties and no longer the embodiment of ideal physical beauty she had once been, introduced three variations of the sheath gown into her touring production of *Wildfire*.[38] Although most critics enthused about Russell's "finesse" and her "complete mastery of the details" of performance, some observers were less convinced about her costuming choices.[39] Alan Dale, for example, quipped that *Wildfire* was little more than "a comedy in three directoire gowns," and that Russell was "a lovely martyr to the exquisite knack of masquerading a '12-inch bust measure' in a 32-inch waist."[40] The caricaturist Moe Zayas shared Dale's sarcastic view of the mature actress and her fashion tastes, implying with his less-than-flattering image (figure 4.4) that Russell's vain attempts to squeeze her body into the form-fitting style had made her an object of ridicule. But accounts of audience behavior offer a different perspective on Russell's performance. The *New York Telegraph*'s Mlle. Manhattan reported that women "sat up and gasped" when Russell stepped onstage in a turquoise satin sheath, thrilled with the attractive if slightly plump actress's

Figure 4.4. A less than flattering depiction of the "American Beauty" Lillian Russell in one of her sheath gowns for the 1908 production of *Wildfire.* Caricature by Moe Zayas. Billy Rose Theatre Division, The New York Public Library for the Performing Arts, Astor, Lenox and Tilden Foundations.

appearance.[41] These women seem to have interpreted Russell's embrace of the sheath as an argument suggesting that neither age nor body size should deter women from expressing their sexuality or experimenting with new looks.

Russell's daring fashion display also complemented *Wildfire*'s message of female self-sufficiency. A light-hearted romantic comedy, *Wildfire* tells the story of Mrs. Henrietta Barrington, a horse-loving widow who inherits a racehorse named Wildfire but must disguise her knowledge and love of the sport to avoid social prejudice. Although, in keeping with the comic genre, Henrietta finds love by the play's end, she nevertheless maintains her independent spirit and proves herself the intellectual equal of her male associates. *Wildfire*'s implicitly feminist message is hardly surprising given Russell's own political views. Although it would be another three years before she publicly declared her support for woman's suffrage—presumably wary of the negative publicity that such a declaration might bring—she nevertheless used her reputation as one of the great beauties of the American stage to encourage women to assert themselves both in love and through dress.[42] Later, in public lectures, in her own line of beauty products, and perhaps most significantly, through her direct involvement with the suffrage cause, she would continue to show how women might advance their personal and political objectives by cultivating a charming appearance.[43] For those intent on counteracting negative stereotypes of suffragists as masculine, man-hating women, Russell's strategy was a highly appealing one.[44]

The African American dancer, singer, and choreographer Aida Overton Walker also put the sheath gown to strategic use in the touring production of *Bandana Land*, a musical starring her husband, George Walker, and the comedian Bert Williams. Walker's most notable number in this production was a sophisticated tribute to the Salome dance craze, a number that carefully deemphasized the transgressive sexuality of the biblical woman in favor of highlighting the actress's skill as a choreographer and dancer.[45] Theater historians have focused extensively on Walker's Salome performance, seeing her appropriation of the sinful woman as an ideal illustration of how African American performers "revise[d] popular constructions of black womanhood onstage."[46] Few scholars, however, have considered Walker's transgressive use of stage fashion in "The Sheath Gown in Darktown," a late addition to *Bandana Land*, which not only elicited positive reactions from the audience but also seems to have been a direct response to accusations of racial appropriation.[47]

In February 1908, the white dramatic editor Burton M. Beach criticized the female performers in *Bandana Land*, arguing that their emulation of what he interpreted as white styles and gestures detracted from the performance: "Several members of the company, possibly out of sheer vanity, make up in imitation of this, that or the other prominent American actress (white), and most of the women in the chorus affect the manners of white folk—from gait and gesture, to rouge pot and powder puff. Imitation is the sincerest form of flattery . . . [b]ut the Negroid illusion is spoiled: the realism which the originators of the work had in view is marred by the affectations of Caucasian traits."[48] It was not the performers' emulation of supposedly white manners, gestures, and beautifying practices in themselves that bothered Beach but rather the way that the women's appropriative acts disrupted the reality effect, calling attention to their attempts at racial passing. Clearly influenced by white stereotypes of black femininity, which equated authentic blackness with a lack of education, a subservient attitude, and limited knowledge of the world, Beach interpreted the women's performances as a refusal to follow the racial script.[49]

The actor Charles D. Marshall of the Walker and Williams Company responded to Beach's complaints, asserting that black performers had just "as much right to imitate white folks as the white have to imitate black folks." He nevertheless concurred that black actresses should not "[spoil] that unusual face of beauty that is generally found in our women of the stage . . . by the covering of powder."[50] In arguing against the use of whiteners and face powder by African American women, Marshall echoed the position of black middle-class reformers who stressed the importance of race pride and encouraged women to spurn bleach and straightening solutions. Those who adopted a more militant stance went so far as to interpret any attempt to emulate white beauty culture as a sign of racial self-hatred and instead promoted traditional African hair and clothing styles as the appropriate aesthetic for uplifting the race.[51] The issue was a charged and complicated one for African American performers, especially women. If they conformed to white expectations of authentic "blackness," they would be reproducing negative racial stereotypes, but if they refused to adopt any "white" fashions or beautifying practices, they would be subscribing to an altogether different stereotype of authentic African beauty.

Aida Overton Walker joined the debate over female appropriation of "white" styles in the fall of 1908 with "The Sheath Gown in Darktown," a satirical comic number written by Tom Lemonier with words by "Mord" Allen. The lyrics recount the story of "Miss Belladonna Sophie Brown," a young woman who, upon her return from a trip to "gay Paree," scandalizes all of Darktown by wearing the controversial sheath style. As the chorus explains:

Oh there's trouble down in Old Darktown,
Since Bella came with the new sheath gown,
Imported walk and smile, and all that foreign style,
And all the girls are badly hurt as they watch her flirt that see-more skirt.
The sheath gown it's got Darktown, and will hold it for a while. [52]

Although the lyrics emphasize the triviality of the sheath fad—in keeping with the musical comedy tradition of parodying women's fashion[53]—Walker's performance may have meant something quite different to female audiences, especially African American women. Indeed, as scholars such as David Krasner, Karen Sotiropoulos, and Daphne Brooks have shown, the members of the Walker and Williams Company often used coding and other subtextual methods to "target a collective black audience, literally and often figuratively 'over the heads' of white patrons seated in the orchestra."[54] This strategic play protected performers from the scorn and criticism of white critics and audiences, while allowing them to engage in a critical dialogue with black theatergoers seated in the gallery seats.

Although there is little direct evidence of Walker's actual performance in "The Sheath Gown in Darktown," her central role in the Walker and Williams Company provides strong circumstantial evidence that she used coding techniques to address black female spectators. On one level, the comic context of the song and the character of Bella worked to distance Walker from the "see-more skirt" and its attendant associations with African American hypersexuality. The lyrics warn against the folly and excesses of foreign fashion and strongly imply that any women wishing to avoid "trouble down in Old Darktown" should avoid such fads at all costs. Taken literally, Walker's portrayal of Bella must have supported this conservative message, simultaneously confirming black reformers' perspective on racial uplift while placating white anxieties about African American women's problematic adoption of white aesthetics. But Walker was no stranger to fashion. Her previous experience teaching the cake walk to New York's social elite had given her access to the semiotics of designer fashion and other aspects of class display.[55] Moreover, as the wife of George Walker, a man who cultivated a stylish persona in both his on- and offstage appearances, she would surely have possessed sophisticated knowledge of fashion's communicative potential.[56] Promotional photographs from *Bandana Land* and earlier Walker and Williams productions offer further evidence that Walker was attentive to the demands of stage spectacle (figure 4.5). Given these considerations, it is certainly possible to read her performance of "The Sheath Gown in Darktown" as a strong response to Beach's racist complaints. Dancing about the stage in what was likely a

Figure 4.5. A promotional photograph of the dancer and musical comedy star Aida Overton Walker, ca. 1900. Photographs and Prints Division, Schomburg Center for Research in Black Culture, The New York Public Library, Astor, Lenox and Tilden Foundations.

designer-made gown, she not only poked fun at "foreign fads" and addressed critics' concerns about racial appropriation but also offered black female audiences an opportunity to examine the provocative style more closely and imagine a world where they too could parade freely through the streets.

Fashioning the Modern Mind

In 1908, the writer Laurette van Varseveld published an article entitled "The Psychology of Stage Clothes," in which she emphasized the actress's artistic responsibility to select clothes that expressed the psychology of the character she was playing. The proper wardrobe aided the "temperamentally sensitive actress" by "put[ting] her psychologically *en rapport* with the role she is interpreting," she explained, arguing further that the actress should design her own costumes: "No dressmaker, however skillful, can accurately design a gown for a part when only the actress herself understands its subtle personality as she intends enacting it on the stage."[57] Van Varseveld criticized performers who challenged the limits of believability by dressing in expensive gowns that belied their character's social and economic status, and instead urged them to "select those that will most forcibly accentuate the psychology of the character she is to enact, while at the same time . . . [emphasizing] the salient and distinctive personality of the woman she intends to portray."[58]

Van Varseveld's intervention seems to have had the desired effect. By the 1910s, Broadway actresses regularly discussed their individual approaches to the "psychology of stage clothes" in interviews and articles. "My gowns have always been a part of my existence," Jane Cowl told the *Boston American* in 1914. "I give them just as much consideration in the planning [for a new role] as I give to memorizing my lines and am just as particular about their outcome."[59] For Cowl, finding the appropriate stage clothes was an integral part of her interpretative process as an actress. Other performers expressed similar ideas, offering detailed explanations for their costume choices. In 1915, the *Green Book Magazine* introduced a series of articles in which actresses shared their personal "philosophies of dress." Supposedly written by the actresses Ruth Chatterton, Anna Held, Alice Brady, Valeska Suratt, Julia Dean, and others widely acknowledged for their beauty, taste, and style, these articles offered female readers "invaluable tips on originality, individuality, and independence in attire."[60]

Theater critics, however, were less than thrilled with Broadway's "clothes mania"—especially the *Cosmopolitan* writer Alan Dale. Dale raged against what he perceived as the gross abuses of the fashionable actress and her dress-maker. "The stage should reflect the dress of real life and not go beyond it," he declared in 1907. According to Dale, Broadway's obsession with fashionable dress threatened the artistic development of American drama and the acting profession by requiring managers to select plays on the basis of costuming opportunity. "How can there be simplicity in acting, grace and naturalness in gesture, sincerity and truth in demeanor," he asked, "when the wretched object of it all has been led to believe that she will 'set the fashions'?"[61] Rather than support a realist theater aesthetic, designer fashions and the women who wore them distracted audience members, pulling them out of rather than into the fictional world onstage. Moreover, the "overdressed drama" trans-formed capable actresses into vain peacocks, drove young stage-struck girls into debt, and compelled directors to typecast on the basis of appearance rather than talent.[62] The blame, as Dale saw it, rested solely with the actress and her "tyrannical" dressmaker. It was the dressmaker who encouraged the vain, weak actress to wear such overblown creations by conferring psycho-logical meaning upon different articles of clothing. "What chance have you and I against the dressmaker?" he queried in 1915. "What we consider appro-priate, she looks upon as dowdy and dowdiness is the greatest crime in the sartorial lexicon."[63]

Yet in attacking the "tyrannical" dressmaker and her vain clients, Dale unwittingly undermined his authority as a critic by admitting that he didn't know a thing about fashion: "The dressmaker knows—what we [men] can never know—the emotional aspirations of the dramatic creatures whom she clothes, and it has often occurred to me that, as the regular dramatic critic is never allowed to assist at the conferences between dressmaker and 'star,' *he can never be thoroughly fitted to fulfill his manifold duties*" (my emphasis).[64] While clearly intended as sarcasm, Dale's comments hint that the source of his frus-tration was his inability to understand the semiotics of stage dress. "Graceful feminine writers describe the clothes worn on the stage in terms that none but the initiated [that is, women] can understand," he continued, implying that as a man, he was one of the uninitiated. Fashion-conscious women could appreciate the "psychology of clothes," but he lacked the knowledge or the "knowingness" to do so.[65]

I am nevertheless wary of disregarding Dale's skepticism entirely. As Jane Cowl herself admitted, many of the actresses who claimed to practice the "psychology of clothes" were "hazy with regard to it" and used the rhetoric of psychology to justify costuming choices that had little to do with character.[66] It is also possible that many of the articles purportedly written by leading stage actresses were in fact ghost written by press agents. What becomes interesting then, is the way that actresses' voices—ventriloquized or not—were used to promote fashion as a means for self-expression and to counter conservative criticism about the dangers of consumption.

In demonstrating fashion's interpretative potential, actresses (or their agents) challenged those who feared that fashion-obsessed women were at risk of losing their individuality. In 1914, the literary magazine *The Craftsman* estimated that women devoted as much as 50 percent of their time to "keeping up with the ever changing, eccentric, artificial styles of the day." This consuming interest in fashion distracted women from "opportunities for intellectual and spiritual progress" and prevented them from contemplating "real" concerns, most notably "the progress and needs of the country and the making of the home as beautiful and comfortable and satisfactory as homes can be made today without extravagance."[67] Women's failure to take their social responsibilities seriously marked a decline in "the beauty, the refinement, [and] the sincerity of life," and the democratic values on which the nation had been founded.[68] More disturbing for these critics, however, was fashion's effect on the intellectual independence of the American woman. With the increased availability of cheap ready-to-wear fashions, most women purchased rather than made their clothing. Some critics felt that this development severely inhibited women's ability to select attractive, comfortable clothes and think for themselves. Hoping to forestall fashion's debilitating effects on the American woman's intellectual and spiritual growth, they urged women to design and make their own clothes, to suit their individual physical, spiritual, and emotional characteristics. Those who did would foster "the kind of civilization we are hoping for and working for in this country today—the democratic civilization in which all our young people are intelligent laborers with trained minds, developed spirits and capable bodies."[69] By developing their own dress styles, American women would become better citizens, better wives, and better mothers.

Actresses addressed the concerns articulated by *The Craftsman* and others by characterizing fashion as a creative, productive process and similarly urging women to select clothes that suited their individual tastes and personalities. "Be yourself" was the predominant theme underlying their "philosophies of dress." "No matter what taste your dressmaker may have," Elsie de Wolfe advised in an 1897 *Cosmopolitan* article, "those certain little touches which alone give originality should come only from one's self. . . . No woman who is truly chic is slave to her dressmaker."[70] Other actresses openly criticized women for their slavish devotion to the latest modes and their "sacrifice of individuality in dress." "Our streets are filled with women in uniforms," Mary Mannering observed in 1910, "uniforms that scarcely differ in color or trimming—and to all appearances the throngs might be composed of persons wearing the livery of a few employers."[71] Valeska Suratt echoed Mannering's complaint in 1915: "There's the secret of why the women of to-day are such holy sights," she explained. "They try to adapt themselves to the styles instead of making the styles adapt themselves to their personalities."[72] Unlike the anti-fashion critics, however, actresses stopped short of suggesting that women should abandon fashion or dress unfashionably, hesitant to undermine their own role in the creation and distribution of fashion ideas. Instead, they advised women to identify (or adapt) styles *within* the existing mode to suit their individuality and emphasized the importance of remaining aware of the latest trends. Actress Julia Dean went so far as to suggest that women who did *not* follow fashion failed in their responsibilities as women: "To dress at marked variance with the prevailing fashion is to strike an inharmonious note. The woman who does this is off key with her surroundings. She creates a discord."[73]

In acknowledging the relationship between fashion and individuality, actresses also articulated the ideas of the contemporary sociologist Georg Simmel, who argued that fashion's power lies in its ability to convey distinction while allowing individuals to seek membership within a larger social group.[74] As he explains in "The Philosophy of Fashion" of 1905, "a certain very broad framework of general style—the current fashion—is strictly observed, so that the individual appearance never *clashes* with the general style, but always *stands out* from it."[75] Individual expression therefore operates within the boundaries of public consensus. To achieve individuality in dress a woman must select clothes that are not only appropriate for her physically and psychologically, but also compatible with the latest styles.[76] Actresses addressed the conflicting desires for individuality and community, promising that those who managed to find the delicate balance would enjoy a renewed sense of confidence and liberation. "I do not care for the bouffant effects: crinolines are unsuited to my personality: so why should I wear them? I have the courage of my individuality," Alice Brady boasted in an article in 1915. Although her early efforts at fashion were dismal failures, she had learned, "through many mistakes in dress that have cost me and my family anguish of spirit," that certain styles do not suit her. Finally confident in her abilities, Brady characterized herself as a fashion revolutionary: "This is my declaration of independence in dress. I take pleasure in adding another to my assertions of freedom from what is generally accepted. I know that it is very nice and ladylike to rave about white. I don't like it."[77] Valeska Suratt similarly invoked the metaphor of liberation, characterizing her decision to cut off the fashionable yet uncomfortable "choke-me-and-get-it-over-with" collar from a new dress as "emancipation from the bondage of Style."[78] In presenting themselves as freethinkers and rebels, Brady and Suratt urged other women to liberate themselves from the tyranny of fashion by thinking for themselves.

Indeed, as Brady, Suratt, and others pointed out, acquiring self-knowledge through careful study and self-analysis was the key to achieving greater personal satisfaction in dress. "To study oneself, one's height, color of hair and eyes, and [select the] material and design accordingly is to be well dressed," Elsie de Wolfe explained to the readers of *Harper's Bazar* in 1900.[79] Jane Cowl repeated the same point thirteen years later, identifying self-analysis as the "one safe rule" for becoming fashionable.[80] Other actresses encouraged women to identify and accentuate their most attractive features, to study the color of their eyes and hair and learn how to bring out the highlights, to "have some definite idea of . . . [the] lines that will best bring out her good points and conceal her bad ones."[81] With hours of careful study, they promised, any woman could become as well dressed as the fashionable women she admired. But knowing oneself involved much more than a physical inventory; it also meant exploring one's inner emotions and desires. "More than the physical conditions must be taken into account," Mary Mannering argued in an article in *Green Book* in 1910. "The mental attitude must be considered . . . it is necessary to take into account one's own mental poise before giving way to an inclination to purchase a dress because it fits well and accords generally with the type of woman who is to wear it."[82] In her use of the term "mental poise," Mannering defined the well-dressed woman as one who examines each potential purchase in an informed, cautious manner, in accordance with her physical, mental, and psychological characteristics.

Other actresses similarly urged women to consider "the psychology of dress" when they selected clothes. "As a matter of fact," Jane Cowl suggested to the readers of *Dress*, "clothes should be considered by the actress as well as the woman in private life, as a very special and important sort of messenger. . . . They are the means of making something known."[83] Through clothing, she continued, women can reveal the "charm and value" of their personalities and impress on others their inner strength and vitality.[84] While sharing Cowl's view that clothing can express individuality, the Russian actress Alla Nazimova explained that certain fabrics could also be used to *conceal* the inner self and create distance from strangers. "With the outsiders of my life, acquaintances who will never be friends," she told *McCall's*, "there must be barriers—stiff, unresponsive fabrics, like serge." However, when she was with those she loved, she dressed in "warm, soft, clinging things, which carry the atmosphere of intimacy, and through which I may express my real self."[85] Both Cowl and Nazimova assured readers that through careful self-analysis and an appreciation of the different messages conveyed by dress, they could highlight certain aspects of their individuality and shape the way others perceived them.

This emphasis on self-analysis and hard work as the secret to a fashionable appearance is significant for several reasons. First, by encouraging women to study themselves, not only physically, but also psychologically, actresses outlined a strategy for achieving self-knowledge and self-fulfillment that was compatible with emerging feminist thought.[86] Rejecting nineteenth-century notions of self-sacrifice and modesty, they validated a woman's right to personal development and urged readers to make bold, public statements about themselves as modern individuals. Second, by defining the well-dressed woman as one who knows how to accentuate her best assets and hide her worst flaws, the actresses acknowledged fashion's potential for disguise and revelation. Although most actresses do not seem to have questioned the notion of identity as inherent—suggested by Nazimova's reference to her "real self"—they nevertheless demonstrated that dressing fashionably was a performative act. Indeed, as closer analysis of their onstage performances suggests, actresses deliberately played with fashion's duality, using it to promote themselves as stylish trendsetters while communicating important information about character. Such performances paradoxically upheld the possibility of conveying individual psychology through dress while demonstrating how a woman might use fashion to experiment with other modes of self-presentation.

Beyond advising women about their own fashion choices, actresses also spoke at length about the importance of selecting the right clothes as a tool for gaining access to the psychology of the characters they were playing. "Dress your part as the character you are playing in real life," Laurette Taylor advised, "and you are sartorially—and perhaps psychologically—in tune with your role."[87] Frances Starr likewise observed that "the sense of feeling appropriately dressed for the part gives a dramatic artist a grasp of her character, a confidence in her ability to portray that character which no amount of skillful stage management could make up for." In an interview with the *Green Book's* John Lopez, she explained that her thinking on the "psychology of stage dress" had been influenced by Thomas Carlyle's *Sartor Resartus*, the first philosophical treatise on clothing's social function, and Helen Zimmern's more recent work, "The Philosophy of Dress."[88] Building on their ideas, she celebrated the transformative nature of dress and its role in the construction of a new, different self.

Indeed, as many actresses emphasized, dressing for a stage role often meant selecting clothes that they would never choose for themselves. "An actress cannot always indulge her personal tastes for dress when she is playing a part," Laurette Taylor explained. "If she could, 95 per cent of the women on the stage would be playing modern, fashionable young girls or matrons."[89] Chrystal Herne agreed: "O, but you must distinguish between stage clothes and personal clothes, you know," she told the *Theatre Magazine's* Anne Archbald. "This 'Dickey Bird' frock is not at all the sort I should chose for myself. But it fits the character I am playing."[90] This apparent willingness to "distinguish between stage clothes and personal clothes" suggests that female performers were more concerned with "being true to character" than appearing in fashionable dress. A glimpse of the photographs and sketches accompanying the interviews, however, reveals that the difference between stage costume and personal dress was, in fact, quite small. While most actresses willingly experimented with the "psychology of stage clothes" when playing wealthy or socially advanced characters, they were less likely to abandon style for realism and psychology when it came to the portrayal of working-class characters.[91] "I recall an actress who, in the part of a painter at her work, wore a gown too magnificent and too elaborate, with an apron of chiffon trimmed with real lace," Annie Russell reported in 1902. When Russell suggested that she might adapt her costume to accord with the reality of the situation, the actress replied that "she did not belong to the natural school of acting."[92] While some performers declined to delve into the uglier side of stage realism—as previously argued, out of a perceived need to perform class status—they nevertheless shared their peers' interest in exploring the relationship between external appearance and inner subjectivity.

For many actresses, color was one of the most significant ways to reveal a character's psychology. Nineteenth-century performers had previously used color to signify a character's morality or social status, but early twentieth-century performers experimented with a wider range of shades and color combinations to suggest greater psychological depths.[93] Abandoning the rather simplistic color symbolism of the nineteenth century, whereby white stood "for purity and innocence; gray for gentleness and modesty; and scarlet, or spangled black, for duplicity and sin," actresses introduced elements of the developing scientific field of color theory into the design process, presenting themselves as sophisticated observers of modern science and technology.[94] According to contemporary scientific studies, each color's varying wavelengths produced a different effect on the body's nervous system, such that individuals associated red with warmth, blue with cold, and violet with sadness.[95] These theories were put to great use by the symbolists in the late 1880s as part of the synthetic style and later influenced the design theory of men like Joseph Urban, but they also seemed to have trickled through to stage performers.[96] "It is absolutely true that colors and human moods are closely related," Dorothy Donnelly told the interviewer John Lopez, "and it is a fact that one may induce any mood at any time by wearing clothes of the appropriate shade." She explained how she had carefully studied her emotions before selecting costumes for the title role in *Madame X*. "[I]n the prologue there is but one shade that precisely fits the mood of the character," she concluded. "That is deep purple. This is conducive to the precise stage of self-hypnosis that is needed for the actress to 'feel' the part."[97] Much more than a fashion statement, Donnelly's deep purple gown became the conduit through which she gained access to her character's thoughts and emotions, and in turn revealed those emotions to the audience.[98]

The "psychology of stage clothes" also allowed actresses to illustrate their characters' emotional and psychological development over the course of a play. In 1915 Ruth Chatterton discussed how she had carefully selected different colors, styles, and fabrics to reflect the growth of her character Judy in *Daddy Long Legs*. When her director hesitated over her decision to wear black in the final act, she pleaded with him to allow her to recognize her artistic vision: "Please let me wear black. I have good reasons," she insisted. "Aside from the appropriateness of her costume, I want to typify her moods by the color of her frocks. Black in the last act will show her development in quietude of spirit, in dignity. At the same time it expresses her mental attitude, a certain depression, a little sadness—a realization of the more serious aspects of life. Mr. Miller yielded. He admitted black was the right color."[99] Chatterton's success in persuading Miller to accept her interpretation suggests one way that actresses used costuming to challenge male authority and define themselves as professionals. Moreover, in her detailed analysis of Judy's psychological journey, Chatterton demonstrated her knowledge of emerging acting theories, which stressed the importance of understanding character motivation and psychology.

Despite winning her director's approval, an actress's desire to express character psychology was occasionally frustrated by a playwright's prescriptive stage directions. For her role as Mrs. Cheveley in *An Ideal Husband*, Constance Collier wore a raspberry gown, although she personally felt that a "low-cut glittering black" dress would have been more suitable. "It is . . . dangerous for the playwright to interfere with mandatory directions for the dress-ing of his characters," *Vogue* argued in 1918, stressing that an inappropriately dressed actress not only "prejudiced the audience against the character she is portraying" but also failed to "feel at home in the role."[100] *Vogue's* insistence that actresses should not have to yield to the dictates of the playwright or director echoes feminist arguments about self-determination. More than giv-ing women the courage to study themselves, actresses' experiments with the "psychology of stage clothes" simultaneously supported and challenged the notion that clothing revealed an essential self. Like vaudeville's quick-change artists, actresses who used clothing to disappear into a role foregrounded its transformative potential, suggesting that the so-called self on display was more construct than reality.

In fact, actresses' onstage play with the "psychology of dress" revealed that a fully transparent semiotics of dress was *only* possible in the imaginary world of the theater. "Few of us, in real life, would care so to reveal our inmost selves, even if we understood them well enough to gown them unerringly," observed *Vogue* in 1918. " 'Show me what you wear and I will tell you what you are,' is a boast that only the charlatan would attempt to make."[101] Moreover, as *McCall's* noted in an interview with Alla Nazimova in 1915, as much as the theory held "endless possibilities," working out "the emotional expression of each adornment of the body would take as big a book as to put in words all the emotions themselves."[102] Onstage, however, actresses could effectively use the "psychology of dress" to illuminate their characters' inner lives *because* the narrative context of the drama limited the range of possible meanings that could be interpreted from their clothing choices.[103]

Staging "Copy Acts"

The challenges of engaging with a complete semiotics of dress did not pre-clude female audience members from developing their own highly imagina-tive approaches to stage fashion. Throughout the 1910s, the *Theatre Magazine* regularly reported sightings of debutantes and society matrons dressed in gowns originally worn by actresses. "No dress seen on the stage has been more widely copied by fashionable women than the fetching pink frock worn by Miss Mary Ryan in *The House of Glass* at the Candler Theatre," the *Theatre Magazine's* Mlle. Manhattan reported in April 1916.[104] While society women were perhaps most likely to purchase replicas of an actress's designer gown, middle-class and even working-class women also attempted to incorporate star styles into their personal wardrobes. Assisted by innovations in the ready-to-wear and pattern industries, the production of cheap fashion products, and the widespread distribution of actresses' photographs in newspapers and magazines, these women successfully staged their own "copy acts."[105]

The prevalence of such acts might seem to contradict previous discussions about female theatergoers' preoccupations with class and authenticity and the actresses' insistence on dressing to suit one's individuality. While working-class women's creative appropriations of stage fashion are perhaps understandable given their ready consumption of knock-off fashions, how are we to understand the society women who instructed their dressmakers, "Make me a replica of Billie Burke's 'fourth act' gown" in *Love Watches*, or ordered, "See Miss [Margaret] Anglin's gray velvet and copy it for me"?[106] Despite the apparent paradox, closer analysis of audience copy acts suggests that female theatergoers drew a critical distinction between clothes that purported to be "authentic" but weren't and clothes that were detailed replicas of designer fashions. My use of the term "copy act" here is intended to highlight the paradoxical nature of theatergoers' participation in fashion consumption.[107] Sending a dressmaker to copy an actress's gown was not the same thing as wearing paste jewels or a fake sealskin coat. Indeed, as much as women copied specific costume elements, their public appearances in copied gowns constituted new acts, public performances that built on, but nevertheless remained independent of, the originals.[108] As avid consumers of fashion and stage gossip, female audiences drew upon the cultural meanings associated with admired actresses to fantasize about alternative lives and make personal statements about themselves as modern women.

Significantly, while most American women had the access and the means to emulate stage fashion, their copy acts varied according to personal taste, financial resources, and perhaps most importantly, age, class, and ethnicity.[109] Although certain fashions seem to have been popular with a diverse group of women, the middle-aged WASP society woman who appeared at a charity ball in an authentic copy of a legitimate actress's designer gown was worlds apart from the seventeen-year-old Jewish working girl who went to a dance dressed in a cheap copy of a vaudeville star's blouse.[110] Moreover, while many female theatergoers were highly attentive to questions of authenticity, not every woman *cared* about wearing designer gowns. In fact, evidence suggests that many women were proud of their copies and saw fashion imitation as a creative act in its own right. Understanding what these copy acts may have meant to the different women who performed them therefore requires an examination not only of who they copied, but also what they copied, how they copied it, and where they staged their performances.[111] Although it is impossible to determine female theatergoers' intentions, it is nevertheless possible to get some sense of how others might have read their performances by looking at the context within which they appeared and the referents upon which they drew.

Stage fashion played an integral role in society women's public performances of leisure and privilege. Tasked with the burden of securing their husband's status through displays of what the contemporary sociologist Thorstein Veblen famously identified as "conspicuous consumption," turn-of-the-century society women turned to the stage.[112] "[I]n the throes of an era of exclusiveness," one contemporary commented, "[t]he women prominent in society are doing the unexpected, the eccentric thing."[113] In fact, these "social belles" seemed to be outperforming actresses with their outlandish displays, "driving down Fifth Avenue in garments of a hue and a fashion that would make [their] aristocratic old ancestors turn over in their graves." Although many women went to the theater for the express purpose of copying stage gowns, only society women had the means to acquire exact replicas. Some dressmakers even specialized in reproducing actress's gowns, promising bona fide copies within twenty-four hours to clients rushing from an opening night with sketches in their hands.[114]

But beyond displaying wealth, society women also seemed to have used their copy acts to negotiate the constraints of society marriage.[115] In August 1916, Mlle. Manhattan reported seeing Mrs. Angier Duke, formerly Miss (Cordelia) Drexel Biddle, at an exclusive country club. According to Mlle. Manhattan, "[Mrs. Duke was wearing] a simple frock that puzzled me with its charm that held a familiarity really confusing. I gasped with complacency when I recalled the original, which was the fetchingly simple little frock of white embroidered net and crepe de chine worn by Irene Fenwick in 'The Co-Respondent,' which recently terminated a run at the Republic Theatre."[116] Mlle. Manhattan's easy identification of Mrs. Duke's "simple frock" suggests that Mrs. Duke *wanted* other women to recognize her copy act, certainly as a way of signaling her wealth and taste but also perhaps as a way of signaling her independence and free-spiritedness even after marriage. *The Co-Respondent*, by Alice Leal Pollock and Rita Weiman, tells the story of Anne Gray, a modern young woman who narrowly averts disaster when a kind married man warns her that her prospective husband has no intention of marrying her. As she is thanking him for his intervention, detectives hired by the man's jealous wife photograph the two in an embrace. Later, in her capacity as a star reporter for the *Daily News*, Gray interviews the wife about her impending divorce and discovers that she is the co-respondent named in the suit. All ends peacefully, however, when her editor, also conveniently in love with her, learns that his managing editor has been running a blackmail scheme. Gray is redeemed and the divorcing couple is reunited.[117]

By dressing as Fenwick/Gray in a play written by two women, Mrs. Duke presented herself as a modern woman both alert to the realities of infidelity, divorce, and scandal and sympathetic to women who, like Anne Gray, opted for the fulfillment of a career over marriage. As the daughter of Anthony J. Drexel Biddle, a leader of Philadelphia society who had trained as a boxer and instructed military trainees in hand-to-hand combat during World War I, Duke was hardly a stranger to unconventional lifestyles.[118] Her country club appearance as Fenwick's double may therefore have allowed her to show her affiliation with adventurous young women even if social and marital expectations prevented her from pursuing such a life herself.

Hiding behind an actress's gown and stage character may also have allowed society women to express ideas that could not be spoken for fear of social censure. In 1916, the newly remarried Madelaine Dick, the widow of John Jacob Astor, who died on the *Titanic*, appeared at a society gathering dressed in a copy of the pink evening gown worn by Margaret Anglin in *Caroline*, a new play by Somerset Maugham.[119] Like Cordelia Duke, Dick seems to have wanted others to recognize the referent for her gown; indeed, when the celebrity photographer Baron de Meyer saw her, he playfully addressed her as "Caroline."[120] Maugham's play tells the story of a woman who has "enjoyed for ten long years all the comforts of grass widowhood, among them a serene ménage, the languishing glances of a melancholy youth, and the steady-devotion of a middle-aged barrister." When her estranged husband finally dies, Caroline finds that she is no longer attracted to the barrister and shirks away from the prospect of marriage, despite friends' insistence that the two should marry. It is only with "a lie of heroic proportions and really magnificent detail," in which she claims that her husband is still alive, that she manages to reclaim her love and find happiness with the barrister.[121] Dick's invocation of Maugham so shortly after her second marriage is rather perplexing. Was she suggesting that she was unhappy with her new husband? What other reason could she have for identifying with Caroline? The circumstances surrounding Dick's second marriage present some possible answers; although few could begrudge her desire for happiness, her decision to remarry meant that she relinquished her claim to the Astor estate, a situation that apparently dismayed many of her family and friends.[122] In thus collapsing her public image with Anglin's portrayal of Caroline, she may have been signaling to others that she shared the "grass widow's" desire for romance and freedom and would not be governed by the dictates of well-intentioned outsiders.

Middle-class girls and women also experimented with the semiotics of fashion, but the means through which they acquired their clothes varied, as did the performers and characters they emulated. Juvenile matinee girls seem to have cared less about individual distinction and more about looking like their friends, signaling their membership within a peer group by copying favorite performers en masse. In 1916, for example, the *Theatre Magazine* reported that hundreds of matinee girls had shifted their allegiance from Laurette Taylor, their favorite of three years, to the teenage actress Phoebe Foster, the star of *The Cinderella Man*. As proof of Foster's newfound popularity, the *Theatre Magazine* noted that matinee girls were making "sketches of the details of her simple dresses between the acts" and purchasing "Phoebe Foster" hats, slippers, and other fashionable accessories inspired by the young star.[123] Foster's simple yet elegant clothes suited young women's increasingly active lifestyles and allowed them to signal their affiliation with other modern girls. Perhaps more importantly, it gave them a way to present themselves as confident members of a new generation of women—educated, confident, self-aware, and nothing like their mothers.[124]

Manufacturers of ready-to-wear garments capitalized on the matinee girl's interest in stage fashion by selling inexpensive, mass-produced copies of actresses' stage gowns and accessories at most major department stores and local dress shops. Gowns worn by prominent stars were especially popular with fashion-conscious consumers, and manufacturers used actresses' names as a key selling point. Billie Burke recalls that after her success in the 1909 production of *My Wife*, department stores throughout the country sold the "Billie Burke Dress," a simplified version of one of her stage gowns, most notable for its flat collar and lace trim.[125] The price of these ready-to-wear garments varied according to the quality of the manufacturer and the reputation of the establishment where they were sold. In 1915, for example, Lord and Taylor sold a copy of the gown worn by Irene Fenwick in *Song of Songs* for the relatively high price of $37.50. That same year, Woolf and Shulhof, Makers of Costumes and Dresses, advertised their reproduction of the dress worn by Irene Castle in *Watch Your Step* for $22.50 (figure 4.6). In 1910, the Liberal Shirt Waist Co. advertised the "Blanche Ring" Frock, an embroidered linen dress endorsed by Blanche Ring and available to consumers for the comparatively low price of $10.00.[126] Despite the varying price range, ready-to-wear gowns allowed middle-class matinee girls to emulate the actresses they admired for much less than the cost of ordering a custom-made gown from a dressmaker.

OTTO B. SHULHOF

JESSE WOOLF

WOOLF & SHULHOF

MAKERS OF

COSTUMES AND DRESSES

PARIS
4 RUE MARTEL
LONDON
29 JEWIN CRESCENT, E.C
BERLIN
ALTE JACOBSTR 20

MADISON AVENUE & 30TH STREET

NEW YORK

CABLE ADDRESS
SHULWOLF, N.Y.

Our #347 at $22 50 is a reproduction of The "Watch Your Step" Dress worn by Mrs Vernon Castle. Dont you want Some.

:CEMBER 27, 1914.

[D,
ETALIATES

"Castles in the Air"
Latest Resort of the
Devotees of Dancing

MISS
GYPSY O'BRIEN in "TO-NIGHTS
the NIGHT" SHUBERT THEATRE

Miss Selma Mantell and Her Associates
Demand More Dignity for
Their Profession.

Folies Marigny Reopened with Well Known Professionals

Figure 4.6. Women who admired the dress designed by Lucile for Irene Castle to wear in *Watch Your Step* could purchase their own copy from Woolf and Shulhof for only $22.50. *Dry Goods Economist*, January 16, 1915, 38.

Pattern companies also gave women a cost-effective way to copy stage gowns.[127] Although most American pattern magazines such as *McCall's* and *The Delineator* sold simplified versions of elite fashions, skilled sewers could add design details to create clothes that more closely resembled those worn by actresses onstage. In fact, as the fashion historian Christopher Breward has shown, many women still preferred to make their clothes rather than buy them out of a desire "to stay outside or ahead of the trends" and to produce garments that were "better and longer-lasting" than manufactured clothes.[128] Fashion illustrations for patterns from *McCall's* and *The Delineator* offer some indication of the kinds of clothes produced by middle-class and working-class women and help to identify some of the most popular stage fashions and performers. In 1915, over twenty-five versions of the blue and green gown designed by the British couturier Lucile (Lady Duff Gordon) for Irene Castle in *Watch Your Step* appeared in the pages of *McCall's* and *The Delineator*. With a tight bodice and flared skirt, this gown marked a dramatic shift away from the narrow silhouette that had predominated for over six years. "Last year one could resuscitate narrow dresses by half hiding them under a long tunic," *The Delineator* explained in May 1915. "This season everything, to be in fashion, must have the new wide, wide swirl at the bottom."[129] When Irving Berlin's *Watch Your Step* opened on Broadway in December 1914, dozens of women reportedly lined up on 57th Street outside Lucile's salon to order copies of the gowns she had designed for the fashionable dancer. "When we were dancing at Castles in the Air on the roof of the Forty-fourth Street Theater after the show," Castle recalls, "it was not unusual to find the same dress (sometimes in different colors) on at least six of the women in the room."[130] The gowns shown in *McCall's* and *The Delineator* illustrate the speed of fashion's trickle down effect. Although none of the sketches credit Lucile or Castle as the original model, the source of the design is nevertheless obvious.[131] The sketch for Dress 7657 in *The Delineator*, for example, depicts a tall, slim woman with bobbed hair held back by a headband wearing a dress with a short bodice and a full skirt with bands of ribbon arranged in a pattern almost identical to that in the dress from *Watch Your Step* (figure 4.7). Despite the addition of short sleeves and a bolero-like vest, Dress 7657 is clearly a copy of the original Lucile gown, something most fashion-conscious women would easily have recognized.[132]

The apparent success of the *Watch Your Step* dress is a testament to Irene Castle's overwhelming popularity with middle-class girls and women. Tall, thin, and effortlessly elegant, she demonstrated that it was possible to look fashionable and be comfortable at the same time. Cecil Beaton writes that

Waist 7371; skirt 7552

Dress 7657

Figure 4.7. These dress patterns were likely modeled after Irene Castle's dress in *Watch Your Step*. "The New Styles with Their Full Skirts Make Dancing and Walking a Joy," *The Delineator* (May 1915): 62.

when Irene and her husband, Vernon Castle, burst onto the New York cabaret scene in 1912, she "was greeted with the shock of recognition that people
always reserve for those who—as Wordsworth once said—create the taste by
which they are to be appreciated."[133] With her boyish figure, bobbed hair, and
preference for simple, free-flowing dresses, Castle offered a distinctly modern
look that was in sharp contrast to the fuller-figured, highly polished glamour
of Broadway's established leading ladies and therefore much more appealing
to middle-class women.[134] Women in towns and cities throughout the United
States adopted her hairstyle, wore Castle-inspired accessories, including hats,
shoes, and headbands, and purchased copies of the designer gowns she wore
for her dancing engagements.[135] Indeed, for those who were perhaps wary of
copying other actresses' gowns, Irene Castle represented a stylish and socially
acceptable role model.

The appeal of Castle's *Watch Your Step* costume among middle-class
women also marks an important move away from the restrictive, form-fitting
silhouette previously promoted by Paris and most notoriously represented by
the hobble skirt of 1910, a style that quite literally hobbled women by binding
their legs with a restrictive band.[136] As a dancer, Castle advocated the adoption of loose, soft dress styles that facilitated ease and freedom of movement.
"The plaited skirt of soft silk or chiffon, or even of cloth, is by far the most
graceful to dance in, and the one which lends itself best to the fancy steps of
these modern days," she advised in 1914's *Modern Dancing*, a guidebook co-
authored with her husband and intended for the lay reader. "Therefore, while
fashion decrees the narrow skirt, the really enthusiastic dancer will adopt
the plaited one."[137] The fuller *Watch Your Step* gowns designed by Lucile enabled greater physical freedom for women, yet they also worked to contain
anxieties about unfettered female sexuality (especially latent concerns about
lesbianism) by marking a return to the hourglass silhouette. In Ira L. Hill's
promotional photograph (figure 4.8), Castle's thin, boyish body and short,
bobbed hair—a sign of deviant sexuality in some circles—are feminized by
layers of chiffon and the intricate ribbon work on the bodice.[138] Her coy pose,
complete with thrust hips and raised shoulder, are effectively immunized by
the excesses of her costume; the tightly laced bodice and layers of crinoline
petticoats keep prying hands away.[139] She is a "child woman," a sweet innocent, decidedly different from the vamp style embodied by other dancers of
the period and hardly a threat to male authority.[140]

Like their middle-class counterparts, working-class women used their
sewing skills to create cheap versions of elite stage fashions. Those who lacked
the time or the sewing skills to make their own clothes could purchase inex-

Figure 4.8. Irene Castle in the much-copied *Watch Your Step* dress designed by Lucile. Photograph by Ira L. Hill. Jerome Robbins Dance Division, The New York Public Library, Astor, Lenox and Tilden Foundations.

pensive ready-to-wear garments from local shops or peddlers.[141] While these clothes were often poorly made and tended to fall apart quickly, they nevertheless approximated the latest styles.[142] When working women could not afford a new dress or skirt, they used accessories, such as hats, shoes, feather boas, and jewelry, to participate in fads inspired by stage productions.[143] This was the case not only in New York but also in smaller towns along the theatrical touring circuit, where factory and mill workers spent long hours trimming hats and remaking old gowns in preparation for a theater outing. The amount of time female mill workers spent preparing their gowns for a theater outing surprised the social reformer Mrs. John Van Vorst:

> After ten hours' work in the mill, [the factory girl] began again, eager to use the last of the spring twilight, prolonged by a quarter moon. . . . A hat took form and grew from a heap of stuff into a Paris creation; a bolero was cut and tucked and fitted; a skirt was ripped and stitched and pressed; a shirt-waist was started and finished. For two nights the girls worked until twelve o'clock so that when the 'show' came they might have something new to wear that nobody had seen. . . . This must have been the unanimous intention of the Perry populace, for the peanut gallery was a bowery of fashion. Styles, which I had thought were new in Paris, were familiarly worn in Perry by the mill hands.[144]

For these women, a theatrical outing was a chance to display their dressmaking skills, appear in something "new that nobody had seen," and perhaps most importantly, enact fantasies of social mobility.

Intriguingly, however, while many working-class women admired stage favorites like Julia Marlowe and Ethel Barrymore, other women seem to have preferred performers who represented a more expressive form of female sexuality.[145] Indeed, as Kathy Peiss has shown, prostitutes and other fallen women "provided a cultural model" that appealed to working women. "Tantalized by the fine dress, easy life, sexual expressiveness, and apparent independence, while carefully marking the boundary between the fallen and respectable," Peiss explains, "a working woman might appropriate parts of the prostitute's style as her own."[146] Understood within this context, working-class women's preference for styles originated by the "so-called 'bad woman of the stage'" suggests that rather than seeking social advancement at the theater, these women wanted excitement and danger.[147]

The Long Day, a fictionalized autobiography of a "New York Working Girl" based on the real-life experiences of the middle-class reformer Dorothy Richardson, offers several striking examples of working-class women's copy acts. In one chapter, Richardson describes a woman dressing her hair in the

"Du Barry," a style originated by Mrs. Leslie Carter in the eponymous David Belasco production.[148] As Kim Marra has shown, this production delighted and scandalized audiences with highly suggestive scenes set in the famous French mistress's boudoir. In keeping with Belasco's hyper-realistic aesthetic, the stage was cluttered with "an orgy of material objects [to] signify the ruinous spendings she elicits from the king," while Carter's "small denuded feet" peeked out from beneath the "luxuriant folds of Du Barry's bedclothes."[149] Reclining on the bed, her flaming red hair piled up on top of her head, Carter as Du Barry embodied luxury, decadence, and sexual immorality—an image that presumably appealed to working-class female audiences. In thus dressing her hair in the Du Barry style, Richardson's working-class friend may have wished to draw a semiotic link between herself and the naughty Du Barry character. Though the wealth and excess represented by Du Barry and realized by Belasco onstage may have been beyond her grasp, the symbol of erotic femininity was an easy one to appropriate and rework.

In a later chapter, Richardson describes a young woman at a dance wearing "three Nethersole bracelets on her wrist," an obvious reference to Olga Nethersole, the English actress famous for portraying a range of "Fallen Women" characters, the most notorious of which was Sapho.[150] While it is impossible to know which Nethersole production inspired the girl's three bracelets, the copy act was likely a response to the scandal surrounding the production of *Sapho* in 1900. Following in the line of *Camille, Carmen, The Second Mrs. Tanqueray*, and other "Fallen Women" plays, *Sapho* is the story of Fanny Legrand, a Parisian *demimondaine* who falls passionately in love with Jean Gaussin, a much younger man, and inevitably suffers for overreaching her social bounds. Nethersole's production, translated and adapted by Clyde Fitch from the original French play, drew considerable notice for its suggestive scenes and the actress's "diaphanous" costumes, including one "so transparent that when she stood with her back to the light you could pretty well see through it."[151] The costume alluded to here was that worn for the costume ball at the end of Act I—a tightly draped white toga made out of layers of gauzy material that exposed both Nethersole's shoulder and her leg (anticipating the sheath gown by eight years). A wide-banded brace worn on her upper left arm—presumably the inspiration for the "three Nethersole bracelets—completed the ensemble, directing spectators' eyes toward Nethersole's naked shoulder and her long, elegant neck (figure 4.9).

Standing atop a pedestal in her guise as an artist's model, Fanny (Nethersole) positioned herself as an object of adoration and worship, but audiences saw considerably more than a goddess onstage. "She appears to be

Figure 4.9. Olga Nethersole as Fanny Legrand (Sapho) dressed in the scandalous Greek gown, 1901. Note the bracelet (likely the inspiration for the "Nethersole bracelet") on her upper arm. Courtesy Library of Congress Prints and Photographs Division.

naked down to the apex of the heart," W. O. Inglis of the *New York World* remarked. "[T]he shoulder is bare right down to the shoulder blade. The rest of the costume is almost transparent and you can see the entire outline of the body."[152] That Nethersole as Fanny was portraying an artist's model—a highly eroticized figure in popular male culture—added yet another layer to her performance. Katie N. Johnson argues that "Nethersole heightened this performative citationality by making explicit her various roles: as muse, as Grecian Goddess, and as eroticized spectacle" in order to "denaturaliz[e] the representational apparatus that objectified her at the very same time she utilized it towards her own ends."[153] In complete control of the image she projected onstage, Nethersole challenged contemporary gender prescriptions and implicated male spectators in the process.

Not surprisingly, given their distaste for feminized spectacle, most theater critics panned *Sapho*, but the production's notoriety, as well as Nethersole's reputation for elegant dressing, ensured its success with female audiences. According to a count made by a reporter for the *New York World*, women outnumbered men at a matinee performance of *Sapho* by 1,509 to 178.[154] For their part, male critics were dismayed and alarmed by the overwhelmingly female presence at the show. "When I am at a play in which an unnatural, idealized courtesan is the principal character," one critic wrote, "and when I look about and see in the audience shop-girls, factory-girls, typewriters and society girls, and when I note the look on their faces, you must forgive me if I decline to believe that these young persons are learning nothing but a great moral lesson."[155] Other critics noted the absence of "the great middle class, which preserves the moral equipoise of the community" and disparaged the "morbid crowds" of "knowing" women, which included "a large proportion of girl bachelors of the Tenderloin" identifiable only by "their gayer attire, their intensely up-to-date air and the fact that they snickered at the risqué lines about half a second earlier than the rest."[156] These women, the critics implied, were no better than *Sapho* herself.

When *Sapho* continued to attract large crowds of pleasure-seeking women, conservative newspapers launched a campaign to close what they perceived to be an immoral and dangerous production. On February 21, 1900, the police arrested and charged Nethersole, her leading man Hamilton Revelle, her manager Marcus Mayer, and Theodore Moss, the lessee of Wallack's Theatre, with indecency. On March 5, *Sapho* was forced to close until after the trial, but when on April 5 a jury found the accused innocent, the production resumed to capacity houses until Nethersole left for Europe at the end of May. Audiences now apparently erupted into spontaneous bursts of applause when the actress appeared in the see-through Greek gown, rewarding her for her legal victory.[157]

Through her erotic portrayal of Fanny Legrand, as well as her role as the show's producer, Nethersole represented an exciting and daring role model for the shop girls, factory girls, typewriters, and society girls who attended *Sapho* in droves. For those who gained entry to the show through a "treating" arrangement, whereby they repaid their male companions with sexual favors, Nethersole's deviant portrayal of a courtesan may have alerted them to the kind of power they could wield through sexual exchange.[158] Some women may also have been attracted to Nethersole herself. Certainly the words "Mama's girlhood crush" found on the back of one of her cabinet photographs hint at the potentially Sapphic nature of "Mama's" imaginary relationship with her "crush."[159] Although the appearance of the word "crush" alone can not be taken as proof of same-sex desire, especially in light of the often passionate declarations of friendship that turn-of-the-century women made to one another, it nevertheless calls attention to the possibility of star-fan relationships infused with sexual desire and longing.[160]

Although it is impossible to know exactly what the girl who wore "three Nethersole bracelets" to a dance intended her friends and dance partners to see—independence, sexual availability, support for Nethersole's court case, sexual desire for the actress, an awareness of stage-inspired fads—her decision to signal Nethersole not once, not twice, but three times on her body indicates that, if nothing else, she wanted others to notice her copy act. Her decision to emulate an actress best known for her "Fallen Women" characters as opposed to an actual prostitute further suggests that she was interested in expressing her sexuality but nevertheless wanted others to recognize that she, like Nethersole, was playing a role.

In 1913, the writer Eleanor Ames enthused that the "psychology of dress" as practiced by actresses and others signaled modern women's growing determination to defy expectations and make meanings for themselves:

It is charged that the modern woman is clothes-mad. In reality she was never so sane. She is daring to be herself. She is defying the bellwether, the fashion arbiter, who has been laying down hard and fast rules, and is asserting in an independence of action the independence of mind she has long kept under subjection. She wears her clothes because they mean something to her. *It is difficult to say just how great an influence the stage has had in helping the modern woman find herself* [my emphasis].[161]

In their embrace of contemporary scientific theories of color and human psychology, actresses proved themselves intellectually astute—modeling a kind of modernity that celebrated a woman's mental capacities as well as her physical attributes. Moreover, by identifying women's inner longings as legitimate and offering very real strategies for individual expression, they positioned women as artistic creators, producers of meaning, and interpreters of their own psyches. Against those who charged that female consumers were becoming mere automatons—slaves to the fashion system—actresses celebrated the art of fashion and encouraged women to engage in productive acts of imagination, vividly demonstrating, in the words of the performance scholar Diana Taylor, that "[n]ot everyone comes to 'culture' or modernity through writing."[162]

But experimentation alone is not enough to bring about social change. Although as Jill Dolan writes, "[T]heatre can move us toward understanding the possibility of something better, can train our imaginations, inspire our dreams and fuel our desires in ways that might lead to incremental cultural change," imagining an alternative reality is quite different from bringing that reality into being.[163] By the mid-1910s, as department store managers and theater producers adopted new techniques for displaying the fashionable body, the limitations of fashion politics became all too clear.

Chapter 5
The Theatrical Fashion Show on Broadway and Sixth Avenue

In December 1914, *Variety*'s "the Skirt" reported that one of the new novelty acts at the New York Roof was a "Fashion Parade." Although she acknowledged that women in the audience liked the display, "the Skirt" was not impressed. To her, the act was little more than a stripped down version of a department store fashion show, and while an effective " 'ad' for the man who had designed the gowns," it was hardly a "novelty." If women "could see the same thing at any of the leading stores where a similar parade occurs at the beginning of each season," she asked, what was the point of staging the same show in a cabaret setting, especially when many of the gowns worn by women in the audience were just as beautiful as those onstage?[1]

"The Skirt's" dismissal of the "Fashion Parade" as an uninspired copy of a department store fashion show points to an interesting shift in the relationship between theaters and department stores in the 1910s. Although store managers continued to use Broadway shows to generate consumer interest, they increasingly challenged the theater's privileged status as a site of elite fashion display with their own highly coordinated spectacles. Not to be outdone, theater managers responded by incorporating imaginative versions of the fashion show into vaudeville, musical comedy, cabaret, and the revue. Yet as "the Skirt's" comments suggest, theatrical fashion shows had to offer much more than the average department store show. Why, then, given the challenges of outdoing the country's leading department stores, did theater managers bother to compete? What did they stand to gain in appropriating the fashion show? The answer, I would suggest, has to do with the way the fashion show's incorporation of assembly line processes presented a new technology for displaying the female body. Positioned as glorified objects, fashion models/showgirls offered a version of female modernity that was alarmingly deficient compared to that advanced by actresses in vaudeville and the legitimate stage and therefore ideal for the purposes of Broadway impresarios intent on building their national brands.[2]

The transformation of the fashion show from an elite salon gathering into mass entertainment radically reoriented the way Americans looked at fashion and viewed themselves as consumers. Throughout the late nineteenth century, most fashion shows were exclusive, private affairs, staged by leading couturiers for wealthy and influential clients. But while "[t]he ideas of showing gowns on models [was] not new," as the *Merchants Record and Show Window* explained in 1909, the "scheme" was still "comparatively new in America."[3] By 1908, however, the rapid growth of the ready-to-wear fashion industry as well as heightened interest in Paris couture made it not only feasible but also highly desirable for department stores and other commercial institutions to produce their own elaborate displays.[4]

The convenience, accessibility, and visual appeal of the department store fashion show made it a popular alternative to going to the theater, where the matinee tickets for "legitimate" drama ranged between seventy-five cents and two dollars.[5] Audiences at a Broadway society drama might see twenty or thirty different ensembles in a three hour period; at a department store fashion show they could see twice as many if not more outfits in half the time.[6] Free and open to the public, these shows provided a more democratic venue, where white-collar workers, matinee girls, suburban housewives, and new immigrants could find membership within the "imagined community of dress" that had once been the exclusive preserve of the rich.[7] United by the collective experience of live performance, these women escaped, if only temporarily, the material realities of their daily lives and entertained the possibility of social advancement through consumption.[8]

The fashion scholar Caroline Evans sees the democratization of the fashion show as "directly linked to the rise of mass production in the wake of industrialization."[9] Combining the glamour and excitement of the society ballroom with Taylorist techniques for regulating the body, the fashion show remade potentially wayward female bodies into standardized commodities. As assembly line, distribution network, and show window in one, it represented the symbolic convergence of production and consumption; yet in its imitation of theatrical spectacle, it concealed the real costs of the labor that had produced it. Unlike society plays, historical dramas, and even musical comedies, the fashion show dispensed with character interpretation or emotional display, fixing the semiotic indeterminacy that female performers often exploited to their advantage. Indeed, as much as the fashion show format provided what Evans describes as a "fluid and theatrical space" for the "performance of gender as image and idea," those performing within that space were carefully monitored by external observers—designers, directors, producers, choreographers—who selected the clothes they wore, choreographed their movements, and created the framework through which audiences viewed their performances.[10]

In thus privileging the work of the designer, choreographer, and director over that of the individual performer, the fashion show profoundly effected gender dynamics within the commercial theater and reoriented the way female audiences related to female performers.[11] Walking in procession along a conveyor-belt-like runway, the fashion show model, and her theatrical sister the showgirl, represented both the loss of individuality within mass culture and the promise that with the appropriate consumption of goods one might find membership within a larger community and perhaps even win a moment in the spotlight. Yet despite diminishing the agency of the individual female performer, the fashion show also opened up new career opportunities for female designers and producers, who used the show to challenge gender hierarchies within the world of theatrical production and refute government efforts to circumscribe consumer behavior. Following the outbreak of World War I, these women also used the framework of the fashion show to offer lively and even controversial opinions about the role of the female consumer in wartime. The goal of this chapter then is to consider the cultural work of the theatrical fashion show as it moved from fashion salon to department store to theater, and to situate its rise within the context of emerging national debates about consumption, citizenship, and patriotism.

The Americanization of the Fashion Show

John Wanamaker was the first department store magnate to realize the fashion show's potential for mass spectacle in the fall of 1908, when he staged a "fashion Fête de Paris" in the theater of his store in Philadelphia. An obvious nod to Paul Poiret and other innovators of the Directoire line, the fête recalled the splendor of the court of Napoleon and Josephine, complete with a detailed re-creation of the emperor's coronation. Designers decorated the store theater in red and black and positioned larger-than-life picture frames on both sides of the stage behind which "living models" posed in *tableaux vivants*. One by one the models were "brought . . . to life" by Napoleon's young pages and escorted down the walkway and onto the stage where they showed their clothes to advantage.[12] Mirroring the commercial theater's subtle promotion of designer goods and other fashion products, the fête's theatricality disguised its more practical function, that is, selling clothes, under the guise of entertainment. Beyond educating customers in the latest style trends, however, Wanamaker's spectacle offered customers something that most commercial theaters could not: the chance to consummate their consumer desires without leaving the building.

As spectacle and advertisement in one, the fashion show represented the ideal solution for department stores looking to attract matinee theatergoers to their establishments and circumvent licensing laws, which prevented department stores from staging plays and other theatrical events on their premises. Indeed, despite their close relationships with Broadway, department stores had tried for years to upstage commercial theaters. As early as 1896, the *Dramatic Mirror* reported that one of the major Sixth Avenue department stores was planning to present vaudeville entertainment as an enticement to consumers. The unnamed Chicago-based firm (most likely Marshall Field's) aimed to keep shoppers from straying outside the premises by offering free admission to "all purchasers of goods" with "seats graded to correspond with the value of purchases."[13] By 1905, *Variety* reported that "half a dozen of the big shops [were throwing] in a free vaudeville with purchases of pickles or patterns . . . in a bid for the Christmas trade." These shows tended to be mediocre affairs—with performers "of the museum grade"—but because they were free *and* staged without a license, Broadway managers viewed them as a commercial menace. "It is not fair to the managers who are compelled to make heavy payments to the city for the privilege of conducting places of amusement that these stores should be permitted to give free performances untrammeled by the exactions of the Police and Building departments," *Variety* argued, "especially when the Christmas shopping makes business bad at the regular houses." Broadway theaters depended on their proximity to department stores to attract female consumers on their way to or from an afternoon of shopping; department store spectacles kept these consumers from coming. "Many persons who go shopping might drop into Proctor's or Keith's on the way home did they not find free entertainment in the places where they spend the rest of their money," *Variety* concluded. Finally, the disgruntled Broadway managers took their case to the police, and the unlicensed shows were forced to close.[14]

Despite licensing restrictions, however, department store managers continued to find ways to bring theatrical acts into their establishments. In 1912, *Variety* reported that "[o]ne of the Sixth avenue department stores" had staged a cabaret show in the store lunchroom, much to the delight of the female shoppers, who "fell for the idea hard." In the same article, *Variety* reported that John R. Butler, the manager of Siegel-Coopers, had spoken with a booking agent at the Knickerbocker Theatre about the possibility of holding cabaret performances in all Siegel-Cooper stores. According to *Variety*, "A tentative agreement was made with the agent to supply attractions when the plan was in shape to be carried through."[15] The department store managers' interest in the cabaret was likely sparked by a recent New York City court decision, which ruled that theatrical licenses were only necessary if the show included the use of scenery and a stage. Restaurants and other cabaret locations, including department stores, could circumvent licensing laws simply by staging the acts in and around dining or shopping patrons.[16]

But whereas cabaret licenses prevented managers from using scenery and a stage, the special licenses required for all "live model" shows do not seem to have placed any such restrictions on department store management.[17] If fact, trade journal descriptions of department store fashion shows indicate that leading stores such as Macy's and Gimbel's spent thousands of dollars staging elaborate spectacles that rivaled anything seen in Broadway's first-class theaters.[18] The fashion show's function as a marketing strategy offers one possible explanation for this regulatory discrepancy. As an event that was essentially a prolonged advertisement for clothing and accessories, the fashion show may have given department stores the perfect excuse for staging theatrical spectacles complete with props, scenery, and a stage.

Echoing the strategies of Charles Frohman, department store managers made much of their relationships with prominent Parisian designers, hoping to simultaneously attract large crowds of middle-class shoppers and the patronage of those who could afford couture fashion. In the fall of 1913, for example, Wanamaker's, Gimbel's, and Macy's promoted the "Minaret" designs created by Paul Poiret for the Paris production of *Le Minaret* and created rival spectacles that recalled the exotic world of the play.[19] Like society dramas and other stage spectacles, these shows acquainted mass audiences with Parisian styles well before their arrival in the United States, helping to create a ready market for foreign luxury goods.

Few department stores could compete with Gimbel's or Wanamaker's on the level of spectacle, but that didn't stop them from producing their own displays. By 1915, "the fashion show could be found in nearly every sizable city in the country" from Murphy's Dry Goods Co. in Sherman, Texas to Pond and Bailey "proprietors of a woman's garments and furnishings store" in Janesville, Wisconsin.[20] Fashion show staging techniques varied from town to town, depending on the individual store's resources and the creative abilities of those responsible for producing the shows. One of the earliest and most innovative shows was the "Style Parade" at L. Dimond and Sons in Providence,

Rhode Island in 1911, which made clever use of the store's show windows to entice passersby. The show began in the suit department on an upper floor like most other fashion shows, but after the models had paraded through the department, they took the elevator to the first floor, where they entered a curtained show window. When the models were in position, the curtain was drawn back, and they were revealed to curious window-gazers outside.[21]

Such display strategies proved troublesome, however, if the crowds grew too large for the stores to handle. "The policy of showing living models *in the window* is open to question," the *Dry Goods Economist* reported in 1911. "In one or two instances, the crowds attracted have been so great as to block the sidewalk and cause the municipal authorities to demand that the living model be taken from the window." In some small towns the sheer novelty of seeing "living models" attracted as many as four thousand to five thousand people in a single afternoon, requiring spectators to stand on counters or tables to see the show.[22] At the height of the craze, fashion shows threatened to disrupt civic order to such an extent that police in New York and other cities required managers to take out licenses for all "live model" shows and even threatened to ban them altogether. In an attempt to prevent overcrowding, some stores began staging their fashion shows in local halls, theaters, and opera houses. This strategy proved problematic, however, when producers in vaudeville, cabaret, and the revue began staging their own shows (a subject I will return to shortly).[23]

Living Models

Although the *Merchants Record and Show Window* expressed some hesitation about the use of "living models" in department store displays, writing in 1909 that "[i]t is not to be understood that living models are in any way to supplant wax figures in the general display of gowns," others recognized that such models were an essential element of the fashion show's success.[24] The appeal of the "live" helps to explain why department stores didn't simply show fashion films from leading couture houses, as they might well have done. In 1913, Paul Poiret toured the United States using a film of his Parisian mannequins to illustrate his fashion lectures, forgoing the costs and logistical challenges of transporting an entire company of mannequins.[25] That same year the American company Kinemacolour produced a popular series of films showing "the newest designs of Paquin and the other French moguls of fashion paraded by living models and in their true colours."[26] Despite their popularity, however, fashion films could not yet compete with the experience of seeing a fashion show live, which perhaps explains why Poiret's rival, Madame Paquin, brought six of her "most attractive manikins [*sic*]" along with her when she toured the United States in 1914.[27]

Public fascination with live fashion show models coincided with recent developments in print advertising, whereby advertising agents argued that the previous practice of associating goods with illustrations of attractive women lacked "real human interest and sincerity." Instead, agents such as William Colgate of the Gagnier Advertising Agency in Toronto argued that photographs of "living models"—real men and women—would "carry a far more convincing appeal."[28] Advertisers had to be careful, though, about selecting appropriate models that would not distract or displease consumers.[29] The Globe-Wernicke Company, makers of office furniture, met this challenge by hiring "men, women and children who type the general run of people who would naturally make up the groups that the pictures portray." The advertising manager, Dave E. Bloch, told *Printers' Ink* that the company believed consumers would find it easier to identify with average-looking men and women than with "a young person of . . . radiant beauty."[30]

Ironically, many of the Globe-Wernicke models were, in fact, up-and-coming actors and actresses. In 1914, the promising ingénue Alice Brady, the daughter of the theater manager William Brady and the actress Grace George, modeled for Globe-Wernicke just as she was beginning to attract public notice. Bloch nevertheless insisted that Brady was "versatile enough to be able to pose in many of the pictures for the Globe-Wernicke campaign." This emphasis on versatility contradicts Bloch's earlier statement, suggesting that Globe-Wernicke's primary criteria for selecting models was *not* average looks per se, but an ability to portray "averageness" convincingly. "The models used in posing [are] endowed with much more than the average ability to act a silent, convincing part in a story-telling picture," he explained. Globe-Wernicke models did not play themselves—they played ideal consumers.[31]

Department store managers adopted a similar strategy, hiring "living models" that represented a variety of looks, shapes, and ages, making it possible for every shopper to find his or her idealized likeness onstage (figure 5.1). "Some of them are short; others are tall," the *Merchants Record and Show Window* observed in 1909. "There are blonds, brunettes, young girls and matured matrons, plump and thin." Although some of these models were trained "demonstrators," many were store employees, saleswomen and cashiers with little or no stage experience, while others were "young ladies of the best society." In hiring a range of physical types, store managers aimed to give "the

Figure 5.1. A model for one of Gimbel Brothers' fashion shows, ca. 1913. Picture Collection, The Branch Libraries, The New York Public Library, Astor, Lenox and Tilden Foundations.

prospective shopper . . . a very accurate idea as to just how a certain gown will appear on herself."[32]

By 1911, however, trade journals strongly discouraged managers from hiring amateur models and laid out a specific set of criteria for the ideal model. "It is essential that the model shall, in the first place, have a *ladylike* appearance and what the actor-folk call 'a good stage presence,'" a writer for the *Dry Goods Economist* advised. "She must not only have a graceful figure, but her face, carriage and expression must accord with the costume and with the style." Managers should avoid hiring their own employees as models, the article continued, "for as a rule, they do not have the appearance that would show off the garments to best advantage and they would be too embarrassed in such a position." By contrast, professional models would "raise the tone of the store" and help educate the customers in proper dress and comportment. Perhaps most importantly, they would retain the patronage and respect of the "discriminating few . . . the ones whose trade is most desired." "Good" models were now expected to possess many of the same qualities expected of young actresses: poise, confidence, and the knowledge of "how a *lady* ought to look and how clothes ought to be worn."[33] It was no longer acceptable for a model to be fat or ungainly; she had to be attractive, fashionable, and thin.

The gradual professionalization of department store modeling in the 1910s signaled a dramatic shift in the way managers viewed their customers and envisioned themselves as cultural arbiters. Rather than encourage women to identify with a range of physical types, they joined theater managers and advertisers in promoting highly standardized yet undeniably appealing images of white American womanhood. But while department store managers may have had aspirations of becoming theatrical impresarios, they could hardly compete with producers like Florenz Ziegfeld and the Shuberts who seized upon the fashion show as a highly promising mechanism for containing, manipulating, and exploiting the female body in the name of fashion. Indeed, the fashion show, a series of gowns displayed in quick succession, was ideally suited for the speed, variety, and continuous action of the modern Broadway revue.[34]

Commodifying the American Girl

Florenz Ziegfeld first introduced the fashion show into the *Follies of 1912* with "A Palace of Beauty," a number that singled out individual showgirls as they slowly walked across the stage to the refrains of "Beautiful, Beautiful Girl" before taking their positions in a group tableau. Noting the increased emphasis on costuming, the *New York Times* described the act as "a gorgeous succession of effective costumes with girls who can carry them with good effect." The *Dramatic Mirror* was similarly impressed with the "[dazzling] array of pretty girls" on the stage. "When they are all there [in the final tableau], it is only a matter of opinion which one appeals most, but Lillian Loraine [*sic*] has the prominence."[35] As this last comment suggests, the showgirl's moment alone onstage was incredibly brief. Once over, she rejoined her fellow showgirls on the stage to provide a pleasing backdrop for the star performer.

The Shuberts also introduced elements of the fashion show into their Winter Garden productions at this time, making optimum use of the theater's new runway, a platform that extended from the middle of the stage into the audience, anticipating the modern catwalk.[36] In a number from *The Passing Show of 1914*, showgirls promenaded up and down the runway, first with evening wraps, and then without them, mimicking the staging of an elite couture show. At the end of the number, they returned to the stage and posed in a line across the stage, confronting the audience with of "a bewildering mass of color and glitter."[37]

Florenz Ziegfeld seems to have recognized the effectiveness of the Winter Garden runway for when he opened *Ziegfeld Midnight Frolic* on the roof of the New Amsterdam Theatre the following year, one of the most unique stage features was a long runway of clear glass that extended above the heads of the audience. Air vents situated randomly along the runway gave theatergoers a titillating glimpse of the chorus girls' legs (and possibly more) as they danced and paraded across it. This runway was the invention of the newly hired Austrian designer Joseph Urban, who would go on to create some of the most elaborate settings for Ziegfeld's *Follies* and *Frolic*. But when he joined the *Follies* in 1915, Urban was also working as a designer for Gimbel's fashion shows, where he had recently "broke[n] new ground . . . splitting the promenade stage into two, one half going stage right, the other stage left."[38] Given the long history of swapping techniques and employees between theaters and department stores, it is certainly possible that the *Midnight Frolic* runway was a "sexed up" version of the Gimbel's runway.

The incorporation of the fashion show into the revue revolutionized the showgirl number by thrusting showgirls, quite literally, into the spotlight.[39] The showgirl herself was not new; indeed, by the turn of the century showgirl numbers were standard fare in most musical comedies.[40] What was new, however, was the presentation and performance of the showgirl. Before the introduction of the fashion show, showgirl numbers usually appeared at the end of the production—a visual accompaniment to the dramatic action intended to overwhelm the audience with "masses of color." This effect was largely achieved by dressing showgirls in gowns that were either identical or complementary in cut, style, and color, and positioning them in a cluster or line near the star performer. For example, in the 1901 production of *The Little Duchess*, a star vehicle for Ziegfeld's common-law wife, Anna Held, twelve statuesque showgirls flanked the diminutive Held in gowns copied from Lillian Russell's latest production, *Hoity Toity* (figure 5.2). Held, of course, appeared in a contrasting gown that further set her apart from the showgirls at her side. This clever staging called attention to Held's exotic beauty and her status as the star of the show—a crown jewel within a setting of semi-precious stones— while poking good-natured fun at Russell, Held's close friend and chief rival at the time. By 1905, the *Theatre Magazine* observed that almost every musical comedy "held as a *pièce de resistance* a number of stunning model dresses, to be exhibited upon as many stunning models at just the precise moment that in a legitimate play would present a big climax."[41]

The fashion show reinvented the traditional showgirl number by promising each girl a moment in the spotlight. Rather than pose behind the star in a mass clump, each "fashion model" showgirl now crossed the stage by herself in a gown that bore little resemblance to the others on display (figure 5.3). No longer the "girl of the crowd," she stood alone, a unique individual who walked in time with others but nevertheless maintained her individuality. The revue's incorporation of the fashion show and the corresponding elevation of the showgirl can thus be seen as the analogue to the star system's advancement of charming or attractive performers. But the showgirl's performance of individuality was limited in a way that the legitimate or vaudeville star's was not. For as much as the technology of the star system circumscribed performers' lives, individual actresses could nevertheless call attention to their feelings and desires through the "psychology of dress" and engage in a lively dialogue with female theatergoers over questions of gender, sexuality, class, and modernity. Showgirls, by contrast, had no public identities other than the ones bestowed upon them by designers, choreographers, and producers.[42] Compared to the semiotically rich actress, ghosted by her fame and visibly public life, showgirls were blank slates, visually appealing alternatives to wax or wooden mannequins without a past or future, the ideal antidote to the highly vocal, politically motivated New Woman.[43]

Indeed, while the fashion revues staged by Ziegfeld and his rivals appealed to women, the displays of scantily yet expensively clad female bodies were clearly intended for the eyes of the "Tired Business Men" (commonly

Figure 5.2. Anna Held and the chorus from *The Little Duchess*, ca. 1902—a crown jewel within a setting of semi-precious stones. Photograph by Gilbert and Bacon, Philadelphia. *Theatre Magazine* (January 1903): 21.

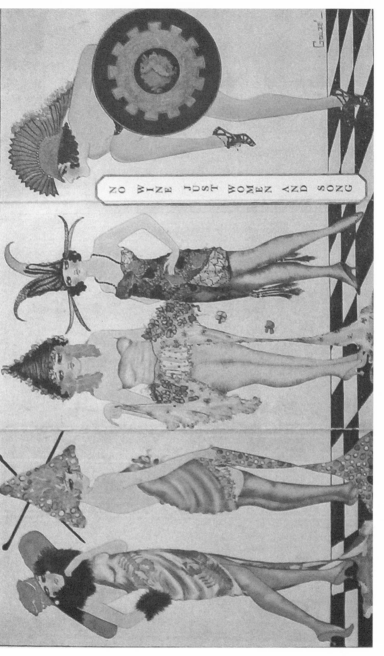

Figure 5.3. Five of the "Ten Types of Winter Garden Beauties" featured in the Shuberts' *Passing Show of 1916*. Individuated showgirls got a moment in the spotlight. Illustration by Gouzé. Courtesy of the Shubert Archives.

referred to by critics and industry writers as the "TBM"). To these down-trodden white-collar workers, many of whom struggled to find new ways to assert their masculinity within the stultifying structures of corporate middle management, the playful *Follies* showgirl represented a voyeuristic reward.[44] Tall and beautiful but without any of her own opinions or the means to communicate them, the showgirl was a finely crafted commodity as available and exchangeable as the clothes on her back. The TBM may not have controlled his own destiny at the office or even the home, but at the theater he could freely fantasize about possessing one of the sexualized objects on display. The scopophilic model of male spectatorship associated with the revue fashion show thus facilitated the production of modern male subjectivity, marking it as distinctly different from the "overdressed dramas" that Alan Dale and other critics decried. Unlike these displays, the raison d'être of the revue fashion spectacle was the female body, not the clothes she wore.[45]

Producers' interest in showcasing individual showgirls to attract male as well as female spectators inevitably translated into more rigorous standards for selecting chorus members. In October 1912, *Variety* reported that sixteen young women had been hired as "models" for Sam Bernard's production entitled *All for the Ladies*, which was choreographed by Ned Wayburn. "Their stage duties," explained *Variety*, "will be principally parading across the stage during the second act, while wearing gowns that cost the management $300 each." For their efforts, the models would receive $50 a week, a significant increase from the standard showgirl wage of $40 a week that reflects the producer's desire to attract "an exclusive collection of young women, with faces not familiar to the Broadway clientele, and forms that can carry the ultra-fashionable mode in 'clothes.' "[46] This willingness to spend more to get an "*exclusive collection* of young women" (my emphasis)—a descriptor most often associated with luxury goods—suggests one way that Broadway managers attempted to outdo department store fashion shows. The commodities in *All for the Ladies*—both the dresses and the women who wore them—would far surpass anything on display in a department store.

The revue's satirical outlook on modern life and its appeal to the cultural elite further distinguished the revue fashion show from similar department store displays.[47] Working from the French "revue" tradition and capitalizing on the popularity of such "smart magazines" as *The Smart Set* and *Vanity Fair*, Broadway revues used the scantiest of plots—for example, a descent into hell, a visit to New York—to make fun of contemporary figures, fads, and events, even lampooning current Broadway hits.[48] The program for *The Passing Show of 1912*, for example, promised audiences "[a] kaleidoscopic almanac in seven scenes presenting the comic aspect of many important events, political, theatrical, and otherwise, and embracing the sunny side of 'Kismet,' 'Bought and Paid For,' 'Bunty Pulls the Strings,' 'A Butterfly on the Wheel,' [etc.]."[49] According to the critic Louis Sherwin, the show possessed "a certain riotous irreverence that takes a fling at everybody and everything that happens to be of topical interest."[50] The historical predecessors of *The Daily Show* and *The Colbert Report*, revues addressed an audience of informed and, for the most part, socially advantaged spectators who enjoyed celebrating and critiquing American culture, politics, and society.

Given the revue's decidedly modern focus, it is certainly no surprise that fashion and the fashion show—which like the revue mimicked the modern city in its structure, complexity, and movement—was a favorite target for jokes, sketches, and songs.[51] Stage directors for the Shubert's *Passing Show* series often integrated fashion shows into a scene or comic number set in a plausible location like a fashion salon. The program for the *Passing Show of 1916*, for example, lists a scene in "Madam Faibisie's Dressmaking Establishment" (a reference to the New York designer Faibisy, who was credited with designing the gowns for the act) with such characters as "Lady Bluff Gordon," an obvious reference to Lucile, Lady Duff Gordon, and "Mons. Tapan," likely a reference to the New York designer Tappé.[52] As the following excerpt from the production script suggests, the centerpiece of the scene was a "burlesque dress parade" with mannequins dressed in bizarre creations:

(*Waltz music is played, curtains are drawn and burlesque dress parade. First two mannikins, one woman with dresses to knee, other woman with dresses to ankle.*)

Tapan: That's the latest style suitable for mother to go walking with daughter. (*Next mannikin advances, girl with hat way over her eyes, furs around neck, dresses to knee, shoes laced up the back, should be as burlesquay [sic] as possible.*) This is the latest stylish creation for summer. This is called "Nature is Cruel." The man who designed this has since been shot. The woman is hiding under her hat, wears fur in the summer. This gives a Turkish bath effect up to her neck. (*Indicates shoes*) You will note the gun boats are tied in the rear. The whole effect is guaranteed to chase men away. (*Next mannikin enters. Woman with bare back dress cut to waist.*) This new style is called "In a draft." If you want to show your backbone try this. This is suitable for bareback dancing by ladies who don't sneeze. (*Next mannikin enters.*) This is a pretty style. It's called the New York, New Haven and Hartford. The train is missing. It turns the lady into a wreck. . . .[53]

The intentionally "burlesquay" act makes the most of its subject, displaying showgirls clad in "bareback dresses" and other revealing outfits, while poking fun at the pretensions of designers like Tappé and Lucile, especially the latter's practice of giving her gowns exotic names.

Subsequent Shubert revues and musical comedies responded in a similarly cheeky manner to consumer trends and the fashion show. In 1915 the production *Maid in America* lampooned the recent "Made in America" campaign with a song that identified a range of supposedly foreign products— "Havana smokes," Russian caviar, Viennese operas—that had all been "made in the U.S.A." Another number parodied Irene Castle's status as a style icon by dressing the lead performer Rosika Dolly in a replica of the dancer's *Watch Your Step* gown.[54] In 1918, the production of *Over the Top* returned to familiar territory with a scene set in the salon of Mlle. Celeste, in which characters named Mlle. Lingeria, Mlle. Gown, Mlle. Corset, and Mlle. Stocking paraded about the stage, representing fashion objects as opposed to fashion models. The scene starred Justine Johnston as herself, Vivien Oakland as Mme. Celeste, and Fred and Adele Astaire, who performed a "Gown Dance."[55] Consistent with the revue's tradition of turning chorus girls into commodities, the mannequins in this scene were conflated with the fashion articles they represented, although names like "Lingeria" and the appellation "Mlle." also suggest that the performers may have managed to maintain some semblance of individual subjectivity.

Yet the gleeful irreverence found in *The Passing Show of 1916* and *Over the Top* is noticeably absent from the later *Follies* fashion parades, most of which seem to have been performed as musical numbers without any accompanying dialogue. In the "Garden of Girls" number from the *Follies of 1917*, for example, showgirls dressed as flowers emerged from a trap door when "the prima donna intrusted [*sic*] with their description in song sprinkles flower-seeds upon their decorated heads."[56] While undoubtedly humorous, this number is a departure from the self-aware sensibility that characterized the Shubert shows and which had in fact been a feature of earlier *Follies*. The *Follies of 1910*, for example, offered a comical commentary on the couturier Paul Poiret's restrictive new style with a number entitled "That Horrible Hobble Skirt." In the act, showgirls identically dressed in Poiret's creation literally hobbled around the stage, demonstrating in a humorously graphic way the folly of the latest Paris trend.[57] By contrast, the later *Follies* fashion parades adopted a much more celebratory view of fashion, glorifying commodities alongside the tall, elegant showgirls who wore them.

This movement away from parodic self-reflexivity can be explained, at least in part, by noting that many of the designers parodied in *The Passing Show* actually *worked* for the *Ziegfeld Follies*. Tappé, for example, designed hats for some of the leading *Follies* stars, including Lillian Lorraine, and Lucile not only designed costumes for *Follies* headliners and showgirls alike but also *staged* the "Garden of Girls" number.[58] Her involvement with the *Follies* from 1915 to 1919 thus precluded the kind of satirical comedy that characterized the *Passing Show* fashion shows, promoting instead a model of fashion spectacle that glorified the female body. Indeed, further investigation of Lucile's work for the *Follies* suggests that the designer may have played a much larger part in the invention of the Ziegfeld Girl than previous accounts have allowed.

Fashioning the Ziegfeld Girl

Historians acknowledge Lucile's role in the "invention" of the *Follies* showgirl, but they tend to attribute greater significance to Ziegfeld, the scenographer Joseph Urban, and the choreographer Ned Wayburn, perhaps influenced by contemporary perceptions of the costume designer's role and Ziegfeld's own persuasive self-promotion. Indeed, as much as Ziegfeld profited from his association with leading designers, he rarely publicized their names, "relegat[ing] costume design credits to the small print in the back of the programme," while simultaneously emphasizing *his* involvement in the creation and selection of stage costumes.[59] In 1915, Lucile's first year with the *Follies*, he told a reporter, "[F]or the last four months I have been spending [eight hours a day] every day with the dressmaker, the bookmaker, and the milliner." In addition to collaborating with designers, Ziegfeld explained that he had a hand in the design process as well:

My process of working out my ideas with clothes is the result of years of experience. I never fail to make a note any time a suggestion for a dress may chance to come to me or which I may see. For instance, I read and study every fashion and society magazine published in this country and Europe, and whenever I see a photograph of a costume that strikes me as pretty or original, or having the germ of an idea which I might subsequently elaborate upon, I clip it and file it away.[60]

By presenting himself as a skilled observer of stylistic trends, Ziegfeld drew attention away from designers like the flamboyant Lucile, whose involvement with the *Follies* may have detracted from his own status as image maker. Although in a 1924 article, Ziegfeld discussed Lucile's contribution to the *Follies*—without actually acknowledging her by name and long after she had ceased working for the *Follies*—he continued to downplay her role in the invention of the Ziegfeld showgirl.[61]

Ziegfeld had reason to worry; Lucile was one of the most influential figures in the development of the modern fashion show, a show woman of exceptional talent who bridged the international worlds of theater and fashion with her elegant, colorful designs (figure 5.4). Born Lucy Christiana Sutherland in 1862, she achieved recognition as a dressmaker in London in the early 1890s when her first husband abandoned her for another woman. Divorced and penniless, she began a dressmaking business out of her home and soon became a favorite with society women, who enjoyed her unique designs, especially her frilly lingerie, and her emphasis on creating gowns to suit her clients' individual "personalities." "I always saw the woman, not the frock as detached from her," she later explained, "and so women loved my clothes, because women are above all other things personal in every thought and action."[62] Lucile's first foray into theatrical costume design came in 1897 when Sir Charles Wyndham hired her to design the gowns for the London production of *The Liars*. The delicate chiffon gowns she created for Irene Vanbrugh, Mary Moore, and Cynthia Brooke, all of which were intended to "harmonize with the characteristics" of the individual performers, established Lucile's reputation as a designer and brought her "a long series of plays to dress."[63]

In 1900, shortly after her second marriage to Sir Cosmo Duff Gordon, Lucile decided to use the knowledge she had gained designing for West End society dramas and musicals to transform her Hanover Square showroom into a mini-theater. "I had a soft, rich carpet laid down in the big showroom, and beautiful, gray brocade curtains to tone with it were hung across the windows," she recalls in her memoirs. "At one end of the room I had a stage, a miniature affair, all hung with misty olive chiffon curtains, as the background, which created the atmosphere I wanted."[64] Specially installed limelights illuminated the stage and focused attention on the intricate details of her gowns. To enliven this theatrical mise-en-scène, Lucile hired six mannequins, "glorious, goddess-like girls . . . who would be able to do justice to my dresses." After an intensive training regime, which involved trips to the hairdressers and long hours spent walking with books on their heads, these former shopgirls and apprentices became "the incarnation of enchanting womanhood."[65] To complete her mannequins' metamorphoses, Lucile renamed each girl, replacing "hopelessly incongruous" (and recognizably working-class) names such as Susie and Kathleen Rose with exotic names such as Gamela, Dolores, and Hebe—names that were "in harmony" with the individual mannequins' personalities.[66]

Although Lucile was hardly the first couturier to hire mannequins to wear her gowns, she was one of the first to fully exploit their theatrical potential and sexual appeal. Throughout the nineteenth century, most designers displayed their models—the term referring to the actual gowns, not the

Figure 5.4. Portrait of Lucile (Lady Duff Gordon) ca. 1915–17. The self-proclaimed inventor of the fashion show, Lucile's stage credits included *Watch Your Step* and the *Ziegfeld Follies*. Courtesy Library of Congress Prints and Photographs Division.

women wearing them—on wooden or wax figures; those who used "live" mannequins insisted that they wear a black satin, tunic-like undergarment to prevent their designs from becoming stained or otherwise tainted by contact with the skin. Deprived of all personality and emotional expression, these mannequins were little more than wooden figures themselves, cold and impersonal.[67] Lucile took the opposite approach, ensuring that her mannequins looked and behaved like ladies, while staging their performances to attract the attention of society men.[68] Lucile further heightened the dramatic and the erotic aspects of the spectacle by breaking away from the tradition of using numbers to distinguish gowns, instead giving her creations flamboyantly erotic titles such as "Passion's Thrall," "Do You Love Me?" and "A Frenzied Song of Amorous Things."[69] When strung together, these titled gowns worked subtextually to communicate ideas that might otherwise have been too risqué for an audience of respectable women.[70]

Lucile's theatrical mannequin parades became the talk of London society and the designer's business flourished (figure 5.5). Women could come to her shows without feeling obliged to buy, but the theatrical mise-en-scène and parade of graceful mannequins made it difficult to resist: "[W]hen the lights are lowered to a rosy glow, and soft music is played and the mannequins parade, there is not a woman in the audience, though she may be fat and middle-aged, who is not seeing herself looking as those slim, beautiful girls look in the clothes they are offering her. And that is the inevitable prelude to buying."[71] In disguising the more prosaic aspects of her business, Lucile encouraged her clients to identify with her models, not as individuals but as idealized bodies, as reflections of what they hoped to become. But as much as her mannequins attracted considerable attention from male spectators and journalists, the undisputed star of the mannequin parade was Lucile herself. Every time she stepped on the stage to welcome her audience or stood at a podium to discuss the gowns on display, she reaffirmed her status as the author of the fashion spectacle. The mannequins were her tools; she was the craftswoman.

In March 1910, at the urging of her close friend, the retired actress and former Frohman "clothes horse" Elsie de Wolfe, Lucile opened a branch of Lucile Ltd. in New York at 57th Street, just off Fifth Avenue.[72] An audience of "the most stylishly dressed of New York women, leaders of fashion, leaders of suffrage, leaders of music, leaders of dramatic art" attended the opening fashion parade.[73] Encouraged by her reception in the United States, after the outbreak of World War I she relocated from London to New York, where she designed extensively for actresses in legitimate drama, vaudeville, musi-

Figure 5.5. A Lucile mannequin parade in the garden of Lucile Ltd. at Hanover Square in London, 1913. Lucile (Lady Duff Gordon), *Discretions and Indiscretions* (New York: Frederick A. Stokes, 1932), 239.

cal comedy, and the revue, including, perhaps most significantly, the *Ziegfeld Follies*.[74]

In addition to designing gowns for the *Follies* stars Ina Claire, Ann Pennington, and Justine Johnson, Lucile designed and directed a number of the *Follies* fashion parades, and she trained many of the mannequins who would later become showgirls. For the *Follies of 1917*, arguably her most influential *Follies*, she designed and directed four numbers: "The Garden of Girls," "The Wedding Morning," "The Arabian Nights" (most likely an adaptation of one of her salon shows), and the "Episode of the Chiffon," a "model or fashion scene" featuring nine showgirls dressed in provocatively named chiffon gowns.[75] In this last number, the theater critic Burns Mantle observed, "the creative modiste really shines."[76] Set to Edith Hallor's rendition of "Jealous Moon," the showgirls slowly emerged from behind chiffon curtains and promenaded across the stage, arms outstretched in typical mannequin style.[77] The climax of the parade came when Lucile's house mannequin Dolores, making her *Follies* debut, emerged as "The Empress of Fashion" dressed in a gown entitled "The Discourager of Hesitancy."[78] Dolores's haughty composure and tall, thin elegance captivated the *Follies* audience who, according to Lucile, "[f]êted and worshiped [*sic*] [her] as though she had been a queen."[79] Other mannequins from Lucile's salon soon followed Dolores in crossing over to the stage, signaling what the cultural historian Linda Mizejewski calls "the formal marriage of model and chorus girl." Trained to show clothes to advantage, these tall, thin women set a new standard of beauty for *Follies* showgirls that firmly "relocate[d] the chorus girl within codes of avant-garde fashion."[80]

The question of training is important for it suggests one area where Lucile may have had as much influence as the *Follies* choreographer Ned Wayburn. Most historians credit Wayburn with coordinating the look and movement of the Ziegfeld Girl, pointing to his incorporation of militaristic training techniques into chorus-girl choreography, his establishment of four classes or "types" of chorus girl, and his creation of the Ziegfeld Walk to showcase their talents. In 1913, Wayburn explained his method to the *Theatre Magazine:*

There are four kinds of girl of the chorus: the "A"; type, a tall, good-looking girl, of brains, education and refinement, what we might call a "well brought up" girl. . . . The next grade, the "B" girl, is a grown-up dancer. She has the attributes of the show girl, but can dance, too, which is very useful. . . . The "C" girl is much like the "A" girl, but smaller and younger. [She] is, in fact, an undeveloped "A" girl. She and the "B" girl are very useful for the picture dances. The "D" girl is a dancer. She is small, healthy and trained for vigorous dancing.[81]

Like eggs or beef, Wayburn graded chorus girls according to quality, intent on matching each physical type with movements and characters that showed off her particular skills. Of these, the "A" girl was clearly the cream of the crop. Tall, thin, attractive, and obviously white, she bore the marks of class and education and was ideally suited to wearing an array of designer costumes. To showcase the "A" girl, Wayburn devised the Ziegfeld Walk, a slow stately glide that the historian Robert Baral describes as a "combination of Irene Castle's flair for accentuating the pelvis in her stance, the lifted shoulder, and a slow concentrated gait."[82] Representing at once the eroticization and regimentation of the female body, the Ziegfeld Walk transformed showgirls into glamorous commodities, carefully packaged products floating across the assembly line of the stage.

Scholars are virtually unanimous in acknowledging Wayburn's role in the invention and institutionalization of the Ziegfeld Walk.[83] Yet while I have no wish to deny his influence, I nevertheless question the tacit assumption that he was operating alone, especially given Lucile's extensive influence on Broadway costuming practices in this period. Wayburn joined the *Follies* in 1915, the same year as Lucile, and while there is very little evidence of direct collaboration between the two, they were undoubtedly aware of one another. Although Dolores and Lucile's other house mannequins did not appear in the *Follies* until 1917, Wayburn would certainly have been aware of these women, especially in light of the extensive media coverage they received; he may even have attended Lucile's in-house mannequin parades along with Ziegfeld and his wife, Billie Burke, who was a client of Lucile's.[84] Even if Wayburn devised the Ziegfeld Walk of his own accord, he had well-trained bodies to command, especially in 1917 when Dolores and Lucile's other mannequins entered the *Follies*. Unlike untrained chorus girls arriving from the country, these professional mannequins had years of experience walking in the slow, stately manner that was the hallmark of the Walk. Figure 5.6 shows two photographs from the key sheet for the *Follies of 1917*, in which a showgirl, probably Dolores, emerges from a curtain and then glides across the stage while facing the front and with her arms outstretched. This, presumably, is a scene from Lucile's "Episode of the Chiffon" number and an example of the Ziegfeld Walk described by Baral.[85] Compare this photograph with the photograph of Lucile's salon mannequins in the garden of Lucile's salon in Hanover Square (see figure 5.5). Although stationery, the mannequins' carriage and poise, especially the one in the center of the photograph (possibly Dolores), suggest a bodily awareness that is strikingly like that of the showgirl in figure 5.6. Although inconclusive, such evidence suggests that the choreography of the Ziegfeld Girl was not the product of a single

Figure 5.6. A showgirl, most likely Dolores as the "Empress of Fashion," emerges from a curtain in a number from the *Ziegfeld Follies of 1917*. Billy Rose Theatre Division, The New York Public Library for the Performing Arts, Astor, Lenox, and Tilden Foundations.

man but rather the result of a complicated exchange between Wayburn, Lucile, and her salon mannequins.[86]

But if Lucile was a major player in the commodification of the Ziegfeld Girl, she also used the fashion show to actively refute the government's attempts to shame women for purchasing dresses, jewels, and other display commodities in wartime. In a six-month tour of the vaudeville circuit, she offered a vision of the modern female "citizen consumer" that urged women to see fashion consumption as a patriotic act.[87]

Lucile's Vaudeville Turn

Between December 1917 and May 1918, one of the leading acts on the Keith vaudeville circuit was *Fleurette's Dream at Peronne*, a fashion show starring a dozen mannequins and a million dollars in clothing. Staged by Lucile while on hiatus from the *Follies* and other Broadway engagements, the twenty-eight minute "playlet" was an obvious celebration of fashion's excesses and a clever promotional vehicle for the designer's gowns. But as Lucile repeatedly emphasized in her stage appearances and newspaper interviews, *Fleurette's Dream* was *not* a fashion show: it was a war drama created for the express purpose of raising money to rebuild French homes destroyed in the war. Set in the French town of Peronne, a commune within the *départemente* of the Somme and the recent site of a major German offensive, *Fleurette's Dream* told the story of a young mannequin hiding out in a cellar with her family. As German bombs explode overhead, Fleurette dreams of her former life in Paris; she shops with friends, strolls through the city, and prepares for an evening out, all the while trying on new clothes and watching other women parade before her in their finery. The act concluded with Fleurette awakening from her dream to once again face the horrors of war.

In framing *Fleurette's Dream at Peronne* as a war drama and insisting that the majority of the money made by the act was going to support displaced French citizens, Lucile aligned theatrical spectatorship and fashion consumption with the ideals of philanthropy, humanitarianism, and patriotism. Although critics were skeptical about Lucile's motives and questioned whether a million dollar spectacle was really the most appropriate way to assist war refugees, Lucile remained adamant about the connection between fantasy, consumption, and altruism. In her equation, going to the theatre, dreaming about purchasing pretty dress, and ogling beautiful women gained political significance when the cause was right.

Lucile originally created *Fleurette's Dream at Peronne* as a one-time only charity event for New York's social elite at the behest of her sister, the novelist Elinor Glyn. Glyn had recently been appointed vice president of Secours Franco-American Pour la France Devastée, a war society created to "enabl[e] [French] refugees to resettle in recaptured areas" and had written to her sister about meeting a family hiding out in a cellar after the Germans had destroyed the town of Peronne. The daughter, a young woman named Fleurette, was a Parisian mannequin who had returned to the countryside at the outbreak of the war to be with her family.[88] Inspired by the story, Lucile agreed to organize a charity event for Secours Franco-American, using the mannequin's dream of her life prior to the war as the touchstone for a lavish fashion spectacle.[89]

The two-and-a-half-hour version of *Fleurette's Dream* premiered at the Little Theatre in the fall of 1917. Phyllis Francatelli, the sister of Duff Gordon's secretary "and a born mannequin," played Fleurette, and Lucile's studio mannequins, several of whom had already appeared as showgirls in the *Ziegfeld Follies*, filled other roles. A crowd of spectators, including many members of New York's social elite, filled the theater to capacity; Florenz Ziegfeld himself was present, having apparently sold hundreds of tickets for "not less than five dollars" each on Lucile's behalf. Lucile reports that "people stood up and cheered, and the Four Hundred . . . does not often cheer, and rushed out to buy flowers to throw upon the stage."[90]

Also in the audience that afternoon was George Gottlieb, the booker for the Palace Theater. When the curtain came down, he approached Lucile and insisted on having "that act just as it is for the halls."[91] Gottlieb was not the first vaudeville booker to try to entice Lucile onto the vaudeville boards. According to *Variety*, tour managers had been after her for two years to appear in vaudeville, but to no avail. The situation with Secours Franco-American, however, apparently changed her mind and she agreed to embark on a twenty-five week tour.[92] For her pains, she received $2,500 a week, the majority of which she claims to have given to "various war charities."[93]

While Lucile continued to insist that Secours Franco-American was her only reason for taking *Fleurette's Dream* on the road, evidence of financial difficulties suggests another possible motivation.[94] The theater historian M. Alison Kibler has shown that going on the vaudeville circuit was often a last resort for respected legitimate actresses and other esteemed personalities who were down on their luck.[95] Although Lucile's memoirs contain few references to financial trouble, Elinor Glyn claims that Lucile lost all her money in 1917 when the London branch of Lucile Ltd. failed, presumably as a result of the war.[96] That same year, she lost a lawsuit to Otis F. Wood for failing to comply with the terms of a business contract.[97] This is not to suggest that Lucile's intentions with *Fleurette's Dream* were wholly mercenary or that she did not care deeply about the plight of French refugees but rather that her decision to undertake a six-month tour of the vaudeville circuit was motivated in part by a desire to recoup some of her recent financial losses.

On December 3, 1917 *Fleurette's Dream*—the vaudeville version—opened to a capacity audience at the Palace Theater, New York's preeminent vaudeville house.[98] Before the playlet began, Lucile appeared onstage accompanied by her dog Mahmud to deliver a short curtain speech, in which she stressed her relationship with Secours Franco-American and encouraged the audience to read the fashion spectacle as part of the war effort. In accordance with vaudeville's emphasis on fast-paced, nonstop action, *Fleurette's Dream* was shortened to twenty-eight minutes, during which time sixty-eight dresses were modeled by a team of elegant mannequins.[99] Four of these mannequins—Phyliss (who played Fleurette), Mauricette, Dinarzarde, and Dolores—had recently performed in Ziegfeld's production of *Miss 1917* in costumes designed by Lucile.[100] Chief among these was Dolores, the six-foot-tall beauty who had electrified audiences at the *Follies of 1917* with her appearance as the "Empress of Fashion" (figure 5.7). In fact, every performer in *Fleurette's Dream* was a Lucile house mannequin, trained to display clothes in the cold, aloof manner that was the designer's signature.

As Gottlieb had anticipated, the act was a huge hit. During its first week at the Palace, *Fleurette's Dream* "drew unusually large crowd[s]," and with advance sales and complete sell-outs it quickly proved an important "drawing card."[101] On December 15, the *New York Clipper* announced: "Lady Duff Gordon, the dictator of fashion, registered such a distinct hit at the Palace Theater last week . . . that the management has decided to hold her over for a second week."[102] Even poor weather conditions and the approach of Christmas did not deter eager women and men from attending the show.[103] After a successful two-week stay at the Palace, Lucile and her mannequins headed onto the circuit under the direction of A. Paul Keith and E. G. Albee.[104] In most locations, *Fleurette's Dream* was the headliner, bumping such acts as the hula dancer Doraldina and the minstrel performer Lew Dockstaeder from the privileged spot, and appearing alongside such acts as Meehan's Dogs, Ragtime Reilly, 3 Chums, 4 Bards, and Deiro.[105]

With *Fleurette's Dream*, Lucile followed a number of enterprising theater producers, many of them female, in capitalizing on middle-class obsession with the fashion show. Significantly, whereas revue fashion shows centered around the female body, vaudeville fashion shows very much remained spec-

Figure 5.7. Dolores in one of Lucile's costumes for *Fleurette's Dream*. Sketch Supplement, *Fleurette's Dream*, Harry Ransom Humanities Research Center, The University of Texas at Austin.

tacles about clothing targeted primarily at women. These shows tended to follow the same formula as the department store fashion show and found their greatest success in smaller towns where the fashion show was still very much a novelty. But in offering audiences a series of up-to-date fashions, vaudeville fashion shows also provided a platform for emerging and established designers to showcase their work, and participated in contemporary debates about consumption and female citizenship.

The vaudeville performer-turned-producer May Tully brought the fashion show to vaudeville in April 1915, introducing a new act simply titled "The Fashion Show." Featuring a reported $50,000 in gowns and jewelry "from abroad and from the salons of leading dressmakers at home," the act filled vaudeville's premiere theater, the Palace, to capacity four times in its first week, equaling the opening week success of the famed actress Alla Nazimova. As *Variety* reported, "The Fashion Show" "combines a gigantic advertising proposition with one of the grandest feminine sights extant." In the space of twenty-six minutes, twenty-five models, "perfect thirty-sixes," stepped through an enlarged cover of *Vogue* magazine and promenaded about the stage dressed in the latest styles for morning, afternoon, and evening. Program notes and advertisements informed audience members that they could purchase these gowns at nearby department stores or salons.[106] After its initial run at the Palace, the show toured the vaudeville circuit for several months before returning to New York in October to showcase the newest fall fashions. The revamped "Fall Fashion Show" was now fifty-seven minutes long, an almost unheard-of length for a vaudeville act, and continued to tour the circuit until March 1916.[107]

The success of "The Fashion Show" clearly owed much to Tully's artistic vision, business acumen, and networking abilities. Her first major achievement was convincing "the celebrated artist-modistes of Fifth Avenue," including Harry Collins, Bonwit Teller, Hickson, and Nardi, as well as the Paris couturiers Lanvin and Redfern to lend her gowns for the show.[108] Throughout the lengthy run of "The Fashion Show," Tully acquired new gowns and encouraged different designers to participate. In July 1915, for example, Lucile contributed two gowns to the show: "Dear Lady Disdain," which featured a hoop skirt, and "A Discourager of Hesitancy," "a clinging evening gown of mauve paon velvet, lined with rich rose chiffon." In exchange for their donations, participants received free print and program advertisements as well as mention onstage, making the production both "the most expensive and the cheapest act in vaudeville." By October 1915, the *Variety* editor Sime Silverman acknowledged Tully's skills and credibility as a producer, concluding that "Miss Tully's credit must be A1 or she keeps her word to return goods, for the Fifth avenue firms have allowed her to amass all the clothes and jewelry that could be held in one taxi."[109] Whether through personal connections or a persuasive sales pitch, Tully managed to secure some of New York's most exclusive designs and thereby set her fashion show apart from standard department store fare.

Tully's most ingenious promotional strategy, however, was making a direct connection between her "Fashion Show" and *Vogue* magazine's recent Fashion Fête in celebration of American fashion. For years groups such as the United Tailor Association of America had urged American dressmakers to "stop pretending that they are following strictly the Paris fashions when, as a matter of fact, they are using their own creations."[110] Reputable publications including the *New York Times* and the *Ladies' Home Journal* had similarly launched campaigns to encourage consumers to "buy American." But it was not until the threat of German invasion forced the Paris salons to close that *Vogue*, the leader of the fashion industry, embraced the notion of fashion nationalism.[111] In November 1914, the magazine sponsored an exclusive charity fashion show at the Ritz-Carlton to promote the work of New York designers—an event described by one historian as "the beginning of America's stylistic coming-of-age."[112] By positioning an enlarged cover of *Vogue* onstage, Tully implied in a none-too-subtle way that her "Fashion Show" had received *Vogue*'s endorsement, an association the magazine tacitly acknowledged. The June 1, 1915 issue of *Vogue* includes a photograph of a scene from the "Fashion Show" with a caption that playfully highlights the symbiotic relationship between the worlds of theater and fashion: "Vogue Plays a New Role: Fashion, Becoming Stagestruck, Dramatizes Vogue Fashions, Cover and All, for an Extended Road Tour."[113]

As with most successful vaudeville acts, Tully's "Fashion Show" soon spawned a series of imitators. By October 1915, *Variety* reported that a "Flood of Fashion Shows" was "Swamping New York Theatres."[114] In addition to Tully's revamped "Fall Fashion Show," complete with a new set, cast, and scenario, there was also "Mrs. Whitney's Fashion Show," sponsored by Selwyn and Co., and a show staged at the Carnegie-Lyceum sponsored by the *Evening Globe*.[115] The Shuberts had also expressed interest in producing a fashion show and had approached Condé Nast about staging one under the auspices of *Vogue* and *Vanity Fair*.[116] By December, "Catherine Crawford's Fashion Show" was touring the Loew Circuit, and a fashion show musical comedy titled *Nothing to Wear* was scheduled to open at the Auditorium in February.[117] Like Tully's "Fashion Show," many of these later spectacles promoted the work of

American designers and gave local dressmakers a chance to appeal to a new clientele. In May 1916, Castles in the Air, the popular cabaret named after the ballroom dancers Vernon and Irene Castle, ran a series of fashion shows that culminated in a competition between seven New York dressmakers, who each displayed three gowns (a precursor to *Project Runway*). On the last night of the competition, the popular vaudeville performer Irene Fenwick awarded the prize to Mme. Kahn, who subsequently took out a full-page advertisement in *Variety* to announce her win.[118]

Although fashion shows continued to tour vaudeville throughout the 1910s, theater critics and New York audiences seemed to tire of the spectacle rather quickly. In October 1915, *Variety* reported that "The 'Fashion Show,' despite its unusual splendor and luxurious surroundings, seems to have lost its novelty for Broadway theatergoers, who can view practically the same display two blocks east on almost any afternoon."[119] If department stores offered the same spectacle for free every day, the writer suggested, why would anyone bother paying to see a fashion show? Moreover, as *Variety*'s female columnist "the Skirt" argued in a separate column, many of the gowns featured in the new "Fashion Show" "looked like 'ringers' from a wholesale house" and paled in comparison to the "gorgeous" gowns worn by the dancer Evelyn Nesbit, the other major act on the bill.[120] Without exciting new fashions, she implied, the "Fashion Show" had very little to offer New York audiences.

If audiences were already tiring of vaudeville fashion shows in October 1915, why was *Fleurette's Dream* such a success two years later? Part of the answer lies with Lucile. While May Tully's "Fashion Show" boasted designs from European couturiers and New York's elite salons, *Fleurette's Dream* starred the famous couturier herself. Glowingly referred to by the *New York Times* as "the Artist-Aristocrat-Autocrat of Style" and the "Supreme Law-Maker in the Lovely Land of Fine Feathers," Lucile's light, frothy designs, often made of chiffon and lace, were emulated by dressmakers across the United States.[121] "Probably not more than three thousand women in all the United States had the money or temerity to cross her thresholds," explains Howard Greer, the Hollywood designer and a one-time apprentice with Lucile, "yet she was [as] well known during the giddy opulence of World War I as was America's sweetheart."[122] In addition to designing for the stage and running her own design salons, Lucile endorsed a wide range of products from taffeta petticoats to automobiles, wrote a syndicated column for William Randolph Hearst's *New York American* as well as a monthly series for *Harper's Bazar*, and signed an exclusive deal with Sears Roebuck and Company to design a special line of patterns.[123] Her involvement in such a diverse range of activities attests to

Lucile's ability to strike the right balance between appealing to a mass audience and securing her status as a designer of exclusive fashion.[124]

Yet while many women would have known Lucile's name, few would have seen her designs in person, except perhaps those worn by an actress or showgirl onstage. Unlike department store fashion shows, Lucile's salon mannequin parades were restricted to her elite clientele. Even the initial performance of *Fleurette's Dream* was limited to members of the Four Hundred or those who could afford a five-dollar ticket. More people had an opportunity to see her designs in the *Follies*, but these spectacles also tended to appeal to the social elite. *Fleurette's* appearance on the vaudeville circuit, however, where ticket prices ranged between 25 and 75 cents, meant that anyone could see Lucile's designs *and* hear her speak about them. But more than offering middle- and lower-class audiences an opportunity to see the famous designer and her corps of elegant mannequins, *Fleurette's Dream* presented a compelling argument in favor of consumption in wartime.

Patriotic Acts of Consumption

Between September 1914 and April 1917, Americans enjoyed a boom economy thanks to the government's neutral stance on the war and the resurgence of economic and cultural nationalism. The "Made in America" campaign, launched in 1914 as a widespread effort to get consumers to buy American-made goods, drew an explicit connection between consumption and citizenship, picking up on a long-standing rhetorical argument that dated back to the American Revolution.[125] Industries that had languished against foreign competitors, including the silk and textiles industries, now profited from the turmoil overseas.

Lucile was a strong advocate of fashion nationalism. Writing in *Harper's Bazar* in October 1914, a month after the closure of the Paris salons, she advised American women to create gowns for themselves (with some tips from her, of course), declaring that it was "their moment to show independence."[126] The following month, she addressed American dressmakers, urging them "to prove to her countrywomen just what her creative ability is worth. I know they will rise to the occasions splendidly, and that poor Paris, when she has come into her own again, will have a great rival in America and no longer will be able to stand unequalled in fashion's world as hitherto she has done."[127]

Although somewhat surprising considering her British citizenship, Lucile's pro-American stance makes sense when considered alongside *Vogue's* recent endorsement of American-made fashion and the resurgence of fashion nationalism in American magazines and newspapers. As a British designer and rival to leading Paris couturiers such as Paul Poiret and Jeanne Paquin, Lucile had little to lose. Even after *Vogue* abandoned its nationalist agenda in 1915 under pressure from the reopened Paris salons, and *Harper's Bazar* proclaimed that Paris "is and always will be the source of fashion inspiration for the world," Lucile continued to write about the need for American fashion in her monthly column.[128] In June 1915, she published the results of a design contest she had helped to coordinate and judge at the New York School of Fine and Applied Arts (now Parsons New School of Design). "Don't you think it is equal to anything that Paris can produce, taking into the occasion for which the dress is to be worn?" she asked the magazine's readers.[129]

In addition to boosting young talent, Lucile called upon American manufacturers to develop a much stronger public profile. At the First National Silk Convention in the fall of 1915, she delivered a paper entitled "The Relation of Silk to Style," in which she urged silk manufacturers to recognize the contribution they could make to the development of an American fashion industry. "Silk manufacturers of America," she concluded, "rise to the opportunity, to your duty, and fulfill the tradition of American enterprise and progress."[130] More than advocating for change, Lucile also made a point of using American-made fabrics, dress goods, and laces for her own designs. In January 1915, she premiered her spring collection in which "75 per cent of the fabrics and accessories were supplied by American firms," including M. C. Migel and Co., B. Altman and Co., and Quaker Lace Mills.[131] Photographs in *Harper's Bazar* and the *American Silk Journal* of performers and mannequins dressed in Lucile's gowns made from American silk offer further proof of the designer's dedication to the industry, not to mention her interest in developing her brand identity.[132]

The "Made in America" movement supported by Lucile and numerous others captured the attention of American consumers, manufacturers, trade publications, and mass-circulation periodicals.[133] But with the declaration of war in April 1917, the terms of the debate over American consumption shifted considerably. The issue was no longer whether Americans should consume foreign products over American ones but whether Americans should consume at all. As American troops prepared to go overseas, President Woodrow Wilson called for citizens to practice thrift and conservation, equating good citizenship with self-sacrifice and the creative use of existing resources. As he explained in his Proclamation to the People: "This is the time for America to correct her unpardonable fault of wastefulness and extravagance. Let every man and every woman assume the duty of careful, provident use and expenditure as a public duty, as a dictate of patriotism which no one can now expect ever to be excused or forgiven for ignoring."[134]

Joined by men such as Bernard Baruch, the chairman of the War Industries Board, and Herbert Hoover, the head of the Wartime Food Administration, Wilson launched an anti-consumption campaign targeted primarily at women, which made effective use of recent innovations in commercial advertising. "[M]uch can be done by national propaganda to limit extravagance," Hoover had observed in an interview with the *Saturday Evening Post* several months before the United States joined the war. "We need some phrase that puts the stamp of shame on wasteful eating, dressing and display of jewelry."[135] Gendering the wasteful American consumer as female through references to dress and jewelry, Hoover presented the ultimate solution to the problem of excessive consumption as an updated version of the scarlet letter: "the stamp of shame."

Women's magazines like the *Ladies' Home Journal*, previously one of the loudest voices in the "American Fashions for American Women" campaign, took up the president's call for thrift, promising readers that "[w]ar in Europe has made it both fashionable and patriotic to practice thrift."[136] Newspapers also jumped on the conservation bandwagon and began reporting interesting uses for old clothing and other consumer goods.[137] The underlying argument was that denying consumer desire was patriotic, a position made explicit by Bernard Baruch, the chairman of the War Industries Board. "[T]he most patriotic woman will be the one who finds happiness in what she does without rather than what she consumes," Baruch explained to the readers of the *Ladies' Home Journal*, urging them to limit their spending for the sake of their brothers, lovers, and husbands fighting overseas.[138]

The government's new stance on consumption posed a major problem for the fashion and theater industries. How could they pitch new items and promote new shows when the government was encouraging consumers to practice thrift? Desperate to prevent their businesses from failing, these industries argued for an even stronger link between consumption and patriotism, adopting much of the same rhetoric used by the government. In June 1917 the *Theatre Magazine* issued a statement beneath the banner headline "True Patriotism!" that justified wartime consumption:

Let every man and woman, says President Wilson, assume the duty of careful, provident use and expenditure as a public duty. But it is not meant that we must close our purse strings altogether, nor that we must hoard our money . . . if husbands, wives and daughters stop ordering from tailors, shirtmakers, milliners and dressmakers; if the big stores, the restaurants, the theatres, and concert halls are deserted; if there comes a sudden cessation of business activities, such wide-spread distress would result in the business life of the community that no man can say what the outcome would be, and millions of innocent persons would suffer.[139]

In raising the specter of economic depression, the *Theatre Magazine* defined spending money on entertainment and fashion as a patriotic act and a "public duty." The fashion designer and columnist Faibisy made a similar argument in an ad published in the *Theatre Magazine* the following month, expressing his hope "that the American women will not heed the hysterical cry which has spread across the land with the advent and discussion of war and be deluded into embracing and practicing a false economy, in neglecting her wardrobe." Instead, he argued, "Let us express the spirit of the flags waving on Fifth Avenue, the confidence of victory, the triumph of peace, not only in our secret hearts but in our outward personality, expressed in the manner of our raiment."[140] According to this logic, it was a woman's natural right and national responsibility to dress as beautifully as possible.

Advertisers also reworked war rhetoric to encourage rather than deter consumption, invoking the ideals of patriotism and duty, irrespective of the actual function of the product.[141] For example, an ad for the Nemo Self-Help Corset No. 333 claimed, "Our Contribution to War-Efficiency/Real Economy-Hygienic Service . . . To preserve your health and efficiency, you need the support of a truly hygienic corset now more than ever."[142] Another ad for Redfern Corsets reminded women that "[y]ou can wear an old gown with a new corset better than a new gown with an old corset."[143] Given the choice between a gown and a corset, the ad suggests, the corset is the most sensible, and therefore patriotic, choice.

The complex relations between wartime rhetoric, commercial advertising, and the desire to at once suppress, appease, and encourage consumer desires converged in the presentation of *Fleurette's Dream*. Clearly anticipating criticism from those who would see displays of "costly stuffs" and "priceless furs" as frivolous and unpatriotic, Lucile made a point of playing up the act's association with Secours Franco-American both onstage and in her column in *Harper's Bazar*. As she explained to readers in January 1918, "Every one in the country is doing his bit for the war, so when the managers asked me to repeat the sketch that I gave for 'La Secours Franco-American pour la France Devastee,' why I was only too happy to find another opportunity for collecting more funds as the salary of four figures which I am receiving makes it all worth while."[144] She even arranged for a French officer to introduce her to the Palace audience when she made her official debut, grounding *Fleurette's Dream* in the reality of wartime service and sacrifice. Standing before the capacity crowd, the officer "explain[ed Lucile's] mission as being one of charity more than self-exploitation, as her weekly wage for arranging her vaudeville act would go to a French war charity."[145] In response to those who questioned her decision to reference the actual town of Peronne in her act, Lucile argued that if it hadn't been for Peronne, "there would have been no stage presentment by her and in consequence there could have been no incentive to appear in aid of her sister's charities for the homeless French in the battle zones."[146] In Boston shortly after the act opened, she once again asserted her position, agreeing to hand out autographed pictures of herself to any audience member who joined the Red Cross. "I have been working so long for others that I propose doing my very best now for myself and France," she informed the full house.[147]

Public and media reactions to the charity aspect of the show were mixed. According to one *Variety* review, "[A]s Lady Duff is giving the proceeds to war charities, her vaudeville debut has good grounds as far as the public is concerned, and the public seems only to be concerned in Lady Duff and her stuff."[148] Another writer surmised, "Lady Duff's effort goes, in spite of its splendor in these times, for it's all for charity."[149] Other reviewers, however, were less willing to accept the act as a legitimate charity fundraiser. *Variety* noted that "if Lady Duff wishes to aid war charities in these days of suggested economy she could secure more through saving in gowns than she could earn upon the stage. As an economical thought, there has never been such a waste displayed as in the materials and labor of Lady Duff's fashion parade. But as an act Lady Duff is a financial success, at least for the theater."[150] The writer here makes a good point: given her connections and reputation Lucile could just as easily have raised funds for Secours Franco-American without going on the vaudeville circuit. The real beneficiaries of the act seemed to be Lucile and the Keith vaudeville circuit. The *Boston Herald and Journal* also criticized the inclusion of the war drama, arguing that it "would be much more interesting were she [Lucile] to eliminate the feeble attempt at a story. The first scene, depicting the dream of Fleurette in the cellar during the bombardment of Peronne was far from convincing."[151] A Philadelphia critic expressed similar reservations: "Lady Duff Gordon pulls a bit of a camouflage at the start when she makes her introductory speech and says her offering is a little play and not a fashion show.... *Fleurette's Dream* is a fashion show, and that's all."[152] The *New York Times* cut straight to the chase: "[*Fleurette's*] military environment is rather unnecessary; and an equally striking effect would have been achieved by dropping all pretense of narrative and merely parading the mannequins across the stage."[153]

Lucile's continued efforts on stage and in print to associate *Fleurette's Dream* with Secours Franco-American hint that she may also have been aware of the tenuous connection of the two. Rather than eliminate the war drama, however, Lucile responded to her critics by heightening the act's relationship to the war charity dramaturgically, concluding the act with the intervention of the Secours Franco-American charity. Earlier accounts of the *mise en scene* make no reference to the presence of the Secours Franco-American volunteers as actual characters in the playlet. Yet an April 1918 review from the *Toronto World* describes the young mannequin awakening to hear "the kind women of the Secours Franco-Americaine [*sic*] coming down the cellar steps with food and clothing for the much-enduring sufferers of Peronne, one of the most terribly devastated cities of fair France, which at this writing has just endured another awful war assault."[154] Given the recent events of the war, Lucile may have wished to make a stronger emotional connection between the real and the fictional Peronne to avoid criticism for treating the town's devastation frivolously. By showing the women of Secours Franco-American aiding the victims of Peronne, she tightened the connection between the world of the play and the efforts of the charity.

There is very little evidence to indicate whether vaudeville audiences were receptive to Lucile's message or whether they accepted her argument that consumption was patriotic. Most reports of audience behavior emphasize women's interest in the clothing and men's interest in the attractive models.[155] The costliness of the show also attracted commentary. "Perhaps the man in the seat behind gave the best criticism of this delightfully camouflaged show," *Variety* critic wrote. " 'Gee,' he remarked with fervor and feeling. 'A million dollars worth of gowns!' "[156] From these (admittedly limited) accounts, it seems likely that audiences accepted Lucile's war drama "camouflage" for the simple reason that it camouflaged their *own* consumer desires. Just as the women who purchased the "efficient" and "hygienic" Nemo Self-Help Corset could assuage their guilt by accepting the company's promise that they were contributing to the war effort, audiences at *Fleurette's Dream* could reassure themselves that it was all for a good cause.

In fact, despite her continued protestations that *Fleurette's Dream* was a war drama, Lucile could hardly deny its function as fashion spectacle. While emphasizing the charity association, both she and the Keith circuit promoters made extensive use of advertisements and other promotional materials to frame the act as *haute couture* fantasy, using the very language that justified *Fleurette's* excesses to *celebrate* those excesses as well: "Charity to rebuild French Villages *Alone* Brings Lady Duff-Gordon to vaudeville and Justifies This Amazing Richness of Display of Costly Stuffs, Priceless Furs and Precious Stones in War Time (my emphasis)" ran the headline for a preview article in the *New York Times*.[157] Newspapers were kept well informed of the value of the costumes, which increased dramatically during the act's first two weeks in New York, from $500,000 to a reported $1,000,000.[158] This emphasis on "beauty and costliness" helped raise audience expectations, reassuring eager observers that the clothes on display were more than stylish copies of elite fashions—they were Lucile originals. Ultimately, it was the "Amazing Richness of Display of Costly Stuffs, Priceless Furs and Precious Stones" that drew audiences to *Fleurette's Dream*, not the war drama or Secours Franco-American.

Lucile's celebratory stance on fashion and consumption also worked its way into the dramatic narrative. In the "real world" of the playlet, Fleurette is an impoverished, victimized woman. The German army has deprived her of her former life of fashionable clothes and expensive outings, and now her only escape from the terror of bombardment is the dream world that awaits her when she sleeps. But, the narrative seems to suggest, Fleurette's dream *is* the American woman's reality. Rather than denying herself the pleasure of shopping with friends and dressing fashionably, she should embrace the freedom to consume for the sake of those who cannot.

Lucile's dream metaphor extended to *Fleurette's* costumes as well. Recognizing the importance of stirring audience fantasies and perhaps anticipating a certain degree of hesitation to her more extreme couture designs, she explained to the audience in Toronto that "these creations about to be shown are not fashions, they are just dreams."[159] Photographs and fashion sketches of the *Fleurette* gowns (figures 5.8 and 5.9) further suggest that Lucile made optimum use of the vaudeville tour to experiment with new ideas for her couture collections. " 'Fleurette' and her friends they are all wearing my 'last cries' in line, color and form," she informed the readers of *Harper's Bazar* in February 1918, reassuring the fashion savvy that she had not abandoned her elite salons. Ironically, for all her talk of American innovation, Lucile's designs suggest a lingering interest in the kinds of Orientalist subjects that had fascinated Paris couturiers before the war. "The Chinese vibration has completely hypnotized me," she enthused in her fashion column. "In the present state of chaos of feminine fashions, I bethought of a perfect haven of safety and perfection—China!"[160] Within the context of *Fleurette's Dream*, Lucile's invocation of a distant country— "a perfect haven of safety and perfection"—was

Lady Duff-Gordon's Latest Styles

Drawn for the Post-Dispatch by Marguerite Martyn.

Figure 5.8. The illustrator Marguerite Martyn's sketches of some of the Lucile gowns displayed in the vaudeville version of *Fleurette's Dream at Peronne*. *St. Louis Dispatch*, April 6, 1918.

entirely consistent with the other elements of escapist fantasy. Although some critics complained that the gowns were "bizarre" and "wildly incongruous" and wondered why Lucile had not "dressed her girls as sensibly as she dressed herself" to allow "ordinary mortals" to adopt her designs, they seem to have missed the point.[161] Unlike other commercial-oriented fashion shows, *Fleurette's Dream* was an escapist fantasy that celebrated fashion's potential for inspiring dreams.

With *Fleurette's Dream*, Lucile advanced a philosophy of dress that positioned female consumers as powerful citizens capable of influencing their nation's future. Outside the theater, she continued to advocate for luxury spending in speeches, articles, and interviews, flagrantly disregarding the government's call for economy in dress. In April 1918, while appearing in Pittsburgh, she made one of her boldest pro-consumption speeches at the Press Club's "Economy Dinner"—an event at which Herbert Hoover was the guest of honor. After Hoover delivered an address on "economy in food," the toast-

Figure 5.9. Other examples of Lucile's costumes from *Fleurette's Dream*, in which the Orientalist influence is particularly strong. Sketch Supplement, *Fleurette's Dream*, Harry Ransom Humanities Research Center, The University of Texas at Austin.

master asked Lucile to speak on "economy in dress." Rather than speaking on the assigned topic, however, she presented a strong argument against it: " 'Ladies and Gentlemen, the first thing I am going to tell you is that I don't believe in economy in dress at any time, and above all in war-time.' Then I went on to tell them that I thought it was the duty of every wife, sweetheart and mother to spend as much on dress as they could possibly afford in order to make the best of themselves for the sake of the men in the trenches."[162] By insisting that the truly patriotic woman was the one who continued consuming in order to present an image of flawless beauty and enduring youth, Lucile challenged the government's definition of good citizenship. In her equation, shopping, spending, and displaying commodities were not wasteful or frivolous activities: they were significant, patriotic acts. After her speech, Lucile apologized to Hoover for her oppositional stance, to which he responded, "Never mind dear, you have done very well," a polite if patronizing gesture that tacitly acknowledged the designer's influence over women's consumer habits.[163]

While his views on consumption differed markedly from hers, Hoover shared Lucile's interest in clothing's semiotic potential and its communicative power for propaganda purposes. In 1917, he introduced the "Hoover costume" or "uniform," an outfit worn by women who had agreed to join his Food Administration. The sturdy blue material and detachable collars and cuffs were intended to save time, energy, and money, while the adjustable cap with the Food Administration's insignia allowed women to declare their allegiance to Hoover's policies. The administration's headquarters in Washington sold patterns for 10 cents each and the whole outfit cost approximately $1.25 to make.[164] The "Hoover uniform" thus served as an active signifier of a woman's commitment to her country and the conservation cause, and a powerful tool for exerting peer pressure on others. Going from house to house, "Hoover's helpers" encouraged housewives to sign a pledge to follow Hoover's conservation "suggestions" to the best of their abilities. Their sales tactics were highly persuasive. At the end of a two-week campaign, the female volunteers had managed to collect over ten million pledges, representing almost 50 percent of the nation's families. In October 1917, over three thousand members of the Maryland Food Conservation Army gathered in Baltimore to hear Hoover speak. Dressed in the "Hoover costume," they created a startling spectacle of mass uniformity and patriotic devotion.[165]

In spite of these impressive displays of conformity, many women simply refused to adopt any kind of uniform. In January 1918, the *Washington Evening Star* reported that an event in Washington attended by President Wilson included "the usual smart contingent from out of town. There was the flash of jewels. There were gowns that bore the hallmark of the Parisian atelier."[166] Newspaper cartoons of young women decked out in the height of fashion and fashion reports in the Sunday papers offer further proof that many women were as interested in fashion during the war as they had been before it.[167] Educated by Broadway actresses and fashion designers like Lucile to see dress as a site for the expression of individual identity, female consumers did not take kindly to the notion of standardization in dress. When, in January 1918, the commercial economy board of the Council of National Defense announced plans to standardize clothing for men, one observer noted that "the commercial economy board, with a wisdom that is veritably uncanny makes no move towards standardization of women's clothes. This war is a big job. There is no need to add to its pains and difficulties."[168] Despite wanting to control consumer behavior, the government recognized that it could not afford to interfere in the closets of American women.

Although there is no direct evidence that *Fleurette's Dream* had any effect on government policy, it nevertheless stood as a powerful counter-spectacle to the uniformed members of the Maryland Food Conservation Army and may even have alerted men like Hoover and Wilson to the practical dangers of enforcing a dress code on American women. It is worth noting that President Wilson himself attended *Fleurette's Dream* when it played in Washington in January 1918, the same month that the Council of National Defense made its decision. After the bill concluded, he came backstage to congratulate Lucile for "the best vaudeville show he had ever seen."[169] These words—as represented by Lucile in her memoirs—are telling. By referring to the act as a "vaudeville show" instead of a war drama or a fashion show, Wilson seems to have quite deliberately overlooked Lucile's pro-consumption agenda, perhaps in an effort to contain her problematic politics within the fictional realm of theatrical entertainment. As a "vaudeville show," *Fleurette's Dream* could do little damage; as a war drama, it threatened to undermine the government's campaign for thrift and conservation.

The government's decision not to restrict women's fashion suggests one possible reason why Lucile finally abandoned the war angle when she arrived in New York for her final week at the Palace Theatre in May 1918. Rather than pushing Secours Franco-American, advertisements for the triumphant return of *Fleurette's Dream* reframed the show as a delightful fashion extravaganza:

Spring & Summer Edition of Vaudeville's Loveliest Feature—Frocks & Frills and Girls like Peach Blossoms/A Glorified Fashion Show representing the exquisite Art of Lucile in its ultimate perfection and revealed by Beautiful Girls, all graduates of Milady's

School of Sartorial Perfection. The essence of smart modes and manners—the aristocratic dressing of the Social Register—the haute mode garb and grooming that every woman loves. *Also a thrilling war drama interwoven* [my emphasis].[170]

Consistent with the general trend in vaudeville to move away from war acts, Lucile acknowledged the act's charity origins but did not make it the focus of her promotional efforts. Freed of the war drama disguise, *Fleurette's Dream* emerged as a marvelous consumer fantasy, a dream accessible to "every woman" who entered vaudeville's Palace.

But by 1918 fancy clothes and dreams of mass consumption were no longer enough to sustain the millions of disenfranchised American women who had helped the country to victory, nor were they enough for the thousands of actors and actresses who had withstood years of abuse from theater producers. As the war drums slowly faded into the background, suffragists, union leaders, and members of Actor's Equity prepared to wage new battles, this time on domestic soil.

Epilogue

Although New York theaters and department stores continued to work collaboratively well into the 1920s and beyond, a number of developments in the late 1910s signaled a change in Broadway's designation as *the* premiere site for displaying elite fashion. The department store's embrace of the fashion show was one such development. Others included the emerging art theater movement; the death of the manager Charles Frohman in 1915; the Actor's Equity strike in 1919; and the rise of the Hollywood star system.

In the mid-1910s, a group of young American designers began experimenting with a new approach to costume, set, and lighting design. Inspired by Wagner's notion of "total theatre" (*gesamtkunstwerk*) whereby all elements in a production work together to produce a unified, harmonious interpretation, these designers argued against dividing design responsibilities among a group of individuals with differing ideas and insisted that a single designer should "endeavor to grasp the whole, to discover its inner meaning and to reveal its unity and purpose, to select the essential and repeat it constantly."[1] Eschewing the realistic detail for which Belasco had been celebrated, art theater designers emphasized specific design elements that, according to their reading, would illuminate the play's inner meaning.

The first effects of the art theater movement on Broadway became apparent in 1912 when the German director Max Reinhardt brought his production of *Sumurun*, with Ernst Stern's costumes and set, to the Casino Theatre. The theater critic Clayton Hamilton noted that Stern's "costumes are designed not as dresses, in reference to life, but as blocks of color, in reference to art, and the colors are simple in themselves and harmonious with one another."[2] Instead of giving theatergoers a flirtatious glimpse of upcoming trends, these costumes supported Reinhardt's artistic conception of the play with small regard to contemporary fashions. In November 1914, the Stage Society of New York's "Exhibition of the Art of the Theatre" gave New York audiences a more extensive look at the "latest technical improvements in European stage lighting and construction," showcasing the work of such innovators as Reinhardt and Edward Gordon Craig.[3] The following year, the American designer Robert Edmond Jones aped Stern's innovation, using blocks of color to create costumes that stood out in strong relief against a black and white set for Harley Granville Barker's New York production of *A Man Who Married a Dumb Wife*. Avant-garde groups like the Washington Square Players and the Neighborhood Playhouse similarly experimented with design in this period, paving the way for a new generation of designers that included Jones, Lee Simonson, and Aline Bernstein.[4]

Theater critics welcomed the new developments in design, seeing them as a sign of "what our theatre may become."[5] After railing against the debilitating influence of the matinee girl for years, these men seem to have welcomed the male-dominated art theater movement as the long-awaited answer to the commercialization and feminization of the American theater. Indeed, the art theater movement's emphasis on unity and the notion that all design elements "should be the work of one mind" represented a dramatic departure from previous costuming practices, which had emphasized the charm and personality of individual female performers.[6] "Costuming is not dressmaking," the designer Robert Edmond Jones asserted. "It is a matter of understanding the dramatist's inner idea, of knowing how the actors carry out this intention in their movements and of arranging drapery to make these movements seem more expressive and more heroic."[7] While the new designers created costumes to *assist* actors in their work, their primary goal was to illuminate the meaning of the play, not advance individual careers.[8]

It would take several years for the commercial theater to adopt design practices similar to those introduced by the art theater movement, but the theatrical hierarchy was nevertheless beginning to shift. Directors and producers increasingly looked to professional theater designers to give their productions a unified look, and the fashion designers who had once dominated Broadway retired or moved on to other projects. In 1919, Lucile, arguably the most influential designer on Broadway, left the *Ziegfeld Follies*, sold Lucile Ltd. to a manufacturer (much to her later regret), and returned to Europe. Her work on the *Frolics* of 1919 "was the last spurt of my flagging energies," she explains in her memoirs. "I knew that the time had come for me to take a rest."[9] Following Lucile's departure, Ziegfeld and other revue producers continued to work with innovative designers such as Erté, Pascaud, Charles LeMaire, and Gilbert Adrian (before he left for Hollywood).[10] Such designers rarely worked for the legitimate theater, however, with the exception of several prominent dressmakers, who continued to design for female stars. The formation of the Stage Painters Union in 1923 further amplified the designer's place within the industry by persuading producers to view design as an integral part of the production process. Although the union did not establish a separate section for costume designers until 1936, designers on the whole received greater public recognition, a trend that is evident in production playbills from 1915 onward.[11]

The unexpected death of Charles Frohman aboard the *Lusitania* in 1915 and the subsequent decline of the Theatrical Syndicate further signaled the end of the era of fashionable stage dress on Broadway. Though Frohman had initiated and sustained the "revolution in modern gowns" by agreeing to provide actresses with the funds necessary to purchase them, and though the impetus for producers to spend lavishly on costumes for society dramas and other "legitimate" stage productions declined after his death, the vogue for fashionable dress certainly persisted long after 1915 in vaudeville and musical comedy.[12] Therefore, while Frohman's prolific work as a producer had encouraged his rivals to stage elaborate spectacles and ensured the aesthetic dominance of the Theatrical Syndicate, his death was but one of many factors in the reordering of business and spectacle on Broadway.

Perhaps more than Frohman's death, the Actor's Equity Strike of 1919 dramatically altered Broadway costuming practices as actors and actresses finally addressed decades of managerial abuse. In 1913, a group of actors concerned about the absence of a standard theatrical contract formed the Actor's Equity Association. Although initially reluctant to allow women to join the AEA, the founding members soon yielded under pressure from politically minded actresses.[13] In fact, Equity made its first arbitration settlement on behalf of a female performer, Mrs. Grace Thorne Coulter, who in 1913 was awarded the cost of dresses she had purchased for an acting job that fell through. According to the Equity Council Minutes, Coulter "had spent about $200 for dresses for the engagement and she asked to be at least reimbursed for that outlay. She could not get even an acknowledgment from the Manager [Al. H. Woods] to her 'phone calls or letters."[14] With the intervention of the lawyer Nathan Burkan, conveniently "both an Associate Attorney of the Actor's Equity Association and counsel for Mr. Woods," the matter reached a successful conclusion, and Mrs. Coulter received the money for the dresses.[15]

Despite this early success, however, contractual arrangements varied considerably from manager to manager, and while most managers paid for a leading actress's costumes, they generally expected supporting actresses to pay for their own gowns. Equity responded to the apparent emergence of a two-tier class system among actresses by identifying an "adjustment of the situation with regard to women's costumes" as one of the key points to be addressed in ongoing contractual discussions with management.[16] In October 1917, Equity and the United Managers Protection Association, a loose management coalition, finally agreed on the terms for a standard minimum contract, which included costuming provisions for all actresses earning less than $150 a week. But the ongoing struggle between the Shuberts and rival producers Klaw and Erlanger all but nullified the contract, as neither group was willing to keep it.[17]

With little hope of resolving the matter without some form of action, Equity voted to strike in August 1919. For one month, thousands of actors and actresses staged public demonstrations in the Times Square district, making the most of their training and talent to enlist support for their cause and demand that management take their concerns seriously.[18] Ironically, the strikes and spectacles of labor unrest that theaters (and their department store counterparts) had tried for years to avoid had finally arrived at their doorsteps. Yet while Equity staged many of its strike activities outside Broadway theaters, its leaders also recognized the need to take the strike to the streets of the city beyond Times Square. To that end, they arranged for cars filled with attractive chorus girls billed as "the prettiest strikers in history" to tour Manhattan's financial district, where, according to the theater historian Sean P. Holmes, they "gained admission to the offices of brokerage houses and merchant banks and distributed pamphlets setting out Equity's demands" (figure E.1).[19] Indeed, whereas striking laborers in other industries were often represented by management and the media as threats to civil order, Equity's highly theatrical public protests seemed "entirely consonant with popular perceptions of actors as natural exhibitionists unbound by conventional notions of propriety."[20] Audiences already familiar with the names and faces of the striking stars willingly agreed to support the cause.

Throughout the strike, actresses shared stories about their troubles with management over costuming and argued that managers, not performers, should bear the responsibility for costuming expenses.[21] In fact, the social and economic gap between female performers was all too evident in the clothing they wore to participate in strike rallies and marches. Holmes notes that "the contrast between the French-heeled slippers of the leading ladies and the unfashionable boots of their less-successful sisters brought home to the spectators lining the sidewalks the economic gulf which divided those at the top of the acting profession from those at the bottom."[22] But with the support of actresses like Marie Dressler, who had herself risen through the ranks of the chorus to become a star, chorus girls found the voice that they lacked onstage and called upon management to make amends for years of financial and sexual exploitation.[23]

Finally, on September 6, 1919, the managers gave in to Equity's demands

Figure E.1. Chorus-girl strikers bring their spectacle of labor unrest to the Tired Business Men of Wall Street. Alfred Harding, *The Revolt of the Actors* (New York: William Morrow and Co., 1929), 83.

and agreed to abide by the terms of Equity's proposed contract. According to this new contract, managers were expected to furnish "all costumes, wigs, shoes and stockings" for chorus girls and "all artists' gowns" for female performers "in both dramatic and musical companies."[24] The new Equity contract was a victory for the thousands of actresses who had struggled for years to provide their costumes, but it also, ironically, marked a major change in the star actress's status as a "clothes artist." Whereas the previous system had given actresses considerable control over the way they looked onstage, the new contract placed the responsibility in the hands of managers, directors, and designers, who could now insist that performers wear the costumes selected for them. Although star actresses continued to have some say in costuming decisions, their influence over the design process gradually diminished, as the costume designer assumed a more prominent position.

The development of the motion picture star system in the mid-1910s further challenged Broadway's special status as a site of fashion spectacle. Although audiences continued to go to the theater to see elaborate costume displays, most notably in revues like the *Follies*, American women increasingly looked to film rather than stage actresses for fashion inspiration, especially after 1914. In fact, motion picture actors were known to the public by name as early as 1909, but these "picture personalities" were not yet full-fledged "stars." This all changed in 1914, when studios, presumably inspired by the star-making efforts of Charles Frohman, began circulating stories about performers' private lives in newspapers and magazines, transforming previously unknown "personalities" into stars in their own right.[25]

Public fascination with film stars coincided with and was aided by the popularity of movie fan magazines like *Photoplay* and *Motion Picture Magazine*. Recognizing the growing number of middle-class women who made up the movie-going audience, these magazines redesigned their content to appeal to female consumer desires, complete with fashion spreads, beauty product advertisements, and articles detailing the consumer preferences of film stars.[26] Not surprisingly, many of the actresses who first established reputations for fashionable dress on Broadway—Billie Burke, Irene Castle, Alice Brady, Hazel Dawn, Marion Davies, Peggy Hopkins Joyce—moved into film in the late 1910s and 1920s, where they continued to set trends and expand their existing fan bases.[27] They were joined by a new generation of faces—Gloria Swanson, Clara Bow, Mary Pickford, Constance Talmadge—who similarly modeled modern clothes, hairstyles, and attitudes.

Central to film's success as a medium for distributing style ideas was its reproducibility; women could go to their local movie houses and see the same actresses and films that thousands of women in other cities across the United States were seeing. Although the appeal of observing performers and clothing in a live setting was lost at the cinema, the technology of the close-up, which brought design details into focus, as well as the possibility of seeing the same film multiple times for considerably less than the price of a theater ticket, gave female fans an opportunity to view fashion in a way that was impossible in most proscenium-style theaters. By the mid-1920s, Hollywood had effectively replaced Broadway as the dream factory of modern consumption.

Despite these changes, however, the relationships forged between theaters, department stores, manufacturers, and other commercial sites did not simply fade away. From the 1920s well into the 1960s, a period often referred to as the Golden Age of the Broadway musical, producers made the most of their proximity to major retailers, music publishers, record companies, and radio and television studios to reach a mass audience that now numbered in the millions.[28] The phenomenon of the cast recording, a relatively new development in the 1950s, and the huge success of variety programs such as *The Ed Sullivan Show* brought Broadway musicals into the home and, like the touring combination company seventy years before, supported an imagined community of Broadway theatergoers that extended from coast to coast. In 1947, for example, the original cast album for *South Pacific*, by Richard Rodgers and Oscar Hammerstein II, sold one million copies and remained on top of the record charts for sixty-nine weeks. One of the show's major hits, "I'm Gonna Wash That Man Right Out of My Hair," sung by the tom-boyish star Mary Martin as she quite literally washed her hair onstage, provided the ideal promotional connection for shampoo companies looking to retrain female consumers to wash their hair on a daily basis.[29] Later Broadway musicals encouraged similar collaborations with national corporations and helped to educate and inform a nation of consumers.

The so-called corporatization of Broadway in the 1990s heralded a new stage in the relationship between theater and commerce. With the encouragement of Mayor Rudolph Giuliani, who aimed to rid Times Square of the strip clubs, prostitutes, and junkies who had moved into the area in the 1970s, multinational corporations like Disney, Time Warner, Clear Channel, and Fox Searchlight entered the arena of theatrical production. Critics responded with horror and skepticism; echoing the dire predictions of William Winter and Harrison Grey Fiske, they warned that the "Mickey Mousing" of Broadway would spell disaster for the development of home-grown talent, forever ruin the tastes of American audiences, affect regional theaters looking to keep audiences happy, and turn Times Square into little more than a tourist zone.[30]

Like Winter and Fiske before them, many of these critics failed to note that the corporatization of Broadway was not particularly new or that the golden age whose passage they lamented had, in many ways, been just as commercial. Indeed, one of the unspoken anxieties behind the attacks seems to have been the perception that theater critics were once again losing their privileged position as cultural arbiters. Whereas in previous decades, a bad review from one of the major New York critics could close a show in a matter of days, now, thanks to online advertising campaigns, fan blogs, and Facebook clubs, even shows that are panned by numerous critics can become huge popular hits.[31]

This is not to dismiss concerns about the widespread influence of corporatization and the commodification of bodies and experiences that many recent Broadway shows seem to advocate. Certainly the practices of corporations like Disney and Time Warner, which skillfully use one commercial product to promote a series of other products, demand further analysis and critique.[32] Yet if fan blogs for shows like *Wicked*, a musical largely dismissed by the critics but embraced by young female audiences, are any indication, the new generation of Broadway theatergoers are smart and savvy consumers, hardly mindless dupes of corporate seduction. Like the generation of matinee girls who flooded Times Square a century ago, these excited teens relate in a deeply emotional way to the musical's female stars and remain confident in their right to see the kind of theater they want to see.[33] They may not be the ideal audience desired by critics, but as highly vocal, influential consumers, they are nevertheless fitting descendants of the matinee girls who defied gender norms in pursuit of pleasure, companionship, and the promise of a Merry Widow hat.

Notes

Introduction

1. "Merry Widow Hats Galore," *New York Times* (hereafter *NYT*), May 22, 1908, 7.
2. Richard Traubner, *Operetta: A Theatrical History* (London: Victor Gollancz Ltd., 1984), 247; Gerald Bordman, *American Operetta: From "H.M.S. Pinafore" to "Sweeney Todd"* (New York: Oxford University Press, 1981), 247. "Merry Widow Making a Million," *NYT*, December 22, 1907: C8; "'Merry Widow' Burlesques," *NYT*, December 28, 1907, 7.
3. Quoted in Andrew Lamb, "America's Merry Widow Craze," http://www.josef-weinberger.co.uk/mw/frame.html, accessed April 17, 2008.
4. Lady Duff Gordon (Lucile), *Discretions and Indiscretions* (New York: Frederick A. Stokes Co., 1932), 108–9.
5. "Merry Widow Hats Outdone," *NYT*, June 13, 1908, C1.
6. "Mr. Henry W. Savage: The Yankee Impresario," *NYT*, December 29, 1907, SM7.
7. "Hot Skirmish over 'Merry Widow' Hats," *NYT*, June 14, 1908, 11; "Women in Hard Battle for Free 'Merry Widows,'" *New York World*, June 14, 1908, 1.
8. "Hot Skirmish over 'Merry Widow' Hats"; "Women in Hard Battle for Free 'Merry Widows.'"
9. On women in department stores, see Rachel Bowlby, *Just Looking: Consumer Culture in Dreiser, Gissing and Zola* (New York and London: Methuen, 1985); Susan Porter Benson, *Counter Culture: Saleswomen, Managers and Customers in American Department Stores: 1890–1940* (Urbana and Chicago: University of Illinois Press, 1986); Elaine S. Abelson, *When Ladies Go A-Thieving: Middle-Class Shoplifters in the Victorian Department Store* (New York and Oxford: Oxford University Press, 1989), 11; William R. Leach, *Land of Desire: Merchants, Power, and the Rise of a New American Culture* (New York: Pantheon Books, 1993); Erica D. Rappaport, "'The Halls of Temptation': Gender, Politics, and the Construction of the Department Store in Late Victorian London," *Journal of British Studies* (January 1996): 58–83.
10. Angela M. Blake, *How New York Became American* (Baltimore: Johns Hopkins University Press, 2006), 5–6. See also Charles Lockwood, *Manhattan Moves Uptown: An Illustrated History* (Boston: Houghton Mifflin, 1976); William R. Taylor, *In Pursuit of Gotham: Culture and Commerce in New York* (New York and Oxford: Oxford University Press, 1992); George J. Lankevich, *American Metropolis: A History of New York City* (New York: New York University Press, 1998).
11. Elizabeth Ewen, *Immigrant Women in the Land of Dollars: Life and Culture on the Lower East Side* (New York: Monthly Review Press, 1985); Kathy Peiss, *Cheap*

Amusements: Working Women and Leisure in Turn-of-the-Century New York (Philadelphia: Temple University Press, 1986); Susan A. Glenn, *Daughters of the Shtetl: Life and Labor in the Immigrant Generaustion* (Ithaca, N.Y., and London: Cornell University Press, 1990); Barbara A. Schreier, *Becoming American: Clothing and the Jewish Immigrant Experience, 1880–1920* (Chicago: Chicago Historical Society, 1991); David Nasaw, *Going Out: The Rise and Fall of Public Amusements* (reprint; Cambridge, Mass.: Harvard University Press, 1999); Lawrence B. Glickman, *A Living Wage: American Workers and the Making of Consumer Society* (Ithaca, N.Y.: Cornell University Press, 1997); Nan Enstad, *Ladies of Labor, Girls of Adventure* (New York: Columbia University Press, 2000).

12. Lankevich, *American Metropolis*, 126; Taylor, *In Pursuit of Gotham*, 96; David C. Hammack, "Developing for Commercial Culture," in *Inventing Times Square: Commerce and Culture at the Crossroads of the World*, ed. William R. Taylor (New York: Russell Sage Foundation, 1991), 37; Alan Trachtenberg, *The Incorporation of America: Culture and Society in the Gilded Age* (New York: Hill and Wang, 1982); Nancy L. Green, *Ready-to-Wear and Ready-to-Work: A Century of Industry and Immigrants in Paris and New York* (Durham, N.C.: Duke University Press, 1997), 2, 46, 48.

13. Mona Domosh, *American Commodities in an Age of Empire* (New York: Routledge, 2006), 22; Jack Poggi, *Theater in America: The Impact of Economic Forces, 1870–1967* (1966; Ithaca, N.Y.: Cornell University Press, 1968), 6; Philip C. Lewis, *Trouping: How the Show Came to Town* (New York: Harper and Row, 1973), 9.

14. Trachtenberg, *The Incorporation of America*, 4; Tony Freyer, "Legal Restraints on Economic Coordination: Antitrust in Great Britain and America, 1880–1920," in *Coordination and Information: Historical Perspectives on the Organization of Enterprise*, ed. Naomi R. Lamoreaux and Daniel M. G. Raff (Chicago and London: University of Chicago Press, 1995), 183–202; Peter A. Davis, "The Syndicate/Shubert War," in *Inventing Times Square: Commerce and Culture at the Crossroads of the World*, ed. William R. Taylor (New York: Russell Sage Foundation, 1991), 151.

15. Susan Strasser, *Satisfaction Guaranteed: The Making of the American Mass Market* (New York: Pantheon Books, 1989), 89–123; Stephen Fox, *The Mirror Makers: A History of American Advertising and Its Creator* (New York: William Morrow, 1984), 40–77; Jackson Lears, *Fables of Abundance: A Cultural History of Advertising in America* (New York: Basic Books, 1994), 380. For more on the history of advertising, see Michael Schudson, *Advertising: The Uneasy Persuasion* (New York: Basic Books, 1984); Roland Marchand, *Advertising the American Dream: Making Way for Modernity, 1920–1940* (Berkeley: University of California Press, 1985); Lears, *Fables of Abundance*; Richard S. Tedlow, *New and Improved: The Story of Mass Marketing in America* (New York: Basic Books, 1990); Juliann Sivulka, *Soap, Sex, and Cigarettes: A Cultural History of American Advertising* (Belmont, Calif.: Wadsworth Publishing Co., 1998); Roland Marchand, *Creating the Corporate Soul: The Rise of Public Relations and Corporate Imagery in American Big Business* (Berkeley: University of California Press, 1998); Pamela Walker Laird, *Advertising Progress: American Business and the Rise of Consumer Marketing* (Baltimore and London: Johns Hopkins University Press, 1998); Charles F. McGovern, *Sold American: Consumption and Citizenship, 1890–1945* (Chapel Hill: University of North Carolina Press, 2006).

16. Jennifer Scanlon, *Inarticulate Longings: The "Ladies' Home Journal," Gender,*

and the Promises of Consumer Culture (New York: Routledge, 1995), 169–96; Simone Weil Davis, " 'Complex Little Femmes': Ad Women and the Female Consumer," in *Living Up to the Ads: Gender Fictions of the 1920s* (Durham, N.C.: Duke University Press, 2000), 80–104.

17. On women's magazines, see Helen Woodward, *The Lady Persuaders* (New York: I. Obolensky, 1960); Sally Stein, "The Graphic Ordering of Desire: Modernization of a Middle-Class Women's Magazine, 1919–1939," in *The Contest of Meaning: Critical Histories of Photography*, ed. Richard Bolton (Boston: MIT Press, 1989), 145–62; Helen Damon-Moore, *Magazines for the Millions: Gender and Commerce in the "Ladies' Home Journal" and the "Saturday Evening Post," 1880–1910* (Albany: State University of New York Press, 1994); Matthew Schneirov, *The Dream of a New Social Order: Popular Magazines in America, 1893–1914* (New York: Columbia University Press, 1994); Ellen Gruber Garvey, *The Adman in the Parlor: Magazines and the Gendering of Consumer Culture, 1880s to 1910* (New York and Oxford: Oxford University Press, 1996); Richard Ohmann, *Selling Culture: Magazines, Markets, and Class at the Turn of the Century* (London and New York: Verso, 1996); Scanlon, *Inarticulate Longings*; Carolyn L. Kitch, *The Girl on the Magazine Cover: The Origins of Visual Stereotypes in American Mass Media* (Chapel Hill and London: University of North Carolina Press, 2001); Nancy A. Walker, *Shaping Our Mother's World: American Women's Magazines* (Jackson: University Press of Mississippi, 2000).

18. Caroline Seebohm, *The Man Who Was Vogue* (New York: Viking Press, 1982), 259, 260–61, 418.

19. Nancy J. Troy, *Couture Culture: A Study in Modern Art and Fashion* (Cambridge, Mass., and London: MIT Press, 2003), 223.

20. Ibid.; Kristin Hoganson, "The Fashionable World: Imagined Communities of Dress," in *After the Imperial Turn: Thinking with and Through the Nation*, ed. Antoinette M. Burton (Durham, N.C.: Duke University Press, 2003), 260–78; Kristin Hoganson, *Consumers' Imperium: The Global Production of American Domesticity, 1865–1929* (Chapel Hill: University of North Carolina Press, 2007).

21. Leach, *Land of Desire*, 93.

22. Wendy Gamber, *The Female Economy: The Millinery and Dressmaking Trades; 1860–1930* (Urbana: University of Illinois Press, 1997), 111; Jane Mulvagh, *Vogue History of Twentieth Century Fashion* (London: Viking, 1988), 9; Nicholson Baker and Margaret Brentano, *The World on Sunday: Graphic Art in Joseph Pulitzer's Newspaper* (New York: Doubleday, 2005), 9; Valerie Steele, *Paris Fashion: A Cultural History* (New York: Oxford University Press, 1988).

23. See "Gowns Seen on the Stage," *Harper's Bazar* (hereafter *HB*) (July 1913): 28–29; Seebohm, *The Man Who Was Vogue*, 259, 260–61, 418; "The Stage as the Mirror of Fashion," *HB* (October 1914): 53; "Mrs. Vernon Castle and Her Husband Will Appear in the New Play 'Watch Your Step,' " *Vogue* (December 1914): n.p.

24. Edna Woolman Chase and Ilka Chase, *Always in Vogue* (New York: Doubleday and Company, Inc., 1954), 132.

25. Nancy Hall-Duncan, *The History of Fashion Photography* (New York: Alpine Book Co. Inc., 1979), 14, 32, 40.

26. This arrangement eventually backfired on *Vanity Fair*. When the magazine failed to publish photographs of Castle as promised, she threatened to cancel her sub-

scription and withdraw her support. The *Vanity Fair* editorial staff had to work hard to keep her happy and published several photographs and illustrations as compensation. See the caption under the photograph of Irene Castle in *Vanity Fair* (January 1916): 47, and the caption under the photograph of "Mrs. Vernon Castle," *Vanity Fair* (April 1917): 45.

27. See "Stage Fashions of the Month: Maude Adams, Leslie Carter, Julie Opp, Frances Starr, Maxine Elliott," *Theatre Magazine* (March 1909): n.p.; Anne Archbald, "Clothes Seen on the Stage," *Theatre Magazine* (August 1916): 104; Mlle. Manhattan, "Footlight Fashions," *Theatre Magazine* (January 1917): 52; Anne Archbald, "Clothes Seen on the Stage," *Theatre Magazine* (May 1915): 268; "Another 'Liberal' Success . . . The 'Blanche Ring' Frock," *Dry Goods Economist* (hereafter *DGE*), April 16, 1910, 13; "Announcing the Hazel Dawn Debutante Dress," *DGE*, January 16, 1915, 46–47.

28. Rob Schorman, *Selling Style: Clothing and Social Change at the Turn of the Century* (Philadelphia: University of Pennsylvania Press, 2003), 51–57; Claudia B. Kidwell and Margaret C. Christman, *Suiting Everyone: The Democratization of Clothing in America* (Washington, D.C.: Smithsonian Institution Press), 137; Barbara Burman, "Made at Home by Clever Fingers: Home Dressmaking in Edwardian England," *The Culture of Sewing: Gender, Consumption and Home Dressmaking*, ed. Barbara Burman (Oxford and New York: Berg, 1999), 35, 49.

29. Elizabeth Wilson, *The Sphinx in the City: Urban Life, the Control of Disorder, and Women* (Berkeley: University of California Press, 1999), 7. See also Deborah L. Parsons, *Streetwalking the Metropolis: Women, the City, and Modernity* (Oxford: Oxford University Press, 2000), 26, 28, 38.

30. See, for example, Benson, *Counter Culture*; Leach, *Land of Desire*; Lauren Rabinovitz, *For the Love of Pleasure: Women, Movies, and Culture in Turn-of-the-Century Chicago* (New Brunswick, N.J., and London: Rutgers University Press, 1998). One notable exception is Andrew L. Erdman's work on American vaudeville, which suggests that vaudeville impresarios like B. F. Keith adopted many of the same marketing strategies as consumer goods manufacturers to attract mass audiences. Erdman focuses primarily on the production and distribution of borderline performances and other forms of "blue vaudeville" and is less concerned with analyzing the specific business relationships that developed between theater managers and manufacturers or the promotion of actual commodities onstage. Andrew L. Erdman, *Blue Vaudeville: Sex, Morals and the Mass Marketing of Amusement, 1895–1915* (Jefferson, N.C., and London: McFarland and Company, Inc., Publishers, 2004). Kim Marra, Susan Glenn, and Linda Mizejewski have also offered commentaries on the relationship between theater and fashion in the United States. Kim Marra, "Elsie de Wolfe, *Circa* 1901: The Dynamics of Prescriptive Feminine Performance in American Theatre and Society," *Theatre Survey* 35.1 (May 1994): 108; Susan A. Glenn, *Female Spectacle: The Theatrical Roots of Modern Feminism* (Cambridge, Mass.: Harvard University Press, 2000); Linda Mizejewski, *Ziegfeld Girl: Image and Icon in American Culture* (Durham, N.C.: Duke University Press, 1999), 91. Studies by cultural, art, and theater historians have gone further to highlight the symbiotic relationship between the fashion and theater industries in Britain and France, but there has not yet been a full-length study of the multiple and multidirectional relationships that developed between producers, manufacturers, performers, and audiences/consumers in the United States. On the British

context, see Joel H. Kaplan and Sheila Stowell, *Theatre and Fashion: Oscar Wilde to the Suffragettes* (Cambridge: Cambridge University Press, 1994). On the French context, see Troy, *Couture Culture*.

31. Hoganson, "The Fashionable World," 260–78; Hoganson, *Consumers' Imperium*; Domosh, *American Commodities in an Age of Empire*. In its exploration of the overlapping, competing exchanges that occurred between theater managers, department store entrepreneurs, consumer goods manufacturers, theater critics, female audiences, and stage performers, *When Broadway Was the Runway* is a response to David Savran's call for theater and performance scholars "to specify the relation between a given performance and its *habitus*, the 'cultural unconscious' or set of 'principles which generate and organize practices and representations.' " Citing Bourdieu, Savran calls for works that pay closer attention to "the social structures in which *habitus* operates, the 'arenas of production, circulation, and appropriations of goods, services, knowledge, or status, and the competitive positions held by [social] actors." Such an approach requires an emphasis on the messiness of cultural processes, on the multiple factors that lead to a particular cultural expression, and on the cross-industry alliances and tensions that develop between producers, distributors, and consumers. Indeed, what is so appealing about this approach, especially for an analysis of theater's engagement with consumer culture, is the way that it avoids an overemphasis on consumption's transgressive possibilities by acknowledging the material, everyday challenges that limit the freedom of the disempowered, while opening up new ways of seeing resistance and agency in actions that might otherwise escape notice. In its more expansive consideration of intersecting identities and interests, this approach also represents a movement away from the potentially limiting argument that involvement in the culture industries binds and liberates simultaneously. David Savran, "Choices Made and Unmade," *Theater* 31.2 (2001): 89–95; James W. Cook, "The Return of the Culture Industry," in *The Cultural Turn in U.S. History*, ed. James W. Cook (Chicago: University of Chicago Press, forthcoming 2008), page unavailable; Emily Allen, "The Circus and Victorian Society [review]," *Theatre Survey* (May 2007): 194–96.

Maurya Wickstrom's recent *Performing Consumers: Global Capital and Its Theatrical Seductions* critiques previous tendencies within cultural studies to celebrate the potential for consumers to dismantle corporate structures through the acquisition of commodities. Although highly compelling, Wickstrom's argument does not take into account more nuanced work by cultural historians such as Nan Enstad and Margaret Finnegan who, in their work on early twentieth-century working-class laborers and suffragists, point to the many ways that historical actors have used consumer culture as a "material resource" to resist oppressive power structures but nevertheless acknowledge the limitations of living in a consumer society. In thinking through questions of resistance and agency, I have also found helpful Alison Piepmeier's insistence on asking "not whether [women] are victims or agency, but ... how do *acts* of agency and resistance emerge within a social, cultural, and perhaps a personal context of disempowerment and even oppression?" Maurya Wickstrom, *Performing Consumers: Global Capital and Its Theatrical Seductions* (New York: Routledge, 2006); Enstad, *Ladies of Labor, Girls of Adventure*; Margaret Finnegan, *Selling Suffrage: Consumer Culture and Votes for Women* (New York: Columbia University Press, 1999); Alison Piepmeier, *Out in Public: Configurations of Women's Bodies in Nineteenth-Century America* (Chapel Hill: University of North Carolina Press, 2004), 9.

In its focus on the commercial aspects of theatrical production, this book joins other theater historians in returning to the stereotypically prosaic yet illuminating subjects of business and economics. In recent years scholars such as Michael McKinnie, Sally Charnow, Steven Alder, and Ric Knowles have taken heed to Tracy C. Davis's warning that "[i]f culture's historians ignore business, they overlook the resources that make or break an artist choice" (1). Theater and performance scholars have often shied away from projects that deal with commercial theater and its products in favor of tackling subjects deemed more "worthy" of scholarly analysis. "[T]his scholarly myopia has very real consequences for the project of inclusivity," Susan Bennett warns, "and, indeed, for how we devise our approaches to understanding contemporary theatre and performance in both its production and reception contexts" (3). Anti-commercial prejudices have also had a profound influence on the writing of early twentieth-century American theater history and continue to inform the way we read and interpret commercial theater today. Recent work on the relationship between theater and commerce includes Tracy C. Davis, *The Economics of the British Stage, 1800–1914* (Cambridge: Cambridge University Press, 2000); Steven Adler, *On Broadway: Art and Commerce on the Great White Way* (Carbondale: Southern Illinois Press, 2004); Sally Charnow, *Theatre, Politics, and Markets in Fin-de-Siècle Paris: Staging Modernity* (New York: Palgrave, 2005); Michael McKinnie, *City Stages: Theatre and Urban Space in a Global City* (Toronto: University of Toronto Press, 2007); Ric Knowles, *Reading the Material Theatre* (Cambridge: Cambridge University Press, 2004); Susan Bennett, "Theatre/Tourism," *Theatre Journal* 57.3 (October 2005): 407–28; Thomas Postlewait, "George Edwardes and Musical Comedy: The Transformation of London Theatre and Society, 1878–1914," in *The Performing Century: Nineteenth-Century Theatre's History,* ed. Tracy C. Davis (London: Palgrave Macmillan, 2007), 80–102; Vincent Landro, "Media Mania: The Demonizing of the Theatrical Syndicate," *Journal of American Drama and Theatre* 13 (spring 2001): 23–50.

32. Jeffrey D. Mason, "Curtain Raiser," in *Performing America: Cultural Nationalism in American Theater,* ed. Jeffrey D. Mason and J. Ellen Gainor (Ann Arbor: University of Michigan Press, 1999), 1; Philip Auslander, *Liveness: Performance in a Mediated Culture* (London and New York: Routledge, 1999), 1–9; Jill Dolan, *Utopia in Performance: Finding Hope at the Theatre* (Ann Arbor: University of Michigan Press, 1999), 36–41; David Román, "Tragedy and the Performing Arts in the Wake of Sept. 11, 2001," in *Performance in America: Contemporary U.S. Culture and the Performing Arts* (Durham and London: Duke University Press, 2005): 226–79.

Chapter 1

1. "American Stage in Danger, Says William Winter," *Theatre Magazine* (September 1907): 89.

2. See John Frick, "A Changing Theatre: New York and Beyond," in *The Cambridge History of the American Theatre,* ed. Don B. Wilmeth and Christopher Bigsby

(Cambridge: Cambridge University Press, 1999), 2: 215; Monroe Lippman, "The Effect of the Theatrical Syndicate on Theatrical Art in America," *Quarterly Journal of Speech* (April 1940): 275–82. Many of the Theatrical Syndicate's greatest critics reiterated their attacks in memoirs and books of criticism. See, for example, John Rankieri Touse, *Sixty Years of the Theatre* (New York: Funk and Wagnalls, 1916), 462–63; William Winter, *Other Days* (New York: Moffett, Yard, 1908), 330; Sheldon Cheney, *The Theatre: Three Thousand Years of Drama, Acting, and Stagecraft* (New York: Longmans, Green, 1929), 500; Walter Prichard Eaton, *At the New Theatre and Others* (Boston: Small, Maynard, and Co., 1910), 1–10. For a list of newspapers opposed to the Syndicate, see "Newspapers Opposed to the Theatre Trust," *New York Dramatic Mirror* (hereafter *NYDM*), January 1, 1898, 2.

3. "The Great Theatrical Syndicate: How Six Dictators Control Our Amusements IV: To-day and To-Morrow," *Leslie's Monthly Magazine* 59.3 (January 1905): 335.

4. Mark Hodin, "The Disavowal of Ethnicity: Legitimate Theatre and the Social Construction of Literary Value in Turn-of-the-Century America," *Theatre Journal* 52 (2000): 214–16; Vincent Landro, "Media Mania: The Demonizing of the Theatrical Syndicate," *Journal of American Drama and Theatre* 13 (spring 2001): 23–50; Benjamin McArthur, *Actors and American Culture: 1880–1920* (1984; Iowa City: University of Iowa Press, 2000), 146. On nineteenth-century theater criticism, see Tice L. Miller, *Bohemians and Critics: American Theatre Criticism in the Nineteenth Century* (Metuchen, N.J., and London: Scarecrow Press, Inc., 1981); Tice L. Miller, "Alan Dale: The Hearst Critic," *Educational Theatre Journal* (March 1974): 69–80.

5. On antimodernism, see Jackson Lears, *No Place of Grace: Antimodernism and the Transformation of American Culture: 1880–1920* (Chicago: University of Chicago Press, 1981).

6. Lawrence W. Levine, *Highbrow Lowbrow: The Emergence of Cultural Hierarchy in America* (Cambridge, Mass.: Harvard University Press, 1988), 30, 101, 176–77, 184. Although the word "legitimate" had long been used to distinguish classical plays from "popular" melodramas, it was during this period of shifting hierarchies that it came to refer to theater that connoted greater cultural and literary value. Hodin, "The Disavowal of Ethnicity," 212. Vaudeville's designation as lowbrow theater helps to explain why critics failed to express similar concerns about the incorporation and systemization of vaudeville theaters. Operating independently of "legitimate" theater, with their own theaters and booking agencies, vaudeville managers drew inspiration from the Syndicate and began a similar process of streamlining booking processes in the 1890s. In 1900, the impresario B. F. Keith oversaw the formation of the Association of Vaudeville Managers of the United States, which brought the eastern and western branches of the existing vaudeville circuits under the control of a centralized booking system. This is not to suggest that the incorporation of vaudeville went uncontested. Sime Silverman, the publisher of *Variety*, and Harry Mountford, the leader of the White Rats union for vaudeville performers, challenged the monopolistic tactics and oppressive conditions that Keith and others imposed on performers. Arthur Frank Wertheim, *Vaudeville Wars: How the Keith-Albee and Orpheum Circuits Controlled the Big Time and Its Performers* (New York: Palgrave Macmillan, 2006), 50–66; 181–93; Robert W. Snyder, *The Voice of the City: Vaudeville and Popular Culture in New York* (New York and Oxford: Oxford University Press, 1989), 37; M. Alison Kibler, *Rank*

Ladies: Gender and Cultural Hierarchy in American Vaudeville (Chapel Hill: University of North Carolina Press, 1999), 15–21.

7. Charles F. McGovern, *Sold American: Consumption and Citizenship, 1890–1945* (Chapel Hill: University of North Carolina Press, 2006), 36; Roland Marchand, *Advertising the American Dream: Making Way for Modernity, 1920–1940* (Berkeley: University of California Press, 1985).

8. "Lackaye Blames the Women: Declares They Are Responsible for the Degenerating of the Stage," *New York Times* (hereafter *NYT*), February 23, 1910, 6.

9. Hodin, "The Disavowal of Ethnicity"; Landro, "Media Mania." On the feminization of mass culture, see Janice Radway, "On the Gender of the Middlebrow Consumer and the Threat of the Culturally Fraudulent Female," *South Atlantic Quarterly* 93.4 (fall 1994): 883, 886; Andreas Huysson, "Mass Culture as Woman: Modernism's Other," in *After the Great Divide: Modernism, Mass Culture, Postmodernism* (Bloomington and Indianapolis: Indiana University Press, 1986), 53, 55; Ann Douglas, *The Feminization of American Culture* (New York: Alfred A. Knopf, 1977); Dorothy Chansky, *Composing Ourselves: The Little Theatre Movement and the American Audience* (Carbondale: Southern Illinois University Press, 2004), esp. 107–48; Stacy Wolf, "*Wicked* Divas, Musical Theater and Internet Fans," *camera obscura* 65.22.2 (2007): 38–71.

10. Isaac F. Marcosson and Daniel Frohman, *Charles Frohman: Manager and Man* (New York and London: Harper and Brothers, 1916), 186; Mark [sic] Klaw, "The Theatrical Syndicate's Reply to Its Critics," *NYT*, March 26, 1905, 36; Jack Poggi, *Theater in America: The Impact of Economic Forces, 1870–1967* (1966; Ithaca, N.Y.: Cornell University Press, 1968), 12–13; Alfred L. Bernheim, *The Business of the Theatre: An Economic History of the American Theatre, 1750–1932* (New York: Benjamin Blom, Inc., 1932), 46–47; Frick, "A Changing Theatre," 212; Hodin, "The Disavowal of Ethnicity," 217 n. 12. On theatrical management in Australia, see Veronica Kelly, "A Complementary Economy? National Markets and International Product in Early Australian Theatre Managements," *New Theatre Quarterly* 21.1 (February 2005): 77–95.

11. Bernheim, *The Business of the Theatre*, 30–31; Poggi, *Theater in America*, 6–7; Peter A. Davis, "From Stock to Combination: The Panic of 1873 and Its Effects on the American Theater Industry," *Theater History Studies* 8 (1988): 1–9; McArthur, *Actors and American Culture, 1880–1920*, 5, 9.

12. Poggi, *Theater in America*, 6; Philip C. Lewis, *Trouping: How the Show Came to Town* (New York: Harper and Row, Pub., 1973), 9. On economic incentives for touring in Britain, see Tracy C. Davis, *The Economics of the British Stage, 1800–1914* (Cambridge: Cambridge University Press, 2000), 348–54.

13. Poggi, *Theater in America*, 3. Margaret Knapp, "Introductory Essay," in *Inventing Times Square: Commerce and Culture at the Crossroads of the World*, ed. William R. Taylor (New York: Russell Sage Foundation, 1991), 122.

14. John Frick, *New York's First Theatrical Center: The Rialto at Union Square* (1983; Ann Arbor: UMI Research Press, 1985), esp. 107–50.

15. "The 'Rialto' a Generation Ago," *Theatre Magazine* (July 1912): 57.

16. Mary Henderson, *The City and the Theatre* (1973; New York: Back Stage Books, 2004), 106–47; Wertheim, *Vaudeville Wars*, 95–99.

17. Bernheim, *The Business of the Theatre*, 34–35; Mark Klaw, "The Theatrical

Syndicate—the Other Side," *Cosmopolitan* 38 (December 1904): 201; Klaw, "The Theatrical Syndicate's Reply to Its Critics."

18. Bernheim, *The Business of the Theatre*, 37, 40–43; Marcosson and Frohman, *Charles Frohman*, 187; Klaw, "The Theatrical Syndicate's Reply to Its Critics."

19. Marcosson and Frohman, *Charles Frohman*, 24–66; Kim Marra, *Strange Duets: Impresarios and Actresses in the American Theatre, 1865-1914* (Iowa City: University of Iowa Press, 2006), xiv; "That Theatrical Syndicate," *NYDM*, March 7, 1896, 17.

20. "Does Not Think There Will Be Trouble" and "Will Stand Aloof," *NYDM*, March 7, 1896, 17; "The New Booking System," *NYDM*, April 10, 1897, 15. For other reactions, see "Views in Various Cities," *NYDM*, October 16, 1897, 17; "That Theatrical Syndicate," 17.

21. "Theatrical Trust Supplement no. 2," *NYDM*, November 20, 1897, 4; "Theatrical Trust Supplement no. 4," *NYDM*, December 4, 1897, 2; "Theatrical Trust Supplement no. 8," *NYDM*, January 1, 1898, 1, 3.

22. Bernheim, *The Business of the Theatre*, 49, 59; "The Great Theatrical Syndicate [II]," *Leslie's Monthly Magazine* (November 1904): 41; Montrose J. Moses, "The Disintegration of the Theatre," *Forum* (April 1911): 466; "The Theatre Trust Must Go to Pieces," Supplement no. 4, *NYDM*, December 4, 1897, 1; Monroe Lippman, "The First Organized Revolt Against the Theatrical Syndicate," *Quarterly Journal of Speech* (December 1955): 343–51; Peter A. Davis, "The Syndicate/Shubert War," in *Inventing Times Square: Commerce and Culture at the Crossroads of the World*, ed. William R. Taylor (New York: Russell Sage Foundation, 1991); Landro, "Media Mania," 39.

23. Some accounts suggest that the Syndicate's commission was much higher, ranging between 20 and 50 percent. See Poggi, *Theater in America*, 14; Bernheim, *The Business of the Theater*, 50.

24. "The Great Theatrical Syndicate [II]," 34.

25. Lippman, "The First Organized Revolt Against the Theatrical Syndicate," 349. Minnie Maddern Fiske was the lone exception.

26. Lewis, *Trouping*, 9; "The Unknown 'C.F.'—And the Manner of Man He Is," *NYT*, August 9, 1908, SM5; Samuel E. Moffett, "Charles Frohman," *Cosmopolitan* (July 1902): 293; "A Busy Day with Charles Frohman," *Theatre Magazine* (September 1912): 91.

27. "The Great Theatrical Syndicate [II]," 41; "Belasco Drops Agencies," *NYT*, September 24, 1903, 5.

28. Norman Hapgood, *The Stage in America, 1897–1900* (New York: Macmillan Co., 1901), 29–30.

29. On the Syndicate's confrontation with James S. Metcalfe, a theater critic for *Life* magazine whom it banned from its theaters for his anti-Semitic attacks, see "The Managers' Predicament," *NYDM*, June 17, 1905, 10; Hodin, "The Disavowal of Ethnicity," 220–23; Landro, "Media Mania," 37–38; Harley Erdman, *Staging the Jew: The Performance of an Ethnicity, 1860-1920* (New Brunswick, N.J.: Rutgers University Press, 1997), 94, 99; John Flautz, *Life: The Gentle Satirist* (Bowling Green, Ohio, 1972), 166.

30. Moses, "The Disintegration of the Theatre," 466.

31. Hapgood, *The Stage in America*, 30; George H. Douglas, *The Golden Age of the Newspaper* (Westport, Conn., and London: Greenwood Press, 1999), 143–56.

32. Benedict Anderson, *Imagined Communities: Reflections on the Origin and Spread of Nationalism* (1983; London and New York: Verso, 1991), 44.

33. Hapgood, *The Stage in America*, 31; Susan Strasser, *Satisfaction Guaranteed: The Making of the American Mass Market* (New York: Pantheon Books, 1989), 89–123; Stephen Fox, *The Mirror Makers: A History of American Advertising and Its Creator* (New York: William Morrow, 1984),40–77; Andrew L. Erdman, *Blue Vaudeville: Sex, Morals and the Mass Marketing of Amusement, 1895–1915* (Jefferson, N.C., and London: McFarland and Company, Inc., Publishers, 2004), 8, 16–18.

34. "Misrepresentation: Misleading Advertising Exposed by a Boston Newspaper," Theatrical Trust Supplement no. 2, *NYDM*, November 20, 1897, 3; "The Theatre Trust Must Go to Pieces," Theatrical Trust Supplement no. 4, *NYDM*, December 4, 1897, 1.

35. Strasser, *Satisfaction Guaranteed*, 44–46.

36. Landro, "Media Mania," 29–30.

37. "It Makes the Blood Boil," Theatrical Trust Supplement, no. 5, *NYDM*, December 11, 1897, 2. See also the editorial in the *Buffalo Evening News*, October 6, 1897, quoted in "Views in Various Cities" *NYDM*, October 16, 1897, 17. On anti-Semitic representations, see Bram Dijkstra, *Evil Sisters: The Theatre of Female Sexuality and the Cult of Manhood* (New York: Alfred A. Knopf, 1996); Andrea Dworkin, *Scapegoat: The Jews, Israel, and Women's Liberation* (New York: Free Press, 2000).

38. "The Usher," Theatrical Supplement no. 12, *NYDM*, January 29, 1898, 3.

39. Hans Krabberdom, *The Model Man: A Life of Edward William Bok, 1863–1930* (Amsterdam: Rodopi, 2001), 104.

40. Winter, quoted in Hodin, "The Disavowal of Ethnicity," 218.

41. "The Department Store Theatre," *NYDM*, June 17, 1905, 10.

42. George J. Lankevich, *American Metropolis: A History of New York City* (New York: New York University Press, 1998), 122.

43. Susan A. Glenn, *Daughters of the Shtetl: Life and Labor in the Immigrant Generation* (Ithaca, N.Y., and London: Cornell University Press, 1990); Nan Enstad, *Ladies of Labor, Girls of Adventure* (New York: Columbia University Press, 2000); Elizabeth Ewen, *Immigrant Women in the Land of Dollars: Life and Culture on the Lower East Side* (New York: Monthly Review Press, 1985).

44. Hodin, "The Disavowal of Ethnicity," 223.

45. Harrison Grey Fiske, "Evidently—Not," Theatrical Trust Supplement no. 1, *NYDM*, November 13, 1897, 1.

46. "W. D. Howells Against the Trust," Theatrical Trust Supplement no. 9, *NYDM*, January 8, 1898, 2.

47. Quoted in McArthur, *Actors and American Culture*, 146.

48. "As to Trusts," *NYDM*, September 4, 1897, 12. Moses, "The Disintegration of the Theatre"; "The Great Theatrical Syndicate [IV]," *Leslie's Monthly Magazine* 59.3 (January 1905): 225.

49. Hodin, "The Disavowal of Ethnicity," 216; Landro, "Media Mania," 23–50.

50. Alan Dale, "Alan Dale's Recipe for Making 'Stars,'" *Cosmopolitan* (December 1906): 195; Alan Dale, "Nazimova and Some Others," *Cosmopolitan* (April 1907): 674–76.

51. Marcosson and Frohman, *Charles Frohman*, 291, 127, 136, 139, 143.

52. Ibid., 139. On Daly, see Dora Knowlton Ranous, *Diary of a Daly Debutante:*

Being Passages from the Journal of a Member of Augustin Daly's Famous Company of Players (New York: Duffield and Company, 1910); Kim Marra, "Taming America as Actress: Augustin Daly, Ada Rehan, and the Discourse of Imperial Frontier Conquest," in *Performing America: Cultural Nationalism in American Theater*, ed. Jeffrey D. Mason and J. Ellen Gainor (Ann Arbor: University of Michigan Press, 1999), 60, 63; Marra, *Strange Duets*, 1–30, 31–71.

53. Moffett, "Charles Frohman," 293; "A Busy Day with Charles Frohman," 91; "The Unknown 'C.F.,'" SM5.

54. Marcosson and Frohman, *Charles Frohman*, 217, 283; Moffett, "Charles Frohman," 294.

55. Marcosson and Frohman, *Charles Frohman*, 279; Billie Burke (with Cameron Shipp), *With Powder on My Nose* (New York: Coward-McCann, Inc., 1959), 18.

56. Marcosson and Frohman, *Charles Frohman*, 139.

57. "Art vs. Commercialism," *Theatre Magazine* (July 1901): 16; Hapgood, *The Stage in America*, 32.

58. "The Drama in New York During 1907–8," *New York World*, May 17, 1908, 4M; Frick, "A Changing Theatre," 215; "The Great Theatrical Syndicate [II]," 31; "Art vs. Commercialism," 16; "American Stage in Danger," 269.

59. "American Stage in Danger," 269; Hapgood, *The Stage in America*, 35.

60. T. J. Jackson Lears, "From Salvation to Self-Realization: Advertising and the Therapeutic Roots of the Consumer Culture, 1810–1930," in *Culture of Consumption: Critical Essays in American History, 1880–1980*, ed. T. J. Jackson Lears and Richard Wightman Fox (New York: Random House, 1983), 37; James Livingston, "Modern Subjectivity and Consumer Culture" in *Getting and Spending: European and American Consumer Societies in the Twentieth Century*, ed. Susan Strasser, Charles McGovern, and Matthias Judt (Cambridge and New York: Cambridge University Press, 1998), 422–24. On white masculinity in this period, see Michael Kimmel, *Manhood in America: A Cultural History* (New York: Free Press, 1996); Kristin L. Hoganson, *Fighting for American Manhood: How Gender Politics Provoked the Spanish-American and Philippine-American Wars* (New Haven, Conn., and London: Yale University Press, 1998); Gail Bederman, *Manliness and Civilization: A Cultural History of Gender and Race in the United States, 1880–1917* (Chicago and London: University of Chicago Press, 1995); Gaylyn Studlar, *This Mad Masquerade: Stardom and Masculinity in the Jazz Age* (New York: Columbia University Press, 1996); John F. Kasson, *Houdini, Tarzan, and the Perfect Man: The White Male Body and the Challenge of Modernity in America* (New York: Hill and Wang, 2001).

61. Marra, *Strange Duets*, 250 n. 4, xiii–xxii.

62. Studlar, *This Mad Masquerade*. On matinee idols, see David Caroll, *Matinée Idols* (New York: Arbor House, 1972). On female performers, see "Women and the American Theatre," *The Nation*, June 1, 1918, 665; Marra, *Strange Duets*, xv; Susan A. Glenn, *Female Spectacle: The Theatrical Roots of Modern Feminism* (Cambridge, Mass.: Harvard University Press, 2000).

63. Lears, *No Place of Grace*, 30.

64. Theodore Roosevelt, "On American Motherhood," http://www.bartleby.com/268/10/29.html, accessed July 3, 2007.

65. Thomas G. Dyer, *Theodore Roosevelt and the Idea of Race* (Baton Rouge: Lou-

isiana State University Press, 1980). See also Kimmel, *Manhood in America*; Bederman, *Manliness and Civilization*; Kasson, *Houdini, Tarzan, and the Perfect Man*.

66. "American Stage in Danger," 269.

67. McArthur, *Actors and American Culture*, 28–29.

68. On the politics of whiteness in early twentieth-century American culture, see Michael Rogin, *Blackface, White Noise: Jewish Immigrants in the Hollywood Melting Pot* (Berkeley: University of California Press, 1996); Matthew Frye Jacobson, *Whiteness of a Different Color: European Immigrants and the Alchemy of Race* (Cambridge, Mass.: Harvard University Press, 1998); David R. Roediger, *The Wages of Whiteness: Race and the Making of the American Working Class* (New York: Verso, 1998); Laura Wexler, *Tender Violence: Domestic Visions in an Age of U.S. Imperialism* (Chapel Hill: University of North Carolina Press, 2000); David R. Roediger, *Working Towards Whiteness: How America's Immigrants Became White; The Strange Journey from Ellis Island to the Suburbs* (New York: Basic Books, 2005).

69. While booming Yiddish theaters in the Lower East Side provided ample opportunity for Jewish actors and impresarios, many performers also sought mainstream success. Nina Warnke, "Immigrant Popular Culture as Contested Sphere: Yiddish Music Halls, the Yiddish Press, and the Processes of Americanization, 1900–1910," *Theatre Journal* 48.3 (1996): 321–35; Judith Thissen, "Reconsidering the Decline of the New York Yiddish Theatre in the Early 1900s," *Theatre Survey* 44.2 (November 2003): 173–97. On early twentieth-century Jewish stage stars, see Joan Sochen, "Fanny Brice and Sophie Tucker: Blending the Particular with the Universal," in *From Hester Street to Hollywood: The Jewish-American Stage and Screen*, ed. Sarah Blacher Cohen (Bloomington: Indiana University Press, 1983), 44–57; Barbara W. Grossman, *Funny Woman: The Life and Times of Fanny Brice* (Bloomington and Indianapolis: Indiana University Press, 1991); Rogin, *Blackface, White Noise*; Andrea Most, *Making Americans: Jews and the Broadway Musical* (Cambridge, Mass.: Harvard University Press, 2004).

70. Glenn, *Female Spectacle*, 33. See also Erdman, *Staging the Jew*; Hodin, "The Disavowal of Ethnicity," 220.

71. Although many of his discoveries were American, Frohman also imported new talent and arranged tours for such well-established foreign stars as Mrs. Patrick Campbell, Olga Nethersole, and Sir Charles Wyndham. Indeed, as much as he claimed to enjoy developing performers, he later explained that his extensive business operations did not permit him to "conduct a theatrical kindergarten" and he therefore preferred to work with skilled experts who could give him the "quick results" he needed. Marcosson and Frohman, *Charles Frohman*, 225, 297.

72. "Foreign and Native Stars," *NYT*, April 1, 1895, 8.

73. Franklin Fyles, "The Invasion of the American Stage," *Leslie's Monthly Magazine* (December 1904): 145, 151.

74. McArthur, *Actors and American Culture*, 28–29; Arthur Klauber, "Ibsen and Shakespeare as First-Night Lures," *NYT*, March 27, 1910, X8.

75. Hapgood, *The Stage in America*, 33.

76. Marcosson and Frohman, *Charles Frohman*, 133, 151; Moffett, "Charles Frohman," 293; Letter to Haddon Chambers, November 19, 1901; Letter to Elizabeth Marbury, November 25, 1901, Frohman (Charles) Letter-press Copybook Collection, New York Public Library. See also Marcosson and Frohman, *Charles Frohman*, 230–31;

"The Unknown 'C.F.,'" SM5; "French Can't Sing or Dance," *New York World*, March 22, 1908, E3. Frohman's position within the Syndicate, which guaranteed the best routing possible for his productions, was critical to his success in securing foreign rights. "The Rise and Fall of the Theatrical Syndicate," quoted in Bernheim, *The Business of the Theatre*, 59. On the British franchising system, see Davis, *The Economics of the British Stage*, 346–54.

77. "The Great Theatrical Syndicate [IV]," 333.

78. Moffett, "Charles Frohman," 294–95.

79. Charles Frohman, "The Lure and Lesson of the Foreign Playwright," *NYT*, September 5, 1909, X2.

80. "The Great Theatrical Syndicate [II]," 31–32; "Brazen Shows," Theatrical Trust Supplement no. 8, *NYDM*, January 1, 1898, 2.

81. Kristin Hoganson, "The Fashionable World: Imagined Communities of Dress," in *After the Imperial Turn: Thinking with and Through the Nation*, ed. Antoinette M. Burton (Durham, N.C.: Duke University Press, 2003): 260–78. For more on the relationship between fashion and national identity, see Alison Goodrum, "Land of Hip and Glory: Fashioning the 'Classic' National Body," in *Dressed to Impress: Looking the Part*, ed. William J. F. Keenan (Oxford: Berg, 2001), 85–104; Wendy Parkins, ed., *Fashioning the Body Politic* (London: Berg, 2002); Maria Makela, "The Rise and Fall of the Flapper Dress: Nationalism and Anti-Semitism in Early-Twentieth-Century Discourses on German Fashion," *Journal of Popular Culture* (June 2003): 183–208; Sandra A. Niessen, *Re-orienting Fashion: The Globalization of Asian Dress* (Oxford and New York: Berg, 2003); Jean Allman, ed. *Fashioning Africa: Power and the Politics of Dress* (Bloomington: Indiana University Press, 2004).

82. "What We Mean by 'American Fashions,' by the Editors," *Ladies' Home Journal* (hereafter *LHJ*) (October 1910): 3.

83. Ibid.; "Nazimova for American Modes," *NYT*, December 14, 1912, 10; Justia, "Nationalism in Dress [letter to the editor]," *NYT*, January 1, 1909, 10.

84. "Would Bar Foreign Play," *NYT*, November 11, 1910, 9.

85. F. Mackay, F. Edwin Elwell, and Edwin Markham, "A National Art Theater for America: A Symposium," *The Arena* (July 1904): 48. On the endowed theater, see also Edward Fuller, "An Independent Theatre," *Lippincott's Monthly Magazine* (March 1892): 371–75; Helena Modjeska, "Endowed Theatres and the American Stage," *Forum* (November 1892): 337–44; "On the Endowing of Theaters," *Current Literature* 22.2 (August 1897): 140–42; Mackay, Elwell, and Markham, "A National Art Theater for America," 48–53; Robert Stodart, "The Endowed Theater Idea," *The Independent*, November 1, 1900, 2629–32; F. William Randolf, "Endowed Theatres," *Lippincott's Monthly Magazine* (February 1912): 283–84. Ironically, many of the critics who opposed the Syndicate's importation of foreign products seem to have been quite willing to adopt a model from the European art theater movement and to support plays by foreign authors of the avant garde. This apparent hypocrisy further suggests that what was really at stake in the war against the Syndicate was an idealized vision of elite white culture, untrammeled by commerce.

86. "Art vs. Commercialism," 12–16.

87. "It Will Not Be Tolerated," Theatrical Trust Supplement no. 8, *NYDM*, January 1, 1898, 1.

88. J. Dennis Rich and Kevin L. Sullivan, "The New Theatre of Chicago, 1906–1907," *Educational Theatre Journal* (March 1974): 53–68. See also James Highlander, "America's First Art Theatre: The New Theatre of Chicago," *Educational Theatre Journal* (December 1959): 285–90.

89. William Archer, "The New Drama and the New Theater," *McClure's Magazine* (November 1909): 3–16.

90. "American Stage in Danger," 270; "The Great Theatrical Syndicate [IV]," 335; "The Great Theatrical Syndicate [II]," 42, M137.

91. "The American Drama," *Current Literature* (August 1902): 137.

92. Charlton Andrews, "Elevating the Audience," *Theatre Magazine* (February 1907): 102.

93. Marra, *Strange Duets*, 178–79; Erdman, *Staging the Jew*, 94, 99.

94. Miller, *Bohemians and Critics*; Miller, "Alan Dale," 69–80.

95. Moses, "The Disintegration of the Theatre," 466.

96. "As an Actor Sees Women: A Successful Actor Frankly Analyzes the Women Who Attend," *LHJ* (November 1908): 26, 70.

97. On the British response to the matinee girl, see Susan Torrey Barstow, " 'Hedda Is All of Us': Late-Victorian Women at the Matinee," *Victorian Studies* (spring 2001): 391.

98. "The Matinee Girl," *Munsey's* (October 1897/1898): 35. "Matinee girls" were also sometimes referred to as "Matinee Millies," "Matinee Marthas," and "Matinee Madames," although "Matinee girl" was most common. Caroll, *Matinée Idols*, 15. See also Arthur T. Williamson, "Matinee Audiences," *Green Book Album* (June 1911): 1237.

99. Albert Auster, *Actresses and Suffragists: Women in the American Theatre, 1890–1920* (New York: Praeger, 1984), 40. Although the term was largely used to describe adolescents, "matinee girl" also referred to older, even middle-aged, women. Barstow, " 'Hedda Is All of Us,' " 392; Caroll Smith-Rosenberg, "The New Woman as Androgyne: Social Disorder and Gender Crisis, 1870–1936," in *Disorderly Conduct: Visions of Gender in Victorian America* (New York: A. A. Knopf, 1985), 245, 253–56; Kathy Peiss, *Cheap Amusements: Working Women and Leisure in Turn-of-the-Century New York* (Philadelphia: Temple University Press, 1986); Enstad, *Ladies of Labor, Girls of Adventure*. For more on the regendering of the urban environment, see Mary Ryan, *Womanhood in America: From Colonial Time to the Present* (New York: Alfred A. Knopf, 1984); Lauren Rabinovitz, *For the Love of Pleasure: Women, Movies, and Culture in Turn-of-the-Century Chicago* (New Brunswick, N.J., and London: Rutgers University Press, 1998); Richard Butsch, "Bowery B'hoys and Matinee Ladies: Re-Gendering of Nineteenth Century American Theater Audiences," *American Quarterly* 46.3 (September 1994): 374–405.

100. Florence Lothair, "Gallery Gods and Goddesses," *Green Book Album* (August 1909): 415.

101. "The Matinee Girl," 34.

102. Butsch, "Bowery B'hoys and Matinee Ladies," 374. See also Richard Butsch, *The Making of American Audiences from Stage to Television, 1750–1990* (Cambridge and New York: Cambridge University Press, 2000). For more on the "gentrification" of the nineteenth-century theater, see Levine, *Highbrow Lowbrow*; Robert C. Allen, *Horrible Prettiness: Burlesque and American Culture* (Chapel Hill: University of North

Carolina Press, 1991); Albert F. McLean Jr., *American Vaudeville as Ritual* (Lexington: University of Kentucky Press, 1965); Robert N. Snyder, *The Voice of the City: Vaudeville and Popular Culture in New York* (New York and Oxford: Oxford University Press, 1989); Kibler, *Rank Ladies*; Neil Harris, *Humbug: The Art of P. T. Barnum* (Chicago: University of Chicago Press, 1973); A. H. Saxon, *P. T. Barnum: The Legend and the Man* (New York: Columbia University Press, 1989); Bluford Adams, *E Pluribus Barnum: The Great Showman and The Making of U.S. Popular Culture* (Minneapolis: University of Minnesota Press, 1997). For more on the regendering of urban geography, see Frick, *New York's First Theatrical Center*; Susan Porter Benson, *Counter Culture: Saleswomen, Managers and Customers in American Department Stores: 1890–1940* (Urbana and Chicago: University of Illinois Press, 1986); Elaine S. Abelson, *When Ladies Go A-Thieving: Middle-Class Shoplifters in the Victorian Department Store* (New York and Oxford: Oxford University Press, 1989); John Kasson, *Rudeness and Civility: Manners in Nineteenth-Century America* (New York: Hill and Wang, 1990); William R. Leach, *Land of Desire: Merchants, Power, and the Rise of a New American Culture* (New York: Pantheon Books, 1993); Henderson, *The City and the Theatre*, 131; Christine M. Boyer, *Manhattan Manners: Architecture and Style, 1850–1900* (New York: Rizzoli, 1985); Rabinovitz, *For the Love of Pleasure.*

103. Butsch, "Bowery B'hoys and Matinee Ladies," 390, 377.

104. Ibid., 377; Rabinovitz, *For the Love of Pleasure*, 6, 7, 102. See also Karen Halttunen, *Confidence Men and Painted Women: A Study of Middle-Class Culture in America* (New Haven, Conn.: Yale University Press, 1982); Faye E. Dudden, *Women in the American Theatre: Actresses and Audiences 1790–1870* (New Haven, Conn.: Yale University Press, 1994).

105. See Butsch, "Bowery B'hoys and Matinee Ladies"; Dudden, *Women in the American Theatre*; Allen, *Horrible Prettiness*, 142; Maria Elena Buszek, *Pin Up Grrrls: Feminism, Sexuality, Popular Culture* (Chapel Hill: University of North Carolina Press, 2006); Lois W. Banner, *American Beauty* (Chicago and London: University of Chicago Press, 1983), 123–24; Kathy Peiss, *Hope in a Jar: The Making of America's Beauty Culture* (New York: Harry Holt and Co., 1998), 48.

106. Butsch, "Bowery B'hoys and Matinee Ladies," 394; Auster, *Actresses and Suffragists*, 40; Shirley Burns, "The Afternoon Theatre," *Green Book Album* (April 1910): 846. The percentage of women in vaudeville audiences was generally lower but still considerable; a study in 1911 by the Russell Sage Foundation reported that "women form on the average 40% of the audience and at times are in the majority"; quoted in Auster, *Actresses and Suffragists*, 38. In the same period, women in England outnumbered men by a margin of twelve to one. Barstow, " 'Hedda Is All of Us,' " 387.

107. Clayton Hamilton, "Woman Takes the Stage," *Green Book Album* (May 1909): 1106.

108. Clayton Hamilton, "The Drama: The Psychology of Theatre Audiences," *The Forum* 39 (1907): 245; Burns, "The Afternoon Theatre," 846.

109. Hamilton, "Woman Takes the Stage," 1106.

110. Quoted in Auster, *Actresses and Suffragists*, 41–42.

111. Anna Marble, "Woman in Variety," *Variety*, December 22, 1906, 14.

112. "As an Actor Sees Women," 26.

113. Peiss, *Cheap Amusements*, 53–55. See also Peiss, " 'Charity Girls' and City

Pleasures: Historical Notes on Working-Class Sexuality, 1880–1920," in *Passion and Power: Sexuality in History*, ed. Kathy Peiss and Christina Simmons (Philadelphia: Temple University Press, 1989), 57–69.

114. Marion Earle, "Bachelor Girls Guests of Miss Elsie De Wolfe," *New York Evening World* (1 March 1902), Elsie de Wolfe, v. 160, p. 40, Robinson Locke Collection (hereafter RLC), Billy Rose Theatre Collection (hereafter BRTC).

115. Burns, "The Afternoon Theatre," 845. Barstow, " 'Hedda Is All of Us,' " 389, 394.

116. A similar discourse surrounded novel reading by women in late eighteenth-century America. See Katherine Binhammer, "The Persistence of Reading: Governing Female Novel-Reading in Memoirs of Emma Courtney and Memoirs of Modern Philosophers," *Eighteenth-Century Life* 27.2 (spring 2003): 1–22.

117. "As an Actor Sees Women," 26.

118. Elizabeth McCracken, "The Play and the Gallery," *Atlantic Monthly* 89 (1902): 497–98.

119. Shannon Jackson, *Lines of Activity: Performance, Historiography, Hull-House Domesticity* (Ann Arbor: University of Michigan Press, 2001), 238.

120. McCracken, "The Play and the Gallery," 498–99, 504, 500–501.

121. Davis, "The Syndicate/Shubert War," 155.

122. Marcosson and Frohman, *Charles Frohman*, 324.

123. Burns, "The Afternoon Theatre," 850.

124. "More Money in Matinees Than Night Shows, 'Tis Said," *Variety*, March 13, 1914, 10.

125. "The American Girl's Damaging Influence on the Drama," *Current Literature* 43 (December 1907): 673.

126. Alan Dale, "Our Overdressed Drama," *Cosmopolitan* (May 1907): 64, 66.

127. Walter Prichard Eaton, "Women as Theater-goers," *Woman's Home Companion* (October 1910): 13.

128. "The Young Person Is the Tyrant of the Theatre," *NYT*, November 20, 1910, P5.

129. Hamilton, "The Drama," 245; "The American Girl's Damaging Influence," 673.

130. Shelley Stamp, *Movie-Struck Girls: Women and Motion Picture Culture after the Nickelodeon* (Princeton, N.J.: Princeton University Press, 2000), 25, 39.

131. "The Matinee Girl," 37. See also Mrs. Richard Mansfield, "Metropolitan Audiences," *Cosmopolitan* (April 1904): 667.

132. Edward Bok, "The Young Girl at the Matinee," *LHJ* (June 1903): 16. For more positive responses to the matinee girl, see "Is Woman Responsible for Salacious Plays," *NYT*, February 27, 1910, X8; "When Audiences Are a Help," *NYT*, March 13, 1910, SM5.

133. Bok, "The Young Girl at the Matinee," 16.

134. Burns, "The Afternoon Theatre," 845.

135. Franklin Fyles, *The Theatre and Its People* (New York: Doubleday, Page and Co., 1900), 92–93.

136. "As an Actor Sees Women," 26.

137. "What a Cartoonist Saw of Maxine Elliott at the Matinee," Maxine Elliott,

v. 179, p. 28, RLC, BRTC. See also James L. Ford, "The Ethel Barrymore Following," *Appleton's* (November 1908): 546–50; Lothair, "Gallery Gods and Goddesses," 415; John Corbin, "Perilla at the Matinee," *NYT*, May 4, 1902, SM8.

138. Juliet Wilbor Tompkins, "The Brutality of the Matinee Girl," *Lippincott's* (November 1907): 688; "Some Hard Truths about the People-Out-Front," *NYT*, December 31, 1905, pt. 4, pg. 4. According to M. Alison Kibler, women in vaudeville audiences occasionally appropriated "more masculine behaviours," cheering loudly at staged boxing matches and other displays by male athletes. Kibler, *Rank Ladies*, 51–52.

139. Smith-Rosenberg, "The New Woman as Androgyne," 245, 253–56, 258.

140. Edward Marshall, "Scathing Arraignment of Women by Mrs. John A. Logan," *NYT*, December 11, 1910, SM3.

141. Marshall, "Scathing Arraignment of Women," SM3.

142. Burns, "The Afternoon Theatre," 850.

143. "The Matinee Girl," 35; May Buckley, "Matinee Audiences," *Green Book Album* (June 1911): 1237.

144. Enstad, *Ladies of Labor, Girls of Adventure*, 79–80. For more on women's hats, see Fiona Clark, *Hats* (London: B. T. Batsford Ltd., 1982); Susie Hopkins, *The Century of Hats: Headturning Style of the Twentieth Century* (London: Aurum Press Ltd., 1999); Jenna Weissman Joselit, *A Perfect Fit: Clothes, Character and the Promise of America* (New York: Henry Holt and Company, 2001), 125–26.

145. " 'The Skirt' Says, Speaking of Woman, Mostly," *Variety*, April 29, 1911, 19.

146. "The Theatre Hat in California," *NYT*, February 21, 1895, 3; "Hats Barred in Wisconsin," *NYT*, March 25, 1897, 1; "Ohio's Anti-High Hat Law," *NYT*, April 6, 1896, 9; "The Theatre Hat Nuisance," *NYT*, February 1, 1905, 8. See also "High Hat's Narrow Escape," *NYT*, February 24, 1897, 1; "Chicago's High Hat Law," *NYT*, January 7, 1897, 1.

147. "A Legislative Jest," *NYDM*, April 10, 1897, 12.

148. " 'The Skirt' Says, Speaking of Woman, Mostly," *Variety*, April 8, 1911, 15; Auster, *Actresses and Suffragists*, 41.

149. Buckley, "Matinee Audiences," 1237; "The Woman in Variety, by 'the Skirt,' " *Variety*, May 15, 1909, 13; "Safety Measure for the New Hats," *NYT*, April 13, 1908: 7; illustration and caption, *Theatre Magazine* (April 1909): 117.

150. "The Matinee Girl," 14.

151. "Boston Woman's Queer Demand," *NYT*, April 3, 1898, 6. Shelley Stamp identifies a similar power struggle between female audience members and cinema managers at this time. Stamp, *Movie-Struck Girls*, 33–35.

152. "The Woman in Variety, 'by the Skirt,' " *Variety*, October 22, 1915, 6.

Chapter 2

1. Thompson, quoted in William R. Taylor, *In Pursuit of Gotham: Culture and Commerce in New York* (New York and Oxford: Oxford University Press, 1992), 101. On the Hippodrome, see Margaret Werry, "Politics, Spectacle, and the American Pacific," *Theatre Journal* 57 (2005): 355–82.

2. "The Department Store Is a Stage," *Theatre Magazine* (February 1917): 108.

3. Richard Butsch, "Bowery B'hoys and Matinee Ladies: Re-Gendering of Nineteenth Century American Theater Audiences," *American Quarterly* 46.3 (September 1994): 390, 377. For more on the development of the Ladies' Mile, see Mary C. Henderson, *The City and the Theatre* (1973; New York: Back Stage Books, 2004), 131; Christine Bonner, *Manhattan Manners: Architecture and Style, 1850–1900* (New York: Rizzoli, 1985); John Frick, *New York's First Theatrical Center: The Rialto at Union Square* (1983; Ann Arbor: UMI Research Press, 1985); Susan Porter Benson, *Counter Culture: Saleswomen, Managers and Customers in American Department Stores: 1890–1940* (Urbana and Chicago: University of Illinois Press, 1986); Elaine S. Abelson, *When Ladies Go A-Thieving: Middle-Class Shoplifters in the Victorian Department Store* (New York and Oxford: Oxford University Press, 1989); John Kasson, *Rudeness and Civility: Manners in Nineteenth-Century America* (New York: Hill and Wang, 1990).

4. Andrew L. Erdman, *Blue Vaudeville: Sex, Morals and the Mass Marketing of Amusement, 1895–1915* (Jefferson, N.C., and London: McFarland and Company, Inc., Publishers, 2004), 8.

5. Rozel Gotthold, "Smartness in Stage Settings," *Theatre Magazine* (February 1916): 84.

6. Zeta Rothschild, "The Home Follows the Stage," *Theatre Magazine* (August 1918): n.p.

7. Ellen Gruber Garvey has similarly shown how department stores, along with mail-order catalogs, ladies' magazines, and children's scrapbooks, "swapped techniques for display and organization among themselves." Ellen Gruber Garvey, *The Adman in the Parlor: Magazines and the Gendering of Consumer Culture, 1880s to 1910* (New York and Oxford: Oxford University Press, 1996), 5.

8. Charles F. McGovern, *Sold American: Consumption and Citizenship, 1890–1945* (Chapel Hill: University of North Carolina Press, 2006), 36–37; Roland Marchand, *Advertising the American Dream: Making Way for Modernity, 1920–1940* (Berkeley: University of California Press, 1985; Susan Strasser, *Satisfaction Guaranteed: The Making of the American Mass Market* (New York: Pantheon Books, 1989), 89–123; Roger Miller, "*Selling Mrs. Consumer*: Advertising and the Creation of Suburban Socio-Spatial Relations, 1910–1930," *Antipode* 23.1 (1991): 263–301; Jackson Lears, *Fables of Abundance: A Cultural History of Advertising in America* (New York: Basic Books, 1994); Jennifer Scanlon, *Inarticulate Longings: The "Ladies' Home Journal," Gender, and the Promises of Consumer Culture* (New York: Routledge, 1995). Although, as more recent histories have shown, men continued to play important roles as consumers, especially with respect to luxury goods, shopping and other aspects of consumption were persistently gendered as female. See, for example, Roger Horowitz, ed., *Boys and Their Toys? Masculinity, Technology and Class in America* (New York: Routledge, 2001); Carole Turbin, "Fashioning the American Man: The Arrow Collar Man, 1907–1931," *Gender and History* 14.3 (November 2002): 470–91; Tom Pendergast, *Creating the Modern Man: American Magazines and Consumer Culture, 1900–1950* (Columbia: University of Missouri Press, 2000).

9. N. W. Ayer and Son, quoted in McGovern, *Sold American*, 76–78. See also Regina Lee Blaszczyk, *Imaging Consumers: Design and Innovation from Wedgwood to Corning* (Baltimore: Johns Hopkins University Press, 2000).

10. Mcgovern, *Sold American*, 36–37. On the shift from "reason why" to "soft sell" copy, see Elspeth H. Brown, "Rationalizing Consumption: Lejaren à Hiller and the Origins of American Advertising Photography," *Enterprise and Society* 1 (December 2000): 720, 722; Elspeth H. Brown, *The Corporate Eye* (Baltimore: Johns Hopkins University Press, 2006), esp. chap. 4; Roland Marchand, *Advertising the American Dream*; Scanlon, *Inarticulate Longings*.

11. On the problem of the female urban spectator or *flâneuse*, see Lauren Rabinovitz, *For the Love of Pleasure: Women, Movies, and Culture in Turn-of-the-Century Chicago* (New Brunswick, N.J., and London: Rutgers University Press, 1998), 49; Susan Buck-Morss, "The Flaneur, the Sandwichman and the Whore: The Politics of Loitering," *New German Critique* 39 (1986): 99–140; Anne Freidberg, *Window Shopping: Cinema and the Postmodern* (Berkeley: University of California Press, 1993); Janet Wolff, *Feminine Sentences: Essays on Women and Culture* (Oxford: Polity Press, 1990); Deborah L. Parsons, *Streetwalking the Metropolis: Women, the City, and Modernity* (Oxford: Oxford University Press, 2000).

12. Angela M. Blake, *How New York Became American* (Baltimore: Johns Hopkins University Press, 2006), 68–69. See also *Inventing Times Square: Commerce and Culture at the Crossroads of the World*, ed. William R. Taylor (New York: Russell Sage Foundation, 1991). For more on the relationship between theater and geography, see Michael McKinnie, *City Stages: Theatre and Urban Space in a Global City* (Toronto: University of Toronto Press, 2007); Una Chaudhuri, *Staging Place: The Geography of Modern Drama* (Ann Arbor: University of Michigan Press, 1997); Gay McAuley, *Space in Performance: Making Meaning in the Theatre* (Ann Arbor: University of Michigan Press, 1999); Marvin Carlson, *Places of Performance: The Semiotics of Theatre Architecture* (Ithaca, N.Y.: Cornell University Press, 1989); David Wiles, *A Short History of Western Performance Space* (Cambridge: Cambridge University Press, 2003).

13. For more on New York's emergence as a cultural center, see Taylor, "Launching a Commercial Culture: Newspaper, Magazine, and Popular Novel as Urban Baedekers," *In Pursuit of Gotham: Culture and Commerce in New York* (New York and Oxford: Oxford University Press, 1992); Blake, *How New York Became American*.

14. Bonner, *Manhattan Manners*, 62.

15. Osgood, quoted in Bonner, *Manhattan Manners*, 62; Henderson, *The City and the Theatre*, 133.

16. For an example study of the relationship between urban planning and theater companies in Toronto, see McKinnie, *City Stages*.

17. Abelson, *When Ladies Go A-Thieving*, 67. Hone, quoted in Charles Lockwood, *Manhattan Moves Uptown: An Illustrated History* (Boston: Houghton Mifflin Company, 1976), 89.

18. Bonner, *Manhattan Manners*, 91.

19. Robert A. M. Stern, Thomas Mellins, and David Fishman, *New York 1880: Architecture and Urbanism in the Gilded Age* (New York: Monacelli Press, 1999), 663; John Kenrick, "New York Theatres, Past and Present: Demolished Broadway Theatres," 2003–2005, http://www.musicals101.com/bwaypast6.htm, accessed May 15, 2008.

20. "Matinees: What They Are, and Their Influence," *NYT*, October 1, 1860, 5.

21. "A Word for Matinees," *NYT*, October 3, 1860, 4.

22. "Amusement," *NYT*, September 13, 1866, 4.

23. *New York Clipper*, quoted in Robert C. Allen, *Horrible Prettiness: Burlesque and American Culture* (Chapel Hill: University of North Carolina Press, 1991), 112. See also Faye E. Dudden, *Women in the American Theatre: Actresses and Audiences 1790–1870* (New Haven, Conn.: Yale University Press, 1994), 164–65.

24. Quoted in Allen, *Horrible Prettiness*, 115.

25. Twain, quoted in Dudden, *Women in the American Theatre*, 154.

26. Dudden, *Women in the American Theatre*, 151, 154; Allen, *Horrible Prettiness*, 115.

27. Butsch, "Bowery B'hoys and Matinee Ladies," 394; Henderson, *The City and the Theatre*, 114; Vanderheyden Fyles, "Clothes and the Actress," *Green Book Album* (June 1911): 1182.

28. Genevieve Richardson, "Costuming on the American Stage, 1751–1901: A Study of the Major Developments in Wardrobe Practice and Costume Style" (Ph.D. diss., University of Illinois, 1953), 82, 111–12.

29. Ibid., 75–77, 82, 92, 111–12.

30. Quoted in ibid., 92.

31. Otis Skinner, *Footlights and Spotlights: Recollections of My Life on the Stage* (New York: Blue Ribbon Books, 1923), 138.

32. Robert W. Snyder, *The Voice of the City: Vaudeville and Popular Culture in New York* (New York and Oxford: Oxford University Press, 1989), 20; M. Alison Kibler, *Rank Ladies: Gender and Cultural Hierarchy in American Vaudeville* (Chapel Hill: University of North Carolina Press, 1999), 10; Arthur Frank Wertheim, *Vaudeville Wars: How the Keith-Albee and Orpheum Circuits Controlled the Big Time and Its Performers* (New York: Palgrave Macmillan, 2006), 71; "What Next?" *New York Dramatic Mirror* (hereafter *NYDM*), August 15, 1896, 12.

33. Quoted in Stern et al., *New York 1880*, 670.

34. Ibid., 670–72, 677; Henderson, *The City and the Theatre*, 130.

35. Bonner, *Manhattan Manners*, 96; Stern et al., *New York 1880*, 725; William R. Leach, *Land of Desire: Merchants, Power, and the Rise of a New American Culture* (New York: Pantheon Books, 1993), 31.

36. Stern et al., *New York 1880*, 722.

37. Henderson, *The City and the Theatre*, 145.

38. Nancy L. Green, *Ready-to-Wear and Ready-to-Work: A Century of Industry and Immigrants in Paris and New York* (Durham, N.C.: Duke University Press, 1997), 2, 46, 48.

39. David C. Hammack, "Developing for Commercial Culture," *Inventing Times Square: Commerce and Culture at the Crossroads of the World*, ed. William R. Taylor (New York: Russell Sage Foundation, 1991), 43–44; Betty Blackmar, "Uptown Real Estate and the Creation of Times Square," *Inventing Times Square: Commerce and Culture at the Crossroads of the World*, ed. William R. Taylor (New York: Russell Sage Foundation, 1991), 58.

40. Quoted in Hammack, "Developing for Commercial Culture," 37.

41. Green, *Ready-to-Wear and Ready-to-Work*, 49. See also Hammack, "Developing for Commercial Culture," 43.

42. Taylor, *In Pursuit of Gotham*, 97.

43. Hammack, "Developing for Commercial Culture," 43, Blackmar, "Uptown

Real Estate and the Creation of Times Square," 61; Margaret Knapp, "Introductory Essay," in *Inventing Times Square: Commerce and Culture at the Crossroads of the World*, ed. William R. Taylor (New York: Russell Sage Foundation, 1991), 120–32.

44. Knapp, "Introductory Essay," 121; Blackmar, "Uptown Real Estate and the Creation of Times Square," 61.

45. Katie N. Johnson, *Sisters in Sin: Brothel Drama in America, 1900–1920* (Cambridge: Cambridge University Press, 2006), 13; Gilfoyle, "Policing of Sexuality," in *Inventing Times Square: Commerce and Culture at the Crossroads of the World*, ed. William R. Taylor (New York: Russell Sage Foundation, 1991), 299. For more on early twentieth-century prostitution, see Ruth Rosen, *The Lost Sisterhood: Prostitution in America, 1900–1918* (Baltimore and London: Johns Hopkins University Press, 1982); Marilyn Wood Hill, *Their Sisters' Keepers: Prostitution in New York City, 1830–1870* (Berkeley: University of California Press, 1989), 294–315; Kevin J. Mumford, *Interzones: Black/White Sex Districts in Chicago and New York in the Early Twentieth Century* (New York: Columbia University Press, 1997). On early twentieth-century attitudes toward sexuality, see Timothy J. Gilfoyle, *City of Eros: New York City, Prostitution, and the Commercialization of Sex, 1790–1920* (New York: Norton, 1992); John D'Emilio and Estelle B. Freedman, *Intimate Matters: A History of Sexuality in America*, 2nd ed. (Chicago and London: University of Chicago Press, 1997), 171–238; George Chauncey, *Gay New York: The Making of the Gay World* (1994; London: Flamingo, 1995); Sharon R. Ullman, *Sex Seen: The Emergence of Modern Sexuality in America* (Berkeley: University of California Press, 1997).

46. Lewis A. Erenberg, *Steppin' Out: New York Nightlife and the Transformation of American Culture* (Chicago and London: University of Chicago Press, 1981), 61.

47. Frederick Cople Jaher, "Style and Status: High Society in Late Nineteenth-Century New York," in *The Rich, the Well Born, and the Powerful: Elites and Upper Classes in History*, ed. Frederick Cople Jaher (Urbana and Chicago: University of Illinois Press, 1973), 265. See also Steven J. Diner, *A Very Different Age: Americans of the Progressive Era* (New York: Hill and Wang, 1998).

48. Gilfoyle, "Policing of Sexuality," 297, 310.

49. Taylor, *In Pursuit of Gotham*, 97.

50. Hammack, "Developing for Commercial Culture," 47; see also ibid., 51; Peter A. Davis, "The Syndicate/Shubert War," in *Inventing Times Square: Commerce and Culture at the Crossroads of the World*, ed. William R. Taylor (New York: Russell Sage Foundation, 1991); Knapp, "Introductory Essay," 124; Henderson, *The City and the Theatre*.

51. Henderson, *The City and the Theatre*, 131, 186; Leach, *Land of Desire*, 31.

52. Jeanne Allen, "The Film Viewer as Consumer," *Quarterly Review of Film Studies* 5.4 (fall 1980): 482; Catherine Gudis, *Buyways: Billboards, Automobiles, and the American Landscape* (New York: Routledge, 2004).

53. Gustav Kobbé, "The Stage as a School of Costume," *The Delineator* (January 1905): 64.

54. Max Freeman, "Fin De Siècle Stage Costumes," *Cosmopolitan* (January 1897): 290, 292.

55. X, "Costly Dressing on the Stage," *Theatre Magazine* (December 1906): 321; Freeman, "Fin De Siècle Stage Costumes," 292; Roland Phillips, "Costuming the Modern Play," *Cosmopolitan* (March 1902): 488.

56. Fyles, "Clothes and the Actress," 1181; Janet Loring, "Costuming on the New York Stage from 1895 to 1915 with Particular Emphasis on Charles Frohman's Companies" (Ph.D. diss., State University of Iowa, 1961), 5.

57. Fyles, "Clothes and the Actress," 1183.

58. Ibid.

59. Ibid., 1180, 1184; Freeman, "Fin de Siècle Stage Costumes," 291–92; Franklin Fyles, *The Theatre and Its People* (New York: Doubleday, Page and Co., 1900), 166–67.

60. Elsie de Wolfe, v. 151, p. 13, Robinson Locke Collection, Billy Rose Theatre Collection (hereafter RLC, BRTC); Jane S. Smith, *Elsie de Wolfe: A Life in the High Style* (New York: Atheneum, 1982), 53–55.

61. Kobbé, "The Stage as a School of Costume," 63; "Valeska Suratt Has the Gowns," *New York Telegraph*, December 12, 1907, Locke Envelope #2203 [Suratt, Valeska], RLC, BRTC. Broadway theater was much like the *trompe l'oeil* gallery, amusement park, exhibition hall, cinema, and other modern amusements in that it challenged viewers' perceptual awareness and taught them to see the world in a new way. On visual culture, see Rabinovitz, *For the Love of Pleasure*; Jonathan Crary, *Techniques of the Observer: On Vision and Modernity in the Nineteenth Century* (Cambridge, Mass.: MIT Press, 1990); Leo Charney and Vanessa R. Schwartz, eds., *Cinema and the Invention of Modern Life* (Berkeley: University of California Press, 1995); James W. Cook, *The Arts of Deception: Playing with Fraud in the Age of Barnum* (Cambridge, Mass.: Harvard University Press, 2001).

62. Maureen E. Montgomery, *Displaying Women: Spectacles of Leisure in Edith Wharton's New York* (New York: Routledge, 1998), 137; de Wolfe quoted in Montgomery, *Displaying Women*, 138. See also Smith, *Elsie de Wolfe*; Elsie de Wolfe, *After All* (New York: Arno Press, 1974); Kim Marra, "Elsie de Wolfe Circa 1901: The Dynamics of Prescriptive Feminine Performance in American Theatre and Society," *Theatre Survey* 35.1 (May 1994): 100–120.

63. "Clothes Seen on the Stage," *Theatre Magazine* (March 1915): n.p.

64. Loring, "Costuming on the New York Stage from 1895 to 1915 with Particular Emphasis on Charles Frohman's Companies," 5–6. Like British society drama, the lavish costumes in George Edwardes's Gaiety musicals anticipated similar displays in American musicals by several years; A. E. Wilson, " 'Choked with Musical Comedy,' " in *Edwardian Theatre* (London: Arthur Baker Ltd., 1951), 211–22; Joel H. Kaplan and Sheila Stowell, *Theatre and Fashion: Oscar Wilde to the Suffragettes* (Cambridge: Cambridge University Press, 1994), 104, 115–16.

65. Allen Churchill, *The Great White Way: A Re-creation of Broadway's Golden Era of Theatrical Entertainment* (New York: E. P. Dutton and Co., Inc., 1962), 9; "Fashions on the Stage," *Theatre Magazine* (advertising section) (February 1905): v.

66. "May Graduate to Jeweled Corset Hooks Themselves," *Cleveland News*, Anna Held, v. 265, p. 67, RLC, BRTC.

67. Anna Marble, "The Woman in Variety," *Variety*, October 13, 1906, 7; "The Woman in Variety, by the 'Skirt,' " *Variety*, January 16, 1909, 11; "Women's Clothes, by the 'Skirt,' " *Variety*, December 25, 1914, 36.

68. Mary C. Henderson, *Theater in America: 200 Years of Plays, Players and Productions* (New York: Harry N. Abrams, Inc. Publishers, 1996), 224.

69. X, "Costly Dressing," 322; Fyles, *The Theatre and Its People*, 166; Freeman,

"Fin De Siecle Stage Costumes"; Phillips, "Costuming the Modern Play"; Letter from Alf Hayman to Charles Frohman, May 27, 1909, p. 4, Box 3, Hayman, Alf, Frohman (Charles) Letter press copies, March 12, 1908–May 31, 1910, 54M107, New York Public Library (hereafter NYPL); "Calls Tariff Benighted," *NYT*, June 14, 1908; "Payne-Alrdich Bill Revision Upward," *NYT*, August 2, 1909.

70. Letter from John Wanamaker to Shubert brothers, November 11, 1911, 2224 Wanamaker, 1910–1926, Box 431–448, Shubert Archives (hereafter SA); Letter from J. M. Gidding and Co. to Lee Shubert, May 24, 1918, Folder 436 (J. M. Gidding and Co.), SA; Letter from Henry Lehman, Corsets to Lee Shubert, August 5, 1912, Folder 1020, October 1910–April 1913, SA.

71. Loring, "Costuming on the New York Stage from 1895 to 1915 with Particular Emphasis on Charles Frohman's Companies," 47–51; Billlie Burke, *With a Feather on My Nose* (New York: Appleton-Century-Crofts, 1949), 80.

72. Box 3, Hayman, Alf, Letter press copies, March 12, 1908–May 31, 1910, 54M107, p. 412, April 14, 1910 [3]; Hayman, Alf, Letter press copies, May 31, 1910–June 20, 1913, 54M107, p. 186, May 2, 1911, NYPL.

73. Letter from J. M. Gidding and Co. to Lee Shubert, May 24, 1918, 1910–1926, Box 431–448, Folder 436 (J. M. Gidding and Co.), SA; Letters between Lichtenstein Millinery Co. and J. J. Shubert, 1911–1912, Box 1556 (Lichtenstein Millinery Co.), SA.

74. "Fashion Hints from the New York and Paris Stage," *Theatre Magazine* (May 1909): xiv; "A Fool There Was; No Doubt of That," *NYT*, March 25, 1909, 9.

75. Most stores capitalized on this free publicity by selling cheaper variations of stage costumes, often naming certain clothing items after a star performer or character. For a more detailed discussion, see Chapter 4.

76. Jack Poggi, *Theater in America: The Impact of Economic Forces, 1870–1967* (1966; Ithaca, N.Y.: Cornell University Press, 1968), 16.

77. Davis, "The Syndicate/Shubert War," 154–55.

78. Poggi, *Theater in America*, 16–17, 19.

79. Davis, "The Syndicate/Shubert War," 155.

80. Quoted in Maryann Chach, "The New York Review," in *Performing Arts Resources*, ed. Barbara Naomi Cohen-Stratyner (New York: Theatre Library Association, n.d.), 14: 93. See also Brooks McNamara, *The Shuberts of Broadway: A History Drawn from the Collections of the Shubert Archive* (New York and London: Oxford University Press, 1990), 60–63.

81. Chach, "The New York Review," 92–93; Letter from Charles Daniel to [J. J.] Shubert, October 28, 1916, "The New York Review," (4) SA; Letter from Daniel to J. J. Shubert, October 17, 1911, quoted in Chach, "The New York Review," 93–94; Letter from Charles Daniel to [J. J.] Shubert, February 4, 1914; Letter from Charles Daniel to [J. J.] Shubert, April 7, 1915; Letter from J. J. Shubert to Charles Daniel, September 2, 1916; Letter from Lee Shubert to Charles Daniel, January 18, 1916, "The New York Review," (4) SA; Letter from Charles Daniel to [J. J.] Shubert, February 2, 1916, (4) SA.

82. Foster Hirsch, *The Boys from Syracuse: The Shuberts' Theatrical Empire* (Carbondale and Edwardsville: Southern Illinois University Press, 1998), 76–78.

83. Letter from J. J. Shubert to Charles Daniels, May 11, 1916, "The New York Review"; Letter from Charles Daniel to [J. J.] Shubert, May 24, 1916, "The New York Review," (4) SA.

84. Letter from Procter and Gamble to Charles Daniel, May 18, 1916; Letter from the Fleischmann Co. to Charles Daniel, May 19, 1916; Letter from the Coca-Cola Company, May 16, 1916; Letter from Pillsbury Flour Mills Company, May 15, 1916; Letter from Colgate and Company, May 16, 1916, "The New York Review" (4) SA. For other examples of collaboration between theaters and advertisers, see "Advertised Goods on the Stage," *Printers' Ink* (hereafter *PI*), July 17, 1913, 46; "Advertising Show Off," *Variety*, July 18, 1913, 1; Carolyn L. Kitch, *The Girl on the Magazine Cover: The Origins of Visual Stereotypes in American Mass Media* (Chapel Hill and London: University of North Carolina Press, 2001), 41.

85. Letter from Charles Daniel to J. J. Shubert, May 20, 1916; Letter from Charles Daniel to J. J. Shubert, May 24, 1916, "The New York Review" (4) SA.

86. Letter from James W. Young, J. Walter Thompson Company to Charles Daniel, June 6, 1916 (4) SA.

87. Other "commodity costumes" by Conant include "Postage Stamp Girls" for the *Passing Show of 1916*, and a "Beer Girl" and "Manhattan Cocktail" for the *Passing Show of 1917*. See the costume sketches CS.07.03.07 (Homer Conant), CS.07.03.06 (Homer Conant), CS.16.03.02 (Homer Conant), Costume Designs—Photos—CS, SA.

88. CS.15.04.02, Conant, Homer, Cities, St. Paul (Minn.), SA.

89. CS.15.04.01, Conant, Homer, Cities, Detroit Girl, SA.

90. See Leach, *Land of Desire*, 27.

91. Quoted in ibid., 29.

92. California and New York introduced laws in the 1890s that were intended to level out the playing field. Leach, *Land of Desire*, 29; "Fighting the Department Stores," *Illustrated American*, cited in "Current Literature," *NYT*, March 28, 1897, 15.

93. Leach, *Land of Desire*, 26.

94. Quoted in Allis Rosenberg Wolfe, "Women, Consumerism, and the National Consumers' League in the Progressive Era," *Labor History* (1975): 384.

95. Ibid., 384–85.

96. Annie Marion MacLean, "Two Weeks in Department Stores," *Journal of Sociology* (May 1899): 740–41. MacLean's article represented but one of a series of articles on the plight of the shop girl. Between 1890 and 1920, over fifty articles on shop girls appeared in popular magazines like *McClure's* and the *Ladies' Home Journal*, urging middle-class readers to consider the unseen costs of their consumer purchases. Johnson, *Sisters in Sin*, 86.

97. Kathryn Kish Sklar, "The Consumers' White Label Campaign of the National Consumers' League, 1898–1918," in *Getting and Spending: European and American Consumer Societies in the Twentieth Century*, ed. Susan Strasser, Charles McGovern, and Matthias Judt (New York: Cambridge University Press, 1998), 22, 25, 27, 30–31. See also Wolfe, "Women, Consumerism, and the National Consumers' League in the Progressive Era," 378–92.

98. Sklar, "The Consumers' White Label Campaign," 31.

99. Peter Bailey, "Musical Comedy and the Rhetoric of the Girl, 1892–1914," in *Popular Culture and Performance in the Victorian City* (Cambridge: Cambridge University Press, 1998); Tracy C. Davis, *The Economics of the British Stage, 1800–1914* (Cambridge: Cambridge University Press, 2000), 341–42; Thomas Postlewait, "George Edwardes and Musical Comedy: The Transformation of London Theatre and Soci-

ety, 1878–1914," in *The Performing Century: Nineteenth-Century Theatre's History*, ed. Tracy C. Davis (London: Palgrave Macmillan, 2007), 80–102.

100. Kaplan and Stowell, *Theatre and Fashion*, 103–4, 130–32.

101. Johnson, *Sisters in Sin*, 83–84.

102. Bailey, "Musical Comedy and the Rhetoric of the Girl," 181.

103. "Lew Fields Tends the Soda Fountain," *NYT*, October 2, 1907, 11.

104. Johnson, *Sisters in Sin*, 86–87; Kaplan and Stowell, *Theatre and Fashion*, 104.

105. Most shop-girl musicals offered bright depictions of the department store environment, but some, such as *Only a Shop Girl* (1902), raised the specter of labor exploitation. "More Theatres to Open Up," *NYT*, August 31, 1902, 8; "Morals in the Comedy Drama 'Only a Shop Girl,'" *NYT*, May 3, 1903, 22; Johnson, *Sisters in Sin*, 84–85; Kaplan and Stowell, *Theatre and Fashion*, 82–114.

106. "Say Loiterers Kill Fifth Ave Business," *NYT*, April 8, 1910, 5.

107. "Fifth Avenue to Be the Best of Streets," *NYT*, January 2, 1912, 2.

108. Hammack, "Developing for Commercial Culture," 44; "To Keep Loiterers Off Fifth Ave," *NYT*, February 3, 1911, 8.

109. "Decrease in Fifth Avenue Workers," *NYT*, July 11, 1915, xxi; "Factory Law to End 5th Ave. Congestion," *NYT*, February 5, 1914, 10. It was only with the New York City Zoning Resolution of 1916 that Fifth Avenue north of Thirty-Fourth Street received official designation as a commercial district, making it permanently inaccessible to factories and other industrial businesses. Hammack, "Developing for Commercial Culture," 44. See also Todd W. Bressi, *Planning and Zoning New York City: Yesterday, Today and Tomorrow* (New Brunswick, N.J.: Center for Urban Policy Research, 1993); Keith D. Revell, *Building Gotham: Civic Culture and Public Policy in New York City, 1898–1938* (Baltimore: Johns Hopkins University Press, 2003).

110. Nan Enstad, *Ladies of Labor, Girls of Adventure* (New York: Columbia University Press, 2000); Susan A. Glenn, *Daughters of the Shtetl: Life and Labor in the Immigrant Generation* (Ithaca, N.Y., and London: Cornell University Press, 1990).

111. Glenn, *Daughters of the Shtetl*, 167–69; Enstad, *Ladies of Labor*, 84, 85, 93.

112. "Suffragists to Aid Girl Strikers," *NYT*, December 2, 1909, 3.

113. "The Rich Out to Aid Girl Waistmakers," *NYT*, December 3, 1909, 1.

114. "Girl Strikers Tell the Rich Their Woes," *NYT*, December 16, 1909, 3.

115. Lackaye, quoted in Sean Patrick Holmes, "Weavers of Dreams, Unite: Constructing an Occupational Identity in the Actor's Equity Association, 1913–1934" (Ph.D. diss., New York University, 1994), 53. For more on the Shuberts' treatment of actors, see Alfred Harding, *The Revolt of the Actors* (New York: W. Morrow, 1929); Hirsch, *The Boys from Syracuse*, 109–13.

116. Blackmar, "Uptown Real Estate and the Creation of Times Square," 52.

117. Mary Doane, "The Economy of Desire: The Commodity Form in/of the Cinema," *Quarterly Review of Film and Video* 11 (1989): 31. See also Wolfgang Schivelbusch, *The Railway Journey: The Industrialization of Time and Space in the 19th Century* (Berkeley: University of California Press, 1986).

118. Blackmar, "Uptown Real Estate and the Creation of Times Square," 64; see also Gudis, *Buyways*, 9–22.

119. Charles Taylor, "Modern Social Imaginaries," *Public Culture* 14.1 (2002): 106.

120. Quoted in Leach, *Land of Desire*, 76.

121. Benson, *Counter Cultures*, 44, 47; Leach, *Land of Desire*, 75.

122. Anne Friedberg, *Window Shopping: Cinema and the Postmodern* (Berkeley and Los Angeles: University of California Press, 1993), 2. See also Rachel Bowlby, *Just Looking: Consumer Culture in Dreiser, Gissing and Zola* (New York and London: Methuen, 1985), 3.

123. Abelson, *When Ladies Go A-Thieving*, 11; Bowlby, *Just Looking*; Benson, *Counter Culture*; Erica D. Rappaport, " 'The Halls of Temptation': Gender, Politics, and the Construction of the Department Store in Late Victorian London," *Journal of British Studies* (January 1996): 58–83.

124. Abelson, *When Ladies Go A-Thieving*; Rabinovitz, *For the Love of Pleasure*; Benson, *Counter Culture*; Jeanne Catherine Lawrence, "Geographical Space, Social Space, and the Realm of the Department Store," *Urban History* 19 (1992): 64–83.

125. Rabinovitz, *For the Love of Pleasure*, 76.

126. Susan Porter Benson notes that theatrical metaphors became "a staple" for early twentieth-century retail writers. Benson, *Counter Culture*, 67.

127. Leach, *Land of Desire*, 57–60. Katharine M. Rogers, *L. Frank Baum: Creator of Oz* (New York: St. Martin's Press, 2002), 55–58.

128. Fraser, quoted in Leach, *Land of Desire*, 69.

129. *Women's Wear Daily* quoted in Ableson, *When Ladies Go A-Thieving*, 71; Leach, *Land of Desire*, 69–70. For more on show windows and female spectators, see Charles Eckert, "The Carol Lombard in Macy's Window," in *Fabrications: Costume and the Female Body*, ed. Jane Gaines and Charlotte Herzog (New York: Routledge, 1990), 100–121; Jane Gaines, "The Queen Christina Tie-Ups: Convergence of Show Window and Screen," *Quarterly Review of Film and Video* 11 (1989): 35–60; Allen, "The Film Viewer as Consumer," 481–501; Miriam Hansen, "Adventures of Goldilocks: Spectatorship, Consumerism, and Public Life," *camera obscura* 22 (1990): 51–71; Friedberg, *Window Shopping: Cinema and the Postmodern*.

130. Leach, *Land of Desire*, 70.

131. A. T. Worm to Lee Shubert, November 14, 1912, Box 76, Toxen Worm, SA.

132. Leach, *Land of Desire*, 65.

133. A. T. Worm to Lee Shubert, November 28, 1910, Box 76, Toxen Worm, SA.

134. Letter from Nellie Revell to J. J. Shubert, October 23, 1916, Box 4265 (August 1912–December 1912)—Nellie Revell, SA. See also Letter from Nellie Revell to J. J. Shubert, October 16, 1912, Box 4265 (August 1912–December 1912) —Nellie Revell, SA. Charles W. Hurd, "Putting the Dramatic Punch into Window Display: Using the Stage Manager's Method," *PI*, December 16, 1915, 60. For more on this campaign and other examples of Revell's work, see Marlis Schweitzer, "Singing Her Own Song: Writing the Female Press Agent Back into History," *Journal of American Drama and Theatre* 20.2 (spring 2008): 87–106.

135. Orville K. Larson, *Scene Design in the American Theatre from 1915 to 1960* (Fayetteville and London: University of Arkansas Press, 1989): 21–26.

136. Quoted in Lise Lone Marker, *David Belasco: Naturalism in the American Theatre* (Princeton, N.J.: Princeton University Press, 1975), 60.

137. Ibid., 62; "Staging a Popular Restaurant," *Theatre Magazine* (October 1912): 104.

138. Leach, *Land of Desire*, 60.

139. Ibid., 80–81, 85–90, 99–111. See also Nancy J. Troy, *Couture Culture: A Study in Modern Art and Fashion* (Cambridge, Mass., and London: MIT Press, 2003; Linda L. Tyler, " 'Commerce and Poetry Hand in Hand': Music in American Department Stores, 1880–1930," *Journal of the American Musicological Society* 45 (spring 1992): 75–120.

140. On this point with respect to cinematic spectatorship and audience consumption of fan magazines, see Gaylyn Studlar, " 'The Perils of Pleasure?' Fan Magazine Discourse as Women's Commodified Culture in the 1920s," *wide angle* 13.1 (January 1991): 6–33.

141. Montgomery, *Displaying Women*, 123.

142. Maurya Wickstrom, *Performing Consumers: Global Capital and Its Theatrical Seductions* (New York: Routledge, 2006), 39.

143. Leach, *Land of Desire*, 5. Rosalind Williams first used the term "dream world of mass consumption" in "The Dream World of Mass Consumption," in *Rethinking Popular Culture: Contemporary Perspectives in Cultural Studies* (Berkeley: University of California Press, 1991), 198–235. Gaines, "The Queen Christina Tie-Ups," 36.

144. Quoted in Garvey, *The Adman in the Parlor*, 5. See also Wickstrom, *Performing Consumers*, 13–42.

145. Snyder, *The Voice of the City*, 195–97.

146. Kim Marra, *Strange Duets: Impresarios and Actresses in the American Theatre, 1865-1914* (Iowa City: University of Iowa Press, 2006), 74.

147. Henderson, *The City and the Theatre*, 210–11.

148. Ibid., 220–21. See also Mary C. Anderson, *New Amsterdam Theatre: The Biography of a Theatre* (New York: Hyperion, 1997).

149. Quoted in Nicholas Van Hoogstraten, *Lost Broadway Theatres*, rev. ed. (1991; Princeton, N.J.: Princeton Architectural Press, 1997), 73.

150. Henderson, *The City and the Theatre*, 256–57. See also Maryann Chach et al., *The Shuberts Present: 100 Years of Great Theatre* (New York: Henry N. Abrams in association with the Shubert Organization, Inc., 2001).

151. Charlotte Herzog, "The Movie Palace and the Theatrical Sources of Its Architectural Style," *Cinema Journal* 20.2 (spring 1981): 21, 22. See also Charlotte Herzog, "The Archaeology of Cinema Architecture: The Origins of the Movie Theater," *Quarterly Review of Film Studies* (winter 1984): 11–32.

152. Wertheim, *Vaudeville Wars*, 204–5. See also Marion Spitzer, *The Palace* (New York: Atheneum, 1969).

153. Shelley Stamp, *Movie-Struck Girls: Women and Motion Picture Culture After the Nickelodeon* (Princeton, N.J.: Princeton University Press, 2000), 20.

154. Ibid., 21. On lobbies, see Carlson, *Places of Performance*, 161.

155. Shirley Burns, "The Afternoon Theatre," *Green Book Album* (April 1910): 850; "The Matinee Girl," *Munsey's* (October 1897/1898), 34–35. See also Herzog, "The Movie Palace and the Theatrical Sources of Its Architectural Style," 21; Henderson, *The City and the Theatre*, 210–11.

156. Quoted in Carlson, *Places of Performance*, 159–60.

157. "When Audiences Are a Help," *NYT*, March 13, 1910, SM5.

158. Burns, "The Afternoon Theatre," 845; "The Bargain Idea," *NYDM*, May 8, 1897, 12.

159. "Professional Doings," *NYDM*, December 11, 1909; "Silk Stocking Souvenirs," *Variety*, October 14, 1911, 8.
160. "Souvenirs at Matinees," *Variety*, May 9, 1913, 6.
161. Ibid.
162. *Broadway Magazine* (May 1906): 119; Ms. Coll. 30—Dreiser, Theodore, 1871–1945, Papers, ca. 1890–1965, Rare Books and Manuscripts Room, University of Pennsylvania.
163. "The Callboy's Comments," *NYDM*, September 11, 1897, 22.
164. A program from Maxine Elliott's Theatre for the 1912–13 season included advertisements for Revillon Frères (furriers), the Hotel Rudolf, Oppenheim, Collins and Co. (corset makers), and Lucile Ltd. (couturier). "Maxine Elliott's Theatre, New York," Box 3, "Theater," Warshaw Collection of Business Americana (hereafter Warshaw), Archives Center, National Museum of American History, Kenneth E. Behring Center, Smithsonian Institution (hereafter NMAH). See also Marvin Carlson, "The Development of the American Theatre Program," in *The American Stage: Social and Economic Issues from the Colonial Period to the Present*, ed. Ron Engle and Tice L. Miller (New York: Cambridge University Press, 1993), 101–14.
165. "The Theater Programme as an Advertising Medium," *PI*, September 11, 1907, 14–15; "A Programme Champion," *PI*, September 22, 1909, 6; "*PI* Does Not Recommend Theatre Programmes," *PI*, August 25, 1909, 24.
166. J. W. Weil, "Theatre Curtain Advertising," *PI*, October 5, 1909, 43.
167. Ibid. In 1914, for example, Gimbel Bros. paid the Shuberts $125 a week for theater curtain advertising at the new Winter Garden show. Letter from Charles Daniel to [J. J.] Shubert, January 5, 1914, "The New York Review," January–December 1914, SA.
168. Letter to C. A. Bird from Clyde W. Riley, July 7, 1908, Box 75, Folder Rid-Ril, 1908–1909, SA.
169. Letter to Clyde W. Riley from C. A. Bird, July 10, 1907, Box 75, Folder Rid-Ril, 1908–1909, SA.
170. "Merely Realism" (reprinted from *Pittsburgh Post*), *PI*, December 8, 1908, 19.
171. Leach, *Land of Desire*, 46–48. Gudis, *Buyways*, 11–34. On nineteenth-century practices, see David M. Henkin, *City Reading: Written Words and Public Spaces in Antebellum New York* (New York: Columbia University Press, 1998).
172. Marra, "Elsie de Wolfe Circa 1901," 112. On the Shuberts' collaborations with the White Automobile Company, see Chach, "The New York Review," 94.
173. Jenn Stephenson, "Singular Impressions: Metatheatre on Renaissance Celebrities and Corpses," *Studies in Theatre and Performance* 27.2 (summer 2007): 137–53; McAuley, *Space in Performance*, 181–82.
174. Philip Francis Nowlan, "Warding Off Saturation Point by Changing Advertising Appeal," *PI*, September 20, 1917, 27–28.
175. "Heatherbloom Is Advertised by Ethel Barrymore in a New Play," *PI*, October 28, 1915, 31–32; "Ethel Barrymore Is Talking" (ad), *The Delineator* (January 1916): 46; "Heatherbloom in Stageland" (ad), *Good Housekeeping* (November 1916): 98; ad in *Theatre Magazine* (October 1916): 237.
176. Neil M. Alperstein, "Imaginary Relationships with Celebrities Appearing in Television Commercials," *Journal of Broadcasting and Electronic Media* 35.1 (winter

1991): 49; Michael Schudson, *Advertising: The Uneasy Persuasion Its Dubious Impact on America Society* (New York: Basic Books, 1984); and J. Reeves, "Television Stars: The Case of Mr. T," in *Television: The Critical View*, 4th ed., ed. H. Newcomb (New York: Oxford University Press, 1987), 445–54; Chris Rojek, *Celebrity* (London: Reaktion Books, 2001), esp. chap. 2.

177. Stanley Resor, quoted in Fox, *The Mirror Makers*, 90. See also Stanley Resor, "Personalities and the Public: Some Aspects of Testimonial Advertising," *New Bulletin* 138 (April 1929): 1–7; "Company Meeting on 'Personality Advertising,' April 5, 1928," Box 4, Testimonial Advertising 1928–1977, J. Walter Thompson Information Center Records, JWT Collection, Hartman Center for Sales, Advertising & Marketing History.

178. William M. Freeman, *The Big Name* (New York: Printers' Ink Books, 1957), 183.

179. Allen, "The Film Viewer as Consumer," 482; Doane, "The Economy of Desire," 23–33; Judith Mayne, "Immigrants and Spectators," *Wide Angle* 5.2 (1982): 34; Gaines, "The Queen Christina Tie-Ups," 38.

180. "Theatre Fashions," *Theatre Magazine* (advertising section) (January 1905): vi.

181. The *Theatre Magazine*'s fashion department underwent a series of changes in its early years, disappearing for months at a time only to return with a new name and focus. In March 1915, Hornblow introduced an enlarged fashion department with the trademarked name "Footlight Fashions," which lasted, relatively unchanged, into the 1920s. "An Important Announcement Concerning Footlight Fashions" (ad), *Theatre Magazine* (February 1918): 67; "The Women Readers of *Theatre Magazine* Are the Best Dressed, Most Up-to-date Women in America" (ad), *Theatre Magazine* (August 1912): n.p.

182. Archbald, "Clothes Seen on the Stage," *Theatre Magazine* (June 1915): 322, 329.

183. "What Were a Spring Without Sport Togs?" *Theatre Magazine* (May 1916): 324; "Do You Like to Have Your Shopping Done for You" (ad), *Theatre Magazine* (June 1915): 65.

184. In 1913, the *Ladies' Home Journal* introduced a monthly series featuring Sarah Bernhardt, Billie, Burke, Laurette Taylor, and other "Famous Actresses as Fashion Editors," Box 46, Folder 4, Gladys Reid Holton Collection, NMAH; ad in *The Delineator* (November 1913): 72.

185. For more on the role of urban guidebooks, see Taylor, "Launching a Commercial Culture" and Blake, *How New York Became American*, 49–79.

186. Charlotte Herzog and Jane Gaines argue that it is this absence of "dramatic ideas" that distinguishes a fashion photograph from a production photograph. Gaines and Herzog, " 'Puffed Sleeves Before Tea-Time': Joan Crawford, Adrian and Women Audiences," *Wide Angle* 6.4 (1985): 33.

187. Simon J. Bronner, "Object Lessons: The Work of Ethnological Museums and Collections," in *Consuming Visions: Accumulation and Display of Goods in America, 1880–1920*, ed. Simon J. Bronner (New York and London: W. W. Norton and Co., 1989), 217–54.

188. "Gowns on the Stage," *Harper's Bazar* (hereafter *HB*) (November 1913): 52.

189. Leslie W. Rabine, "A Woman's Two Bodies: Fashion Magazines, Consumer-

ism, and Feminism," in *On Fashion*, ed. Shari Benstock and Suzanne Ferriss (New Brunswick, N.J.: Rutgers University Press, 1994), 64; Christopher Breward, "Patterns of Respectability: Publishing, Home Sewing and the Dynamics of Class and Gender 1870–1914," in *The Culture of Sewing: Gender, Consumption and Home Dressmaking*, ed. Barbara Burman (Oxford and New York: Berg, 1999), 26; Herzog and Gaines, " 'Puffed Sleeves Before Tea-Time,' " 27–28.

190. Tony Bennett and Janet Wollacott, *Bond and Beyond: The Political Career of a Popular Hero* (London: Macmillan Education Ltd., 1987), 248.

Chapter 3

1. Jane Cowl, "Why a Reputation for Beauty Is a Handicap," *American Magazine* (August 1917): 50.

2. Blanche Yurka, *Bohemian Girl: Blanche Yurka's Theatrical Life* (Athens: Ohio University Press, 1970), 72.

3. Ruth Shepley, "The Life an Actress Leads," *Green Book Magazine* (March 1916): 514. See also X, "Costly Dressing on the Stage," *Theatre Magazine* (December 1906): 322.

4. Mlle. Sartoris, "Stage Fashions of the Month," *Theatre Magazine* (December 1908): xxvi.

5. James L. Ford, "The Ethel Barrymore Following," *Appleton's* (November 1908): 550. See also Sophie Tucker (with Dorothy Giles), *Some of These Days: The Autobiography of Sophie Tucker* (Garden City, N.Y.: Garden City Publishing Co., 1945), 106; Walter Prichard Eaton, "Women as Theater-goers," *Woman's Home Companion* (October 1910): 13.

6. Alan Dale, "Clothes and Drama," *Theatre Magazine* (November 1915): 234.

7. "The Drama," *New York Times—Illustrated Magazine*, December 19, 1897, 6.

8. Vanderheyden Fyles, "Clothes and the Actress," *Green Book Album* (June 1911): 1182; Irene Franklin, v. 217, n.p., Robinson Locke Collection (hereafter RLC), Billy Rose Theatre Collection (hereafter BRTC); May Buckley, "Matinee Audiences," *Green Book Album* (June 1911); Kobbé, "The Stage as a School of Costume." *The Delineator* (January 1905): 64; Max Freeman, "Fin De Siècle Stage Costumes," *Cosmopolitan* (January 1897): 290.

9. Clara Morris, *Stage Confidences: Talks about Players and Play Acting* (Boston: Lothrop Pub. Co., 1902), 72, 148.

10. "The Drama," 6; Freeman, "Fin de Siècle Stage Costumes," 290.

11. Miles Orvell, *The Real Thing: Imitation and Authenticity in American Culture, 1880–1940* (Chapel Hill and London: University of North Carolina Press, 1989), xv, 35. See also Hillel Schwartz, *The Culture of the Copy: Striking Likenesses, Unreasonable Facsimiles* (New York: Zone Books, 1996).

12. Claudia B. Kidwell and Margaret C. Christman, *Suiting Everyone: The Democratization of Clothing in America* (Washington, DC: Smithsonian Institution Press, 1974), 137, 145; Nan Enstad, *Ladies of Labor, Girls of Adventure* (New York: Columbia University Press, 2000), 28–31; Kathy Peiss, *Cheap Amusements: Working Women*

and Leisure in Turn-of-the-Century New York (Philadelphia: Temple University Press, 1986); 65; Stewart Ewen and Elizabeth Ewen, *The Channels of Desire: Mass Images and the Shaping of American Consciousness* (Minneapolis: University of Minnesota Press, 1982), 116.

13. Rob Schorman, *Selling Style: Clothing and Social Change at the Turn of the Century* (Philadelphia: University of Pennsylvania Press, 2003); Enstad, *Ladies of Labor*.

14. Richardson, quoted in Enstad, *Ladies of Labor*, 29.

15. Pastor, quoted in ibid., 29.

16. Lois W. Banner, *American Beauty* (Chicago and London: University of Chicago Press, 1983), 198–99; Peiss, *Cheap Amusements*, 63–65; Nicholson Baker and Margaret Brentano, *The World on Sunday: Graphic Art in Joseph Pulitzer's Newspaper* (New York: Doubleday, 2005), 9.

17. On the professionalization of acting see, Benjamin McArthur, *Actors and American Culture: 1880–1920* (1984; Iowa City: University of Iowa Press, 2000); Albert Auster, *Actresses and Suffragists: Women in the American Theatre, 1890–1920* (New York: Praeger, 1984).

18. Will Marion Cook, quoted in Karen Sotiropoulos, *Staging Race: Black Performers in Turn of the Century America* (Cambridge, Mass.: Harvard University Press, 2006), 47. See also Richard Newman, " 'The Brightest Star': Aida Overton Walker in the Age of Ragtime and Cakewalk," *Prospects* 18 (1993): 465–81; Linda Mizejewski, *Ziegfeld Girl: Image and Icon in American Culture* (Durham, N.C.: Duke University Press, 1999), 109–35; Annemarie Bean, "Black Minstrelsy and Double Inversion, Circa 1890," in *African American Performance and Theater History: A Critical Reader*, ed. Harry J. Elam and David Krasner (Oxford and New York: Oxford University Press, 2001), 171–91; David Krasner, "Black *Salome*: Exoticism, Dance, and Racial Myths," in *African American Performance and Theater History: A Critical Reader*, ed. Harry J. Elam and David Krasner (Oxford and New York: Oxford University Press, 2001), 192–211; Susan A. Glenn, *Female Spectacle: The Theatrical Roots of Modern Feminism* (Cambridge, Mass.: Harvard University Press, 2000), 96–125; Daphne Brooks, *Bodies in Dissent: Spectacular Performances of Race and Freedom* (Chapel Hill: University of North Carolina Press, 2006).

19. Morris, *Stage Confidences*, 147, 149, 152.

20. Anna Held, v. 264, p. 94; v. 265.2, p. 78; v. 266.3, p. 16, RLC, BRTC; "Hazel Dawn's Real $1,000 Gown," *Vanity Fair* (October 1911), series 3, v. 259, p. 27, RLC, BRTC; "Lillian and Her Gowns," *Variety*, January 28, 1916, 2.

21. Auster, *Actresses and Suffragists*, 31; Alan Trachtenberg, *The Incorporation of America: Culture and Society in the Gilded Age* (New York: Hill and Wang, 1982), 87; Sean Patrick Holmes, "Weavers of Dreams, Unite: Constructing an Occupational Identity in the Actor's Equity Association, 1913–1934" (Ph.D. diss., New York University, 1994), 35.

22. David Belasco, "Seeing Four Thousand Stage-Struck Women Every Year," *New York Times* (hereafter *NYT*), September 5, 1909, pt. 6, p. 3; Auster, *Actresses and Suffragists*, 49.

23. David Belasco, "The Girl Who Wants to Go on the Stage," *Ladies' World* (August 1913): 7.

24. McArthur, *Actors and American Culture*, 29; Bureau of the Census, *Fourteenth Census of the United States Taken in the Year 1920*, v. IV, *Occupations*, cited in Holmes, "Weavers of Dreams Unite!" 35; Channing Pollock, "Stage Struck: A Fever Which Afflicts Rich and Poor Alike," *Sunday Magazine of the New York Tribune*, June 21, 1908, 3.

25. Ethel Barrymore, "The Young Girl and the Stage," *Harper's Bazar* (hereafter *HB*) (November 1906): 998. Stage-struck girls were a much-discussed topic in theatrical trade journals, newspapers, and magazines, becoming almost as ubiquitous as the women themselves. Throughout the 1890s, the *National Police Gazette*, a popular newspaper that appealed to male readers with lurid tales of promiscuous burlesque dancers and chorus girls, published accounts of innocent stage-struck girls fleeing their homes in pursuit of theatrical glory only to be "drugged, then robbed of money and jewels." See Robert C. Allen, *Horrible Prettiness: Burlesque and American Culture* (Chapel Hill: University of North Carolina Press, 1991), 198–99; "Stage Struck Girls Skip," *National Police Gazette* 61.792 (November 5, 1892): 6; "Photograph 16—No Title," *National Police Gazette* 76.1199 (August 11, 1900): 9. Although less graphic than the *Police Gazette* stories, short stories in literary and women's magazines supported the general consensus that an acting career was a dangerous pursuit for a young girl. See B. Perkins, "Stage Struck: A Comedy in One Act," *HB* (February 1902): 108–13. Other "stage-struck" stories include Marion Hill, "Jane Duke: A Story of the Stage," *American Magazine* (February 1908): 416–24; Louise Closser Hale, "The Seven Stages to the Stage," *The Delineator* (June 1909): 772–73, 811; "Facing the Footlights: The Autobiography of an Actress," *Green Book Album* (June 1910): 1194–1200; "How I Became an Actress: A Girl's Actual Experiences in Getting on the Stage and What Happened after She Got On" (Part 1), *Ladies' Home Journal* (hereafter *LHJ*) (April 1911): 11–13, 35, and (Part 2) (May 1911): 13–14, 30. For more on anti–New Woman literature in women's magazines, see Jennifer Scanlon, *Inarticulate Longings: The "Ladies' Home Journal," Gender, and the Promises of Consumer Culture* (New York: Routledge, 1995), esp. 137–68. Somewhat surprisingly, given their interest in uplifting the stage, most actresses agreed with the magazines. In articles, columns, and interviews they strongly urged women to avoid the stage and to seek the contentment of the domestic life. The stage beauty Maxine Elliott framed her response to the stage-struck girl as a protective gesture: "If you saw a dozen people struggling in the water, and realized that only one or two could possibly escape drowning, your instinct would be just as ours is to warn others against jumping in. That is why we shout 'don't! don't!' in the hope that it may save someone from drowning" (Elliott, quoted in Auster, *Actresses and Suffragists*, 35). The historian Albert Auster suggests that actress's advice articles should be read "not merely as cautionary literature, but as attempts to upgrade the profession, especially in the minds of the middle class who were more and more becoming both its audience and aspirant" (Auster, *Actresses and Suffragists*, 50). By discouraging stage-struck girls from taking up a career on the stage, actresses presented themselves as moral and empathetic figures, the epitome of middle-class respectability.

26. Frank Wiesberg, "The Chorus Girl," *Variety*, October 3, 1908, 9.

27. "Woman and the Stage," *New York Dramatic Mirror* (hereafter *NYDM*), August 28, 1897, 12.

28. "A Girl's Opportunities for Success on the Stage," *New York World*, April 27, 1903, Grace George, v. 234, p. 12, RLC, BRTC; Brittain and Dexter, cited in Claudia D.

Johnson, *American Actress: Perspective on the Nineteenth Century* (Chicago: Nelson-Hall, 1984), 50, 57; "The Stage Struck Girl: By the People Who Know Best," *Theatre Magazine* (November 1915): 249. See also Wiesberg, "The Chorus Girl," 9; Richard Butsch, "Bowery B'hoys and Matinee Ladies: Re-Gendering of Nineteenth Century American Theater Audiences," *American Quarterly* 46.3 (September 1994): 374–405.

29. Auster, *Actresses and Suffragists*, 36–37; "The Stage Struck Girl," 249.

30. Theodore Dreiser, *Sister Carrie* (1900; New York: Random House, 1997), 230.

31. Gustav Kobbé, "Annie Russell Out-of-Doors," *LHJ* (May 1903): 6; "Stage Favorites at Home," *HB* (October 1901): 576–79; Gustav Kobbé, "The Actress We Know as Julia Marlowe," *LHJ* (February 1903): 7–8; Clara E. Laughlin, "Back of the Footlights with 'Juliet': What a Day Means to Julia Marlowe Behind the Scenes," *LHJ* (May 1907): 13, 76; Annie Russell, "The Stage and Its People," *LHJ* (March 1910): 46.

32. Auster, *Actresses and Suffragists*, 18. Claudia D. Johnson, "That Guilty Third Tier," in *Victorian America*, ed. Geoffrey Blodgett and Daniel Walker Howe (Philadelphia: University of Pennsylvania Press, 1976), 111–20; Johnson, *American Actress*, 3–36; Faye E. Dudden, *Women in the American Theatre: Actresses and Audiences 1790–1870* (New Haven, Conn.: Yale University Press, 1994), 9–26; Katie N. Johnson, "Zaza: That 'Obtruding Harlot' of the Stage," *Theatre Journal* 54 (2002): 222–43; Katie N. Johnson, *Sisters in Sin: Brothel Drama in America, 1900-1920* (Cambridge: Cambridge University Press, 2006); Tracy C. Davis, "The Actress in Victorian Pornography," *Theatre Journal* 41 (October 1989): 294–315. See also Jonas Barish, *The Antitheatrical Prejudice* (Berkeley: University of California Press, 1981), 2, 88, 91, 282–86, 384–89, 466.

33. McArthur, *Actors and American Culture*, 85–122, 145; Banner, *American Beauty*, 177; John Frick, *New York's First Theatrical Center: The Rialto at Union Square* (1983; Ann Arbor: UMI Research Press, 1985), 87; Dudden, *Women in American Theatre*, 130.

34. Johnson, "Zaza," 234; Johnson, *Sisters in Sin*, 29–44.

35. Garff Wilson, *A History of American Acting* (Bloomington and London: Indiana University Press, 1966), 136; David Belasco, "The Truth about the Theater," *LHJ* (September 1917): 52. For a thorough analysis of Belasco's work with Mrs. Leslie Carter, see Kim Marra, *Strange Duets: Impresarios and Actresses in the American Theatre, 1865-1914* (Iowa City: University of Iowa Press, 2006), esp. chaps. 5–7; and Johnson, *Sisters in Sin*, 29–44.

36. The Loss of Personality," *Atlantic Monthly* 85 (February 1900): 195–204. See also Warren I. Susman, "Personality and the Making of Twentieth Century Culture," in *Culture as History: The Transformation of American Society in the Twentieth Century* (1974; New York: Pantheon Books, 1984), 271–85; T. J. Jackson Lears, *No Place of Grace: Antimodernism and the Transformation of American Culture: 1880–1920* (Chicago: University of Chicago Press, 1981); Lears, "From Salvation to Self-Realization: Advertising and the Therapeutic Roots of the Consumer Culture, 1810–1930," in *The Culture of Consumption: Critical Essays in American History, 1880–1980*, ed. T. J. Jackson Lears and Richard Wightman Fox (New York: Random House, 1983), 3–38; Gregory W. Bush, *Lords of Attention: Gerald Stanley Lee and the Crowd Metaphor in Industrializing America* (Amherst: University of Massachusetts Press, 1991); Schorman, *Selling Style*, 137, 144.

37. Susman, "Personality and the Making of Twentieth Century Culture," 277, 280.

38. On the actress's questionable status in early twentieth-century France, see Mary Louise Roberts, *Disruptive Acts: The New Woman in Fin-de-Siècle France* (Chicago and London: University of Chicago Press, 2002), 54–57.

39. E. M. Holland, "Personality vs. Technique," *Green Book Album* (February 1911): 374.

40. Valeska Suratt, "Personality—That's Me!" *Green Book Magazine* (September 1915): 420–23; J. E. Dodson, "Personality versus Individuality," *Theatre Magazine* 1.10 (December 1901): 12; George Arliss, "Personality and the Actor," *Vanity Fair* (December 1915): 39; 104d; William Gillette, "Personality: An Essential of Good Acting," *Vanity Fair* (March 1916): 57.

41. Lady Randolph Churchill, "Personality," *HB* (June 1916): 46.

42. Walter Prichard Eaton, "The Vexed Question of Personality (1916)," in *Plays and Players: Leaves from a Critic's Scrapbook* (Cincinnati: Steward and Kidd Co., 1916), 382.

43. Holland, "Personality vs. Technique," 374.

44. Eaton, "The Vexed Question of Personality," 380–81.

45. Walter Prichard Eaton, "Personality and the Player: The Matter of Individual Charm and Technical Efficiency," *Collier's*, October 22, 1910, 34.

46. Eaton, "The Vexed Question of Personality," 385.

47. Kim Marra, "Taming America as Actress: Augustin Daly, Ada Rehan, and the Discourse of Imperial Frontier Conquest," in *Performing America: Cultural Nationalism in American Theater*, ed. Jeffrey D. Mason and J. Ellen Gainor (Ann Arbor: University of Michigan Press, 1999), 52–72; Marra, "Clara Bloodgood (1870–1907), Exemplary Subject of Broadway Gender Tyranny," *American Theatre Quarterly* 7 (spring 1993): 193–216.

48. Marra, *Strange Duets*, 76–77, 98–99, 156–58, 178–79.

49. Tucker, *Some of These Days*, 25–26. The Sophie Tucker "B File" in the Billy Rose Theatre Collection contains a photograph of Tucker, ca. 1906 with the following on the back: "1906 in my wedding dress. I had to wear [it] on my first job. Café job." Sophie Tucker, "B File," BRTC.

50. X, "Costly Dressing on the Stage," 321.

51. Burke, "The Actress and Her Clothes," *Saturday Evening Post*, February 20, 1909, Billie Burke, v. 87, p. 8–9, RLC, BRTC; Diana Forbes-Robertson, *My Aunt Maxine: The Story of Maxine Elliott* (New York: Viking Press, 1964), 65.

52. "The Seven Ages of the Stage," *The Delineator* (June 1909), 811. Marcelle Earle (with Arthur Homme Jr.), *Midnight Frolic: A Ziegfeld Girl's True Story*, [3rd ed.] (Basking Ridge, N.J.: Twin Oaks Publishing Co., 1999), 134–35; Gelett Burgess, "The Second of the Millionaire Girl Stories: The Two Understudies," *LHJ* (September 1905): 5–7.

53. "The Experiences of a Chorus Girl," *The Independent*, July 12 1906, 84. See also Clara Morris, *Stage Confidences*; 146–62; Burgess, "The Second of the Millionaire Girl Stories," 5–7; "The Seven Ages of the Stage," *The Delineator* (June 1909): 811; "Satellites of Stars," *Green Book Album* (March 1909): 613.

54. Burke, "The Actress and Her Clothes."

55. Annie Russell, "The Stage and Its People," *LHJ* (January 1910): 31.

56. Barrymore, "The Young Girl and the Stage," 999; Ethel Barrymore, *Memories: An Autobiography* (New York: Harper & Brothers: 1955), 94. See also Catherine Cornell (as told to Ruth Woodbury Sedgwick), *I Wanted to Be an Actress* (New York: Random House, 1939), 15; Laurette Taylor, "Critics: An Actress Talks Back," *Town and Country* (March 1942): 47, 70; Marguerite Courtney, *Laurette* (New York and Toronto: Rinehart and Company, Inc., 1955), 82–83; Jean Francis, "The Girl Who Would an Actress Be," *Green Book Album* (December 1909): 1183–84; Wiesberg, "The Chorus Girl," 9; Alice Francis, "The Woes of a Chorus-Girl," *Green Book Album* (May 1909): 970.

57. Barrymore, *Memories*, 94; X, "Costly Dressing on the Stage," 321. Arthur Edwin Krows, *Play Production in America* (New York: Henry Holt and Co., 1916), 273.

58. Viola Allen, "What It Means to Be an Actress," *LHJ* (May 1899): 2.

59. "Stage Clothes," *Theatre Magazine* (December 1914): 284.

60. Burke, "The Actress and Her Clothes," 8.

61. Yurka, *Bohemian Girl*, 56.

62. "What It Costs to Be an Actress," *Green Book Album* (December 1910): 1259; X, "Costly Dressing on the Stage," 322.

63. On fashion and discipline, see Joanne Entwistle, "The Dressed Body," in *Body Dressing*, ed. Joanne Entwistle and Elizabeth Wilson (Oxford and New York: Berg, 2001), 55; Alexandra Warwick and Dani Cavallaro, *Fashioning the Frame: Boundaries, Dress and the Body* (London: Berg, 1998), 75.

64. Tucker, *Some of These Days*, 64–65; Peggy Hopkins Joyce, *Men, Marriage, and Me* (New York: The Macaulay Company, 1930), 64–65.

65. Fyles, "Clothes and the Actress," 1180.

66. Tucker, *Some of These Days*, 63–65.

67. "The Matinee Girl," *NYDM*, March 13, 1897, 2.

68. Magda Frances West, "Nobody Stars a Fat Woman," *Green Book Magazine* (August 1912): 230.

69. Ibid., 231.

70. Mike Featherstone, "The Body in Consumer Culture," in *The American Body in Context: An Anthology*, ed. Jessica R. Johnston (Wilmington, Del.: Scholarly Resources Inc., 2001), 83. See also Joan Jacobs Blumberg, *The Body Project: An Intimate History of American Girls* (New York: Random House, 1997); Susan Bordo, *Unbearable Weight: Feminism, Western Culture, and the Body* (1993; Berkeley: University of California Press, 2003); Heather Addison, "Hollywood, Consumer Culture, and the Rise of 'Body Shaping,'" in *Hollywood Goes Shopping*, ed. David Desser and Garth S. Jowett (Minneapolis and London: University of Minnesota Press, 2000), 3–33; Margaret Lowe, *Looking Good: College Women and Body Image* (Baltimore: Johns Hopkins University Press, 2003).

71. Featherstone, "The Body in Consumer Culture," 88.

72. Marie Griffith, *Born Again Bodies: Flesh and Spirit in American Christianity* (Berkeley: University of California Press, 2004), 225.

73. M. Alison Kibler, *Rank Ladies: Gender and Cultural Hierarchy in American Vaudeville* (Chapel Hill: University of North Carolina Press, 1999), 113; Glenn, *Female Spectacle*, 47.

74. Tucker, *Some of These Days*, 33.

75. The historian Susan Glenn questions Tucker's claim that she was forced to

wear blackface, suggesting that by 1946 when she published her autobiography she was embarrassed by her days as a blackface performer and needed to justify her actions. Yet the singer's attempts to remake herself as a fashionable performer after abandoning blackface, seen most vividly in her sheet music covers, suggest that she may have been more distressed than Glenn allows. Glenn, *Female Spectacle*, 52; Tucker, *Some of These Days*, 33–34.

76. Tucker, *Some of These Days*, 35, 40.

77. Rogin, *Blackface, White Noise*, 34, 48.

78. Tucker, *Some of These Days*, 60.

79. Tucker was not alone in the anxiety she felt about blackface. The comedian Eddie Cantor describes similar fears in his autobiography, *My Life Is in Your Hands*. Rogin, *Blackface, White Noise*, 155.

80. Tucker, *Some of These Days*, 63.

81. Tucker, *Some of These Days*, 96; Box 674, DeVincent Sheet Music Collection, Archives Center, National Museum of American History, Kenneth E. Behring Center, Smithsonian Institution (hereafter NMAH).

82. Tucker, *Some of These Days*, 105. For later comments on Tucker's style, see *Variety*, April 2, 1910; *New York Telegraph*, January 24, 1911; *Peoria Journal*, January 30, 1914, Sophie Tucker, Locke Envelope # 2391, p. 25, 33, BRTC.

83. Plain Mary (Vesta Powell), "All for the Ladies: About Women—Mostly," *Variety*, February 6, 1914, 13.

84. Marie Dressler, *The Life Story of an Ugly Duckling: An Autobiographical Fragment in Seven Parts* (New York: Robert M. McBride and Company, 1924), 48–49.

85. Abel Green and Joe Laurie Jr., *Show Biz: From Vaude to Video* (New York: Henry Holt and Company, 1951), 10; "The Woman in Variety, by 'the Skirt,'" *Variety*, March 25, 1910, 11.

86. "The Woman in Variety, by 'the Skirt,'" *Variety*, December 19, 1913, 15.

87. " 'The Skirt' Says, Speaking of Woman, Mostly," *Variety*, November 21, 1913, 9; December 5, 1913, 8; October 11, 1912, 12; Anna Marble, "Woman in Variety," *Variety*, November 24, 1906, 7; "The Woman in Variety, by 'the Skirt,'" *Variety*, March 19, 1910, 12; January 16, 1909, 11.

88. Yurka, *Bohemian Girl*, 72, 75. See also Miriam [Burr] Young, *My Mother Wore Tights* (London and New York: McGraw Hill Books Company, Inc., 1944), 10; Tucker, *Some of These Days*, 26.

89. Fanny Brice (as told to Palma Wayne), "Fannie of the Follies," *Cosmopolitan* (March 1936): 106.

90. Brice, "Fannie of the Follies," 106.

91. Peiss, *Cheap Amusements*, 65.

92. On African American use of color, see Jenna Weissman Joselit, *A Perfect Fit: Clothes, Character and the Promise of America* (New York: Henry Holt and Company, 2001), 40.

93. Barbara A. Schreier, *Becoming American: Clothing and the Jewish Immigrant Experience, 1880-1920* (Chicago: Chicago Historical Society, 1991), 67. See Allen, *Horrible Prettiness*, 33, citing Emmanuel Le Roy Ladurie.

94. Pamela E. Klassen, "The Robes of Womanhood: Dress and Authenticity among African American Methodist Women in the Nineteenth Century," *Religion and*

American Culture 14.1 (Winter 2004): 43–44. See also Shane White and Graham White, *Stylin': African American Expressive Culture from Its Beginnings to the Zoot Suit* (Ithaca and London: Cornell University Press, 1998); Joselit, *A Perfect Fit*, 36–40.

95. Henry T. Sampson, *The Ghost Walks: A Chronological History of Blacks in Show Business, 1865–1910* (Metuchen, N.J., and London: Scarecrow Press, 1988), 118–19.

96. Sotiropoulos, *Staging Race*, 48.

97. "Review: *Freeman*, 10–09–09, Johnson and Dean in Vaudeville, by Bradford," and "Review: *Variety*, 10–02–09," Sampson, *The Ghost Walks*, 477–78.

98. Sotiropoulos, *Staging Race*, 48.

99. Sampson, *The Ghost Walks*, 390.

100. "Stage Clothes," *Theatre Magazine* (December 1914): 283.

101. Warwick and Cavallaro, *Fashioning the Frame*, 60.

102. Kibler, *Rank Ladies*, 178.

103. Bates, quoted in McArthur, *Actors and American Culture*, 226.

104. Other actresses who claimed to design their own costumes include Grace La Rue, Ethel Barrymore, Grace George, and Luisa Tetrazzini. *NYDM*, November 19, 1914, Locke Envelope # 1078 (Grace La Rue); Ethel Barrymore, *Memories*, 134–35; "Gowns on the Stage," *HB* (July 1913): 34; Luisa Tetrazzini, "Should We Design Our Gowns?" *HB* (June 1911): 286.

105. Aston Stevens, "Fame via Furbelows," *Cosmopolitan* (February 1914): 415–16.

106. Brian Dureyea, "Introducing the Real Mrs. Castle," *Green Book Magazine* (December 1915): 1034.

107. "To Understand the Working Girl's Problem Try Putting Yourself in Her Place," *New York Evening News*, February 5, 1913, Jane Cowl, v. 131.1, p. 81, RLC, BRTC.

108. John D. Lopez, "The Actress and Her Clothes," *Green Book Album* (July 1910): 116–17.

109. Eaton, "Women as Theater-goers," 13.

110. Rachel Moseley, "Dress, Class, and Audrey Hepburn," in *Fashioning Film Stars: Dress, Culture and Identity*, ed. Rachel Moseley (London: British Film Institute Pub, 2005), 117. See also Sarah Berry, *Screen Style: Fashion and Femininity in 1930s Hollywood* (Minneapolis and London: University of Minnesota Press, 2000), 1–46.

111. Irene (Mrs. Vernon) Castle, *Castles in the Air* (New York: Doubleday and Co., 1958), 67; Shepley, "The Life an Actress Leads," 515.

112. Phillips, "Costuming the Modern Play," 480. "How I Became an Actress," 19.

113. Shepley, "The Life an Actress Leads," 515. See also "Clothes!" *Variety*, January 30, 1915, 12.

114. " 'I Never Tore or Clawed the Girl' but Miss Valeska Suratt Admits Pulling the Cord on Miss Horton's Neck," *New York Telegraph*, February 15, 1907; "Jeanette Horton Withdraws Her Complaint Against Valeska Suratt"; "She Didn't Claw Stage Rival," February 15, 1907, Locke Envelope #2203 (Suratt, Valeska), RLC, BRTC.

115. *New York Telegraph*, October 15, 1907, Locke Envelope #2203 (Suratt, Valeska), RLC, BRTC.

116. See Susan Strasser, *Satisfaction Guaranteed: The Making of the American Mass Market* (New York: Pantheon Books, 1989), 89–123; Stephen Fox, *The Mirror*

Makers: A History of American Advertising and Its Creator (New York: William Morrow, 1984), 40–77; Roland Marchand, *Advertising the American Dream: Making Way for Modernity, 1920–1940* (Berkeley: University of California Press, 1985); Charles F. McGovern, *Sold American: Consumption and Citizenship, 1890–1945* (Chapel Hill: University of North Carolina Press, 2006); Pamela Walker Laird, *Advertising Progress: American Business and the Rise of Consumer Marketing* (Baltimore and London: Johns Hopkins University Press, 1998).

117. Walter Prichard Eaton, "Footlight Fiction: The Wonders Performed by Press Agents," *American Magazine*(December 1907): 164. For more on press agents, see "A Theatrical Press Agent's Confession and Apology," *The Independent* 59 (July 27, 1905): 191–96; "Why Not Press Agents?" *Variety*, July 14, 1906, 8; "Press Agent in His Melancholy Days," *Printers' Ink*, December 5, 1906, 15; "Press Agent's Advice," *Variety*, February 22, 1908, 9; Hugh Pendexter, "On the Trail of the Press Agent," *Green Book Album* (January 1910): 217–24; Nellie Revell, "Woman's Sphere as a Press-Agent," *Green Book Album* (June 1911): 1328–32; George Sinclair, "Actress' Ready Press-Agent," *Green Book Album* (August 1911): 368–72; "The Autobiography of a Theatrical Press Agent," *American Magazine* (April 1913): 66–70; (May 1913): 78–87; (June 1913): 70–77; Leander Richardson, "Where Are the Press Agents of Yesteryear?: The Decline and Fall of a Noble Profession," *Vanity Fair* (October 1914): 39; Roy S. Durstine, "The Up-to-date Press Agent at Work," *Printer's Ink*, March 9, 1916, 101–2; Vincent Landro, "Faking It: The Press Agent and Celebrity Illusion in Early Twentieth Century American Theatre," *Theatre History Studies* 22 (June 2002): 95–113; Marlis Schweitzer, "Singing Her Own Song: Writing the Female Press Agent Back into History," *Journal of American Drama and Theatre* 20.2 (spring 2008): 87–106; Schweitzer, "Surviving the City: Press Agents, Publicity Stunts, and the Spectacle of the Urban Female Body," in *Performance and the City*, ed. D. J. Hopkins, Shelley Orr, and Kim Solga (London: Palgrave Macmillan, forthcoming 2009).

118. Banner, *American Beauty*, 177; Frick, *New York's First Theatrical Center*, 87; McArthur, *Actors and American Culture*, 145.

119. Revell, "Woman's Sphere as a Press-Agent," 1330.

120. Shepley, "The Life an Actress Leads," 515.

121. Cowl, "Why a Reputation for Beauty Is a Handicap," 50.

122. There are exceptions to this. Throughout the 1880s, Lily Langtry, Sarah Bernhardt, and Lillian Russell regularly posed for photographs in the height of fashion. See Sandra Barwick, *A Century of Style* (London: George Allen and Unwin, 1984), 40. For more on theatrical photography, see Alan Thomas, *The Expanding Eye: Photography and the Nineteenth Century Mind* (London: Croom Helm, 1978); Ben L. Bassham, *The Theatrical Photographs of Napoleon Sarony* (Kent, Ohio: Kent State University Press, 1982); William C. Darrah, *Cartes de Visite in Nineteenth Century Photography* (Gettysburg, Pa.: W. C. Darrah, Publisher, n.d.); Alan Trachtenberg, *Reading American Photography: Images as History, Matthew Brady to Walker Evans* (New York: Hill and Wang, 1989); Barbara McCandless, "The Portrait Studio and the Celebrity," in *Photography in Nineteenth Century America*, ed. Martha Sandweiss (New York: Abrams, 1991); Joan L. Severa, *Dressed for the Photographer: Ordinary Americans and Fashion, 1840–1900* (Kent, Ohio: Kent State University Press, 1995); Maria Elena Buszek, "Representing 'Awarishness': Burlesque, Feminist Transgression, and the Nineteenth-Century

Pin-up," *Drama Review* 43.4 (T164) (winter 1999): 141–61; David Mayer, " 'Quote the Words to Prompt the Attitudes': The Victorian Performer, the Photographer, and the Photograph," *Theatre Survey* 43.2 (November 2002): 223–51; Veronica Kelly, "Beauty and the Market: Actress Postcards and Their Senders in Early Twentieth-Century Australia," *New Theatre Quarterly* 20.2 (May 2004): 99–116.

123. Anna Marble, "Woman in Variety," *Variety*, November 3, 1906, 9.

124. Mrs. Woodrow Wilson, "The Fascination of Being Photographed," *Cosmopolitan* (October 1903): 680–81.

125. Ibid. *Cosmopolitan* was also the first major nontheatrical publication to publish photographs of actors and actresses in contemporary dress. See Mizejewski, *Ziegfeld Girl*, 49.

126. Anna Marble, "The Ex-Headliner," *Variety*, January 6, 1906, 4; Mayer, " 'Quote the Words to Prompt the Attitudes,' " 240.

127. Margaret Illington Banes, "The Mad Search for Beauty: And the Slight Chance That the Average Actress Can Guide the Average Woman," *Green Book Magazine* (May 1912): 956.

128. Forbes-Robertson, *My Aunt Maxine*, 181.

129. "Mary Mannering's New Frocks, with Comments on Recent Stage Costumes," *Theatre Magazine* (December 1909): n.p.

130. "Gowns on the Stage," *HB* (October 1913): 30.

131. "The Stage as a Mirror of Fashion," *HB* (February 1914): 32.

132. See Karen Adele Recklies, "Fashion Behind the Footlights: The Influence of Stage Costumes on Women's Fashions" (Ph.D. diss., Ohio State University, 1982), 137, 162, 166.

133. "Footlight Fashions," *Theatre Magazine* (March 1916): 167.

134. "Stage Fashions of the Month," *Theatre Magazine* (March 1909): xxiv. See also "Jane Cowl Wins Fame by Wonderful Gowns for 'Within the Law,' " *Boston American*, March 15, 1914, Jane Cowl, v. 132.2, p. 15, RLC, BRTC; "Behind the Scenes with Nora Bayes," *Dress* (May 1910), Nora Bayes, v. 46, p. 32, RLC, BRTC.

135. "Advantages in Road Show Travel Told by Eva Tanguay," *Variety*, May 16, 1913, 6; "With the Women," *Variety*, October 10, 1914, 6; Tucker, *Some of These Days*, 94; "Women's Clothes, by 'the Skirt,' " *Variety*, December 25, 1914, 36; "The Woman in Variety, by 'the Skirt,' " *Variety*, February 7, 1909, 14.

136. "With the Women," *Variety*, December 12, 1914, 8.

137. "The 'Single Act,' " *Variety*, December 23, 1911, 50.

138. "Woman in a Riot of—Yes, Wardrobe," *New York Telegraph*, January 12, 1909, Eva Tanguay, v. 450, p. 91, RLC, BRTC; "The Woman in Variety, by 'the Skirt,' " *Variety*, February 7, 1909, 14.

139. " 'The Skirt' Says, Speaking of Woman, Mostly," *Variety*, January 6, 1912, 14; "The Woman in Variety, by 'the Skirt,' " *Variety*, January 28, 1911, 11; "With the Women," *Variety*, April 23, 1915, 7; "The Woman in Variety, by 'the Skirt,' " *Variety*, November 5, 1910, 13; " 'The Skirt' Says, Speaking of Woman, Mostly," *Variety*, October 25, 1918, 15.

140. "Bertha Noss-Russell" (ad), *Variety*, December 14, 1907, 104.

141. Matthew Solomon, " 'Twenty-Five Heads under one Hat': Quick-Change in the 1890s," in *Meta-Morphing: Visual Transformation and the Culture of Quick-Change*, ed. Vivian Sobchack (Minneapolis: University of Minnesota Press, 2000), 5–6.

142. *Variety*, December 23, 1911, 159; " 'The Skirt' Says Speaking of Woman, Mostly," *Variety*, October 28, 1911, 14; "Carrie DeMar," *Variety*, February 1, 1908, 8.

143. "Disrobing acts" began on the burlesque circuit as early as the mid-1890s and were quite common by the early 1910s. By 1911, when DeMar presented her act, male audience members (and possibly female audience members as well) would also have been familiar with "striptease" films like Mutoscope's *The Trapeze Disrobing Act* of 1901. See Allen, *Horrible Prettiness*, 243–44, 265–71.

144. Glenn, *Female Spectacle*, 93.

145. Ibid., 88.

146. "Bertha Noss-Russell" (ad), *Variety*, December 14, 1907, 104.

147. Harris, quoted in Solomon, " 'Twenty-five Heads under one Hat,' " 13.

148. Solomon, " 'Twenty-five Heads under one Hat,' " 13. See also James W. Cook, *The Arts of Deception: Playing with Fraud in the Age of Barnum* (Cambridge, Mass.: Harvard University Press, 2001).

149. "The Woman in Variety, by 'the Skirt,' " *Variety*, April 24, 1909, 14.

150. "The Woman in Variety, by 'the Skirt,' " *Variety*, April 23, 1910, 11.

151. *Julian Eltinge Magazine and Beauty Hints*, v. 1, pp. 17, 60, MWEZ n.c. 4243, BRTC. For more on Eltinge's magazine, see Laurence Senelick, *The Changing Room: Sex, Drag, and Theatre* (London and New York: Routledge, 2000), 309–12.

152. John F. Kasson, *Houdini, Tarzan, and the Perfect Man: The White Male Body and the Challenge of Modernity in America* (New York: Hill and Wang, 2001), 92–98.

153. Mme. Qui Vive, "College Boy as a Chorus Girl," Julian Eltinge, v. 182, p. 15, RLC, BRTC.

154. "How I Portray a Woman on the Stage," *Theatre Magazine* (August 1913): 58, ix.

155. Rennold Wolf, "The Sort of Fellow Julian Eltinge Really Is," *Green Book Magazine* 9–10 (November 1913): 795.

156. Julian Eltinge, "When a Man Becomes a Woman: A Vaudeville Miracle" (*Pittsburgh Sunday Magazine*) (June 23, 1907), Julian Eltinge, v. 182, p. 12, RLC, BRTC.

157. Banes, "The Mad Search for Beauty," 953, 956.

158. The list of cosmetics companies includes Lablache Face Powder, Sutol, Sempre Giovine, Lora S. Gilman, Crème Nerol, Mme. Le Claire, Watkin's Mulsified Coconut Oil, Rigaud, Helena Rubinstein, The Importers Company, El Rado Depilatory Cream, Swift and Co., Julian Eltinge Cold Cream, Lillian Russell's Own Toilet Preparations, Peg o' My Heart Perfume, Pond's Vanishing Cream, and Cutex. Ads for the companies listed above appeared in the pages of *Vogue, Vanity Fair, HB*, the *Theatre Magazine, The Delineator*, and the *Ladies' Home Journal* between 1911 and 1918.

159. Richard Corson, *Fashions in Makeup, from Ancient to Modern Times* (London: Owen, 1972), 410; Kathy Peiss, *Hope in a Jar: The Making of America's Beauty Culture* (New York: Harry Holt and Co., 1998), 50, 104–5, 123.

160. Kathy Peiss uses the term "makeup" to refer to products such as rouge and tinted face powder that could dramatically alter appearance. "Invisible" cosmetics like cold cream were less threatening than "makeup." Peiss, *Hope in a Jar*, 53, 56.

161. Lears, "From Salvation to Self-Realization," 17–30. On other uses of terms like "individuality" and "personality," see Martha Cutler, "Individuality in the Home," *HB* (July 1906): 640–41; David Leslie Brown, "Personality," *Cosmopolitan* (January

1910): 5 (advertising section); "Make Your Walls Reflect Your Personality" (ad), *The Delineator* (April 1911): 342; Ann Haviland, "Personality Expressed in Perfume," *HB* (March 1915): 48; "Individuality in Dress" (ad), *Vogue* (December 1918): 11.

162. Sara A. Hubbard, *The Duty of Being Beautiful* (Chicago: A. C. McClurg and Co., 1908). On nineteenth-century attitudes toward cosmetics, see Karen Halttunen, *Confidence Men and Painted Women: A Study of Middle-class Culture in America* (New Haven: Yale University Press, 1982), esp. 56–91; Peiss, "Making Up, Making Over: Cosmetics, Consumer Culture, and Women's Identity," in *The Sex of Things: Gender and Consumption in Historical Perspective*, ed. Victoria de Grazia and Ellen Furlough (Berkeley: University of California Press, 1996), 311–36; and Peiss, *Hope in a Jar*, 9–60.

163. Peiss, *Hope in a Jar*, 59. For a detailed discussion of the "democratization of beauty," see Dawn H. Currie, *Girl Talk: Adolescent Magazines and Their Readers* (Toronto: University of Toronto Press, 1999), 30–36; Sarah Berry, *Screen Style*, 94–141.

164. Older actresses tended to be somewhat hesitant to admit that they used cosmetics in their offstage lives, presumably fearful of damaging their reputations or making an unsavory association with lower-caliber performers. In a series of beauty articles published in *The Delineator* between February and October 1911, prominent actresses including Maxine Elliott, Elsie Janis, and the legendary Ellen Terry denied using commercial beauty products and instead emphasized the importance of cultivating inner beauty. Maxine Elliott, "Keeping Young and Fresh," *The Delineator* (April 1911): 337–38; Elsie Janis, "My Campaign for Good Looks," *The Delineator* (February 1911): 128; Ellen Terry, "The Woman of Charm," *The Delineator* (May 1911): 428.

165. Annette Kellerman, *Physical Beauty: How to Keep It* (New York: George H. Doran Co., 1918), 16.

166. Anna Held, " 'Make-up'—on the Street and on the Stage: Hints for the Woman at Her Dressing-Table," *Green Book Magazine* (February 1916): 331. See also Anne Archbald, "A Plea for Make-up (No. 1)," *Theatre Magazine* (April 1917): 238.

167. "The Face Beautiful and Créme Nerol" (ad), *Vogue* (October 1911): 69.

168. Women Who Have the World at Their Feet Unite in Praise of Valaze" (ad for Helena Rubinstein), *Vanity Fair* (December 1915): 99.

169. "Le Secret Gaby Deslys" (ad), *Theatre Magazine* (June 1912): xix.

170. Peiss, *Hope in a Jar*, 121–22.

171. Ibid., 126, 137–40; Fox, *The Mirror Makers*, 88, 90. On Resor, see Scanlon, *Inarticulate Longings*, 169–98.

172. The ads also identify Mrs. Fiske, Julia Sanderson, Julie Opp, Rose Stahl, and Jane Cowl as prominent users. "Send 4 cents for two weeks' supply. See for yourself what one application will do!" Advertising Ephemera Collection—Database # P0074, Emergence of Advertising On-Line Project, John W. Hartman Center for Sales, Advertising and Marketing History, Duke University Rare Book, Manuscript, and Special Collections Library (hereafter Hartman Center, Duke), http://library.duke.edu/digitalcollections/eaa.P0074/pg.1/, accessed November 19, 2008.

173. Ellen Gartrell, "More about the Pond's Collection," Emergence of Advertising On-Line Project, Hartman Center, Duke, http://library.duke.edu/digitalcollections/eaa/ponds.html, accessed November 19, 2008.

174. "Gleaming, Soft, Smooth Skin (1915)," Database # P0072, Emergence of Advertising On-Line Project, Hartman Center, Duke, http://library.duke/digitalcollections/eaa.P0072/pg.1/, accessed November 19, 2008.

175. "What a Man Looks for in a Girl (1916)," Database # P0091, Emergence of Advertising On-Line Project, Hartman Center, Duke, http://library.duke/digitalcollections/eaa.P0091/pg.1/, accessed November 19, 2008.

176. "The Charm Every Actress Knows" (ad), *LHJ* (April 1916): 64.

177. On trade characters, see Fox, *The Mirror Makers*, 44, 46–47; Charles W. Hurd, "Different Uses of the Testimonial: Several Varieties of the Real Thing and a Few of the Imaginary Ones," *Printers' Ink*, August 28, 1913, 40.

Chapter 4

1. Laurence W. Griswold, "Value of a 'Star's' Name in Sales Plan: How Several Manufacturers Have Increased Consumer Interest by Featuring Products with the Names of Well-Known Actresses, Etc.," *Printers' Ink* (hereafter *PI*), January 22, 1914, 144. On Rigaud's strategies for moving into American markets, see Kathy Peiss, *Hope in a Jar: The Making of America's Beauty Culture* (New York: Harry Holt and Co., 1998), 98.

2. On Garden, see Susan Rutherford, "The Voice of Freedom: Images of the Prima Donna," in *The New Woman and Her Sisters: Feminism and the Theatre, 1850–1914*, ed. Viv Gardner and Susan Rutherford (Hertfordshire: Harvester Wheatsheaf, 1992), 95–114. See also M. Garden and L. Biancolli, *Mary Garden's Story* (London: Michael Joseph, 1952).

3. Charles W. Hurd, "Putting the Dramatic Punch into Window Display: Using the Stage Manager's Method," *PI*, December 16, 1915, 60.

4. Griswold, "The Value of a 'Star's' Name in Sales Plan," 143, 146.

5. Neil M. Alperstein, "Imaginary Social Relationships with Celebrities Appearing in Television Commercials," *Journal of Broadcasting & Electronic Media* 35.1 (winter 1991): 50.

6. Susan Torrey Barstow, "Ellen Terry and the Revolt of the Daughters," *Nineteenth-Century Theatre* 25.1 (summer 1997): 20–21. See also Kim Marra, *Strange Duets: Impresarios and Actresses in the American Theatre, 1865–1914* (Iowa City: University of Iowa Press, 2006), 99–103; Veronica Kelly, "An Australian Idol of Modernist Consumerism: Minnie Tittell Brune and the Gallery Girls," *Theatre Research International* 31.1 (2006): 17–36. On fandom and stars, see Lisa A Lewis, ed., *The Adoring Audience: Fan Culture and Popular Media* (London and New York: Routledge, 1992); Gaylyn Studlar, " 'The Perils of Pleasure?' Fan Magazine Discourse as Women's Commodified Culture in the 1920s," *Wide Angle* 13.1 (January 1991): 6–33; Jackie Stacey, *Star Gazing: Hollywood Cinema and Female Spectatorship* (London and New York: Routledge, 1994); Richard Dyer, *Heavenly Bodies: Film Stars and Society* (London: Macmillan Education Ltd., 1986), 5; Richard Dyer, *Stars* (London: British Film Institute, 1979); Christine Gledhill, ed., *Stardom: Industry of Desire* (London and New York: Routledge, 1995); Angela Ndalianis and Charlotte Henry, eds., *Stars in Our Eyes: The*

Star Phenomenon in the Contemporary Era (Westport, Conn., and London: Praeger, 2002); Rachel Moseley, *Growing Up with Audrey Hepburn: Text, Audience, Resonance* (New York: Palgrave, 2002).

7. James L. Ford, "The Ethel Barrymore Following," *Appleton's* (November 1908): 546–60; Diana Forbes-Robertson, *My Aunt Maxine: The Story of Maxine Elliott* (New York: Viking Press, 1964); Elizabeth McCracken, "The Play and the Gallery," *Atlantic Monthly* 89 (1902): 497-98; Billie Burke, *With a Feather on My Nose* (New York: Appleton-Century-Crofts, 1949).

8. J. Caughey quoted in Alperstein, "Imaginary Social Relationships with Celebrities Appearing in Television Commercials," 44. Barstow, "Ellen Terry," 8; Chris Rojek, *Celebrity* (London: Reaktion, 2001), chap. 2.

9. Benjamin McArthur, *Actors and American Culture: 1880–1920* (1984; Iowa City: University of Iowa Press, 2000), x, 164, 188.

10. Forbes-Robertson, *My Aunt Maxine*, 182–83.

11. Leslie Goddard, " 'Women Know Her to Be a Real Woman': Femininity, Nationalism, and the Suffrage Activism of Lillian Russell," *Theatre History Studies* 22 (June 2002): 138–42; Susan A. Glenn, *Female Spectacle: The Theatrical Roots of Modern Feminism* (Cambridge, Mass.: Harvard University Press, 2000), 136–37.

12. On the importance of the imagination in the theater, see Jill Dolan, "Performance, Utopia, and the 'Utopian Performative,' " *Theatre Journal* 53 (2001): 460; Jill Dolan, *Utopia in Performance: Finding Hope at the Theatre* (Ann Arbor: University of Michigan Press, 1999). Bert States echoes Dolan's perception of theater's political potential when he observes that "theater is a license for a remarkable exercise in group imagination." Bert O. States, *Great Reckonings in Little Rooms: On the Phenomenology of Theater* (Berkeley: University of California Press, 1985), 157–58. Dolan's theories also find resonance in Arjun Appadurai's insistence that "the imagination, especially when collective, can become . . . a staging ground for action, and not only for escape." Arjun Appadurai, *Modernity at Large: Cultural Dimensions of Globalization* (Minneapolis: University of Minnesota Press, 1996), 7.

13. William R. Leach, *Land of Desire: Merchants, Power, and the Rise of a New American Culture* (New York: Pantheon Books, 1993), 64–65.

14. "Showing Gowns on Living Models." *Merchants Record and Show Window* (November 1909): 39; "Wax Figures That Sell Goods in Windows," *PI* (November 11, 1908), 19; "Biggest Thing in Fashion Displays," *DGE*, April 1, 1911, 45, 49.

15. "Theatrical and Other Fashions," *Theatre Magazine* (June 1909): n.p.

16. "Fashions on the Stage," *Theatre Magazine* (November 1914): 246.

17. "Gowns on the New York Stage," *HB* (January 1909): 88.

18. Alfred Mason, "The Stage as an Educator," *Green Book Album* (February 1909): 328–29.

19. "French Modistes Differ on the Directorie [*sic*] Gowns," *New York Times* (hereafter *NYT*), May 24, 1908; "On the Side," *Puck*, September 9, 1908, 64.

20. Although women continued to wear corsets with the sheath style, the tight lacing necessitated by the S-curve line gave way to a very different encasement of the female body. On changes in corsetry, see Valerie Steele, *Fashion and Eroticism: Ideals of Feminine Beauty from the Victorian through the Jazz Era* (Oxford: Oxford University Press, 1985).

21. Robert C. Allen, *Horrible Prettiness: Burlesque and American Culture* (Chapel Hill: University of North Carolina Press, 1991), 146.

22. John D'Emilio and Estelle B. Freedman, *Intimate Matters: A History of Sexuality in America*, 2nd ed. (Chicago and London: University of Chicago Press, 1997), 224–26, 230, 232, 241.

23. "Calls Dress a Snare," *Chicago Record-Herald*, May 24, 1908, 1.

24. Martha Banta, *Imaging American Women: Ideas and Ideals in Cultural History* (New York: Columbia University Press, 1987).

25. Valerie Steele, *Paris Fashion: A Cultural History* (New York and Oxford: Oxford University Press, 1988), 233; Justia, "Nationalism in Dress" (letter to the editor), *NYT*, January 1, 1909, 10.

26. Loren H. B. Knox, "Our Lost Individuality," *Atlantic Monthly* 85 (February 1900): 195–204; "The Tyranny of Fashion," *The Independent* 58 (March 2, 1905): 509–10; Anna G. Noyes, "A Practical Protest Against Fashion," *The Independent* 63 (August 29, 1906): 504–9; Enid Campbell Dauncey, "The Functions of Fashion," *Living Age*, June 24, 1911, 790–94; "Indicating the Bad Taste of Today," *Literary Digest*, June 20, 1914, n.p.

27. "Trousers Skirt in Texas: Fort Worth Concern's Display Leads to Sale of Two Dozen," *DGE*, April 15, 1911, 33; " 'The Skirt' Says, Speaking of Woman, Mostly," *Variety*, May 20, 1911, 19.

28. That Carlisle appeared in the gown mere days after it appeared in Paris suggests that her gown was almost certainly a copy, perhaps made by a local dressmaker from photographs of Paris mannequins.

29. "Girl in Directoire Gown," *NYT*, May 24, 1908, pt. 2, 1. For more on this fashion stunt, see Schweitzer, "Surviving the City: Press Agents, Publicity Stunts, and the Spectacle of the Urban Female Body," in *Performance and the City*, ed. D. J. Hopkins, Shelley Orr, and Kim Solga (London: Palgrave Macmillan, forthcoming 2009).

30. "Toledo Gets the Sheath," *Variety*, July 11, 1908, 1. Sophie Tucker staged a similar stunt in Dayton, Ohio. Sophie Tucker (with Dorothy Giles), *Some of These Days: The Autobiography of Sophie Tucker* (Garden City, N.Y.: Garden City Publishing Co., 1945), 106.

31. "Tight-Skirt Brings Out Reserves," *NYT*, July 19, 1908, pt. 2, 7; "The Limerick Contest—Winners and Details," *NYT*, July 19, 1908, SM11.

32. "Tight-Skirt Brings Out Reserves," 7.

33. "When the Split Skirt Was Introduced to Ottawa," *Ottawa Daily Republic*, September 5, 1908.

34. On theater semiotics, see Petr Bogatryev, "Semiotics in the Folk Theater," in *Semiotics of Art: Prague School Contributions*, ed. Ladislav Matejka and Irwin R. Titunik (Cambridge, Mass.: MIT Press, 1976), 33–50; Umberto Eco, "Semiotics of Theatrical Performance," *Drama Review* 21 (1977): 107–17; Keir Elam, *The Semiotics of Theatre and Drama*, 2nd ed. (1980; London: Routledge, 2002); Michael L. Quin, *The Semiotic Stage: Prague School Theater Theory* (New York: Peter Land, 1995). Andrew Sofer offers a fascinating study of the semiotic potential of the fan in Restoration comedy. Sofer, *The Stage Life of Props* (Ann Arbor: University of Michigan Press, 2003), 117–65.

35. Jill Dolan, *Geographies of Learning: Theory and Practice, Activism and Performance* (Middletown, Conn.: Wesleyan University Press, 2001), 84.

36. Gay McAuley, *Space in Performance: Making Meaning in the Theatre* (Ann Arbor: University of Michigan Press, 1999), 178.

37. Peter Bailey, "Conspiracies of Meaning: Music-Hall and the Knowingness of Popular Culture," *Past and Present* 144 (August 1994): 138–70.

38. "Alan Dale Calls 'Wildfire' a Comedy of Directoire Gowns" and "Lillian Russell's Sheath," *Toledo Blade*, September 9, 1908, Lillian Russell, v. 413, p. 46, Robinson Locke Collection, Billy Rose Theatre Collection (hereafter RLC, BRTC).

39. "Miss Lillian Russell Wins with 'Wildfire,' " Lillian Russell, v. 413, p. 45, RLC, BRTC.

40. "Alan Dale Calls 'Wildfire' a Comedy of Directoire Gowns," 46.

41. "Lillian Russell's Sehat," *Toledo Blade*, Lillian Russell, v. 413, p. 47, RLC, BRTC.

42. Goddard, " 'Women Know Her to Be a Real Woman,' " 138–42; Glenn, *Female Spectacle*, 136–37.

43. "Lillian Russell" (review), *Variety*, March 7, 1913, n.p.; "Lillian Russell's Own Toilet Preparations" (ad), *Vanity Fair* (January 1914): 87; "To the Women of America, by Lillian Russell" (ad), *HB* (April 1915): 69; John Burke, *Duet in Diamonds: The Flamboyant Saga of Lillian Russell and Diamond Jim Brady in America's Gilded Age* (New York: Putnam's Sons, 1972), 294–96; Armond Fields, *Lillian Russell: A Biography of "America's Beauty"* (Jefferson, N.C., and London: McFarland and Co., Inc. Publishers, 1999), 190.

44. On suffragette stereotypes and attempts to refute the same, see Wendy Parkins, " 'The Epidemic of Purple, White and Green': Fashion and the Suffragette Movement in Britain 1908–14," in *Fashioning the Body Politic: Dress, Gender, Citizenship*, ed. Wendy Parkins (London: Berg, 2002), 107–13; Margaret Finnegan, *Selling Suffrage: Consumer Culture and Votes for Women* (New York: Columbia University Press, 1999); Catherine H. Palczewski, "The Male Madonna and the Feminine Uncle Sam: Visual Argument, Icons, and Ideographs in 1909 Anti-Woman Suffrage Postcards," *Quarterly Journal of Speech* 91.4 (November 2005): 365–94.

45. Glenn, *Female Spectacle*, 112–15.

46. Karen Sotiropoulos, *Staging Race: Black Performers in Turn of the Century America* (Cambridge, Mass.: Harvard University Press, 2006), 176; Glenn, *Female Spectacle*, 114; Daphne Brooks, *Bodies in Dissent: Spectacular Performances of Race and Freedom* (Chapel Hill: University of North Carolina Press, 2006), 333; David Krasner, "Black *Salome*: Exoticism, Dance, and Racial Myths," in *African American Performance and Theater History: A Critical Reader*, ed. Harry J. Elam and David Krasner (Oxford and New York: Oxford University Press, 2001), 192–211.

47. Locke Envelope #2461, "Walker: Aida Overton," RLC, BRTC.

48. "Review, *Freeman*, Williams and Walker's Bandanna Land, by Burton M. Beach," in Henry T. Sampson, *The Ghost Walks: A Chronological History of Blacks in Show Business, 1865–1910* (Metuchen, N.J., and London: Scarecrow Press, 1988), 423–24.

49. Pamela E. Klassen, "The Robes of Womanhood: Dress and Authenticity among African American Methodist Women in the Nineteenth Century," *Religion and American Culture* 14.1 (Winter 2004): 44.

50. "Review, *Freeman*, Williams and Walker's Bandanna Land, by Burton M. Beach," in Sampson, *Ghost Walks*, 423–24.

51. Peiss, *Hope in a Jar*, 92–93, 206–7. See also Shane White and Graham White, *Stylin': African American Expressive Culture from Its Beginnings to the Zoot Suit* (Ithaca and London: Cornell University Press, 1998), 180–219.

52. Locke Envelope #2461, "Walker: Aida Overton," RLC, BRTC; "The Sheath Gown in Darktown," vocal score, "Performing Arts in America, 1875–1923, New York Public Library Digital Arts Collection," http://digitalgallery.nypl.org/nypldigital/id?G99C485_001, accessed May 21, 2008. For more on Walker, see Richard Newman, " 'The Brightest Star': Aida Overton Walker in the Age of Ragtime and Cakewalk," *Prospects* 18 (1993): 465–81; David Krasner, *Resistance, Parody, and Double Consciousness in African American Theatre, 1895-1910* (New York: St. Martin's Press, 1997), 76–98; Sotiropoulos, *Staging Race*, 174–77; Brooks, *Bodies in Dissent*.

53. Glenn, *Female Spectacle*, 165.

54. Sotiropoulos, *Staging Race*, 64. See also Krasner, *Resistance, Parody, and Double Consciousness*; Brooks, *Bodies in Dissent*; Camille F. Forbes, "Dancing with 'Racial Feet': Bert Williams and the Performance of Blackness," *Theatre Journal* 56.4 (December 2004): 603–25.

55. Newman, " 'The Brightest Star,' " 465–81; Krasner, *"Black* Salome," 192–211.

56. Sotiropoulos, *Staging Race*, 48, 63.

57. Laurette van Varseveld, "The Psychology of Stage Clothes," *Theatre Magazine* (January 1908): 16.

58. Ibid., 15.

59. "Jane Cowl Wins Game by Wonderful Gowns for 'Within the Law.'" *Boston American* (15 March 1914), Jane Cowl, v. 132, p. 15, RLC, BRTC.

60. Alice Brady, "This Business of Dressing: Should You 'Wrap Your Clothes Around You' or Should You Put Them On?" *Green Book Magazine* (September 1915): 484–90.

61. Alan Dale, "Our Overdressed Drama: Much of the Odium That Assails the Theater May Be Traced to the Clothes Habit Which Often Makes the Stage Look Like a Spring Opening or a Sartorial Competition," *Cosmopolitan* (May 1907): 65; Alan Dale, "The Tyranny of Clothes: How the Clothes-Mania Affects the Actor and Influences the Modern Drama," *Cosmopolitan* (May 1908): 610–12; Alan Dale, "Clothes and the Drama," *Theatre Magazine* 22.177 (November 1915): 232–34, 254–55.

62. Dale, "Clothes and the Drama," 254.

63. Ibid., 233.

64. Ibid., 232.

65. Bailey, "Conspiracies of Meaning," 138–70; "Jane Cowl's Understanding of the Portrayal of Character by Clothes," *Dress* (June 1913): 19, Jane Cowl. v. 131, p. 125, RLC, BRTC.

66. "Jane Cowl's Understanding of the Portrayal of Character by Clothes," 125.

67. "Fashion and the Development of Women," *The Craftsman* 25 (February 1914): 505. See also "Is a Nation's Character Revealed in Its Dress?" *The Craftsman* 25 (March 1914): 622–25.

68. "Fashion and the Development of Women," 505–6.

69. "Is a Nation's Character Revealed in Its Dress?" 624.

70. Elsie de Wolfe, "The Well-Dressed Woman," *Cosmopolitan* (December 1897): 125.

71. John D. Lopez, "The Actress and Her Clothes," *Green Book Album* (July 1910): 120.

72. Valeska Suratt, "Personality—That's Me!" *Green Book Magazine* (September 1915): 421.

73. Julia Dean, "In Defense of the Modes," *Green Book Magazine* (July 1915): 67.

74. Georg Simmel, "The Philosophy of Fashion," in *Simmel on Culture: Selected Writings*, ed. David Frisby and Mike Featherstone (London: Sage Publications, 1997), 194.

75. Simmel, "The Philosophy of Fashion," 191.

76. Elizabeth Wilson, *Adorned in Dreams: Fashion and Modernity* (New Brunswick, N.J.: Rutgers University Press, 1985), 123.

77. Brady, "This Business of Dressing," 488.

78. Suratt, "Personality—That's Me!" 421–22.

79. "Miss DeWolfe's Exquisite Gowns," *Harper's Bazar* (hereafter *HB*) (February 3, 1900): 94.

80. "Jane Cowl's Understanding of the Portrayal of Character by Clothes," 125.

81. Suratt, "Personality—That's Me!" 420; Ruby Leone, "No Jewels and Spangles," *Variety*, December 10, 1910, 37; Luisa Tetrazzini, "Should We Design Our Gowns?" *HB* (June 1911): 286. See also Karen Halttunen, *Confidence Men and Painted Women: A Study of Middle-Class Culture in America* (New Haven: Yale University Press, 1982); Peiss, *Hope in a Jar*.

82. Lopez, "The Actress and Her Clothes," 121.

83. "Jane Cowl's Understanding of the Portrayal of Character by Clothes," 125.

84. Ruth Chatterton, "Nature as a Guide to Dress: How She Masses and Arranges Her Colors," *Green Book Magazine* (August 1915): 266.

85. Beatrice Crosby, "Dressing the Emotions: Does Your Gown Express Your Soul?" *McCall's Magazine* (January 1915): 53.

86. Glenn, *Female Spectacle*, 5–6; Nancy F. Cott, *The Grounding of Modern Feminism* (New Haven, Conn.: Yale University Press, 1987), 5, 36–39.

87. "Hobble Skirt and Drama," *Pittsburgh Leader*, October 14, 1910, Laurette Taylor, v. 451, p. 26, RLC, BRTC.

88. Lopez, "The Actress and Her Clothes," 116. For a detailed analysis of Carlyle's "Sartor Resartus," see Michael Carter, "Thomas Carlyle and 'Sartor Resartus,'" in *Fashion Classics from Carlyle to Barthes* (London: Berg, 2003), 1–18.

89. "Hobble Skirt and Drama," 26.

90. Anne Archbald, "Clothes Seen on the Stage," *Theatre Magazine* (April 1915): 216.

91. Janet Loring argues that while "[p]sychology of stage clothes was a common phrase, [it] seldom meant more than a consideration of the most simple and obvious color symbolism." I would counter that although this symbolism may not have been complex, it was nevertheless important to the women who employed it. Janet Loring, "Costuming on the New York Stage from 1895 to 1915 with Particular Emphasis on Charles Frohman's Companies" (Ph.D. diss., State University of Iowa, 1961), 126.

92. "Address by Miss Annie Russell to the Students of the American Academy of Dramatic Arts," March 21, 1902, Empire Theatre, New York (National Publishing Co., Washington, D.C.), Warshaw, Theater, Box 17, Folder: Miscellaneous, Archives Center,

National Museum of American History, Kenneth E. Behring Center, Smithsonian Institution (hereafter NMAH).

93. Vanderheyden Fyles, "Clothes and the Actress," *Green Book Album* (June 1911): 1181.

94. Tracy C. Davis, *Actresses as Working Women: Their Social Identity in Victorian Culture* (London and New York: Routledge, 1991), 109, 111. See also Arthur Edwin Krows, *Play Production in America* (New York: Henry Holt & Co., 1916), 197–98.

95. Lillian L. Bentley, "Does Red Make Us Nervous?" *Ladies' Home Journal* (March 1908): 20. See also Howard Kenneth Greer, "The Psychology of Color," *Theatre Magazine* (December 1917): 374–76.

96. Arnold Aronson, "Architect of Dreams," in *Looking Into the Abyss: Essays on Scenography* (Ann Arbor: University of Michigan Press, 2005), 148–49.

97. Lopez, "The Actress and Her Clothes," 118.

98. For other actresses' discussions of color, see Lavinia Hart, "Olga Nethersole," *Cosmopolitan* (May 1901): 24; "Colors and Emotions: Miss Olga Nethersole Explains Her Theories Concerning Their Relations to Each Other," *New York World*, October 30, 1898, Olga Nethersole, v. 361, p. 43, RLC, BRTC; Ethel Barrymore, *Memories: An Autobiography* (New York: Harper & Brothers: 1955), 134; Anna Marble, "The Woman in Variety," *Variety*, October 10, 1908, 9; "Jane Cowl's Understanding of the Portrayal of Character by Clothes," 125; "On and Off the Stage, Frances Starr Subordinates Her Clothes to Her Expressive Personality by Choosing Uni-Colored Costumes, and Those Preferably White," *Vogue* (February 1914): n.p.

99. Chatterton, "Nature as a Guide to Dress," 266. See also Crosby, "Dressing the Emotions," 53–54.

100. "Stage Clothes That Play Successful Roles,'" *Vogue* (November 1918): 92. Actresses could, of course, find other ways to circumvent playwrights' stage directions. Joel Kaplan and Sheila Stowell argue that Mrs. Patrick Campbell used costuming to undermine attempts by Arthur Pinero Jones and George Bernard Shaw to shape her character against her will. Joel H. Kaplan and Sheila Stowell, *Theatre and Fashion: Oscar Wilde to the Suffragettes* (Cambridge: Cambridge University Press, 1994), 45–81.

101. "Stage Clothes That Play Successful Roles," 35.

102. Crosby, "Dressing the Emotions," 54.

103. "Jane Cowl's Understanding of the Portrayal of Character by Clothes," 125.

104. Mlle. Manhattan, "La comedie de salon et de la mode," *Theatre Magazine* (April 1916): 244.

105. Claudia B. Kidwell and Margaret C. Christman, *Suiting Everyone: The Democratization of Clothing in America* (Washington, D.C.: Smithsonian Institution Press, 1974); Nan Enstad, *Ladies of Labor, Girls of Adventure* (New York: Columbia University Press, 2000); Rob Schorman, *Selling Style: Clothing and Social Change at the Turn of the Century* (Philadelphia: University of Pennsylvania Press, 2003).

106. Mlle. Manhattan, "Footlight Fashions," *Theatre Magazine* (November 1916): 301; (January 1917): 57; Billie Burke, v. 87, p. 4–5, RLC, BRTC.

107. The actual practice of copying stage gowns was hardly new. Throughout the late nineteenth century, society women often drew fashion inspiration from international stars like Rachel, Sarah Bernhardt, and Lily Langtry, all of whom were known for their innovative and expensive clothes, as well as "home grown" stars like

Ada Rehan. See Lois W. Banner, *American Beauty* (Chicago and London: University of Chicago Press, 1983), 69; Richard Butsch, "Bowery B'hoys and Matinee Ladies: Re-Gendering of Nineteenth Century American Theater Audiences," *American Quarterly* 46.3 (September 1994): 388–89; Sarah Bernhardt, *My Double Life: The Memoirs of Sarah Bernhardt*, trans. Victoria Tietze Larson (New York: State University of New York Press, 1999), 258–59; Kim Marra, "Taming America as Actress: Augustin Daly, Ada Rehan, and the Discourse of Imperial Frontier Conquest," in *Performing America: Cultural Nationalism in American Theater*, ed. Jeffrey D. Mason and J. Ellen Gainor (Ann Arbor: University of Michigan Press, 1999), 52–72.

108. In her analysis of female film audiences of the 1930s, 1940s, and 1950s, Jackie Stacey charts the "identifactory practices of spectatorship." These practices, which occur outside the cinematic or theatrical realm, "involve the audience engaging in some kind of practice of transformation of the self to become more like the star they admire, or to involve others in the recognition of similarity with the star." Stacey distinguishes between *imitation*, "the partial taking on of part of a star's identity" (for example, adopting a star's physical or vocal mannerisms), and *copying*, the "attempted replication of appearance" (for example, copying a star's hairstyle or clothing), and argues that through these practices female spectators experiment with their identities. Rather than losing themselves in the identification process, she argues, women who engage in identifactory practices incorporate elements of the star's identity into their own. Imitation and copying become productive, creative acts. Jackie Stacey, "Feminine Fascinations: Forms of Identification with Star-Audience Relations," in *Stardom: Industry of Desire*, ed. Christine Gledhill (London and New York: Routledge, 1991), 153, 156–57; Stacey, *Star Gazing*.

109. Adele Recklies demonstrates that women chose to emulate actresses who represented a specific "type" that they felt was compatible with their personality. See Karen Adele Recklies, "Fashion Behind the Footlights: The Influence of Stage Costumes on Women's Fashions" (Ph.D. diss., Ohio State University, 1982), 146.

110. Harriet Edwards Fayes, "Simplicity Is the Keynote of Smart Spring Styles," *Theatre Magazine* (March 1912): xxiv; Anne Archbald, "Clothes Seen on the Stage," *Theatre Magazine* (July 1916): 48.

111. For excellent sociological analyses of consumer interactions with and uses of dress, see Dick Hebdige, *Subculture: The Meaning of Style* (London: Routledge, 1991); Ali Guy, Eileen Green, and Maura Banim, eds., *Through the Wardrobe: Women's Relationships with Their Clothes* (Oxford and New York: Berg, 2001); William J. F. Keenan, ed., *Dressed to Impress: Looking the Part* (London: Berg, 2001).

112. Thorstein Veblen, *The Theory of the Leisure Class* (1899; New York: Prometheus Books, 1998), 83. See also David Scobey, "Anatomy of the Promenade: The Politics of Bourgeois Sociability in Nineteenth-century New York," *Social History* 17.2 (May 1992): 203–27.

113. "Stars in Society: Social Doors Are Always Open to Leading Stage Stars of America," December 15, 1902, Ethel Barrymore, v. 34, p. 54, RLC, BRTC.

114. For example, the dressmaker Mme. Rosenberg promised that she could reproduce models for actresses within twenty-four hours. Ad in *Variety*, September 3, 1915, 28. For more on the relationship between upper-middle-class women and dressmakers, see Gamber, *The Female Economy*, 96–124.

278   Notes to Pages 164–168

115. Wherever possible, Mlle. Manhattan emphasized the *Theatre Magazine's* role as a leading source of fashion information, suggesting that society women drew inspiration from the exclusive photographs published in "Footlight Fashions." Mlle. Manhattan, "Footlight Fashions," *Theatre Magazine* (July 1916): 46.

116. Mlle. Manhattan, "Footlight Fashions," *Theatre Magazine* (August 1916): 102.

117. In 1924, the play was made into the film *Whispered Name*. Janiss Garza, *All Movie Guide*, http://movies2.nytimes.com/gst/movies/movie.html?v_id=116701), accessed May 15, 2008.

118. Joseph R. Svinth, "Anthony J. Drexel Biddle, USMC CQB Pioneer," *Journal of Non-lethal Combatives* (December 2001), http://ejmas.com/jnc/jncart_Svinth_1201.htm, accessed May 15, 2008. Cordelia Duke later wrote a book about her father entitled *My Philadelphia Father*, which was turned into the film *The Happiest Millionaire*, starring Fred McMurray. http://www.newyorksocialdiary.com/socialdiary/2005/04_06_05/socialdiary04_06_05.php, accessed May 15, 2008.

119. "Miss Anglin Seen in Sparkling Comedy," *NYT*, September 21, 1916, 9.

120. Mlle. Manhattan, "Footlight Fashions," *Theatre Magazine* (November 1916): 301.

121. "Miss Anglin Seen in Sparkling Comedy," 9.

122. For more on Madelaine Dick and the Astors, see Virginia Cowles, *The Astors: The Story of a Transatlantic Family* (London: Weidenfeld and Nicolson, 1979), 143–46, 174–75, 197–98.

123. According to the *Theatre Magazine*, soda fountains in the theater district served "Phoebe Foster nut sundaes." Anne Archbald, "Clothes Seen on the Stage," *Theatre Magazine* (August 1916): 104.

124. As early as 1913, *Vogue* started to include fashion articles for "The Younger Generation." In 1915, the *Theatre Magazine* profiled "Fall Fancies" for girls, and in 1917, it introduced a special series targeted at the "Young Person" entitled "the Fashion Adventures of Angelina." "The Younger Generation," *Vogue* (July 1913): 49; "For the School Girl," *Vogue* (September 1913): 6; Anne Rittenhouse, "Sophisticated Seventeen," *Vanity Fair* (January 1914): 61; "Angelina Changes Her Luck," *Theatre Magazine* (August 1917): 58. For more on girl culture, see Sherrie A. Inness, ed., *Delinquents and Debutantes: Twentieth-Century American Girls' Cultures* (New York and London: New York University Press, 1998); Jane H. Hunter, *How Young Ladies Became Girls: The Victorian Origins of American Girlhood* (New Haven, Conn., and London: Yale University Press, 2002).

125. Burke, *With a Feather on My Nose*, 77. See also "The Hazel Dawn Debutante Dress" (ad), *DGE*, January 16, 1915, 46–47; Anne Archbald, "Clothes Seen on the Stage," *Theatre Magazine* (August 1916): 104; Mlle. Manhattan, "Footlight Fashions," *Theatre Magazine* (January 1917): 52; Fayes, "Simplicity Is the Keynote of Smart Spring Styles," xxiv; Anne Archbald, "Clothes Seen on the Stage," *Theatre Magazine* (May 1915): 268.

126. "Clothes Seen on the Stage," *Theatre Magazine* (March 1915): n.p.; "Woolf and Shulhof, Makers of Costumes and Dresses" (ad), *DGE*, January 16, 1915, 38; "Another 'Liberal' Success" (ad for the Liberal Shirt Waist Co.), *DGE*, April 16, 1910, 13.

127. Christopher Breward, "Patterns of Respectability: Publishing, Home Sewing and the Dynamics of Class and Gender 1870–1914," in *The Culture of Sewing: Gender,*

Consumption and Home Dressmaking, ed. Barbara Burman (Oxford and New York: Berg, 1999), 21–31.

128. Barbara Burman, "Made at Home by Clever Fingers: Home Dressmaking in Edwardian England," in *The Culture of Sewing: Gender, Consumption and Home Dressmaking*, ed. Barbara Burman (Oxford and New York: Berg, 1999), 8–9.

129. Anne Page, "The Wide, Wide Swirl of the New Skirts Suits the New Materials," *The Delineator* (May 1915): 47. On the changing silhouette, see also Steele, *Paris Fashion*, 237.

130. Irene Castle, *Castles in the Air* (New York: Doubleday and Co., 1958), 135; Lady Duff Gordon (Lucile), *Discretions and Indiscretions* (New York: Frederick A. Stokes Co., 1932), 247–49.

131. See *McCall's* and *The Delineator* for 1915.

132. "The New Styles with Their Full Skirts Make Dancing and Walking a Joy," *The Delineator* (May 1915): 62. In 1916, one of the Dolly sisters appeared in a replica of this dress, complete with bobbed hair and "Castle band" in the Shubert production *Maid in America*. See "Maid in America," 16540–122 [48717], White Studio Collection, BRTC.

133. Cecil Beaton, *The Glass of Fashion* (London: Weidenfeld and Nicolson, 1954), 108.

134. Lewis A. Erenberg, *Steppin' Out: New York Nightlife and the Transformation of American Culture* (Chicago and London: University of Chicago Press, 1981), 166. When she cut her long brown hair in 1914 in preparation for an operation, fashion-conscious women everywhere demanded the "Castle bob." Castle, *Castles in the Air*, 115–17; "Cabarets," *Variety*, March 12, 1915, 13; "The 'Castle Bob,'" *Ohio State Journal*, October 14, 1917, Irene Castle, series 2, v. 37, p. 83, RLC, BRTC; clipping, *Vogue* (April 1915[?]): 71, Robert Baral Collection, BRTC.

135. "Capping the Theatre Costume," *Vanity Fair* (January 1914): 70; "Highlights on Trinkets," *Theatre Magazine* (April 1915): n.p.; "Told in the Boudoir: Concerning Coiffures in General and in Particular," *Vanity Fair* (February 1915): 74; "With the Women," *Variety*, June 25, 1915, 12; "Mrs. Vernon Castle, and Her New White Wig," *Vanity Fair* (March 1915): 22; "To the Vernon Castles, a Mild Complaint, by J. S.," *Vanity Fair* (June 1915): 52.

136. Paul Poiret, *King of Fashion: The Autobiography of Paul Poiret*, trans. Stephen Haden Guest (Philadelphia: J. B. Lippincott, 1931), 97.

137. Vernon Castle and Irene Castle, *Modern Dancing* (New York and London, 1914), 139. For more on the Castles' dancing and the early twentieth-century "dance craze," see Julie Malnig, *Dancing Till Dawn: A Century of Exhibition Ballroom Dance* (New York and London: New York University Press, 1992).

138. Brigitte Soland, *Becoming Modern: Young Women and the Reconstruction of Womanhood in the 1920s* (Princeton, N.J., and Oxford: Princeton University Press, 2000), 36–40; Laura Doan, "Passing Fashions: Reading Female Masculinities in the 1920s," *Feminist Studies* 24.3 (fall 1998): 663–701.

139. On this point, see Tamar Jeffers, "*Pillow Talk's* Repackaging of Doris Day: 'Under All Those Dirndls . . .'" in *Fashioning Film Stars: Dress, Culture and Identity*, ed. Rachel Moseley (London: British Film Institute Pub, 2005), 52.

140. The *Watch Your Step* gowns were deemed appropriate for fashion-savvy

middle-class women *and* their daughters; indeed, in several of the pattern magazines I looked at, designers for young girls' clothing seem to have adopted the fuller-skirted, tight-bodiced style *before* it made its way into women's fashion.

141. Enstad, *Ladies of Labor*, 63–65. Mrs. John Van Vorst noted the enthusiasm with which young working women discussed stage celebrities, including Sarah Bernhardt, Maude Adams, and Rejane. Mrs. John Van Vorst and Marie Van Vorst, *The Woman Who Toils: Being the Experiences of Two Gentlewomen as Factory Girls* (New York: Doubleday, Page and Company, 1903), 93–94, 193.

142. Kathy Peiss observes that working women frequently rivaled society women in the swiftness with which they adopted the latest styles. Kathy Peiss, *Cheap Amusements: Working Women and Leisure in Turn-of-the-Century New York* (Philadelphia: Temple University Press, 1986), 62; Enstad, *Ladies of Labor*, 78.

143. Banner, *American Beauty*, 74.

144. Van Vorst and Van Vorst, *The Woman Who Toils*, 93–94.

145. Margaret Clarke, "The Pin-Money Club: A Picture of Ethel Barrymore for Every Pin-Money Club Girl," *Woman's Home Companion* (October 1910): 68; Barrymore, *Memories*, 134. See also Kelly, "An Australian Idol of Modernist Consumerism."

146. Peiss, *Cheap Amusements*, 66.

147. The theater critic Archie Bell (1913), quoted in Katie N. Johnson, "*Zaza*: That 'Obtruding Harlot' of the Stage," *Theatre Journal* 54 (2002): 235.

148. Richardson, *The Long Day: The Story of a New York Working Girl as Told by Herself* (New York: The Century Co., 1905), 70–72.

149. Marra, *Strange Duets*, 227, 229.

150. Richardson, *The Long Day*, 232–33; Photo of Olga Nethersole, Negative # 26140, Prints and Photographs Division (Reproduction # A36454), Library of Congress. See also Johnson, "*Zaza*," 223–43.

151. Olga Nethersole, v. 162.2, p. 3, RLC, BRTC.

152. Quoted in Katie N. Johnson, *Sisters in Sin: Brothel Drama in America, 1900–1920* (Cambridge: Cambridge University Press, 2006), 57–58.

153. Ibid., 58.

154. "Shame's Limit: Olga Nethersole Flaunts the Crimson in All Its Vile Effrontery," *New York Evening Journal*, February 6, 1900, Olga Nethersole, v. 161, p. 107, RLC, BRTC.

155. Olga Nethersole, v. 161.1, p. 103, RLC, BRTC.

156. "Shame's Limit," 107; Alan Dale, "Disgraceful Performance That Should Not Be Tolerated, Attended Largely by Women in Loud Costumes, Who Rode in Hired Carriages," *New York Journal*, February 6, 1900, Olga Nethersole, v. 161, p. 112, RLC, BRTC; "Sapho-Crazed Women Throng to See the Nethersole Play," *New York World*, February 18, 1900, Olga Nethersole, v. 161, p. 123, RLC, BRTC.

157. Joy Harriman Reilly, "A Forgotten 'Fallen Woman': Olga Nethersole's *Sapho*," in *When They Weren't Doing Shakespeare: Essays on Nineteenth-Century British and American Theatre*, ed. Judith L. Fisher and Stephen Watt (Athens and London: The University of Georgia Press, 1989), 117–19; John H. Houchin, *Censorship of the American Theatre in the Twentieth Century* (Cambridge: Cambridge University Press, 2003), 40–71.

158. Peiss, *Cheap Amusements*, 53–55; " 'Charity Girls' and City Pleasures: His-

torical Notes on Working-Class Sexuality, 1880-1920," in *Passion and Power: Sexuality in History*, ed. Kathy Peiss and Christina Simmons (Philadelphia: Temple University Press, 1989), 57–69.

159. Photo of Olga Nethersole (gift of Mrs. Rhoda L. Maurice), Box 2, 19th Century Actress Photograph Collection, NMAH.

160. Caroll Smith-Rosenberg, *Disorderly Conduct: Visions of Gender in Victorian America* (New York: A. A. Knopf, 1985), 52, 74. As Kim Marra has recently shown, same-sex desiring actresses like Maude Adams aroused more than admiration in their fans. Through collaborations with the manager Charles Frohman, Adams brought "a subtext of sexual inversion and same-sex desire elaborately into play" in her breeches roles that appealed to this "emerging queer audience." Marra, *Strange Duets*, 103.

161. Eleanor Ames, "The Dressing of the Modern Drama," *Dress & Vanity Fair* (November 1913): 29.

162. Diana Taylor, *The Archive and the Repertoire: Performing Cultural Memory in the Americas* (Durham and London: Duke University Press, 2003), xviii; Wilson, *Adorned in Dreams*, 245.

163. Dolan, "Performance, Utopia, and the 'Performative Utopian,' " 460. On a similar point, see also Mary Louise Roberts, "Samson and Delilah Revisited: The Politics of Women's Fashion in 1920s France," *American Historical Review* 98.3 (June 1993): 684.

Chapter 5

1. "With the Women," *Variety*, December 12, 1914, 8.

2. Susan A. Glenn, *Female Spectacle: The Theatrical Roots of Modern Feminism* (Cambridge, Mass.: Harvard University Press, 2000), 162–63.

3. Specialty houses such as Ehrich Brothers had previously experimented with the fashion show. William R. Leach, *Land of Desire: Merchants, Power, and the Rise of a New American Culture* (New York: Pantheon Books, 1993), 101; "Fashion Show Opening," *New York Times* (hereafter *NYT*), September 1, 1903, 3; "Showing Gowns on Living Models," *Merchants Record and Show Window* (hereafter *MRSW*) (November 1909): 39; "Living Models," *MRSW* (May 1908): 45.

4. Wendy Gamber, *The Female Economy: The Millinery and Dressmaking Trades; 1860–1930* (Urbana: University of Illinois Press, 1997); Leach, *Land of Desire*, 64–65.

5. Frances Lothair, "Gallery Gods and Goddesses," *Green Book Album* (August 1909): 415.

6. See, for example, "Fashion Openings in New York Stores," *Dry Goods Economist* (hereafter *DGE*), April 12, 1913, 61; "Crowded Every Day: Even Standing Room at a Premium During Gimbel's Promenade," *DGE*, March 31, 1917, 7; "At the New York Spring Openings," *Dry Goods* (hereafter *DG*) (April 1914): 69.

7. Kristin Hoganson, "The Fashionable World: Imagined Communities of Dress," in *After the Imperial Turn: Thinking with and Through the Nation*, ed. Antoinette M. Burton (Durham, N.C.: Duke University Press, 2003), 260–78.

8. Many stores nevertheless maintained class distinctions within the supposedly

democratic space of the department store by arranging special closed viewings for society women. Leach, *Land of Desire*, 101–3.

9. Caroline Evans, "The Enchanted Spectacle," *Fashion Theory* 5.3 (2001): 272.

10. Ibid., 273.

11. For work on the fashion show and the revue showgirl, see Leach, *Land of Desire*, 101–11; Joel H. Kaplan and Sheila Stowell, *Theatre and Fashion: Oscar Wilde to the Suffragettes* (Cambridge: Cambridge University Press, 1994), 115–51; Linda Mizejewski, *Ziegfeld Girl: Image and Icon in American Culture* (Durham, N.C.: Duke University Press, 1999), 89–108; Glenn, *Female Spectacle*, 155–87; Evans, "The Enchanted Spectacle," 271–310; Nancy J. Troy, *Couture Culture: A Study in Modern Art and Fashion* (Cambridge, Mass., and London: MIT Press, 2003).

12. Leach, *Land of Desire*, 102–3.

13. "What Next?" *New York Dramatic Mirror* (hereafter *NYDM*), August 15, 1896, 12. The following year, the *Dramatic Mirror* reported that a London department store had gone through with the scheme. *NYDM*, January 4, 1897, 12.

14. "Department Store Shows," *Variety*, January 4, 1905, 3.

15. "Shoppers Like Cabaret," *Variety*, November 1, 1912, 6.

16. Lewis A. Erenberg, *Steppin' Out: New York Nightlife and the Transformation of American Culture* (Chicago and London: University of Chicago Press, 1981), 122. At the height of the dance craze, department stores also held special dancing exhibitions and "tango teas." See C. E. Hutchings, "Drawing Trade with the 'Tango,'" *DG* (June 1914): 29; "Department Store Tango Now Going on at Gimbel's," *Variety*, March 27, 1914, 6.

17. Leach, *Land of Desire*, 103.

18. Gimbel's held its first "Promenade des Toilettes" in 1910. See Leach, *Land of Desire*, 102; "Biggest Thing in Fashion Displays," *DGE*, April 1, 1911, 49; F. F. Purdy, "Notes from New York," *MRSW* (November 1911): 43, 49.

19. Troy, *Couture Culture*, 223.

20. Leach, *Land of Desire*, 103; "Used Living Models," *DGE*, April 29, 1911, 35; "Living Models," *MRSW* (April 1912): 28–29.

21. "Held 'Style Parade,'" *DGE*, April 29, 1911, 35. Bonwit, Teller and Co. in Cincinnati had first used living models in show windows in the early 1890s. See Purdy, "Notes from New York," 42–43.

22. "Use of Living Models," *DGE*, August 19, 1911, 41, 45; Sarah Berry, *Screen Style: Fashion and Femininity in 1930s Hollywood* (Minneapolis and London: University of Minnesota Press, 2000), 55.

23. Leach, *Land of Desire*, 103. See also "Fashion Show in Theatre," *DGE*, April 12, 1913, 15; John E. Mayhew, "Talking Shop: 'Style Lectures,'" *DG* (April 1911): 32; "Used Living Models," *DGE*, October 5, 1912, 113.

24. "Showing Gowns on Living Models," 39.

25. Evans, "The Enchanted Spectacle," 285.

26. Rush, "Paris Fashions," *Variety*, March 7, 1913, n.p.; "Photographing Fashions," *Variety*, May 16, 1913, 13. The company also filmed popular stage actresses in elegant stage clothes. "Stage Stars Photographed in Kinemacolour Pictures," *Variety*, October 25, 1913, 11; "Lillian Russell" (review), *Variety*, March 7, 1913, n.p.; Evans, "The Enchanted Spectacle," 285. For more on "fashion films," and fashion shows *in* films, see

Elizabeth Leese, *Costume Design in the Movies* (Bembridge, Isle of Wight: BCW Pub. Ltd., 1976), 9; Barbara Naomi Cohen-Stratyner, "Fashion Fillers in Silent Film Periodicals," in *Performing Arts Resources: Performances in Periodicals*, ed. Barbara Naomi Cohen-Stratyner (New York: Theatre Library Association, 1989), 14: 127–42; Charlotte Herzog, " 'Powder Puff' Promotion: The Fashion Show-in-the-Film," in *Fabrications: Costume and the Female Body*, ed. Jane Gaines and Charlotte Herzog (New York and London: Routledge, 1990), 134–59; Sumiko Higashi, *Cecil B. DeMille and American Culture: The Silent Era* (Berkeley: University of California Press, 1994), 87–100; Berry, *Screen Style*, 47–93.

27. "Paquin of Paris Coming to New York" (ad), *Theatre Magazine* (March 1914): n.p. For more on Paquin's tour of the United States, see Troy, *Couture Culture*, 248–51.

28. William G. Colgate, " 'Pretty' Pictures in Copy Becoming Passé," *Printers' Ink* (hereafter *PI*), September 15, 1910, 62, 64; Stephen Fox, *The Mirror Makers: A History of American Advertising and Its Creator* (New York: William Morrow, 1984), 67–69.

29. George H. Whitney, "The Personalities of Advertising Models," *PI*, December 15, 1910, 11–13.

30. Dave E. Bloch, "Stage Models to Make Illustrations Life-Like," *PI* (January 1914): 17

31. Ibid.; Whitney, "The Personalities of Advertising Models," 12. John Powers, the founder of the famous Powers Modeling Agency, began his career as an actor in New York in the 1910s. After struggling for several years, he eventually decided to leave acting and start his own modeling agency, which he claims was the first of its kind. See John Robert Powers, *The Powers Girls* (New York: E. P. Dutton Co., 1941), 19–21.

32. Showing Gowns on Living Models," *MRSW* (November 1909): 39; "Used Living Models," 113.

33. "Use of Living Models: Should Be Done Right, If at All—How to Obtain Models," *DGE*, August 19, 1911, 45. On the early twentieth-century modeling industry, see Evans, "The Enchanted Spectacle."

34. Erenberg, *Steppin' Out*, 210–12; Albert F. McLean Jr., *American Vaudeville as Ritual* (Lexington: University of Kentucky Press, 1965), 7.

35. Quoted in Mizejewski, *Ziegfeld Girl*, 93; "Ziegfeld Follies," *NYDM*, October 23, 1912, 6. On the *Ziegfeld Follies*, see also Marjorie Farnsworth, *Ziegfeld Follies* (New York: G. P. Putnam's Sons, 1956); Charles Higham, *Ziegfeld* (Chicago: Regnery, 1972); Richard Ziegfeld and Paulette Ziegfeld, *The Ziegfeld Touch: The Life and Times of Flo Ziegfeld* (New York: H. N. Abrams, 1993); Randolph Carter, *Ziegfeld: The Time of His Life* (London: Bernard, 1998); Eve Golden, *Anna Held and the Birth of Flo Ziegfeld's Broadway* (Lexington: University Press of Kentucky, 2000).

36. "Ragtime and Clothes," September 5, 1912, MWEX +n.c. 21,053, Ned Wayburn Scrapbooks, Billy Rose Theatre Collection (hereafter BRTC).

37. Glenn, *Female Spectacle*, 184–87; Plain Mary (Vesta Powell), "All for the Ladies, About Women—Mostly," *Variety*, January 16, 1914, 13; Mizejewski, *Ziegfeld Girl*, 91; Leach, *Land of Desire*, 145.

38. Mizejewski, *Ziegfeld Girl*, 91; Leach, *Land of Desire*, 145. On Joseph Urban, see Christopher Innes, "Theatrical Fashions," in *Designing Modern America: Broadway to Main Street* (New Haven, Conn.: Yale University Press, 2005), 38–57; Arnold Aronson,

Architect of Dreams: The Theatrical Vision of Joseph Urban (New York: Miriam and Ira D. Wallach Art Gallery, Columbia University, 2000).

39. There has been considerable work on the incorporation of the fashion show and salon mannequins into revues like the *Ziegfeld Follies.* See Mizejewski, *Ziegfeld Girl;* Glenn, *Female Spectacle;* Evans, "The Enchanted Spectacle"; John E. Hirsch, "The American Revue Costume," in *Musical Theatre in America: Papers and Proceedings of the Conference on the Musical Theatre in America,* ed. Glenn Loney (Westport, Conn.: Greenwood Press, 1984), 155-77; Hirsch, "Glorifying the American Showgirl: A History of Revue Costume in the United States" (Ph.D. diss., New York University, 1988); Rosaline Biason Stone, "The Ziegfeld Follies: A Study of Theatrical Opulence from 1907 to 1931" (Ph.D. diss., University of Denver, 1985), esp. 145-277; Geraldine Mascio, "The Ziegfeld Follies" (Ph.D. diss., University of Wisconsin, 1981).

40. Throughout the 1890s and into the 1900s, "chorus girl" and "showgirl" were often used interchangeably, with "chorus girl" as a kind of catch phrase for *all* non-featured female performers. See George Jean Nation, "A Garland of Girls," *The Theatre, the Drama, the Girls* (New York: Alfred A. Knopf, 1921), 308; Mizejewski, *Ziegfeld Girl,* 93.

41. Mizejewski, *Ziegfeld Girl,* 92; "Pretty Girls and Dazzling Gowns Make 'Little Duchess' Brilliant," *New York World,* October 16, 1901, Anna Held, v. 264, p. 115, Robinson Locke Collection (hereafter RLC), BRTC; Liane Carrera (and Anna Held?), *Anna Held and Flo Ziegfeld,* trans. Guy Daniels (1954; Hicksville, N.Y.: Exposition Press, 1979), 99–101; "Fashions on the Stage," *Theatre Magazine* (February 1905): v.

42. Mizejewski, *Ziegfeld Girl,* 90.

43. Glenn, *Female Spectacle,* 162–63; Mizejewski, *Ziegfeld Girl,* 100. On other responses to the New Woman, see Martha Banta, *Imaging American Women: Ideas and Ideals in Cultural History* (New York: Columbia University Press, 1987); Carolyn L. Kitch, *The Girl on the Magazine Cover: The Origins of Visual Stereotypes in American Mass Media* (Chapel Hill and London: University of North Carolina Press, 2001); Martha Patterson, " 'Survival of the Best Fitted': Selling the American New Woman as Gibson Girl, 1895–1910," *American Theatre Quarterly* 9.2 (1995): 73–85.

44. Glenn, *Female Spectacle,* 160. On scopophilia and the male gaze, see Laura Mulvey's seminal article "Visual Pleasure and Narrative Cinema," *Screen* 16.3 (1975): 6–18.

45. In this respect, I disagree with John Hirsch, who argues that costume was the raison d'être of the revue. See Hirsch, "The American Revue Costume."

46. "Show Girls at $50 Weekly: Better Paid Than Actresses," *Variety,* January 23, 1909, 13.

47. Glenn, *Female Spectacle,* 165. Programs and reviews from the period indicate that most revues included some sort of fashion show. Photo of showgirls, *Passing Show of 1914,* Musical/Revues—Credits (Shubert Shows), Shubert Archives (hereafter SA); "Ned Wayburn's New Production Staged in Twenty-Three Scenes at One-Time New Theatre," *New York Herald,* September 24, 1915, and " 'Town Topics' the Wayburn Review, Has Fun with Many Things," *New York Herald,* September 26, 1915, MWEZ + n.c. 21,063, Ned Wayburn Scrapbooks (1916), BRTC; "New 'Midnight Frolic' a Set of Superlatives in Chiffon and Tulle," *New York Evening Mail,* January 25, 1916, MWEZ + n.c. 21,064, Ned Wayburn Scrapbooks (1916), BRTC; program for *Over the Top,* SA.

48. George H. Douglas, *The Smart Magazines: 50 Years of Literary Revelry and High Jinks at "Vanity Fair," the "New Yorker," "Life," "Esquire," and the "Smart Set"* (Hamdon, Conn.: Archon Books, 1991); Glenn, *Female Spectacle*, 160.

49. Program for *The Passing Show of 1912*, Musicals/Revues—Credits (Shubert Shows), SA.

50. Sherwin, quoted in Glenn, *Female Spectacle*, 160.

51. Erenberg, *Steppin' Out*, 212.

52. Program for *The Passing Show of 1916*, Musicals/Revues—Credits (Shubert Shows), SA. Lucile had been previously represented in the *Passing Show of 1912* as Lady Fluff Bored'Un, months after she and her husband infamously escaped the *Titanic*. Robert Baral, *Revue* (New York and London: Fleet Press Association, 1962), 107. For Lucile's account of her experiences on the *Titanic*, see Lady Duff Gordon (Lucile), *Discretions and Indiscretions* (New York: Frederick A. Stokes Co., 1932), 162–204.

53. "Scene IV, Dressmaking Scene," *The Passing Show of 1916* (Shubert Scripts), SA.

54. "Made in the U.S.A (622)," *Lyrics from all revues and Winter Garden Shows*, vol. 1, SA; *American Silk Journal* (February 1916): 45.

55. Advertising Ephemera Collection, Box 12, Drama, John W. Hartman Center for Sales, Advertising and Marketing History, Duke University Rare Book, Manuscript, and Special Collections Library (hereafter Hartman Center, Duke).

56. Burns Mantle, "*Ziegfeld Follies of 1917*," *Green Book Magazine* (September 1917): 388–92, 352.

57. Baral, *Revue*, 48; *Ziegfeld Follies of 1910*, Folder 4, Box 13, Robert Baral Papers, BRTC; Glenn, *Female Spectacle*, 165.

58. Baral, *Revue*, 49.

59. Hirsch, "The American Revue Costume," 155. See also Hirsch, "Glorifying the American Showgirl"; Mizejewski, *Ziegfeld Girl*, 89, 13.

60. Ziegfeld, Florenz Jr., Folder 46, Box 12, Robert Baral Papers, BRTC.

61. "Beauty, the Fashions and the *Follies*," *Ladies' Home Journal* (hereafter *LHJ*) (March 1924): 16–17, 153–54. Theater critics were not so easily blinded by Ziegfeld's tactics, however, and frequently acknowledged the designer's role in staging the *Follies*, although they did not always look favorably upon costume spectacle. Channing Pollock, *Green Book Magazine* (September 1913): 430–32, in *Selected Theatre Criticism*, ed. Anthony Slide (Metuchen, N.J. and London: Scarecrow Press, 1988), 347; Mantle, "*Ziegfeld Follies of 1917*," 352.

62. Duff Gordon, *Discretions and Indiscretions*, 38, 45. On Lucile's theatrical work and influence on fashion, see also Meredith Etherington-Smith and Jeremy Pilcher, *The 'It' Girls: Lucy, Lady Duff Gordon, the Couturière 'Lucile,' and Elinor Glyn, Romantic Novelist* (London: Hamish Hamilton, 1986), 6; Joel Kaplan and Sheila Stowell, *Theatre and Fashion: Oscar Wilde to the Suffragettes* (Cambridge: Cambridge University Press, 1994), 8–44; Joseph Roach, *It* (Ann Arbor: University of Michigan Press, 2007).

63. Duff Gordon, *Discretions and Indiscretions*, 69–70. Lucile was one of a number of independent London dressmakers who used the commercial theater as a promotional vehicle. Kaplan and Stowell, *Theatre and Fashion*, 8–14.

64. Duff Gordon, *Discretions and Indiscretions*, 69-70.

65. Ibid., 69, 71.

66. Ibid., 72, 74, 79.

67. Evans, "The Enchanted Spectacle," 273; Duff Gordon, *Discretions and Indiscretions*, 68.

68. Marie Corelli, quoted in Kaplan and Stowell, *Theatre and Fashion*, 120; Evans, "The Enchanted Spectacle," 277.

69. Kaplan and Stowell, *Theatre and Fashion*, 119; Evans, "The Enchanted Spectacle," 277.

70. Kaplan and Stowell, *Theatre and Fashion*, 119–20; Etherington-Smith and Pilcher, *The 'It' Girls*, 89–90; Evans, "The Enchanted Spectacle," 277; Roach, *It*, 87–88.

71. Duff Gordon, *Discretions and Indiscretions*, 78.

72. Evans, "The Enchanted Spectacle," 277; Troy, *Couture Culture*, 98–99, 101–2, 105, 116.

73. Duff Gordon, *Discretions and Indiscretions*, 149–50; "Puzzled by Gay Models," *NYT*, March 5, 1910, 3, 4. See also Randolph Carter, *The World of Flo Ziegfeld* (New York: Praeger, 1974), 55; "The Whistler of Dress: Lady Duff-Gordon Opens a Studio in New York to Make Dressmaking an Art," *DG* (April 1910): 98.

74. In 1915 alone, Lucile designed for *Chin Chin, Common Clay, The Only Girl, Hands Up, Watch Your Step, A Pair of Silk Stockings*, and *Town Topics*. *Town Topics* program, Ned Wayburn Scrapbooks (1915), MWEZ + n.x. 21,063, BRTC. In *Play Production in America* (1916), Arthur Krows acknowledges Lucile's influence on the look of Broadway productions in the 1910s, noting how she and her staff of designers at Lucile Ltd. designed "whole 'nest[s]' of plays season after season." Krows, *Play Production in America* (New York: Henry Holt & Co., 1916), 195.

75. *Variety*, June 15, 1917, 7; Baral, *Revue*, 60.

76. Burns Mantle referred to the "Episode of the Chiffon" as "The Ladies of Fashion." Mantle, "*The Ziegfeld Follies of 1917*," 352; Ziegfeld and Ziegfeld, *The Ziegfeld Touch*, 276–80.

77. *Variety* reported that "all" of the performers in the "Episode of the Chiffon" were from Lucile's salon. However, the cast list suggests that Dolores may have been the only Lucile mannequin in the number. See Baral, *Revue*, 60; Photos #2–3, Box 16544-78, *Ziegfeld Follies of 1917* (41202), White Collection, BRTC.

78. Between 1917 and 1921, when she finally left the *Follies* to marry a millionaire, Dolores was Ziegfeld's star showgirl. Her most memorable performance was her appearance as a white peacock in the *Midnight Frolic of 1919*. Dolores, Series 3, v. 368, pp. 191–205, RLC, BRTC. For more on Dolores and Lucile's other mannequins, see Dolores, Locke Series 3, v. 368, pp. 191–205, RLC, BRTC; Box 13 (Dolores), Baral Papers, BRTC; Box 9 (Dinarzarde [Petra Clive]), Baral Papers, BRTC; Farnsworth, *Ziegfeld Follies*, 96–103.

79. Duff Gordon, *Discretions and Indiscretions*, 244. Burns Mantle called her a "fleshly rack." Mantle, "*Follies of 1917*," in *Selected Vaudeville Criticism*, ed. Anthony Slide (Metuchen, N.J. and London: Scarecrow Press, 1988), 353.

80. Mizejewski, *Ziegfeld Girl*, 91, 95. Lucile's mannequins Phyliss, Mauricette, Dinarzarde, and Dolores appeared in the Ziegfeld/Dillingham production *Miss 1917* wearing gowns designed by Lucile. See Ziegfeld and Ziegfeld, *The Ziegfeld Touch*, 222.

The list of mannequins who "graduated to the *Follies*" also includes Gamela, Clarie, Anangaraga, Sovia-Moria, Boneta, Iseult, Majanah, Corisand, Delys, and Hildred. See Carter, *The World of Flo Ziegfeld*, 60.

81. "Handling Humanity in the Mass," *Theatre Magazine* (May 1913): 147. For more on Wayburn's methods, see George Vaux Bacon, "Chorus Girls in the Making," *Green Book Magazine* (October 1913): 571–79; Barbara Naomi Cohen-Stratyner, "The Dance Direction of Ned Wayburn: Selected Topics in Musical Staging, 1901–1923" (Ph.D. diss., New York University, 1980); Barbara Naomi Cohen-Stratyner, *Ned Wayburn and the Dance Routine: From Vaudeville to the Ziegfeld Follies*, Studies in Dance History 13 (Madison: University of Wisconsin Press, 1996); Glenn, *Female Spectacle*, 155–87; and Mizejewski, *Ziegfeld Girl*, 89–108. See also Joel Dinerstein, *Swinging the Machine: Modernity, Technology and African American Culture Between the World Wars* (Amherst: University of Massachusetts Press, 2003).

82. Baral, *Revue*, 61.

83. Ibid.; Glenn, *Female Spectacle*, 182; Mizejewski, *Ziegfeld Girl*, 8–9, 97–98, 169–70; Charles Higham, *Ziegfeld*, 108; Ziegfeld and Ziegfeld, *The Ziegfeld Touch*, 64.

84. Ziegfeld's biographers Marjorie Farnsworth and Randolph Carter claim that Ziegfeld met Lucile in 1915 when he visited her salon on 57th Street with his new wife, Billie Burke. Neither gives a date for this meeting, but they agree that it was here that Ziegfeld first witnessed one of Lucile's fashion parades and became captivated with Dolores. Carter, *The World of Flo Ziegfeld*, 5; Farnsworth, *Ziegfeld Follies*, 96.

85. Baral, *Revue*, 61; *Follies of 1917*, B File, BRTC.

86. See, for example, *Harper's Bazar* (hereafter *HB*) and the *American Silk Journal* (1915–18); Duff Gordon, *Discretions and Indiscretions*, 69, 71.

87. On the notion of the "citizen consumer," see Charles F. McGovern, *Sold American: Consumption and Citizenship, 1890–1945* (Chapel Hill: University of North Carolina Press, 2006); Lizabeth Cohen, *A Consumer's Republic: The Politics of Mass Consumption in Postwar America* (New York: Vintage Books, 2003).

88. Elinor Glyn, *Romantic Adventures: Being the Autobiography of Elinor Glyn* (New York: E. P. Dutton and Co., Inc., 1937), 240; Duff Gordon, *Discretions and Indiscretions*, 266. For more on *Fleurette's Dream*, see Lady Duff Gordon (Lucile), "Billie Burke Charms with Daintiness," *HB* (December 1917): 66–67; Lady Duff Gordon, "Chinese Variations Hypnotize the Clothes for Spring," *HB* (February 1918): 56–57; Lady Duff Gordon, "Other Times Other Tea-Gowns," *HB* (January 1918): 42, 92.

89. Duff Gordon, *Discretions and Indiscretions*, 267.

90. Ibid., 268, 273. Lucile claimed that she supervised all design aspects, including set and lighting.

91. Ibid., 274; "Vaudeville Gaining New Acts and Aiding War Charities," *Variety*, November 23, 1917, 1.

92. "With the Women, by 'the Skirt,' " *Variety*, December 7, 1917, 10.

93. "Lady Duff Holds Over," *Variety*, December 7, 1917, 4; Duff Gordon, *Discretions and Indiscretions*, 279.

94. "Lady Duff-Gordon to Make Debut in Fashion Sketch," *Boston Herald*, December 16, 1917, 7.

95. M. Alison Kibler, *Rank Ladies: Gender and Cultural Hierarchy in American Vaudeville* (Chapel Hill: University of North Carolina Press, 1999), 79–109. See also

Leigh Woods, "Two-a-Day Redemptions and Truncated Camilles: The Vaudeville Repertoire of Sarah Bernhardt," *New Theatre Quarterly* 10 (February 1994): 11–21.

96. Glyn, *Romantic Adventures*, 172; Etherington-Smith and Pilcher, *The 'It' Girls*, 197–99.

97. Wood v. Lucy, Lady Duff-Gordon, 222 N.Y. 88, 118 N.E. 214 (1917), http://www.libfind.unl.edu/workslaw/lady_duff.html, accessed January 3, 2009. Howard Greer, *Designing Male: A Nebraska Farm Boy's Adventures in Hollywood and with the International Set* (New York: G. P. Putnam's Sons, 1951), 53. Meredith Etherington-Smith and Jeremy Pilcher suggest that Lucile's spending habits and her refusal to listen to her financial advisors, including Cosmo, also contributed to her financial difficulties. *The 'It' Girls*, 196-98. For more on Lucile's arrangement with Wood, see Marlis Schweitzer, "The Mad Search for Beauty: Actresses' Testimonials and the 'Democratization of Beauty,' " *Journal of the Gilded Age and Progressive Era* 4.3 (July 2005): 255–92.

98. Duff Gordon, *Discretions and Indiscretions*, 274; "Vaudeville Gaining New Acts and Aiding War Charities," 1.

99. Duff Gordon, *Discretions and Indiscretions*, 274; "Lady Duff-Gordon Playing for Charity," *Cincinnati Commercial Tribune*, April 21, 1918, 5.

100. They may even have appeared in both shows simultaneously. *Miss 1917* ran from November 1917 to early January 1918. Ziegfeld and Ziegfeld, *The Ziegfeld Touch*, 222. As with all her mannequins, the *Fleurette* performers had fabulous names—Dolores, Dinazarde, Phyllis, Mauricette, Hildred, Clair, De Lys, Jill Wood, Virginia, Ruthair, Doris, Anangaraga, Sonia, Mona, Iseult, Majanah, Rosalys, Morgan de Fay—that connoted a kind of Orientalist or Romantic exoticism that was entirely consistent with Lucile's designs. Ziegfeld and Ziegfeld, *The Ziegfeld Touch*, 222; "New Acts: Lady Duff Gordon," *New York Clipper*, December 5, 1917, 9; "Doraldina New Feature at Palace," *NYDM*, December 15, 1917, 27; "Fashion Display at Palace," *NYT*, December 2, 1917, XX6.

101. "Fashion Display at Palace," *NYT*, December 4, 1917, 11; "Show Reviews: Palace," *Variety*, December 14, 1917, 20.

102. "Show Reviews: Palace," *New York Clipper*, December 15, 1917, 27.

103. "Show Reviews: Palace," *Variety*, December 14, 1917, 20.

104. "Doraldina New Feature at Palace," *NYDM*, December 15, 1917, 27.

105. *Variety*, December 1917–May 1918. On audience responses to *Fleurette's Dream*, see Len Libbey, "Boston," *Variety*, December 21, 1917, 34; "New Acts: Lady Duff Gordon," *New York Clipper*, December 5, 1917, 9; "Fashion Revue Is Very Novel Act," *Mail and Empire*, March 6, 1918, 10; Duff Gordon, *Discretions and Indiscretions*, 276.

106. "Fashion Plate Novelty Act Something New for Palace," *Variety*, April 9, 1915, 5; "May Tully Agenting," *Variety*, January 23, 1914, 5; "Two Vaudeville Headlines Furnish Peculiar Contrast," *Variety*, April 16, 1915, 6; Wynn, "New Acts This Week," *Variety*, April 16, 1915, 14.

107. Sime Silverman, "New Acts This Week: Fall Fashion Show," *Variety*, October 15, 1915, 15; " 'Fashion Show' Closing," *Variety*, March 3, 1916, 12.

108. *NYDM*, April 15, 1915, Locke Envelope # 2392 (Tully, May Mary) RLC, BRTC; "Dame Fashion Leads Orpheum Parade: Unique Vaudeville Offering Creates a Stir When Seen Here. Girls and Gowns Lovely. And There Are Many Other Good Features

on the Bill," *Brooklyn Daily Eagle*, April 20, 1915, Locke Envelope # 2392 (Tully, May Mary), RLC, BRTC.

109. "With the Women, by Miss Ruby," *Variety*, July 30, 1915, 7. It is worth noting that the gown Dolores wore as the "Empress of Fashion" in the *Ziegfeld Follies of 1917* was also named "the Discourager of Hesitancy." "Two Vaudeville Headlines," *Variety*, 6; Silverman, "New Acts This Week," 14.

110. "Ladies' Tailors Bar Styles from Paris: Their Association Adopts a Declaration of Independence and the American Gown Is Coming," *NYT*, September 7, 1910, 6.

111. "The Editor's Personal Page: Are the Only Clever Women in the World in Paris?" *LHJ* (January 1910): 3; "Can We Make Pretty Hats in America?" (ad for *LHJ*), *HB* (February 1910): 117; "What We Mean by 'American Fashions,'" *LHJ* (October 1910): 3; "Our Views Endorsed," *DGE*, March 8, 1913, 31; "The Origin of Fashion," *DGE*, April 5, 1913, 103. For more on the *Journal*'s campaign, see Marlis Schweitzer, "American Fashions for American Women: The Rise and Fall of Fashion Nationalism," in *Producing Fashion: Commerce, Culture, and Consumers*, ed. Regina Blaszczyk (Philadelphia: University of Pennsylvania Press, 2007), 130–49.

112. Caroline Seebohm, *The Man Who Was Vogue* (New York: Viking Press, 1982), 102.

113. "Vogue Plays a New Role: Fashion, Becoming Stagestruck, Dramatizes Vogue Fashions, Cover and All, for an Extended Road Tour," *Vogue*, June 1, 1915, 33.

114. Silverman, "New Acts This Week," 14.

115. "Flood of Fashion Shows Is Swamping New York Theatres," *Variety*, October 1, 1915, 6.

116. See "Flood of Fashion Shows Is Swamping New York Theatres," 6; Letter from J. J. Shubert to C. Pierre, Esq., February 11, 1916, Box 1360A (Irene Castle), January 1914–November 1922, SA.

117. "The Fashion Show" (ad for Mme. Rosenberg), *Variety*, November 26, 1915, 40; "Catherine Crawford and Her Fashion Girls" (caption), *Variety*, January 21, 1916, 6; "Small Time Fashion Show," *Variety*, October 29, 1915, 11; " 'Nothing to Wear' a Fashion Show," *Variety*, December 24, 1915, 1.

118. See "Cabarets," *Variety*, May 12, 1916, 8. Mme. Kahn went on to design gowns for the *Passing Show of 1916*. Program for *Passing Show of 1916*, Credits, Musicals/Revues, SA.

119. Silverman, "New Acts This Week," 14.

120. "The Woman in Vaudeville, by 'the Skirt,' " *Variety*, October 22, 1915, 6; "Why Study to Be an Emotional Actress When You Can So Easily Be an Emotionless Mannikin [*sic*]?" *Vanity Fair* (December 1915): 70. Following her scandalous involvement in the love triangle with Harry Thaw and Stanford White, Nesbit remade herself into a ballroom dancer. See Julie Malnig, *Dancing Till Dawn: A Century of Exhibition Ballroom Dance* (New York and London: New York University Press, 1992), 32, 59–60.

121. *New York Times*, December 2, 1917, XX6. *Variety*, December 7, 1917, 20.

122. Greer, *Designing Male*, 3-4.

123. Lady Duff Gordon (Lucile), "The Last Word in Fashions," *HB* (October 1914): 34–35; (November 1914): 18–19; (January 1915): 22–23. Lucile's endorsements included Heatherbloom Taffeta Petticoats and the Chalmers Motor Company. "A Word

from Lucile" (ad), *HB* (March 1915): 101; " 'Comfortable and in Excellent Taste'—Says Lady Duff Gordon" (ad), *Vogue* (October 1916): 169.

124. On Paris couturiers and the mass market, see Troy, *Couture Culture*, 6, 192–265.

125. Dana Frank, *Buy American: The Untold Story of Economic Nationalism* (Boston: Beacon Press, 1999).

126. Lady Duff Gordon, "The Last Word in Fashions," *HB* (October 1914): 34–35.

127. Lady Duff Gordon, "The Last Word in Fashions," *HB* (November 1914): 18–19. See also Duff Gordon, "The Last Word in Fashions," *HB* (January 1915): 22–23; Duff Gordon, "Chinese Variations Hypnotize the Clothes for Spring," *HB* (February 1918): 56–57; Duff Gordon, "Billie Burke Charms with Daintiness," 66–67.

128. Duff Gordon, "Billie Burke Charms with Daintiness," 66–67. *Harper's Bazar* made the most of its relationship with Paris in this period, going so far as to send an envoy to Paris with news that *Vogue* had decided to abandon Paris couture altogether. Angered by this (false) revelation, Paquin, Callot, and others threatened to close their doors to *Vogue* and give exclusive coverage rights to *Harper's Bazar*. *Vogue* had little recourse but to promise the Paris designers their own Fashion Fête in New York the following year. Edna Woolman Chase and Ilka Chase, *Always in Vogue Always in Vogue* (New York: Doubleday & Company, Inc., 1954), 125–26.

129. Lady Duff Gordon, "The Last Word in Fashion," *HB* (June 1915): 42–43.

130. "Silk Convention a Big Success," *American Silk Journal* (November 1915): 40; "A Portrait of Lady Duff-Gordon (Lucile), *American Silk Journal* (November 1915): n.p.; "The Last Word in Fashions," *HB* (March 1915): 18–19.

131. "Lady Duff Gordon's Model Collection for Spring, 1915," *DG* (January 1915): 9.

132. See, for example, the *American Silk Journal*, September and October 1915, June 1916.

133. For more on the "Made in America" movement, see "Shall We Label Our Goods 'Made in U.S. of A.'?" *PI*, September 24, 1914, 17–21; " 'Made in U.S.A.' Movement Gathers Strength," *PI*, November 5, 1914, 42; "Paterson's Exposition of 'Made in America' Products a Big Success," *DG* (November 1914): 26; " 'Made in U.S.A.' Tells the Story," *DGE*, November 21, 1914, 24. See also Frank, *Buy American*; Schweitzer, "American Fashions for American Women," 130–49.

134. "True Patriotism," *Theatre Magazine* (May 1917): 260a.

135. Quoted in Stephen Ponder, "Popular Propaganda: The Food Administration in World War I," *Journalism and Media Communications Quarterly* (autumn 1995): 541. See also Susan Voso Lab, " 'War' Drobe and World War I," in *Dress in American Culture*, ed. Patricia A. Cunningham and Susan Voso Lab (Bowling Green, Ohio: Bowling Green State University Popular Press, 1993), 200–219.

136. Dudley Harmon, "Keeping Up with the Times," *LHJ* (June 1917): 30; "Your Clothes This Winter/Solving the Problem with Ease and Thrift," *LHJ* (November 1918): 125.

137. *Philadelphia Inquirer*, May 7, 1918, 9; Joanne Karetsky, *The Mustering of Support for World War I by the "Ladies Home Journal"* (New York: Edward Mellon Press, 1997).

138. "Just What Is Wartime Thrift?" *LHJ* (September 1918): 29.

139. "True Patriotism!" *Theatre Magazine* (June 1917): 322.

140. "Faibisy Points Out New Fashions," *Theatre Magazine* (July 1917): 44.

141. Karetsky, *The Mustering of Support for World War I*, 67; Juliann Sivulka, *Soap, Sex, and Cigarettes: A Cultural History of American Advertising* (Belmont, Calif.: Wadsworth Publishing Co., 1998), 134.

142. "Nemo Welfare Offering," *Philadelphia Inquirer*, May 5, 1918, 17.

143. Ad in *St. Louis Post-Dispatch*, March 11, 1918, 11.

144. Lady Duff Gordon, "Other Times Other Tea-Gowns," *HB* (January 1918): 42, 92.

145. "Show Reviews: Palace," *New York Clipper*, December 5, 1917, 7.

146. "New Acts This Week: Lady Duff Gordon," *Variety*, December 7, 1917, 20.

147. "Lady Duff-Gordon to Make Debut in Fashion Sketch," 24; Duff Gordon, "Other Times Other Tea-Gowns," 42, 92; Duff Gordon, "Chinese Variations Hypnotize the Clothes for Spring," 56–57.

148. "New Acts This Week: Lady Duff Gordon," 20.

149. "Show Reviews: Palace," *Variety*, December 14, 1917, 20.

150. "New Acts This Week: Lady Duff Gordon," 20.

151. "Models Parade at B. F. Keith's," *Boston Herald and Journal*, December 18, 1917, 9.

152. *Variety*, May 10, 1918, 30.

153. "Fashion Display at Palace," *NYT*, December 4, 1917, 11.

154. "Plays, Pictures and Music," *Toronto World*, March 2, 1918, 5.

155. "New Acts: Lady Duff Gordon," *New York Clipper*, December 5, 1917, 9; Libbey, "Boston," 34; "Show Reviews: Palace," *Variety*, December 14, 1917, 20.

156. "Reviews," *Variety*, March 13, 1918, 29.

157. "Fashion Display at Palace," *NYT*, December 2, 1917, 6.

158. "Fashion Display at Palace," XX6; "Reviews," *Variety*, March 15, 1918, 29.

159. "Lady Duff-Gordon in Fashion Revue," *Toronto World*, March 6, 1918, 7.

160. Duff Gordon, "Chinese Variations Hypnotize the Clothes for Spring," 56–57. For more on the Orientalist designs of the Paris couturier Paul Poiret, see Troy, *Couture Culture*.

161. "Show Reviews: Palace," *Variety*, December 14, 1917, 20; "Models Parade at B. F. Keith's," *Boston Herald and Journal*, December 18, 1917, 9.

162. Duff Gordon, *Discretions and Indiscretions*, 278–79.

163. Ibid., 275, 279.

164. Karetsky, *The Mustering of Support for WWI*, 77.

165. George H. Nash, *The Life of Herbert Hoover: Master Emergencies, 1917–1918* (New York: W. W. Norton and Co., 1996), 154–55. On Hoover's use of other promotional tactics, see Ponder, "Popular Propaganda," 539–50. See also Lab, " 'War' Drobe and World War I," 200–219.

166. Virginia Tatnall Peacock, "Society," *Washington Evening Star*, January 13, 1918, 9.

167. Cartoons in the *Chicago Sunday Tribune*, March 3, 1918, iv; *St. Louis Globe-Democrat*, April 1, 1918, 10.

168. *Washington Evening Star*, January 7, 1918, 6.

169. Duff Gordon, *Discretions and Indiscretions,* 275.

170. "Spring and Summer Edition of Vaudeville's Loveliest Feature" (ad), *NYT,* May 26, 1918, X9.

Epilogue

1. Hiram Kelly Moderwell, *The Theatre of Today* (New York, 1914), 222, cited in Eelin Stewart Harrison, "The Rise of the Costume Designer: A Critical History of Costume on the New York Stage from 1934 to 1950" (Ph.D. diss., Louisiana State University, 1968), 20.

2. Clayton Hamilton, quoted in Janet Loring, "Costuming on the New York Stage from 1895 to 1915 with Particular Emphasis on Charles Frohman's Companies" (Ph.D. diss., State University of Iowa, 1961), 296.

3. "America's First Exhibition of the New Stagecraft," *Theatre Magazine* (January 1915): 28; "Art Notes: Exhibition of the Art of the Theatre," *New York Times,* November 9, 1914, 8.

4. Loring, "Costuming on the New York Stage," 303–5. For a complete analysis of Jones, Simonson, and Bernstein, see Donald Charles Stowell Jr., "The New Costuming in America: The Ideas and Practices of Robert Edmond Jones, Norman Bel Geddes, Lee Simonson and Aline Bernstein, 1915–1935" (Ph.D. diss., University of Texas at Austin, 1972).

5. Hamilton, quoted in Loring, "Costuming on the New York Stage," 305.

6. Quoted in Stowell, "The New Costuming in America," 44.

7. Jones, quoted in Jo Mielziner, *The Theatre of Robert Edmond Jones,* ed. Ralph Pendleton (Middleton, Conn.: Wesleyan University Press, 1958), 23.

8. Loring, "Costuming on the New York Stage," 306.

9. Lady Duff Gordon (Lucile), *Discretions and Indiscretions* (New York: Frederick A. Stokes Co., 1932), 290–91; Meredith Etherington-Smith and Jeremy Pilcher, *The 'It' Girls: Lucy, Lady Duff Gordon, the Couturière 'Lucile,' and Elinor Glyn, Romantic Novelist* (London: Hamish Hamilton, 1986), 200–202.

10. Robert Baral, *Revue* (New York and London: Fleet Press Association, 1962), 74, 80–81, 128, 134.

11. Bobbi Owen, *Costume Design on Broadway: Designers and Their Credits, 1915–1985* (New York: Greenwood Press, 1987), xiv; Don Stowell Jr., "The Unionization of the Stage Designer—Male and Female," *Theatre Design and Technology* (October 1974): 6–9, 36.

12. Loring, "Costuming on the New York Stage," 307.

13. Sean Patrick Holmes, "Weavers of Dreams, Unite: Constructing an Occupational Identity in the Actor's Equity Association, 1913–1934" (Ph.D. diss., New York University, 1994), 55–56; Sean Holmes, "All the World's a Stage! The Actor's Strike of 1919," *Journal of American History* (March 2005): 1291–1317. See also Chris Sears, "The Rise of Actors' Unions and Organizations in the United States" (Master's thesis, University of Victoria, 1981); Kerry Segrave, *Actors Organize: A History of Union Formation Efforts in America, 1880–1919* (Jefferson, N.C., and London: McFarland and Co., Inc.,

2008); Benjamin McArthur, *Actors and American Culture: 1880–1920* (1984; Iowa City: University of Iowa Press, 2000), 213–36.

14. Quoted in Harding, *The Revolt of the Actors* (New York: William Morrow and Co., 1929), 18.

15. Ibid.

16. Ibid., 20.

17. Holmes, "Weavers of Dreams Unite," 87–88.

18. Holmes, "All the World's a Stage!" 1305–9.

19. Ibid., 1307.

20. Ibid., 1308.

21. Marguerite Courtney, *Laurette* (New York and Toronto: Rinehart and Company, Inc., 1955), 83; Blanche Yurka, *Bohemian Girl: Blanche Yurka's Theatrical Life* (Athens: Ohio University Press, 1970), 76.

22. Holmes, "Weavers of Dreams," 139; Holmes, "All the World's a Stage!" 1304. According to Nan Enstad, female laborers at the shirtwaist strike in 1909 wore cheap French-heeled slippers on the picket lines. Nan Enstad, *Ladies of Labor, Girls of Adventure* (New York: Columbia University Press, 2000), 1–2.

23. Holmes, "All the World's a Stage!" 1303–4; Susan A. Glenn, *Female Spectacle: The Theatrical Roots of Modern Feminism* (Cambridge, Mass.: Harvard University Press, 2000), 203–9.

24. Quoted in Harding, *The Revolt of the Actors*, 200. For a 1916 version of the "Standard Theatrical Contract" proposed by Equity, see Arthur Hornblow, *Training for the Stage* (Philadelphia and London: J. B. Lippincott Co., 1916), 185–93. See also Owen, *Costume Design on Broadway*, xi.

25. As the film historian Richard deCordova explains, prior to 1914, "[k]nowledge about the picture personality was restricted to the player's professional existence— either to his/her representation in films or to his/her previous work in film and theater." On the development of the Hollywood star system, see Richard deCordova, "The Emergence of the Star System in America," *Wide Angle* 6.4 (1985): 10–11; deCordova, *Picture Personalities: The Emergence of the Star System in America* (Champaign, Ill.: University of Illinois Press, 1990). On early cinema audiences, see Barbara Wilinsky, "Flirting with Kathlyn: Creating the Mass Audience," in *Hollywood Goes Shopping*, ed. David Desser and Garth S. Jowett (Minneapolis and London: University of Minnesota Press, 2000), 38; Robert Sklar, *Movie Made America: A Cultural History of American Movies* (London: Vintage Books, 1975); Kathy Peiss, *Cheap Amusements: Working Women and Leisure in Turn-of-the-Century New York* (Philadelphia: Temple University Press, 1986); Kathryn H. Fuller, *At the Picture Show: Small-Town Audiences and the Creation of Movie Fan Culture* (Washington: Smithsonian, 1997); Lauren Rabinovitz, *For the Love of Pleasure: Women, Movies, and Culture in Turn-of-the-Century Chicago* (New Brunswick, N.J., and London: Rutgers University Press, 1998); Enstad, *Ladies of Labor, Girls of Adventure*; Shelley Stamp, *Movie-Struck Girls: Women and Motion Picture Culture After the Nickelodeon* (Princeton, N.J.: Princeton University Press, 2000).

26. Fuller, *At the Picture Show*, esp. chaps. 7 and 8; Barbara Naomi Cohen-Stratyner, "Fashion Fillers in Silent Film Periodicals," in *Performing Arts Resources: Performances in Periodicals* 14 (New York: Theatre Library Association, 1989), 127–43; Stamp, *Movie-Struck Girls*, 10–40.

27. For more on film, fashion, and consumption in the 1920s and 1930s, see Charles Eckert, "The Carol Lombard in Macy's Window," in *Fabrications: Costume and the Female Body*, ed. Jane Gaines and Charlotte Herzog (New York: Routledge, 1990), 100–121; Jane Gaines and Charlotte Herzog, " 'Puffed Sleeves Before Tea-Time': Joan Crawford, Adrian and Women Audiences," *Wide Angle* 6.4 (1985): 24–33; Heather Addison, "Hollywood, Consumer Culture, and the Rise of 'Body Shaping,' " in *Hollywood Goes Shopping*, ed. David Desser and Garth S. Jowett (Minneapolis and London: University of Minnesota Press, 2000), 3–33; Sara Ross, "The Hollywood Flapper and the Culture of Media Consumption," in *Hollywood Goes Shopping*, 57–81; Cynthia Felando, "Hollywood in the 1920s: Youth Must Be Served," in *Hollywood Goes Shopping*, 82–107; Sarah Berry, *Screen Style: Fashion and Femininity in 1930s Hollywood* (Minneapolis and London: University of Minnesota Press, 2000); Rachel Moseley, ed., *Fashioning Film Stars: Dress, Culture and Identity* (London: British Film Institute, 2005).

28. For more on the Golden Age of Broadway musicals, see Bruce Kirle, *Unfinished Business: Broadway Musicals as Works-in-Process* (Carbondale: Southern Illinois University Press, 2005); Mark N. Grant, *The Rise and Fall of the Broadway Musical* (Vancouver: University of British Columbia Press, 2004); John Bush Jones, *Our Musicals, Ourselves: A Social History of the American Musical Theatre* (Vancouver: University of British Columbia Press, 2004); Stacy Wolf, *A Problem Like Maria: Gender and Sexuality in the American Musical* (Ann Arbor: University of Michigan Press, 2004); Andrea Most, *Making Americans: Jews and the Broadway Musical* (Cambridge, Mass., and London: Harvard University Press, 2004).

29. Most, *Making Americans*, 155–56; Wolf, *A Problem Like Maria*, 89–92.

30. Steven Adler, *On Broadway: Art and Commerce on the Great White Way* (Carbondale: Southern Illinois Press, 2004), 67–101; Maurya Wickstrom, "Commodities, Mimesis and *The Lion King*: Retail Theatre for the 1990s," *Theatre Journal* 51.3 (1999): 285–98; Maurya Wickstrom, *Performing Consumers: Global Capital and Its Theatrical Seductions* (New York: Routledge, 2006), 66–95; Elizabeth L. Wollman, "The Economic Development of the 'New' Times Square and Its Impact on the Broadway Musical," *American Music* 20.4 (winter 2002): 445–65; Vincent Landro, "Media Mania: The Demonizing of the Theatrical Syndicate," *Journal of American Drama and Theatre* 13 (spring 2001): 49–50.

31. Wollman, "The Economic Development of the 'New' Times Square," 451–53.

32. Wickstrom, "Commodities, Mimesis, and *The Lion King*"; Wickstrom, *Performing Consumers*, 66–95; Woolman, "The Economic Development of the 'New' Times Square," 449–51.

33. Stacy Wolf, "*Wicked* Divas, Musical Theater and Internet Fans," *camera obscura* 65.22.2 (2007): 38–71.

Index

Page numbers in italics indicate images.

Acknowledgments

I am addicted to acknowledgment pages. Before this project, I rarely glanced at these pages, preferring instead to go directly to the introduction, the beginning of the "important" part of the book. But as I struggled to work my way through a first draft, I found myself looking to the acknowledgment pages in my favorite books for any indication that the scholars I admired experienced similar pangs of self-doubt and anxiety, hoping to find proof that if they did it, I could do it too. Now years later, I realize that people, not pages, have given me the support, courage, and the confidence to get this far, and I am exceedingly grateful.

Robert Lockhart, my editor at the University of Pennsylvania Press, has been everything I could ever have hoped for in an editor—smart, engaged, and fully supportive throughout the process. Chris Hu and Ashley Nelson, acquisitions assistants, answered so many of my detailed questions, and my no-longer-anonymous readers Nan Enstad and Wendy Gamber made excellent suggestions for revision.

This book would not have been possible without the financial support of a number of institutions and funding bodies, including York University; the University of Pennsylvania; the Graduate Centre for the Study of Drama and the School of Graduate Studies, University of Toronto; the Ontario Graduate Scholarship program; the National Museum of American History, Behring Center, Smithsonian Institution; the American Society for Theatre Research; and the John W. Hartman Center for Sales, Advertising and Marketing History, Duke University Rare Book, Manuscript, and Special Collections Library. A Penn Humanities Forum Andrew W. Mellon Postdoctoral Fellowship in the Humanities and a special course release from the dean of the Faculty of Fine Arts at York University provided me with the time and support for research and writing. A Faculty of Fine Arts Minor/Research Creation Grant, a special start-up fund from Dean Phillip Silver of the Faculty of Fine Arts, York University, and a SSHRC Small Grant from the Social Sciences and Humanities Research Council provided support for acquiring and reproducing images.

I could not have done this work without the assistance of the archivists, librarians, and research staff at the Archives Center, National Museum of American History, Behring Center, Smithsonian Institution; the Library of Congress; the New York Public Library for the Performing Arts; the New York Public Library; the Museum of the City of New York; the Shubert Archives; the Hartman Center, Duke University; the Rare Books and Manuscripts Collection at the University of Pennsylvania; and the Philadelphia Museum of Art. I would especially like to thank the excellent archivists at the NMAH Archives Center, who made many helpful suggestions and kept me laughing (quietly, of course) every time I visited them. Thanks also to Maryann Chach at the Shubert Archives, Barbara Cohen-Stratyner at the New York Public Library for the Performing Arts, Phyllis Magidson at the Museum of the City of New York, and Nancy Shawcross at the University of Pennsylvania for taking time to talk with me about my research project.

As this project developed, I benefited immeasurably from the wonderful advice and encouragement of a group of highly accomplished scholars. Stephen B. Johnson, Elspeth H. Brown, and Charlie Keil pointed me in directions I never imagined going but am certainly glad I did. Their intelligence, attention to detail, and dedication to learning have been a constant source of inspiration. At the National Museum of American History, I was fortunate enough to work with Charles F. McGovern, who met with me countless times to chat about my research. His energetic approach to the fields of history and American studies and his boundless enthusiasm helped me make the most of my time in Washington. At the University of Pennsylvania, Kathy Peiss not only met with me several times to discuss my research interests but also invited my family into her home for Thanksgiving dinner. I would also like to thank Wendy Steiner, Peter Stallybrass, and the other members of the 2005–6 Penn Humanities Forum on Image and Word, especially Marcy Dinius and Alexandra Pappas, for their thoughts and companionship.

At various other stages of the research and writing process, I have had productive conversations with and received helpful comments from Jean-Christophe Agnew, John A. Astington, Sara Alpern, Peter Bailey, Regina Blaszczyk, Dwight Blocker Bowers, James W. Cook, Dilys Blum, Caroline Evans, Shelley Foote, Kathryn H. Fuller, Susan A. Glenn, Amy Henderson, Sarah Johnson, Pamela Walker Laird, Alan Lessoff, Kim Marra, David Saltz, Catherine Schuler, Monica Stuft, and Priscilla Wood. I give special thanks to Caroline Evans for the photograph of the sheath gown. I would also like to acknowledge the members of the American Society for Theatre Research Feminist Historiography Working Group for setting such wonderful examples of feminist scholarship, and the members of my Ontario theater studies reading group, Laura Levin, Jenn Stephenson, and Kim Solga, for their laughter, support, and collegiality.

Institutions do not run effectively without excellent administrators and support staff, and academics are completely lost without them. Many thanks go to Luella Massey, Robert Moses, and Jean Glascow at the University of Toronto; Suzanne McLaughlin at the NMAH; Jennifer Conway and Sara Varney at the University of Pennsylvania; and Suzanne Jaeger, Shawn Kerwin, Rachel Katz, Josie MacLean, Marcia Orlowsky, Mary Pecchia, and Andrea Thomas at York University. Thanks as well go to my two excellent graduate assistants, Dahlia Katz and Nicole Leaman.

Some of the material on testimonial advertising (now much revised) in Chapters 3 and 4 previously appeared in " 'The Mad Search for Beauty': Actresses' Testimonials and the 'Democratization of Beauty,' " *Journal of the Gilded Age and Progressive Era* 4.3 (July 2005): 255–92. Material on the sheath gown and the "Made in America" movement, discussed in Chapters 4 and 5, appears in "American Fashions for American Women: The Rise and Fall of Fashion Nationalism," in *Producing Fashion: Commerce, Culture, and Consumers*, ed. Regina Blaszczyk (Philadelphia: University of Pennsylvania Press, 2007), 130–49. And the story of Lucile's vaudeville tour appeared as "Patriotic Acts of Consumption: Lucile (Lady Duff Gordon) and the Vaudeville Fashion Show Craze," *Theatre Journal* (December 2008): 585–608. My thanks to the presses for allowing me to reprint this material here.

My friends and family kept me buoyed up throughout the research and writing process, even on the darkest days when I felt that I would never make it to this point. Thanks to Brian Arens, Jonaki Bhattacharrya, Kamal Bhattacharrya, Marcy Dinius, Brian Dell, Maxine Dell, Bill Evans, Neal Evans, Elysa Engelman, Steve Garabedian, George Gasyna, Jean Glaister, Sara Gregg, Vicki Howard, Jessica Johnson, Erin Lemon, Laura Levin, the Linden Singers, Allana Lindgren, Neil McLeod, Paul McLeod, Gertrud Michelson, Marina Moskowitz, Alison McElwain, Sarah Nixon-Gasyna, Alexandra Pappas, Stephen B. Peterson, Jim Porter, Lisa Ramey, Lynn Ransom, Alex Russo, Brad Schweitzer, Doug Schweitzer, Jen Schweitzer, Kim Solga, Jenn Stephenson, Theatre SKAM, Sara Topham, Craig Taylor, the ladies of Thompson Markward Hall, Lucas Tromly, Rob Wighton, Lisa Wolford Wylam, and Nancy Yakimoski. Special thanks go to my parents, Karen and Ed Schweitzer, for their unwavering love and faith.

Finally, thanks to my husband, Dan Evans, who has lived and breathed this project with me from the very beginning. His humor, enthusiasm, intelli-

gence, and love, his eagerness to read drafts and talk at length about the project, and perhaps most important, his willingness to take a year off from his
own studies to care for our son Marcus made it possible for me to complete
this book and maintain some semblance of sanity. You are my best friend and
this book is for you.